THE
INNER LIGHT

How India Influenced
the Beatles

Susan Shumsky, D.D.

PERMUTED
PRESS

A PERMUTED PRESS BOOK
ISBN: 978-1-68261-977-3
ISBN (eBook): 978-1-68261-978-0

The Inner Light:
How India Influenced the Beatles
© 2022 by Susan Shumsky, D.D.
All Rights Reserved

Cover art by Tiffani Shea
Front cover collage by Susan Shumsky and Chris Turner. See photo credits on page 469.

PERMUTED
PRESS

Permuted Press, LLC
New York • Nashville
permutedpress.com

Published in the United States of America
1 2 3 4 5 6 7 8 9 10

*This book is dedicated to the heartfelt
visionaries who dare to imagine a world in
peace and harmony. All we need is love.*

CONTENTS

PART VII:
AND IN THE END

NOTES FOR READERS

QR Codes

This book features QR codes—a fun, interactive way to read copyright-protected lyrics, hear songs, and see videos. The codes can be scanned using a smartphone or tablet and any free QR reader. On most devices, by simply turning on your camera and pointing to a QR code, a link will automatically pop up on your screen. Tapping that link will take you to an internet page.

If your camera does not automatically read QR codes, you might have to press a button to snap a picture. If you have no QR reader, please find an App Store or Google Play icon on your device. Then search for "QR reader," download a free app, and launch the app.

Quotations, Photo Credits, and Pseudonyms

For the sake of brevity and clarity, direct quotations made by The Beatles or others are often shortened without using ellipses. For full quotations, please check citations by referring to the Endnotes on page 472. Most photo credits can be found right under the photos. Additional photo credits are on page 469. In a few cases, people's names have been changed to protect their privacy. These names are distinguished with quotation marks.

Maharishi and Prabhupada Lingo

Maharishi Mahesh Yogi founded many organizations and used many terms when referring to Transcendental Meditation, TM teachers, and learning TM. This book mostly uses "TM," "TM

Movement," "Initiators," and "getting initiated," since those terms were in use when The Beatles were involved. Maharishi's Meditation Academy in Rishikesh is referred to as the "ashram."

A. C. Bhaktivedanta Prabhupada (a.k.a. Srila Prabhupada) founded ISKCON (International Society for Krishna Consciousness), also referred to as the Hare Krishna Movement. Members of his organization are referred to "devotees" or as "Hare Krishnas."

THE TIMES THEY WERE A-CHANGIN'

The spiritual journey of The Beatles is the story of an entire generation of visionaries. All boomers were influenced by the sixties spiritual revolution that brought Eastern culture to the Western world. The music of John, Paul, George, and Ringo furthered that revolution.

On November 18, 1963, on the nightly *Huntley-Brinkley Report*, Americans first glimpsed the Liverpool Lads who would soon become an unprecedented, world-shattering phenomenon. Narrator Edwin Newman described a "new sound" from Great Britain by "a quartet of young men with pudding-bowl haircuts who spell *beetles* 'B-E-A-T-L-E-S,'" born during the German blitzkrieg of World War II in Liverpool's Merseyside, the "toughest section of one of the toughest cities in the world."[1]

Newman mocked Beatles fans as compulsive screamers, mostly female, between age ten and sixteen, four thousand of whom camped out all night for tickets to concerts—a "near riot." Newman explained the "Mersey sound" originated in Liverpool, on the River Mersey. As screaming fans drowned out The Beatles singing "From Me to You," Newman joked that the "quality of Mersey is somewhat strained," and bringing the Mersey sound to America will "show us no Mersey."

Despite Newman's less-than-flattering introduction, on January 10, 1964, "I Want to Hold Your Hand" became the first British rock song to ever top American charts. That same day, The Beatles' first American LP, *Introducing...The Beatles*, was issued on the Vee-Jay label. Ten days later, their first Capitol Records LP, *Meet The Beatles!*, was released and rocketed to first place on *Billboard*, remaining eleven weeks (seventy-one total weeks on the charts), and selling over four million copies in 1964.

On February 9, 1964, The Beatles debuted on *The Ed Sullivan Show* to seventy-three million viewers, which launched them to stardom. We boomers watched eagerly as the mop-tops performed "All My Loving," "Till There Was You," "She Loves You," "I Saw Her Standing There," and "I Want to Hold Your Hand."

Beatles appear for the first time on Ed Sullivan's USA variety TV show; l. to r.: Ringo Starr, George Harrison, Ed Sullivan, John Lennon, Paul McCartney.

The Beatles were not another mediocre teeny-bop band. Nothing on the radio could rival them. They were rare as twice-struck lightning. The hysteria evoked by Elvis Presley paled in comparison to the frenzy induced by The Beatles. Like every other teen on earth, I became a Beatlemaniac. The British Invasion had begun.

Becoming Beatles

The Beatles could not read music. John said they composed "by feel." Paul said, "We just did our songs in hotel rooms, whenever we had a spare moment, John Lennon and I, sitting on twin beds with guitars."[2] But that intuitive process spun gold out of straw.

The Beatles honed their craft playing grueling four-hour sets seven days a week for peanuts in Hamburg's red-light district from August 1960 to December 1962. Amid dockworkers, prostitutes, gangsters, and existentialists, they entertained fans at the Indra, Kaiserkeller, Top Ten, and Star-Club. At the Indra, they slept on bunk beds in a stinky unheated storeroom. They washed and shaved in cold water from the urinals in adjacent toilets. Through excessive pressure, the rough carbon of Hamburg, heated in the searing cauldron of Liverpool's Cavern Club (where the band played 274 times), forged the diamond that became The Beatles.

The Beatles wearing leathers at The Hamburg Fun Fair 1960; l. to r.: Pete Best, George, John, Paul, Stuart Sutcliffe. JJs/Alamy Stock Photo.

Beatles at the Indra Club in Hamburg, August 19, 1960; l. to r.: John, George, Pete Best, Paul, Stuart Sutcliffe.

Using equipment that is now antique, the Fab Four created incredibly complex, previously unheard sounds. Ringo said, "You could walk in with an elephant, as long as it was going to make a musical note. Anything was viable."[3] By thinking out of the box, these pioneers in songwriting, recording, and presentation revolutionized pop music.

But as cultural icons, youth leaders, anti-establishment role models, and spiritual symbols, The Beatles were much more. Popularizing psychedelia and Eastern mysticism in the West, they ignited a flame of optimism in a country divided by the Vietnam War. Brighter than the stars, they radiated a rarified, impossible incandescence.

Most songwriters record one or two hits and dozens of mediocre tracks. But every Beatles song takes us on a melodic and lyrical journey that stirs our spirit. Afterwards, we are never the same. From the first chord of "A Hard Day's Night" to the last chord of "Day in the Life," we are spellbound, moved, and transported by each of their musical masterpieces. As Tom Petty said, "There was The Beatles, and then there was everybody else."

The Beatles have sold more records in the USA and have had more number-one hits on *Billboard* than anyone else. These timeless trailblazers speak to all generations. From boomers to whatever teenagers call themselves today, The Beatles' mystique lives on. Today's youth want to relive the magic of the Flower Power era and its four superstars. A new generation is always discovering the enduring message and electrifying, mystical music of this iconic band—The Beatles.

Beat Is Born

In 1964, when my mother heard The Beatles on the car radio, she grimaced, blocked her ears, and complained bitterly about the noise. Thus the generation gap opened by Elvis widened into a chasm. Under the influence of revolutionaries like Bob Dylan, I followed my inevitable destiny: leaving my family and adopting the hippie lifestyle.

Unless you lived through the Flower Power era, you might be wondering what hippies are and how they relate to The Beatles and India.

The post-war fifties' economic boom returned America to rigid roles, societal norms, conventional values, and conformity. The Cold War brought the threat of mass annihilation from the Union of Soviet Socialist Republics (USSR), which tested its first atomic bomb in 1949. Under US Senator Joseph McCarthy's reign of terror, America's most creative minds got blacklisted when the House Un-American Activities Committee (HUAC) accused them of communism.

McCarthyism provoked an anti-conformist counterculture to emerge. Herbert Huncke, a New York writer, hustler, and drug addict (nicknamed "Mayor of 42nd Street"), coined the phrase "Beat Generation" and the concepts "beat" and "square."[4] Freethinking writers in Greenwich Village, New York; North

Beach, San Francisco; and Venice West, Los Angeles, formed a political, cultural, and spiritual underground.

Beat writers favored intuition over reason, expression over repression, and freedom over oppression. They preferred Eastern mystic spirituality to calcified Western religious dogma. They rejected "square" conformity, censorship, and inhibitions, and they shocked straightlaced society by reveling in drugs, jazz, poetry, unbridled creativity, and sexual liberation.

Beat author Jack Kerouac wrote his groundbreaking untamed novel *On the Road*, minus paragraphs and punctuation, on a seventy-five-meter roll of paper. Beat poet Allen Ginsberg's scathing critique of mechanistic civilization, "Howl," and William S. Burroughs's anti-authoritarian novel, *Naked Lunch*, were banned. Both authors prevailed in court.[5]

Kerouac defined the Beat Generation as "a generation of crazy, illuminated hipsters suddenly rising and roaming America, serious, bumming and hitchhiking everywhere, beautiful in an ugly graceful new way."[6] "Beat means beatitude! Beatific!"[7]

Harry "The Hipster" Gibson, a white Jewish Harlem jazz composer (born Harry Raab), originated the terms "hep," "hepcat," and "hip" in the 1940s. Hipsters considered themselves cool, intellectual, sophisticated, and forward thinking. They created an underground artist's faction in lingo, dress, manners, and music.

In the 1950s, jazz shifted to a modal style, influenced by improvisational classical Indian music. Examples of modal jazz included Miles Davis' *Kind of Blue* and *Impressions* by John Coltrane, whose 1957 spiritual awakening initiated his lifelong study of mysticism and his album *A Love Supreme*. Coltrane, who declared "I believe in all religions," studied *The Gospel of Sri Ramakrishna*, Paramahansa Yogananda's *Autobiography of a Yogi*, the Bhagavad Gita, Koran, Bible, Kabbalah, Plato, Aristotle, Zen Buddhism, yoga, and astrology.[8] His cacophonous record *Om* included Indian instruments and chants from the Vedas.

The Folk Revival

As hipsters grooved to experimental jazz in the North, African American culture in the Deep South cultivated its own folk music—the blues, which, in the 1950s, spawned rhythm and blues, rockabilly, rock 'n' roll, and, in January 1959, the melodic Motown chords and harmonies. These genres profoundly influenced early Beatles music.

The charismatic Elvis Presley introduced to white audiences what was viewed by conservatives as the shocking "jungle rhythm" of rock 'n' roll, along with pompadour hairstyle and gyrating hips, spurring accusations of obscenity and juvenile delinquency.

Elvis Presley in film *Jailhouse Rock* (1957).

In the late fifties, lines blurred between beatniks and social activists such as Woody Guthrie, Pete Seeger, Bob Dylan, Joan Baez, Odetta, The Kingston Trio, and Peter, Paul and Mary. Folk-protest music and "hootenanny" gatherings brought cultural change to both intelligentsia and common people into the sixties. Guthrie's "This Land Is Your Land," Seeger's "Where Have All the Flowers Gone," "Turn, Turn, Turn," and "If I Had a Hammer," and gospel songs like "This Little Light of Mine," "We Shall Overcome," and "Kumbaya" were the soundtrack for antiwar, free speech, and civil rights demonstrations.

Scan this code to hear Woody Guthrie's "This Land Is Your Land."

Scan this code to hear Pete Seeger's "Where Have All the Flowers Gone."

Bob Dylan was arguably the most influential leader of the underground revolution. On May 27, 1963, he released *The Freewheelin' Bob Dylan* album, featuring "Blowin' in the Wind," which quickly became the anthem for social reform. Dylan remarked: "I came out of the wilderness and just naturally fell in with the Beat scene, the bohemian, Be Bop crowd, it was all pretty much connected. It was Jack Kerouac, Ginsberg, Corso, Ferlinghetti. I got in at the tail end of that and it was magic; it had just as big an impact on me as Elvis Presley."[9]

Scan this code to hear "Blowin' in the Wind."

Joan Baez and Bob Dylan: civil rights March on Washington for Jobs and Freedom: August 28, 1963

Rebels with a Cause

The Folk Revival crossed the Atlantic to Great Britain, where "skiffle" emerged in the 1950s, led by Scottish musician Lonnie Donegan, and influenced by bluegrass, folk, blues, and jazz. Skiffle groups played acoustic guitar, banjo, and homemade instruments like the washboard, jug, washtub bass, tea-chest bass, cigar-box fiddle, cigar-box guitar, musical saw, and comb-and-paper kazoo. George Harrison recalled, "Lonnie Donegan and skiffle just seemed made for me."[10]

 Scan this code to hear Lonnie Donegan's biggest US hit, "Does Your Chewing Gum Lose Its Flavour (On the Bedpost Overnight?)."

The Quarrymen at Woolton Village Rose Queen procession, St. Peter's Church Fete, July 6, 1957; l. to r.: Pete Shotton (washboard), Eric Griffiths (guitar), Len Garry (back to camera: tea-chest bass), John Lennon (eyes closed, singing), Colin Hanton (drums), Rod Davis leaning against truck cab, his banjo in its case at his feet. Photo by James L. Davis.

The Quarrymen play at New Clubmoor Hall in late 1957; l. to r.: Colin Hanton (drums), Paul McCartney, Len Garry (tea-chest bass), John Lennon, Eric Griffiths (guitar). Photo by Leslie Kearney/The Quarrymen.

John Lennon's band, the Quarrymen, joined the craze, playing guitar, banjo, tea-chest bass, and drum. Paul joined the band in 1957, and George in 1958. In 1957, the first youth music television show on BBC, *Six-Five Special*, featured skiffle groups. Dozens of superstars started their careers in one of fifty thousand skiffle groups in 1950s Britain. To name a few: Mick Jagger, Barry Gibbs, Van Morrison, David Gilmour, Roger Daltrey, Jimmy Page, and Graham Nash.

Marlon Brando in *The Wild One*. Entertainment Pictures/Alamy Stock Photo.

"Teddy Boys" and "Ton-up Boys" formed an underground postwar counterculture in Britain. Ton-up Boy motorcycle gangs (a.k.a. "Café Racers," "Leather Boys," or "Coffee-Bar Cowboys") aspired to "do the ton"—exceed 100 mph on their bikes. Emulating Marlon Brando in *The Wild One* (motorcycle-gang film banned in Britain), they dressed head to toe in cliché motorcycle couture. In 1950s Liverpool, the Quarrymen followed this trend.

Scan this code to see photos of the Quarrymen and Beatles in Teddy Boy and Ton-up Boy fashions.

In the fifties, Ton-ups congregated at cafés and listened to the jukebox, where they could hear Rockabilly and rock 'n' roll, which were not played on BBC radio. Or they tuned in to Radio Luxembourg, a pirate radio broadcast from the Continent. Some favorites: Eddie Cochran, Elvis Presley, Gene Vincent, and Bill Haley & His Comets.

 Scan this code to hear "Be-Bop-A-Lula," John Lennon's favorite fifties song and the first record Paul McCartney bought.

The Mersey Beat

In 1960, John Lennon changed the name "Quarrymen" to "The Beatles." Jack Kerouac claimed John personally told him "Beatles" referenced the Beat Generation. "Beatles" also alluded to the British beat, beat music, and Mersey beat—the unique, driving rhythms from Liverpool. John Lennon explained, "It was beat and beetles, and when you said it people thought of crawly things, and when you read it, it was beat music."[11] The Mersey beat was characterized by a heavy beat with driving emphasis on all four beats of the 4/4 bar. An example is "You Can't Do That."

 Scan this code to watch this song performed by the Fab Four in concert, and see firsthand the reason for all the hysteria triggered by these enchanting, irresistible lads.

In the early sixties culture, still stuck in an uptight era of repression, the world was ripe for a sound and message that reflected teenage rebellion and free expression. Both Bob Dylan and The Beatles, with their sounds of the times, fit that bill. Dylan's album *The Times They Are A-Changin'* was released in January 1964, three days after The Beatles' first album, *Introducing...The Beatles* dropped. Dylan's finger was squarely on the pulse of the sixties revolution and perfectly reflected its heartbeat. I was one of the millions of teens to whom Dylan's lyrics spoke volumes.

 Scan this code to hear "The Times They Are A-Changin."

Ginsberg Brings India to the West

In the early sixties, Beat Generation poet and counterculture icon Allen Ginsberg studied Hindu and Buddhist religious texts, including the Bhagavad Gita ("Song of God"), Mahabharata, Ramayana, Vedas, Upanishads, Tibetan Book of the Dead, and writings of Ramakrishna Paramahamsa, Jiddu Krishnamurti, and Paramahansa Yogananda. During his psychedelic experiments, Ginsberg had seen Tibetan mandalas and the universal form of the Hindu deity Lord Krishna. (See Ginsberg's photo: page 131.)

In 1962, Ginsberg and his partner Peter Orlovsky spent over a year in India seeking a guru. India's visionary energy fascinated Ginsberg: "An entire culture suffused with respect for that mythology, that religion and its practices, that was a revelation: how deeply the sense of a spiritual existence could penetrate everyday relations, the streets and street signs."[12]

The Beat poet marveled at ash-smeared *naga sadhus*, smoking hashish openly, wandering about naked, renouncing materialism. In America, they would be charged with indecent exposure.

Ginsberg extolled the cremation *ghats* on the Ganges riverbanks in Varanasi, where death was in the open, not hidden in coffins and masked with make-up. He met many yogis and gurus. He learned to chant *Om* from Swami Sivananda and discussed the psychedelic drug LSD (lysergic acid diethylamide) with the Dalai Lama. He met Chögyam Trungpa Rinpoche, who later founded Naropa Institute in Boulder, Colorado, and became Ginsberg's guru.

After returning to the USA in 1963, Ginsberg became the first to lead public chanting of mantras such as *Om, Hare Krishna Hare Rama, Hare Om Namah Shivaye, Shri Rama Jai Rama Jai Jai Rama, Om Shri Maitreya, Om Mani Padme Hum,* and *Gate Gate Paragate.*

On June 3, 1965, Ginsberg celebrated his thirty-ninth birthday at Barry Miles's flat in Chester Square, London. There, he first met John and Cynthia Lennon, George Harrison, and Pattie Boyd (George's wife). However, by the time they arrived, Allen had stripped down to his birthday suit for his birthday, his underwear perched on his head, and a "Please Do Not Disturb" sign hung around his penis! John and George made sure no photographers were present and only stayed for one drink. Later, however, The Beatles became lasting friends with Ginsberg in supporting the antiwar movement and endorsing Indian philosophy.[13]

By the mid-sixties, the banners of beatnik, folk revival, skiffle, and activism gave way to the next anti-establishment iteration, namely "hippies," who gathered in Haight-Ashbury, San Francisco; Old Town, Chicago; and Greenwich Village, New York. Ginsberg brought Indian mysticism to the hippies and coined the term "Flower Power" to encourage nonviolent protests in the manner of Mahatma Gandhi.

My Life as a Hippie

In 1966, I lived in the San Francisco Bay Area—counterculture central. I enrolled in a college with more hippies per square inch than Golden Gate Park—California College of Arts and Crafts. My English teacher was famed Beat Generation poet Michael McClure.

As a hippie during that pivotal time, I can attest the hippie revolution was not just about sex, drugs, and rock 'n' roll. Seeking inspiration from Buddhism and Hinduism, and led by Allen Ginsberg, Ken Kesey, Timothy Leary, and Richard Alpert, we flower children sought one primary objective—higher consciousness.

The Beatles grew up in my generation and subscribed (in theory anyway) to this same sixties Flower Power philosophy. We embraced psychedelics, free love, women's liberation, civil rights, free speech, nuclear disarmament, worker's rights, environmental causes, communal living, natural lifestyle, health foods, vegetarianism, and artistic freedom. Our slogan was "Make Love, Not War." We rejected the "Establishment" of nine-to-five robots living plastic lives in cookie-cutter suburbs.

The hippie movement was modeled after wandering mendicants of India (the real dropouts)—complete with dreadlocks, hashish pipes, candles, incense, brass idols of Hindu deities, skinny-dipping, Indian clothing, mantra, tantra, meditation, chanting, and the Kama Sutra.

I embraced Indian philosophy wholeheartedly. As a rare insider, I spent two decades in various ashrams of The Beatles' guru, Maharishi Mahesh Yogi (founder of Transcendental Meditation, a.k.a. TM) and served on his personal staff for six years in Europe. That journey is chronicled in my memoir *Maharishi & Me: Seeking Enlightenment with The Beatles' Guru.*

This ad for the first "Human Be-In," January 1967, mimicked Indian sadhus—complete with dreadlocks and a third eye.

I lived through the same era and sought the same spiritual growth as The Beatles, through the same experimentation. Before The Beatles ever met Maharishi, I was already practicing TM. Using their song lyrics as a compass, this book reveals the inside story of The Beatles' pathway through psychedelic exploration, sojourn with spiritual mentors, flirtation with Indian music, and passage to spiritual awakening. Here we will discover how the spell India cast on The Beatles changed their music and transformed the world.

PART I

EVERYBODY MUST GET STONED – EVEN PAUL

CHAPTER 1

TURN ON, TUNE IN, DROP ACID

"There's a Place"

Written: February 1963
Recorded: February 11, 1963
Released: March 22, 1963: Single UK, July 22, 1963:
Single US; January 10, 1964: Introducing...The Beatles

The Beatles' first American album, *Introducing...The Beatles*, was released soon after the Fab Four first arrived in the USA. The Beatles had not yet embraced Indian philosophy, but they were already members of the avant-garde Beat Generation. That enclave of counterculture authors and poets, led by Allen Ginsberg, brought the esoteric philosophy of India into the forefront of intellectual thought in the sixties.

One track on The Beatles' debut album foreshadowed the deeper lyrical direction The Beatles would eventually take: "There's a Place." John said in 1980, "'There's a Place' was my attempt at a sort of Motown black thing, but it says the usual John Lennon things: 'In my mind there's no sorrow.' It's all in your mind."[14] John declared a similar sentiment years later in the lyrics of "Rain": "It's just a state of mind."

Scan this code to read the lyrics for "There's A Place."

The Lyrics

In this early example of Lennon/McCartney songwriting, "There's a Place" expressed some profound explorations of the mind. Here is an interpretation:

The ancient scriptures of India say there is a place of silence within, experienced in meditation. It is transcendental consciousness—beyond time, space, and causality. In this exalted state of awareness, there is no duality—no sorrow or joy, black or white, male or female, yin or yang. It is perfect unity, where polarities do not exist. John said, "I believe God is like a power station, a supreme power, and he's neither good nor bad, left, right, black, or white. He just is."[15]

This higher awareness is not bleak or lonely. It is fullness. Alone in the cave of our mind, we experience inner peace, deep relaxation, perfection, wholeness, and bliss. The Upanishads of India declare this lofty level of consciousness is oneness, a non-dual state of ultimate fulfillment: "Only that which is, was in the beginning, one only, without a second."[16]

Paul McCartney lifted the title "There's a Place" from the song "Somewhere" in Leonard Bernstein's 1957 musical *West Side Story*. Paul elaborated: "But in our case the place was in the mind, rather than round the back of the stairs for a kiss and a cuddle. This was the difference with what we were writing, we were getting a bit more cerebral."[17]

The Beatles were way ahead of their time releasing "There's a Place" in 1963, amid teeny-bop hits like "He's So Fine," "My Boyfriend's Back," and "Be My Baby." In fact, "There's a Place" was ahead of The Beatles' *own* time, amid their 1963 teen hits "Love

Me Do," "I Wanna Hold Your Hand," and "All My Loving." The 1963 Beatles releases were all love songs, but "There's a Place" was a self-love song.

"Got to Get You into My Life"

Written: August 1964 to March 1966
Recorded: April 7, 8, 11, May 18, June 17, 1966
Released: August 5, 1966: Revolver

The Beatles were keen admirers of Bob Dylan. They invited him to New York's Delmonico Hotel on August 28, 1964, where, after their concert at Forest Hills Tennis Stadium in Queens, the Fabs were dining in their suite with manager Brian Epstein and roadies Malcolm Evans and Neil Aspinall. There, The Beatles first met the bard.

After Mal Evans ushered Dylan, his road manager Victor Maymudes, and *New York Post* journalist Al Aronowitz into the suite, Dylan declined the wine and "purple heart" (Drinamyl) pills. He suggested they smoke pot instead. Epstein admitted they had never imbibed. (The Beatles had actually smoked cannabis in 1960 at a gig in Southport but felt no effects.)

Dylan asked, "But what about your song? The one about getting high?" John Lennon asked what he was referring to. Dylan replied, "And when I touch you, I get high, I get high."

John retorted, "Those aren't the words. The words are, 'I can't hide, I can't hide!"[18]

Apparently, it was high time for The Beatles to get high. Dylan, Aronowitz, Maymudes, John, Paul, George, Ringo, Epstein, Aspinall, and Evans all crammed into the bedroom. To avoid scrutiny from fans, reporters, and police guards, they drew the blinds, locked the door, and rolled towels to seal the door gap.

Dylan rolled a joint, lit it, and passed it to John. Unfamiliar with the ritual of taking a toke and passing it on, John gave it to

Ringo, and dubbed him "my royal taster." Ringo, also ignorant of stoner etiquette, kept it and smoked it like a cigarette.

Aronowitz asked Maymudes to roll more joints. With each person getting a separate joint, they quickly got stoned out of their minds. Brian Epstein kept saying, "I'm so high I'm up on the ceiling."[19] They spent the next few hours laughing hysterically.

Paul was on his own trip—"Thinking for the first time, really thinking."[20] He fantasized himself a Liverpool newspaper reporter on assignment to reveal the "Meaning of Life." He kept asking Mal for a pencil and paper. But everyone was so wasted they could produce neither. Paul described, "I'd been going through this thing of levels. And at each level I'd meet all these people again. 'Hahaha! It's you!' And then I'd metamorphose on to another level."[21]

The next morning, Mal handed Paul a little slip of paper that read, "There are seven levels!" Paul recalled, "It wasn't bad for an amateur. And we pissed ourselves laughing. I mean, 'What the fuck are the seven levels?'"[22]

George commented, "It was such an amazing night and I woke up the next day thinking, *What was that? Something happened last night!* I felt really good."[23]

On that night, Dylan tried to convince John that the lyrics were of primary importance in songwriting, but John insisted that was not his priority. The rhythm was. Later, John changed his tune (so to speak). He took Dylan's advice and composed meaningful, purposeful "philosorock" songs.

Throughout their career, Dylan greatly influenced The Beatles. Since the Liverpool Lads held the poet in high esteem, Paul said they felt proud to get introduced to pot by Dylan—the man who publicly declared in 1966, "Everybody must get stoned." Paul likened it to the status of learning meditation and getting his mantra from Maharishi.

This fortuitous meeting of minds marked a breakthrough when The Beatles began writing more reflective lyrics, influenced by Dylan, and Dylan switched from acoustic to electric, influenced by The Beatles. "Got to Get You into My Life" was The Beatles' first psychedelic song, composed under the influence of their budding cannabis romance.

 Scan this code to read the lyrics.

The Lyrics

Paul said "Got to Get You into My Life" expressed his love affair with pot, as an "ode to pot," like writing "an ode to chocolate or a good claret." He fell in love with pot and described his "first flush of pot" like smoking a peace pipe with "native tobacco."[24]

In 1966, we hippies played *Revolver* on the turntable while on psychedelics. We were taking a ride (tripping) with other hippies to connect with other kinds of minds. Just as Paul returned to people repeatedly on "seven levels," some of us on LSD moved through levels on a spiral, circling back to the same people again and again. This spiral symbolizes the Hindu belief in reincarnation, the cycle of birth and death, or the wheel of karma repeating for lifetimes, where we meet the same people over and over until we reach the top of the spiral and attain spiritual liberation.

Paul wrote "Got to Get You into My Life" soon after meeting Dylan. Though he considered himself a "straight working-class lad," he found pot to be "quite uplifting," without the side effects of alcohol or pills: "I didn't have a hard time with it and to me it was literally mind-expanding."[25]

After the Fab Four smoked grass that day in 1964, their lyrics often described getting "high," "turned-on," or ingesting drugs. Examples included "With a Little Help from My Friends," "Doctor Robert," "Because," and "A Day in the Life." Paul said, "Once pot was established as part of the curriculum, you started to get a bit more surreal material coming from us, a bit more abstract stuff."[26]

In 1997, Paul sang a different tune: "I haven't really changed my opinion too much except, if anyone asks me for real advice, it would be, 'Stay straight. That is actually the best way.'"[27]

"She Said She Said"

Written: August 1965 to June 1966
Recorded: June 21, 1966
Released: August 5, 1966: Revolver

After Bob Dylan turned on The Beatles to marijuana, their experience with pot informed the reflective, hypnotic album, *Rubber Soul*. John Lennon dubbed it their "pot album." But LSD was another story.

Dr. John Riley expected to become a UK National Health Service dentist, until he attended Northwestern University in Chicago and returned as a Harley Street cosmetic dentist to the stars. His clients included George Harrison and actor Dudley Moore. One night in April 1965, the thirty-four-year-old Riley and his twenty-two-year-old girlfriend Cyndy Bury invited John and Cynthia Lennon, George Harrison, and Pattie Boyd to dine at his home: Flat 1, 2 Strathearn Place, London.[28]

As the guests were leaving, Dr. Riley said, "You haven't had any coffee yet."[29] They drank the coffee but were anxious to get to the Pickwick Club at 15–16 Great Newport Street, where a trio would premiere: Klaus Voormann (bass guitarist and artist who illustrated the *Revolver* album cover), Gibson Kemp (Rory Storm's drummer after The Beatles stole Ringo), and a guy named Paddy.

Dr. Riley told the Beatles, "You can't leave," then dropped a bombshell—he had spiked their coffee with LSD-laced sugar cubes.

John snapped furiously, "How dare you fucking do this to us!"[30] John had been taking amphetamines to stay awake since the Hamburg days, but LSD, though legal, was virtually unknown in Britain. The Beatles suspected Riley thought acid was an aphrodisiac (nicknamed the "Love Drug," after all) and had tried to trick them into an orgy.

To escape, the Beatles piled into George and Pattie's Mini, and the dentist followed after them to the club. George later quipped, "We were innocent victims of the wicked dentist whom we'd met and had dinner with a few times."[31]

What we might call a transcen-*dental* experience, George described an "overwhelming feeling of well-being, that there was a God, and I could see him in every blade of grass."[32] A light bulb turned on in George's head: "The question and answer disappeared into each other. In ten minutes I lived a thousand years." His awareness expanded "like an astronaut on the moon, or in his spaceship, looking back at the Earth from my awareness."[33]

After the Pickwick closed, they moved on to the Ad Lib club on 7 Leicester Place to meet Ringo, Mick Jagger, and Mick's girlfriend and pop star Marianne Faithfull. After several hours of bizarre hallucinations, George drove his mates to his house in Esher, crawling at 10 mph, though it felt like 1000 mph.

John described it as terrifying but fantastic: "George's house seemed to be just like a big submarine. It seemed to float above his wall, which was eighteen foot, and I was driving it." John made drawings of four faces saying, "We all agree with you." John ended up "pretty stoned for a month or two."[34]

Though George had always looked up to John, after this head-warping experience, he viewed John as his equal and they bonded on a soul level: "John and I spent a lot of time together from then on and I felt closer to him than all the others, until his death." Even after the advent of Yoko, "on the odd occasion I did see him, just by the look in his eyes I felt we were connected."[35] George repeatedly pointed to this first LSD trip as being responsible for his interest in spirituality and Hinduism.

For John, LSD was the self-knowledge that pointed the way. "I was suddenly struck by great visions when I first took acid. But you've got to be looking for it before you can possibly find it.

Perhaps I was looking without realizing it. Perhaps I would have found it anyway. It would have just taken longer."[36]

After LSD, John and George could no longer relate to their Beatle-mates. They decided Paul and Ringo must turn on also. George remembered, "It was such a mammoth experience that it was unexplainable. It was all too important to John and me."[37] So during their 1965 North American tour, they scored sugar cubes wrapped in tinfoil in New York with that intention.

Unabashed LSD Bash

On August 29 and 30, 1965, The Beatles performed at the Hollywood Bowl. During a five-day break before that, they rented actress Zsa Zsa Gabor's French country-style house at 2850 Benedict Canyon Drive, Beverly Hills. George remembered, "It had a little gatehouse, which Mal and Neil stayed in, decorated by Arabian-type things draped on the walls."[38]

That is where John and George planned to break out the sugar cubes on August 24, 1965. Ringo agreed with the plan: "I'd take anything!"[39] But Paul did not. Despite extreme peer pressure, Paul refused the drug because the idea of permanent change, to "never get back home again," frightened him. John said, "Paul felt very out of it, because we are all slightly cruel: 'we're all taking it and *you're* not.'"[40]

Attending the LSD party: Neil Aspinall (Beatles personal assistant), Mal Evans, Tony Barrow (Beatles press secretary), David Crosby and Jim McGuinn of The Byrds, actor Peter Fonda, Joan Baez, Eleanor Bron (co-star in *Help!*), Peggy Lipton (*The Mod Squad* actress), and some female groupies. Mal remained straight so he could guard the house from hundreds of fans at the gate.

George described his LSD out-of-body experience: "I'd go 'out there'; I'd be gone somewhere, and then, bang! I'd land back in my body. I'd look around and see that John had just done the same thing. You go in tandem, you're out there for a while and then, BOING!"[41]

Scan this code to
read the lyrics.

The Lyrics

While sitting on the outdoor deck, George told Peter Fonda he felt he was dying. That feeling is not uncommon on LSD. Timothy Leary, Ralph Metzner, and Richard Alpert's book *The Psychedelic Experience: A Manual Based on the Tibetan Book of the Dead*, is a guide for the LSD ego-death. Alpert described: "I got this terrible panic that precedes the psychological death, because indeed Richard Alpert was dying."[42]

Fonda advised George not to worry, there was no need to fear, and he just needed to relax: "This is what this drug does, it puts your mind, your brain, out of activity of the function you think it's in. It unlocks the doors of perception."[43] Then Fonda told George that he knew what it was like to be dead because, at age ten, he had accidentally shot himself in the stomach with an antique pistol. On the operating table, his heart stopped three times.[44] George recalled: "Peter Fonda was showing us his bullet wound. He was very uncool."[45]

John described the day as epitomizing the sixties—beautiful, in the sunshine, high on acid, having fun with The Byrds and dancing girls (some from *Playboy*). But then Fonda, wearing shades, kept coming over and whispering, "'I know what it's like to be dead,' and we were saying, 'For Christ's sake, shut up! We don't care, we don't want to know!'"[46] John told Fonda, "You're making me feel like I've never been born.[47] Who put all that shit in your head?"[48]

"We kept leaving him, because he was so boring," John recalled. "It was scary when you're flying high."[49]

McGuinn of The Byrds remembered, "We were all on acid and John couldn't take it. John said, 'Get this guy out of here.' It was morbid and bizarre."[50]

Later that day, several starlets arrived and the movie *Cat Ballou* was screened—a release print for drive-ins, with canned laughter and applause. The Beatles hated it. McGuinn said, "We'd just finished watching *Cat Ballou* with Jane Fonda, and John didn't want anything to do with any Fondas. He was holding the movie against Peter and then what he said just added to it."[51]

So the song "She Said She Said" was born of this bizarre LSD trip. The tale is told in the song's lyrics. But something else happened at the party of great significance to George, which is revealed next.

CHAPTER 2

SURRENDER TO AVOID

"Norwegian Wood (This Bird Has Flown)"

Written: January 25 to October 1965
Recorded: October 21, 1965
Released: December 3, 1965: Rubber Soul

In an interview by Beatles fan Robert Bartel, George's sister Louise Harrison said that during World War II, Winston Churchill played music on the radio for one hour per day to soothe the population. She believed George's love for Indian classical music began in his mother's womb: "Mum used to listen to the Sunday morning program from AIR India [All-India Radio] on BBC (all the sitar music and that kind of stuff) and she really loved it. She would dance around the kitchen pretending she was an Indian dancer. And this was partially during the time she was pregnant with George, so that was probably the first time he started hearing the music!"[52]

"Norwegian Wood" was the first pop song where a rock musician played (improperly, but nevertheless played) an Indian musical instrument. It also ostensibly marked the birth of "raga rock"—a term referring to Indian musical instruments used in rock 'n' roll, or to Indian sounds made by Western instruments. How this occurred was a collision of George, some musicians from India, and the movie *Help!*

Help! *(film)*

The Beatles began filming *Help!* on February 23, 1965, on Paradise Island, Bahamas. They were uninvolved with the movie's storyline, which parodied an ancient Indian cult. Because of Parlophone producer George Martin's association with Indian session musicians at the AMC (Asian Music Circle), Indian music embellished the soundtrack. However, the film mocked Indians with atrocious bigoted stereotypes.

"Thuggee" itinerant highway robber gangs operated in India from the seventeenth to nineteenth centuries. These conmen worked in groups, flattering and distracting unsuspecting tourists, strangling them with a handkerchief or noose, then robbing, mutilating, and burying them. *Thug* means "concealment" in Sanskrit.

Thugs considered themselves children of the Hindu goddess Kali—created from her sweat. Oddly, they believed that feeding human blood to Kali would protect and save humanity from slaughter. Even Muslim Thugs worshipped Kali.

THE THUGS WORSHIPPING KALEE.

The 1956 film *Around the World in 80 Days*, winner of five Oscars, had employed a Thuggee theme. So did the film *Help!*, where a high priest "Clang" (addressed as "Swami") is about to sacrifice a woman to the goddess "Kahili" (mocking Kali). But Ringo is wearing her sacrificial ring. To retrieve the ring, Clang and cult members locate Ringo in an Indian restaurant. Ringo discovers, to his horror, that he will be sacrificed unless he surrenders the ring, which gets stuck on his finger.

The remainder of the film could be likened to a Keystone Cops chase cum James Bond parody cum travelogue, where the police, a mad scientist, and cult members pursue The Beatles through the Alps, Buckingham Palace, and the Bahamas. Finally, as Ringo is about to be sacrificed, the ring falls off. Ringo sticks it on Clang's finger and yells, "Get sacrificed. I don't subscribe to your religion." Fights, chaos, and pratfalls ensue.

Beatles on movie set of *Help!*—Idol of "Kahili." (AP/Shutterstock.)

For an interior scene at so-called "Rajahama restaurant," filmed at Twickenham Film Studios in Middlesex on April 4 and 5, 1965, Ken Thorne, the score composer, assembled Indian musicians to play a medley, "Another Hard Day's Night," to the tune of "A Hard Day's Night," "Money Can't Buy Me Love," and "I Should Have Known Better."

George recalled, "We were waiting to shoot the scene in the restaurant when the guy gets thrown in the soup, and there were a few Indian musicians playing in the background. I remember picking up the sitar and trying to hold it and thinking, 'This is a funny sound.'"[53]

None of these Indian musicians who played the medley were credited on the *Help!* album or film: Pandit Shiv Dayal Batish on *vichitra veena*, Pakistani musician Diwan Motihar on sitar, Keshav Sathe on tabla drums, and Qasim on *bansuri* (bamboo flute). Sathe had moved to London from Mumbai (then known as Bombay) in 1956 and joined the AMC. Sathe and Motihar later pioneered Indo-jazz fusion music in America.[54]

At the recording studio, the Indian musicians who played on the *Help!* soundtrack received great respect from the British musicians, who immediately made them feel at home with a tea break. Fascinated by Batish's vichitra veena with its carved peacock head, they joked around by pretending to feed the bird.[55] (See page 431 for a photo of vichitra veena and page 432 for a QR code to see the instrument played).

Later that year, George asked Batish to order a *dilruba* (cello-like instrument) from India and tutor his wife, Pattie Boyd. Under Batish's guidance, she soon mastered the fundamentals. Batish found the couple to be open, friendly, and respectful. His association with The Beatles made him famous in the West and also increased his standing within the Indian community.[56]

 Scan this code to see a musician playing dilruba and its cousin the tar-shehnai (with amplifying horn).

An extraordinary vocalist and virtuoso of multiple instruments, Batish composed hundreds of Bollywood songs and broadcast regularly on television and All-India Radio (AIR). He taught at University of California Santa Cruz and founded Batish Institute of Music and Fine Arts. In 1969, he tutored actor Michael York in sitar for his role in *The Guru*, based on George Harrison, about a musician's search for a guru in India.[57]

"If we all spent more time studying music and other arts, the world would be heaven," Batish said.[58]

The Byrds and B's

Later that year, George learned of the world's foremost sitar player—Pandit Ravi Shankar. On August 24, 1965, in Beverly Hills, an LSD party was underway. The Beatles had invited David Crosby and Jim McGuinn of The Byrds to trip with them. The musicians were sitting in a large bathroom, taking turns playing their favorite tunes on acoustic guitar.

George Harrison called Ravi Shankar the "Godfather of World Music." Here Ravi is performing in 1969.

McGuinn and Crosby had made their first demos in 1964 on World Pacific Records, a label founded by Transcendental Meditators that had produced Ravi Shankar since 1962. An early fan of Indian music, Crosby showed George "some Ravi Shankar stuff that he'd just been into."[59] Crosby demonstrated classical Indian raga scales on guitar and suggested that George check out the sitarist. Crosby often carried one of Ravi's albums around and would say to other musicians, "You ain't heard nothing, try this."[60]

George gave Crosby credit for introducing him to Ravi's music. McGuinn said, "We planted the seeds. We loved Indian music and did some things in that vein, but not as much as The Beatles. Later they went out there [to India], got some sitars, met Ravi Shankar and learned to play them, and got into the whole Eastern thing. We didn't really realize it but it had an impact."[61]

The next time McGuinn encountered George was on a plane. McGuinn recalled, "We talked about Transcendental Meditation and he looked like he was somewhere else. I asked him 'what's going on?' and he said he was 'transcending.'"[62]

Fledgling Sitar Attempts

A few weeks after the LSD party, in September 1965 George bought a sitar from a little shop named Indiacraft at the top of Oxford Street in London, which featured Indian carvings and incense. George recounted, "It was a real crummy-quality one, but I bought it and mucked about with it a bit. We'd recorded the 'Norwegian Wood' backing track, and it needed something. I picked the sitar up—it was just lying around; I hadn't really figured out what to do with it. It was quite spontaneous: I found the notes that played the lick. It fitted and it worked."[63]

Shawn Phillips, an American folk rock, funk, and jazz-fusion musician, shared a flat with Donovan Leitch in London in the sixties. Shawn wrote the music, uncredited, for "Season of the Witch" and other Donovan songs. In 1966, he played sitar on six songs for Donovan's *Sunshine Superman* album. In 1967, he played sitar on

"Sunny South Kensington" on the album *Mellow Yellow*. Through Donovan, Shawn met The Beatles and claims he sang backup on "Lovely Rita."

Shawn recalled first meeting Ravi Shankar after his concert in Toronto: "He was kind enough to sit down with me for about four hours. He showed me how to sit with the instrument, how to hold it, the very basics of the sitar, and that hooked me."[64]

Shawn said, "I started playing the sitar in Canada about 1963 or '64. I gave George Harrison his first lessons, before he met Ravi Shankar. Donovan and I got invited to George's house, and I sat him down and said 'Look, here's the basics, this is the way you sit with it.'"[65] "I spent three weeks with George. I'd go over to his house. We'd have dinner and play some songs, and I was teaching him about the instrument."[66]

After "Norwegian Wood" appeared on *Rubber Soul*, many pop stars released "raga rock" sounds, including The Rolling Stones, The Byrds, Hollies, Donovan, Moody Blues, Them, The Doors, Pretty Things, Traffic, Grateful Dead, Paul Butterfield Blues Band, Box Tops, Monkees, B. J. Thomas, and The Paul Winter Consort.

The Beatles continued to explore Indian sounds on their albums *Revolver*, *Sgt. Pepper's Lonely Hearts Club Band*, *The Beatles* (a.k.a. the White Album), and *Abbey Road*.

Beatles Weigh In

"It was such a mind-blower that we had this strange instrument on a record," Ringo said. "We were all open to anything when George introduced the sitar. Our whole attitude was changing."[67]

John said, "[George] was not sure whether he could play it yet because he hadn't done much on the sitar, but he was willing to have a go, as is his wont, and he learnt the bit."[68]

"Even though the sound of the sitar was bad, they were still quite happy with it," George remembered. "I played the sitar very badly."[69]

Sitar maestro Ravi Shankar recalled: "My nieces and nephews made me hear 'Norwegian Wood' after I had met George [June 1, 1966]. Before this, I had not heard anything [by The Beatles] and was not much impressed by it. But I saw the effect on the young people. I couldn't believe it. They were lapping it up. They loved it so much."[70]

Indian commentators claim "Norwegian Wood" was based on a famous raga, "Raag Bageshri," from the sixteenth century.[71] There is a resemblance to the melody in the *jhala*—the final climactic movement, where the tempo increasingly accelerates until its peak. Ragas are traditionally played at specific times of day. This one, played after midnight, has a romantic theme of a lady waiting hopefully for her lover to return.

 Scan this code to hear George play sitar on "Norwegian Wood."

Who Really Invented Raga Rock?

The Beatles may have been influenced by raga rock (and raga avant-garde). But they did not invent it. In the early sixties, avant-garde musicians of La Monte Young's Theatre of Eternal Music recorded experimental drone music and often performed at Yoko Ono's loft in New York. George Harrison's *Wonderwall Music* resembles Young's compositions. La Monte Young, John Cale, Terry Riley, Tony Conrad, Don Cherry, and others studied Kirana Indian music with master vocalist Pandit Pran Nath.

In the early sixties as well, British folk guitarist Davey Graham (student of Hindu guru Bhagwan Shree Rajneesh, a.k.a. Osho) combined jazz, folk, blues, and Indian ragas and pioneered DADGAD tuning. In 1963, he arranged a traditional Irish folk song, "She Moves Through the Fair" as a guitar raga, which Jimmy Page plagiarized as "White Summer," failing to credit Graham.[72]

Scan this code to hear Graham's brilliant wonder, "She Moved Thru' the Bizarre/Blue Raga."

The Yardbirds featured a sitar on their February 1965 unreleased demo "Heart Full of Soul." In June 1965, Jeff Beck imitated the sitar part using a fuzzbox on his guitar. The song became a hit. In the Kinks' single "See My Friend," recorded April 1965, Dave Davies' guitar replicated an Indian drone sound. On a Kinks tour stopover in India in December 1964, early morning chanting heard on a beach near Bombay (now Mumbai) had inspired Ray Davies.[73] "The Inner Light" (March 1968) by The Beatles resembles its Indian-style melody.

Surprisingly, the birth of raga rock should be attributed to Davey Graham, the Yardbirds, and the Kinks—not The Beatles!

Scan this code to hear the sitar demo of "Heart Full of Soul."

Scan this code to hear "See My Friend."

Beatles Beat Themselves

In the race for first raga rock genre record, The Beatles beat themselves! Their album *Help! (Original Motion Picture Soundtrack)*, released August 13, 1965, preceded "Norwegian Wood" in featuring Indian instruments on these tracks: "James Bond Theme," "From Me to You Fantasy," "Another Hard Day's Night," and "The Chase."

Scan this code to hear
"Another Hard Day's Night."

Along with The Beatles, sixties flower children fell in love with all things Indian, equating Indian music, dress, jewelry, food, crafts, culture, hashish, and Hindu and Buddhist religions with "Flower Power," "free love," and the psychedelic revolution—to the horror of Ravi Shankar, aghast that his classical Hindustani music was associated with LSD and that stoned druggies populated his concerts. Ravi joked with Dick Cavett: "I request my listeners to be in a clear mind, because I like to make them high with my music, and I feel rather cheated when they're already high."[74]

After all, Ravi grew up in the sacred Hindu "City of Temples," Benares (later Varanasi), home to three thousand temples. There, his passion for Nada Brahma ("Sound of God") awakened. He studied under strict tutelage of sarod (like a fretless guitar) maestro Allauddin Khan, far from the hippie subculture of Haight-Ashbury.

How Yoga Found The Beatles

George celebrated his twenty-second birthday on February 25, 1965, while filming *Help!* in the Bahamas. That morning, The Beatles were waiting for their shoot of circling round on bicycles to an instrumental of "Just to Dance with You."

Suddenly, an Indian swami in orange robes approached them. John described, "A little yogi runs over to us. We didn't know what they were in those days, and this little Indian guy gives us a book each, signed to us, on yoga."[75] Foremost Hatha Yoga exponent Swami Vishnudevananda, who founded the Sivananda Ashram Yoga Retreat on Paradise Island, handed each Beatle an autographed copy of the first Hatha Yoga how-to manual published in the West.

John said The Beatles' interest in Indian music and yoga "all [came] from that crazy movie. All of the Indian involvement came out of the film *Help!*"[76] George recalled that meeting the swami was "the start of it all for me." He felt "somebody must have whispered in his inner ear to give us his book, *The Illustrated Book of Yoga*."[77]

Years later, when George desired to visit Rishikesh, India, he picked up the book and was amazed to find the swami's yoga center was a branch of Sivananda Ashram in Rishikesh, right across the Ganges River from Maharishi Mahesh Yogi's Meditation Academy. After becoming vegetarian, George read in the swami's book, "Monkeys don't get headaches; all human ailments and diseases come from an unnatural diet."[78]

The "Flying Swami" on his peace flights.

In his twin-engine Piper Apache plane, decorated by artist Peter Max, "The Flying Swami" conducted peace flights over the world's trouble spots on "boundary-breaking missions." His message, "Man is free as a bird," challenged all manmade borders and mentally constructed boundaries. Marching through the streets of Belfast with Peter Sellers, he chanted, "Love thy neighbor as thyself." Swami Vishnudevananda issued "Planet Earth passports" to the four Beatles.

On February 18, 1968, while The Beatles were studying at Maharishi's ashram in India, the swami broadcast from Los Angeles, criticizing Maharishi for teaching watered-down yoga: "He tells young people that it is easy to find inner peace, that you can drink, smoke, and eat anything you want and need only meditate fifteen minutes a day." He also disparaged Maharishi's beard: "It is only for attracting attention."[79]

"Nowhere Man"

Written: September and October 1965
Recorded: October 21 to 22, 1965
Released: December 3, 1965: Rubber Soul
UK; February 21, 1966: Single US

"Nowhere Man" was a major turning point for The Beatles to realize their music could be about "more than just holding hands." This work of genius was one of The Beatles' first that explored deeper themes. Three years later, the song appeared brilliantly in the movie *Yellow Submarine*. It broke the mold and opened possibilities previously never "imagined."

Revelation of John the Divine Beatle

John described that one morning, he tried to write a good, meaningful song for five hours. Finally, he gave up. "Then 'Nowhere Man' came, words and music, the whole damn thing, as I lay down. So letting it go is what the whole game is."[80] John said that once he let go, "Then I thought of myself as Nowhere Man—sitting in this Nowhere Land."[81]

Receiving instant revelations from a non-physical source is a uniquely Eastern idea. In the West, we respect logic, science, and left-brain activities. But in India and the Far East, feeling, intuition, and right-brain activities are valued. Such geniuses as Einstein and composers Mozart and Beethoven received their brilliant insights from their inner genius—the higher mind. Though The Beatles were already creative masterminds, psychedelic experimentation opened them even further to the unlimited possibilities of tapping "inner space."

Scan this code to
read the lyrics.

The Lyrics

The brilliant music and lyrics that John received in his somnambulant state, between waking and dreaming, continue to inspire generations of Beatles fans with its message of empowerment.

Buddha tells us, in the first verse of the first chapter of the Dhammapada (the essential Buddhist scripture): "All that we are is the result of what we have thought: it is founded on our thoughts, it is made up of our thoughts. If a person speaks or acts with an evil thought, pain follows him or her. If a person speaks or acts with a pure thought, happiness follows him or her."[82]

This verse says we create our own destiny primarily through our thoughts and feelings, but also speech and actions. It might be difficult to control random thoughts streaming through our mind. But we can easily control our words and deeds. For example, if we constantly say, "I am so poor, I am so unhappy, I am so sick," and so on, then these negative results will appear in our life. If, on the other hand, we often say, "I am wealthy, I am happy, I am healthy," and the like, then these positive results will manifest.

Wearing blinders, Nowhere Man (who is a bit like all of us) wanders around wallowing in negativity, without viewpoint or direction, like a boat with no rudder tossing about on the sea. To become the conscious captain of his ship of destiny, he must take command of his thoughts, words, and deeds.

All possibilities are available to him, and he is not alone. With friends lending a helping hand, he can steer his ship, go somewhere, and be something just by making a plan, following through, and persevering with determination.

John's Inner Reflection

Paul believed that John wrote the song about himself, his own feelings of going nowhere, and his dissatisfaction about his marriage.[83] In 1994, Paul explained, "I think at that point in his life, he was wondering where he was going."[84]

John confessed to childhood mate Pete Shotton: "The more I have, the more I see, and the more experience I get, the more confused I become as to who I am, and what the hell life is all about."[85]

John's 1965 breakthrough "Nowhere Man" was our first glimpse at his impassioned activism that he championed in later years. With a little help from his bandmates, and with inspiration from Bob Dylan, John transcended teeny-bop pop and invented his own meaningful lyrical style.

"The Word"

Written: October to November 1965
Recorded: November 10, 1965
Released: December 3, 1965: Rubber Soul

There is no doubt The Beatles' essential message could be summed up in one word: Love. "The Word" was arguably their first venture into a universal definition of "love" beyond the teenage crush. But what is astounding is this song's prescience of the Indian concept of *mantra*.

What Is Mantra?

Usually, the term *mantra* refers to words in the Sanskrit language—potent vibrational sounds, chanted audibly or repeated mentally to produce beneficial effects. But mantras are affirmations and they can be in any language. They can help us achieve our heart's desires, attain higher consciousness, and realize the truth. Ultimately, they can bring liberation—freedom from chains of the illusory material world.

The word *mantra* was not in the English language in 1965. Two years later, The Beatles received their own mantras from Maharishi Mahesh Yogi on August 26, 1967. "The Word" was released pre-Maharishi, pre-Ravi Shankar, and pre-"Summer of Love." We might wonder whether John Lennon knew what he was writing.

The Beatles were way ahead of their time by suggesting a word could change hearts and minds. Two years later, the motto "Make Love, Not War" would define the hippie counterculture. The anti-war movement would advocate universal love, planetary brotherhood, world peace, and "Flower Power." At the pinnacle of the "Summer of Love," The Youngbloods' "Get Together," released July 1967, reflected those times. But The Beatles got there two years earlier with what Beatles biographer Barry Miles called "one of the first hippie anthems"—"The Word."[86]

 Scan this code to read the lyrics.

Love Is the Word

John said, "It's the marijuana period. It's love. It's a love and peace thing. The word is 'love,' right?"[87] According to the Masters and Houston study presented in *The Varieties of Psychedelic Experience*, a common experience of subjects who took psychedelic drugs was a feeling of universal love and harmony—Christ-like love of all beings.[88]

"*Rubber Soul* was the first one where we were fully-fledged potheads," George declared. During his first LSD trip in April 1965, "Suddenly the most incredible feeling [came] over me. It was fantastic. I had an overwhelming desire to go round the club telling everybody how much I loved them—people I'd never seen before."[89]

In John's final interview, he recalled, "It sort of dawned on me that love was the answer, when I was younger, on *Rubber Soul*. My first expression of it was a song called 'The Word.'"[90] "'The word is love' seemed like the underlying theme to the Universe or to everything that was worthwhile. I wanna be as loving as possible. In the Christian sense, as Christ-like as possible. In the Hindu sense, as Gandhi-esque as possible."[91]

"Day Tripper"

Written: September to October 1965
Recorded: October 16, 1965
Released: December 3, 1965: Single UK;
June 15, 1966: Yesterday and Today

In 1970, John Lennon said "Day Tripper" was a drug song.[92] He admitted The Beatles always needed drugs to survive, but he "always took more pills and more of everything, 'cause I'm more crazy."[93] In 1980, John explained, "Day trippers are people who go on day trips, right? Usually on a ferryboat or something. But the song was, kind of, 'You're a weekend hippie.'"[94]

In 2004, Paul declared "Day Tripper" was a psychedelic wink and nod to LSD, a tongue-in-cheek song about tripping on acid. He loved hidden messages for the in-crowd who could decipher them—"putting in references that we knew our friends would get but that the Great British Empire might not. The mums and dads didn't get it but the kids did."[95]

However, two years later, The Beatles no longer minced words. In 1967, John sang: "blew his mind," "had a smoke," "went into a dream," and "turn you on."

 Scan this code to read the lyrics.

Paul said the song described "someone who was a day tripper, a Sunday painter, Sunday driver, committed only in part to the idea. Whereas we saw ourselves as full-time trippers, fully committed drivers, she was just a day tripper."[96]

While writing the song, Paul and John agreed it would be fun to sing "big teaser," actually meaning "prick teaser": "That was one of the great things about collaborating, you could nudge-nudge, wink-wink a bit," said Paul.[97]

Who Was the Real Day Tripper?

It is highly ironic that the Day Tripper/Sunday driver best described the song's composer himself, Paul—the only Beatle who had not taken LSD before the song's release, December 3, 1965. Paul took LSD ten days later: December 13, 1965. Here is how it happened:

After The Beatles' final performance in Cardiff on December 12, 1965, at the end of their UK tour, they celebrated at the Scotch of St James nightclub. The following night, John and Paul returned to the club. There, they met The Who's bassist John Entwistle, Pretty Things' drummer Viv Prince, and also ran into Nicky Browne, wife of the Honorable Tara Browne (heir to the Guinness beer fortune and son of a seventy-two-year House of Lords member). The Beatles' "Day in the Life" portrayed Tara's car accident that took his life a year later, December 18, 1966.

Nicky invited the in-crowd to party at her home in Eaton Row in Belgravia. John bowed out and returned home to Weybridge. Paul, Viv Prince, and dancer Patrick Kerr from *Ready Steady Go!* (pop music TV show) accepted Nicky's invitation. Upon their arrival, Nicky's husband Tara suggested they all take LSD.

Paul did not want to take acid. But as part of a band, there was more than peer pressure. He described it as "fear pressure. It becomes trebled, more than just your mates, it's, 'Hey, man, this whole band's had acid, why are you holding out?'"[98] Realizing he would have to succumb eventually, Paul figured this time was as good as any. So he agreed. He spent the entire trip staring at an art book called *Private View*.

John said The Beatles were never the same after taking LSD, and Paul agreed. "I don't think any of us ever were. It was such a mind-expanding thing." Paul described feeling deeply emotional, wanting to cry, and "seeing God or sensing all the majesty and emotional depth of everything."[99] "God is in everything. God is in the space between us. God is in the table in front of you. I realized all this through acid."[100]

Fifteen months later, on March 21, 1967, Paul finally took an LSD trip with John. When they locked eyes, Paul had a "mind-boggling" experience of dissolving into each other: "You're looking into each other's eyes and you could see yourself in the other person. It was a very freaky experience and I was totally blown away. You ask yourself, 'How do you lead a normal life after that?' And the answer is, you don't."[101]

On December 13, 1965, Paul decided to give up the life of marijuana Day Tripper and became a full-time LSD Tripper.

"Tomorrow Never Knows"

Written: April 1966
Recorded: April 6, 7, and 22, 1966
Released: August 5, 1966: Revolver

When John and George arranged the LSD party in Beverly Hills for Paul and Ringo, Paul declined the drug. Yet Beatles producer George Martin considered Paul the most progressive Beatle. Paul viewed his Beatle-mates as very square—married and living in the suburbs.

At the hub and heartbeat of London's hip scene, Paul explored cutting-edge pop music and avant-garde culture. He ascribed to Bertrand Russell's philosophy, became a pacifist anti-war protester, and influenced John to become a peacenik. In quest of all things countercultural, Paul followed experimental classical composers

Karlheinz Stockhausen, Luciano Berio, and Edgard Varèse, and jazz musicians Albert Ayler and John Cage. Paul said: "People are saying things and painting things and writing things and composing things that are great, and I must know what people are doing."[102]

Indica Books and Gallery opened in November 1965 at 6 Mason's Yard, St James's, London. The name "Indica" referred to *cannabis indica*, a marijuana species. This underground shop was founded by John Dunbar, Barry Miles, and silent partner Peter Asher (half of British pop duo Peter and Gordon). At the time, Paul was living with his girlfriend Jane Asher (Peter's sister) at her family home, 57 Wimpole Street. Paul invested £5,000 in Indica; created flyers to promote it; designed wrapping paper; designed, sawed, plastered, and painted the shop; and was their first and best customer. He rifled through esoteric books at night, keeping some and sending others to fellow Beatles.

On April 1, 1966, Paul and John visited Indica. John said he was seeking "Nitz Ga." Despite the mispronunciation, Barry Miles handed John *The Portable Nietzsche*—along with a portion of ridicule. John retorted, "Tell Ginsberg I did it first!" (In 1955, John filled his school exercise book with funny cartoons, poems, and stories, and named it "the Daily Howl." Allen Ginsberg's *Howl and Other Poems* was published a year later.)

While scanning the Indica bookshelves, John stumbled across *The Psychedelic Experience*. Miles recalled, "John was delighted and settled down on the settee with the book."[103] He finished reading it in the shop.

Published January 1, 1964, *The Psychedelic Experience: A Manual Based on the Tibetan Book of the Dead* was authored by Timothy Leary, Ralph Metzner, and Richard Alpert (a.k.a. Ram Dass, author of the 1971 classic *Be Here Now*). In 1963, these professors got dismissed from Harvard for conducting experimental psychedelic therapy sessions on students and hosting "tripping" parties with LSD, psilocybin, and mescaline.

Based on the ancient Buddhist text Bardo Thodol (Liberation by Hearing on the After-Death Plane), a.k.a. the Tibetan Book of the Dead, Leary's guidebook navigated the "ego death" experienced on acid trips—a shortcut to the "void."

According to Indian philosophy, consciousness is not material. It is spiritual. Every living thing is an eternal being: *atman,* which was never born and never dies. When the physical body dies, the soul transmigrates into another womb and takes rebirth. Trapped by the illusory physical plane, souls reincarnate time after time. By mistakenly identifying ourselves as the false self (ego), we repeatedly revolve around the grindstone of relentless recurring reincarnation, known in Buddhism as *samsara,* the "Wheel of Birth and Death." When we realize our true self (atman) and attain liberation (moksha), we no longer return to the physical world. We merge with "the void"—universal consciousness.

Timothy Leary commented: "'Book of the Dead' really means 'Book of the Dying' but it's your ego rather than your body which is dying. The concept of Buddhism is of the void and of reaching the void."[104]

The Psychedelic Experience flew off the bookshelves because hippies needed a roadmap to chart their otherworldly experiences induced by LSD.

More Popular Than Jesus

Though George was considered the Beatle most influenced by Indian religion, John was just as fervent in his quest for enlightenment. One month before his visit to Indica, on March 4, 1966, John was quoted: "Christianity will go. It will vanish and shrink. We're more popular than Jesus now; I don't know which will go first—rock 'n' roll or Christianity. Jesus was all right but his disciples were thick and ordinary. It's them twisting it that ruins it for me."[105]

These remarks garnered no reaction in Europe, but caused a firestorm in the USA, as those dubbed by John "fascist Christians" burned Beatles albums en masse. John apologized to the press on August 12 in Chicago, but declared, "I view God not as an old man in the sky. I believe that what people call God is something in all of us."[106] To many Christians, that Eastern view of God was blasphemy.

The Title

The working title for "Tomorrow Never Knows" was "The Void." But John decided he would use "one of Ringo's malapropisms as the title, to take the edge off the heavy philosophical lyrics."[107]

After The Beatles returned from their first tour to America in early 1964, David Coleman of BBC Television asked Ringo, "I hear you were manhandled at the Embassy Ball. Is this right?"

Ringo replied, "Not really. Someone just cut a bit of my hair. I looked 'round, and there was about four hundred people just smiling. So, you know—what can you say?"

Then John chimed in: "What can you say?"

Ringo then replied, "Tomorrow never knows."[108]

George explained, "Ringo would always say grammatically incorrect phrases and we'd all laugh."[109] But John would write them down and use them, such as "A Hard Day's Night."

 Scan this code to read the lyrics.

The Lyrics

In "Tomorrow Never Knows," John conveyed the meaning of the following passage from *The Psychedelic Experience*: "Beyond the restless flowing electricity of life is the ultimate reality—The Void. Your own awareness, not formed into anything possessing form or color, is naturally void. The Final Reality."[110]

The song is a meditation manual. John sang about letting go of the mind and discovering inner meaning in the infinite void, beyond fluctuating thoughts. In that state of harmony in deep meditation, all is love, peace of mind, relaxation of body, and compassion of heart—free from discord.

George interpreted, "From birth to death all we ever do is think. Even when you are asleep you are having dreams. But you can turn off your mind, and go to the part which Maharishi described as: 'Where was your last thought before you thought it?'"[111]

In Hindu and Buddhist belief, we are never born and never die. Grieving the dead is an illusion, since the deathless state is truth and death is untruth. In the Bhagavad Gita, Lord Krishna said, "The wise lament neither for the living nor for the dead. Never was there a time when I did not exist, nor you, nor all these kings; nor in the future shall any of us cease to be."[112]

John described our physical existence as a phantasmic dream. We generally experience waking, dream, and deep sleep states of awareness. In meditation, we attain higher consciousness—*turiya* (literally "fourth state") beyond these three illusory states. Turiya is known as transcendental awareness, nirvana, or samadhi—the void. A common expression in India is "The waking state is a long dream." To awaken from that dream, we must attain moksha (liberation).

George explained, "The goal of meditation is to go beyond (that is, transcend) waking, sleeping and dreaming. The true nature of each soul is pure consciousness. So the song is really about transcending and the quality of the transcendent. [John] knew he was onto something when he saw those words and turned them into a song. But to have experienced what the lyrics are actually about? I don't know if he fully understood it."[113]

The Psychedelic Experience dealt with various ego "games," which take the soul away from liberation. The term "game" appeared 124 times in the text. John referred to a "game" he called "Existence" in his lyrics. Here is a passage from the book:

"'Games' are behavioral sequences defined by roles, rules, rituals, goals, strategies, values, language, characteristic space-time locations and characteristic patterns of movement. Any behavior not having these nine features is non-game: this includes physiological reflexes, spontaneous play, and transcendent awareness."[114]

John's Experiment

The Psychedelic Experience stated repeatedly that to attain liberation, the free consciousness needs only to hear and remember the teachings. So John recorded passages from the book, then played them back while on acid. One passage said, "Do not cling in fondness and weakness to your old self. Even though you cling to your old mind, you have lost the power to keep it. Trust your divinity, trust your brain, and trust your companions. Whenever in doubt, turn off your mind, relax, float downstream."[115]

In 1980, John said, "Leary was going round saying, take it, take it, take it. And we followed his instructions in his 'how to take a trip' book. I did it just like he said in the book, and then I wrote 'Tomorrow Never Knows.'"[116]

LSD Pioneers

The Psychedelic Experience was rooted in Indian mysticism. Its introduction included a dedication to Aldous Huxley and tributes to American anthropologist W. Y. Evans-Wentz, Swiss psychiatrist Carl G. Jung, and German Lama Anagarika Govinda. These twentieth-century pioneers brought much of the wisdom of India to the West.

Lifelong student of Indian Vedanta philosophy, Aldous Huxley, author of *Brave New World*, correlated Western and Eastern mysticism in his book *The Perennial Philosophy*. His *The Doors of Perception* chronicled his mescaline experiments (inspiring Jim Morrison to name his group The Doors, as well as a line in John Lennon's "Help!" about opening up those doors).

Walter Yeeling Evans-Wentz studied Madame Blavatsky's Theosophy and met spiritual masters Paramahansa Yogananda, J. Krishnamurti, and Ramana Maharshi. Evans-Wentz's books, including those he translated or edited, topped the sixties counterculture booklist: The Tibetan Book of the Dead, *Tibet's Great Yogi Milarepa*, *Tibetan Yoga and Secret Doctrines*, *The Tibetan Book of the Great Liberation*, and preface to Yogananda's *Autobiography of a Yogi*.

Carl Gustav Jung postulated a "collective unconscious." His "Jungian archetypes" were multi-cultural, universal symbols in religious art, mythology, and fairy tales. Jung stated, "The Bardo Thodol has been my constant companion, and to it I owe many stimulating ideas and discoveries, [and] many fundamental insights."[117]

Lama Anagarika Govinda, German painter, poet, and teacher of Tibetan Buddhism, Abhidharma, and Buddhist meditation, founded the Arya Maitreya Mandala order. Govinda and his wife Li Gotami were initiated into the Drukpa Kagyu lineage. Govinda rented Evans-Wentz's house on "Crank's Ridge," near Kasar Devi temple, above Almora, Uttarakhand, India. This "Hippie Hill" was an alleged "power center" and landmark on the "Hippie Trail," supposedly due to a gap in the Van Allen Belt (more likely, due to abundant cannabis cultivation).

Spiritual masters Anandamayi Ma and Neem Karoli Baba visited Lama Govinda on the pine-covered ridge. Danish mystic Alfred Sunyata Sorensen was granted land there. Spiritual seekers flocked there, including Beat poets Allen Ginsberg, Gary Snyder, and Joanne Kyger; musicians Bob Dylan and Cat Stevens; LSD Gurus Timothy Leary, Ralph Metzner, and Richard Alpert (Ram Dass); and psychiatrist R. D. Laing. Leary famously streaked on the ridge.

Tibetologist Robert Thurman with his wife Nena von Schlebrügge (former wife of Timothy Leary), and their three-year old child Uma Thurman (the Oscar-nominated actress), studied with Lama Govinda at Hippie Hill for six months in 1971.

Visitors became so overbearing that signs were posted to keep tourists away. Evans-Wentz's estate later became a Buddhist ashram: Bodh Ashram.

With these psychedelic forerunners associated with *The Psychedelic Experience*, LSD gained credibility as a viable spiritual practice. But it gained even greater respect when The Beatles sang about it.

The Beatles on LSD

George saw LSD as a blessing. It saved him many years of indifference.[118] "After much success in The Beatles, the question came: What is it all about? Then, purely because of the force-fed LSD experience, I had the realization of God. The ego identity fools us into thinking, 'I am this body.' LSD gave me the experience of: 'I am not this body. I am pure energy soaring about everywhere.'"[119]

With childlike enthusiasm, George believed everyone who took LSD became enlightened. But he eventually discovered it did not make people spiritual. Many just experienced an Alice-in-Wonderland chimera. He warned drugs are not a path to self-realization and can be dangerous: You might "go so far out in your mind that you think you've lost your grip. In a way, you don't ever really return to how you were before."[120]

Ringo believed LSD changes everyone: "It makes you look at yourself and your feelings and emotions. And it brought me closer to the force of nature and its beauty. You realize it's not just a tree; it's a living thing."[121]

Paul said, "It opened my eyes. Just think what we could accomplish if we could only tap that hidden part [of our brain]! If politicians would take LSD, there wouldn't be any more war, poverty, or famine."[122]

George agreed: "If I had half a chance, I'd put acid in the Government's tea."[123]

"Acid is only real life in CinemaScope. Whatever experience you had is what you would have had anyway," John said.[124] "I must have had 1000 trips. I used to eat it all the time. I stopped taking it because of bad trips. I got a message on acid that you should destroy your ego. I was reading that stupid book of Leary's, all that shit. I destroyed myself and I didn't believe I could do anything, and I was nothing; I was shit."[125]

John was unaware that by giving up the false ego and embracing our true Self, we lose nothing. Instead, we gain contentment, confidence, happiness, and fulfillment. The "void" is not nihilism. It is our magnificent true divine nature.

Recording the Song

Shortly after John's visit to Indica, he composed "Mark 1"—later retitled "Tomorrow Never Knows." John made two requests to arranger George Martin: for his voice to sound like "the Dalai Lama singing from a mountaintop twenty-five miles away from the studio,"[126] and for "thousands of monks chanting" on the track.[127]

The Hammond organ in the studio was connected to a Leslie speaker—an amp and two sets of revolving speakers: one for low bass and another for high treble frequencies. A vocal had never been fed through it. The Beatles' new engineer Geoff Emerick double-tracked John's vocals and amplified them through the Leslie speaker to achieve an exotic echoing effect.

Geoff recalled that John's "voice sounded like it never had before, eerily disconnected, distant yet compelling. The effect seemed to perfectly complement the esoteric lyrics he was chanting. Everyone in the control room looked stunned. Through the glass we could see John begin smiling. He gave an exuberant thumbs-up and McCartney and Harrison began slapping each other on the back. 'It's the Dalai Lennon!' Paul shouted."

John, clearly bowled over, kept repeating, "That is bloody marvelous."[128]

Inspired by avant-garde composer Karlheinz Stockhausen, Paul's tape loops of guitar-tuning and odd shrieks produced a mesmerizing, seagull-like squawk when George Martin played them forward and backward, then ran them through several interconnected tape machines simultaneously.

George suggested a tambura Indian drone stringed instrument. He said, "It's perfect for this track, John. It's just kind of a droning sound and I think it will make the whole thing quite Eastern." John nodded his head.[129]

"George showed up with the tambura he had so eagerly talked of during the first night's session," recalled Geoff. "Actually, he'd been talking about it almost nonstop since then, so everyone was really curious."[130]

Reluctant to let roadies handle the precious instrument, George transported it in his Porsche and lugged it upstairs himself. "He staggered into the studio under its weight—the case was the size of a small coffin—and brought it out with a grand gesture, displaying it proudly as we gathered around," Geoff said. "I recorded him playing a single note on the huge instrument—using a close-miking technique—and turned it into a loop. It ended up becoming the sound that opens the track."[131] (See pages 72 and 73 for photo of a tambura.)

"'Tomorrow Never Knows' was a great innovation," George Martin said. "John wanted a very spooky kind of track, a very ethereal sound."[132] But John reflected later he would have preferred the chanting monks.

PART II

SITARS AND HASH PIPES FOREVER

CHAPTER 3

ROAD TO RAPTURE

"Love You To"

Written: March to April 1966
Recorded: April 11 and 13, 1966
Released: August 5, 1966: Revolver

"Love You To" was the first song George Harrison wrote for Indian musical instruments. He said, "The sitar sounded so nice and my interest was getting deeper all the time. I wanted to write a tune that was specifically for the sitar."[133]

George believed Indian music made Western music seem dead, with its three or four beats to a measure: "When I first heard Indian music I just couldn't really believe that it was so, so great. And the more I heard of it, the more I liked it. And it just got bigger and bigger, like a snowball."[134] "You can get so much more out of it if you are prepared really to concentrate and listen. I hope more people will try to dig it."[135]

Asian Music Circle leaders with George; l. to r.: George, Ayana Angadi, Patricia Fell-Clark, Pattie Boyd.

Asian Music Circle

In 1946, Indian writer and activist Ayana Angadi and his British wife Patricia Fell-Clark founded the Asian Music Circle (AMC), at their home in Fitzalan Road, Finchley, North London. The organization promoted Asian arts and culture. Inspired by meeting Ravi Shankar in India, American violin virtuoso Yehudi Menuhin became president of AMC in 1953. By inviting B. K. S. Iyengar (founder of Iyengar Yoga) to teach at AMC, Menuhin introduced yoga to Britain.

In 1955, AMC hosted the first classical Indian music concerts in the West at the "Living Arts of India Festival" in New York, which introduced Ali Akbar Khan (on sarod), Ravi Shankar (Khan's brother-in-law, on sitar), and Vilayat Khan (on sitar). This led to the first Indian music album in the West: *Music of India: Morning and Evening Ragas* (Angel 1955), and to Ravi Shankar's popularity in the jazz community.

Ustad Ali Akbar Khan playing sarod. Courtesy of Ali Akbar Khan Foundation.
Photograph by Betsey Bourbon Bruner.

George Martin, staff producer at EMI's Parlophone Records, had previously gotten referrals from AMC's Ayana Angadi to hire local Indian musicians for film and recording work, including Goon Show comedy records, such as "Wouldn't It Be Loverly" by Peter Sellers.[136] In 1962, Martin began working with The Beatles when they signed with Parlophone. Under Martin's influence, their film *Help!* featured an Indian-themed script and musicians.

As George Harrison was playing sitar on "Norwegian Wood" in the recording studio on October 21, 1965, a string broke. Martin suggested contacting Ayana Angadi for a replacement. Ringo made the phone call and Angadi's daughter asked loudly, "Ringo who?" Angadi rushed to the phone, and then brought the string, along with his wife and four children, to EMI's Abbey Road Studios, to watch The Beatles record.[137]

For the next six months, George and Pattie spent every weekend at the Angadi home, discovering Indian music. They attended recitals at AMC and watched Indian sitar virtuoso Ravi Shankar perform at the Royal Festival Hall.[138] With enthusiasm to master sitar, George began studying with an AMC sitar player.[139]

George learning to play tambura from AMC teacher. Photograph by Thomas Picton, Camera Press London.

In Sept. 1970 George would open the Indian Music and Dance Festival with Ravi at Royal Festival Hall; l. to r.: tambura stringed drone instrument, unknown man, North Indian classical singer Girija Devi, Ravi Shankar, Kathak dancer Uma Sharma, George Harrison. Pictorial Press Ltd/Alamy Stock Photo.

Recording the Song

"Love You To" was arranged in a classical Hindustani structure. For the recording session on April 11, 1966, George hired unidentified musicians referred by Angadi to play the Indian music track. Instruments on the track included sitar (like slide guitar), tabla (bass and treble drums), *swarmandal* (box zither), and tambura (drone lute).

 Scan this code to watch these same instruments played by classical musicians Ravi Shankar, Alla Rakha, and Kamala Chakravarty.

Anil Bhagwat was hired to play tabla drums—the first time tabla ever appeared on a Beatles song. Bhagwat recalled, "Angadi called and asked if I was free that evening to work with George. He didn't say it was Harrison. It was only when a Rolls Royce picked me up that I realized I'd be playing on a Beatles session.

"When I arrived at Abbey Road, there were girls everywhere with Thermos flasks, cakes, sandwiches, waiting for The Beatles to come out."[140] "George told me what he wanted and I tuned the tabla with him. He suggested I play something in the Ravi Shankar style, sixteen-beats, though he agreed that I should improvise. Indian music is all improvisation. It was one of the most exciting times of my life."[141]

Sound engineer Geoff Emerick placed a sensitive ribbon mike inches from the tabla drums, and heavily compressed the signal, which produced an intense sound. This was a first. Tabla had always been miked from a distance. George and the Indian musicians commented on it afterward.

Other than Anil Bhagwat, AMC musicians that performed on "Love You To" have never been identified. Bhagwat claimed, "I can tell you here and now—100 percent it was George on sitar throughout."[142] Considering that George did not begin studying sitar with Ravi Shankar until June 1966, it would be quite a stretch to imagine he was the only sitar player on this recording in April 1966.

Sitarist Ted Morano told me that to strengthen what George played, another sitarist probably overdubbed the main melody and also played the fadeout at the end. Ted believes George played the middle solo and the introduction, because "it is very unconventional to repeatedly strum the open main playing strings in reverse order (low to high), and to punctuate each phrase with a harmonic note. No trained sitarist would play that way."

"Love You To" was the first pop song to present Indian music in an authentic structure and arrangement, which earned George the title "The Mystic Beatle." George's hypnotic, drone-like vocals, along with double tracking, augmented the Indian effect.

Meeting Ravi Shankar

George Harrison first met Ravi Shankar on June 1, 1966, during the sitar maestro's AMC tour of England that featured a duet with Yehudi Menuhin at Bath Musical Festival. Ayana Angadi hosted a dinner in Ravi's honor. Paul McCartney arrived early and crashed the party.

Ravi's immediate impression of George was of a "sweet, straightforward young man" asking questions and genuinely interested in Indian music and religion. When Ravi told George he had not heard "Norwegian Wood," George seemed embarrassed about lacking skill. He admitted his attempts at playing sitar on Beatles' records were merely experiments. Ravi commented, "I felt strongly that there was a beautiful soul in him, and recognized one quality which is considered the principal one in our culture—humility."[143] Ravi felt that, considering George's enormous fame, he remained quite unassuming, with a childlike quality that he continued to retain.

When George expressed his desire to study with Ravi, the maestro said it takes ten to fifteen years to become a good sitar player, like mastering classical violin or cello, but also having to learn the entire Indian musical system. George promised to do his best to devote the time and effort required.[144] Ravi reflected, "When George Harrison came to me, I didn't know what to think. But I found he really wanted to learn."[145]

George had no idea what he was getting into. Sarod maestro Ali Akbar Khan said, "If you practice for ten years, you may please yourself, after twenty years you may please the audience, after thirty years you may please your guru, but you must practice for many more years before you become a true artist—then you may please even God."[146]

Ravi remarked that rock musicians just picked up sitars and plucked them, as a random person might pick up a violin, scratch on it, and ask whether you like the scratches: "It takes a long time to produce the real sound and play the real music."[147]

The first time Ravi visited George and Pattie's home at Kinfauns in Surrey, he gave George a lesson, and then performed a private recital for all The Beatles along with his accompanist, famed tabla player Ustad Alla Rakha.

Ustad Alla Rakha playing tabla and Pandit Ravi Shankar playing sitar.
© Jack Vartoogian/Front Row Photos.

Twice in one week, with tremendous patience, compassion, and humility, Ravi gave George basic lessons: sitting properly, holding the sitar, wearing the pick, fingering, and elementary scales and melodies. Ignorant of basic etiquette in Hindustani classical music, George horrified Ravi by stepping over his sitar to answer the phone. Ravi gave him a sharp whack on his leg for disrespecting his instrument.[148]

After his first lesson, George remembered: "I wanted to walk out of my home that day and take a one-way ticket to Calcutta. I would even have left Pattie behind in that moment and all I would have taken would have been my sitar."[149]

Ravi recalled, "'Norwegian Wood' was supposedly causing so much brouhaha, but when I eventually heard the song, I thought it was a strange sound that had been produced on the sitar."[150] "It was strange to see pop musicians with sitars. I was confused at first. It had so little to do with our classical music. I never thought our meeting would cause such an explosion—that Indian music would suddenly appear on the pop scene. It's peculiar. But out of this, a real interest is growing."[151]

Though Ravi was well known, his association with The Beatles raised his status from sitarist to "rock star sitarist." Worldwide popularity in Indian music skyrocketed.

Scan this code to
read the lyrics.

The Lyrics

"Love You To" is about the fleeting, ephemeral nature of the physical world. Indian philosophy says material life is not permanent
and therefore not real. This corporeal body we temporarily inhabit
is not our true nature. Attachments to the physical plane bind us
to chains of ignorance. Divine love, free from ego-attachment, is
key to letting go of material bonds. By embracing the simplicity
of pure love, we realize our true divine nature—absolute bliss consciousness (*satchitananda*)—beyond the physical.

This physical body is just one of five sheaths we inhabit during
our brief earthly sojourn. Subtle sheaths of pure liquid light, in
myriad brilliant crystalline hues, vibrating at various frequencies,
pervade our physical frame and extend beyond it. The sheaths are
like veils that hide our luminous higher Self, our true nature—the
unchanging, eternal "I Am" (atman), which vibrates at the highest
frequency. We believe ourselves to be our physical body, thoughts,
feelings, intellect, ego, or experiences. But that is not who we
really are. We are the unbounded, undifferentiated radiance of
Brahman—pure consciousness.

Paul and John Weigh In

In 1966, Paul said The Beatles liked the drone sound in Indian
music and used it on previous songs. "Ticket To Ride" (released
April 9, 1965) was one of the first rock examples of a raga-like drone
chord sustained over the verses. "If I Needed Someone" (released
December 3, 1965) continued that trend, achieved with a twelve-
string guitar. "It's nice to start bridging the two kinds of music.

And it helps people to understand it too—because it's very hard to understand. But once you get into it, it's the greatest," Paul said.[152]

John expressed to Maureen Cleave of the *London Evening Standard*, "It's amazing, this. Don't the Indians appear cool to you? This music is thousands of years old; it makes me laugh, the British going over there and telling them what to do." [153]

"Strawberry Fields Forever"

Written: September and November 1966
Recorded: November 28, 29 and December 8, 9, 15, and 21, 1966
Released: February 13, 1967: Single; November
27, 1967: Magical Mystery Tour

As in many Beatles songs, "Strawberry Fields Forever" is a real place, used as a metaphor. When John Lennon's mother Julia separated from Alfred Lennon, she and John moved in with John Albert "Bobby" Dykins. However, Julia's sister Mimi reported to Social Services that the child was sleeping in the same bed as Julia and Bobby.

In 1946, Julia gave Mimi custody of John, and the five-year-old moved in with Auntie Mimi and her husband George Toogood Smith in a middle-class suburb of Liverpool in a semi-detached house, "Mendips," at 251 Menlove Avenue, Woolton. John described it as a nice house "with a small garden and doctors and lawyers all living around. Not the poor, slummy image that was projected in all The Beatles' stories."[154] Though the other three Beatles lived in government-subsidized housing, the Smiths owned their home.

Mimi admitted to not wanting children, but always wanted John: "He's the one I've waited for."[155] Mimi and George provided John with a stable home, but, unlike John's mother Julia, who encouraged him to become a musician, Mimi treated John with disdain, mocked his ambitions, and drained him of self-confidence.[156]

Strawberry Field, Beaconsfield Road, Woolton was a five-minute walk from Auntie Mimi's house. For seventy years, the imposing Victorian mansion was a Salvation Army children's home. On the grounds, John often played with friends Nigel Whalley and Pete Shotton: "We always had fun at Strawberry Fields. But I used [the name] as an image. I have visions of Strawberry Fields [as] anywhere you want to go."[157]

Paul described Strawberry Fields as a wild, unmanicured garden, "a secret garden like in *The Lion, the Witch and the Wardrobe*. It was a little hideaway where [John] could maybe have a smoke, live in his dreams; so it was a getaway for John."[158]

 Scan this code to
read the lyrics.

The Lyrics

As a youngster, John had a penchant for creative activities like writing and drawing. A visionary, he saw what others could not see: "I would say, 'But this is going on!' and everybody would look at me as if I was crazy. I was so psychic or intuitive or poetic that I was always seeing things in a hallucinatory way." John's other-dimensional perceptions were scary. He read about Oscar Wilde, Dylan Thomas, and Vincent van Gogh, who suffered due to their visions. When John realized society tortured such visionaries for expressing themselves, "I saw loneliness."[159]

Strawberry Fields was John's symbol for an Elysian paradise—a blissful realm beyond the world of suffering. In his metaphoric childhood field of escape, he dreamed of utopia in his mind.

In India, it is believed nothing in this relative world of duality is real and everything is a dream—an illusion of maya (described on page 97–98). Vasistha, a seer of ancient India, described, "I declare again and again: This world-appearance is like a long dream. Wake up, wake up. Behold the self which shines like the sun."[160]

Edgar Allan Poe mused, "All that we see or seem is but a dream within a dream."[161]

Lewis Carroll wrote, "Life, what is it but a dream?"[162]

Albert Einstein opined, "Reality is merely an illusion, although a very persistent one."[163]

John said in his final interview, "In a way, nothing is real. As the Hindus or Buddhists say, it's an illusion. It's *Rashomon*. The agreed-upon illusion is what we live in."[164] Since nothing is real, there is no reason to get disturbed about anything. In the sixties counterculture vernacular, a "hang-up" meant a psychological block. We hippies aspired to be free spirits, unfettered by inhibitions, habits, phobias, or fixations. We wanted nirvana, with no hang-ups attached. The term *nirvana* means "to extinguish"—to let go of the false ego and realize our higher Self.

John could not close his eyes to his higher perceptions. He sought the truth, and truth-seekers rarely have it easy. He took the road less traveled that Robert Frost described in "The Road Not Taken." John accepted his difficult role, and that choice "made all the difference."

John was an individual, unique and different, a trendsetter and a genius. No one but John climbed his tree. It was not scaled by anyone else: "I'm saying, in my insecure way, 'Nobody seems to understand where I'm coming from.'"[165] "Nobody seems to be as hip as me. Therefore, I must be crazy or a genius or an egomaniac for claiming to see things other people didn't see."[166]

In the second and third verses, to express John's self-doubts and uncertainty, the lyrics were expressed haltingly. "'Strawberry Fields' was psychoanalysis set to music," John said. "I think everyone's blocked. Why shouldn't we cry? They tell us to stop crying about [age] twelve. 'Be a man.' What the hell's that? Men hurt."[167]

The Sound

On "Strawberry Fields Forever," another raga-rock track, George played an Indian *swarmandal*, a box zither with about forty metal strings played with one or more plectrums. This instrument was also played on "Love You To," "Within You Without You," and "Wonderwall Music." (See page 421 for a photo of a *swarmandal*.)

Beatles lyrics and sounds in songs like "Strawberry Fields," "Lucy in the Sky with Diamonds," and "Day in the Life" evoke surrealistic images and feelings. John said surrealism affected him greatly, "because then I realized that the imagery in my mind wasn't insanity. Surrealism to me is reality. Psychic vision to me is reality." Even as a child, John would see hallucinations of his face in the mirror "changing and becoming cosmic and complete."[168]

"Within You Without You"

Written: March 1967
Recorded: March 15 and 22, April 3 and 4, 1967
Released: May 26, 1967: Sgt. Pepper's Lonely Hearts Club Band

In July 1966, on their way to London from the Philippines, The Beatles stopped in New Delhi, India, for a couple of days. During this first India visit (other than a Calcutta airport layover in 1964), they visited two music stores. On July 6, they stopped at Lahore Music House in the Daryaganj district. The proprietors, Sardar Harcharan Singh and his brother Gyan Singh, said they gave The Beatles a sitar lesson at their hotel. The Beatles asked Harcharan to teach them Indian classical music. But he refused and referred them to Ravi Shankar.[169]

The following day, on July 7, 1966, The Beatles visited Rikhi Ram and Sons, in Delhi's crowded Connaught Circus shopping center. The master-handcrafter of instruments for sitarist Pandit Ravi Shankar and other legendary musicians, and musical instrument expert for AIR (All-India Radio), proprietor Pandit Bishan Dass Sharma, declared, "This is not a shop; it is a temple."[170]

As Ravi Shankar himself explained, "Music can be a spiritual discipline on the path to self-realization, for we follow the traditional teaching that sound is God—Nada Brahma: By this process individual consciousness can be elevated to a realm of awareness where the revelation of the true meaning of the universe—its eternal and unchanging essence—can be joyfully experienced."[171]

George checking out a sitar in The Beatles' suite at the Oberoi Hotel. TopFoto.

George trying out a sitar. Rikhi Ram proprietor Bishan Dass Sharma in foreground, Bishan's friends Mr. S.L. Kapoor on left, and Sardar Harbhajan Singh (Marina Taxi Service co-owner who transported the instruments) in background. Photo courtesy of Rikhi Ram.

George holding a tambura and Bishan Dass Sharma holding a sarod. Photo courtesy of Rikhi Ram.

From l. to r.: Paul signing an "appreciation letter" thanking Rikhi Ram for its high-quality musical instruments, Bishan Dass Sharma, Sardar Mahendar Singh (Marina Taxi Service co-owner), George, and Mr. S.L. Kapoor. Photo courtesy of Rikhi Ram.

From l. to r.: Bishan Dass Sharma, George, and Paul playing tambura.
Photo courtesy of Rikhi Ram.

Bishan Dass visited The Beatles in their hotel, gave George a sitar lesson, and sold him a superb sitar. Ajay Rikhiram (Bishan's son) told me that when the Fab Four asked Bishan who his teacher was, he answered "Pandit Ravi Shankar" and suggested The Beatles study with him. John bought a sarod (fretless lute), Paul acquired a tambura (drone lute), and Ringo got tabla (drums).[172] Bishan Dass said of his craft, "You will not understand the nuances of music if you are untrained. It is a science that has to be mastered."[173]

In 1995, Ravi Shankar was having trouble tuning his sitar during his seventy-fifth birthday celebration at Siri Fort Auditorium in Delhi. He called out to the crowd, "Bishan Dass *kahan ho* [Where are you]?" The craftsman, who was in the audience, came to his aid. On Ravi's eighty-second birthday in 2002, his sitar-shaped cake broke in half as it was placed on the table. Ravi joked, "Bishan Dass *kahan ho?*"[174]

Travels with Ravi and Shambhu

George related that after an incredible LSD trip where he traveled across time and space, a lingering thought stuck with him: "It was like somebody was whispering to me, 'The yogis of the Himalayas.'"[175] "That was part of the reason I went to India. Ravi and the sitar were excuses. Although they were a very important part of it, it was a search for a spiritual connection."[176] George had heard stories about yogis in the Himalayan caves, hundreds of years old, "doing all sorts of wondrous things."[177] Yogis and saints could levitate and "be buried underground for weeks and stay alive. Now I wanted to see it all for myself."[178]

In quest of this connection, on September 14, 1966, George and his wife Pattie flew to India to study with Ravi Shankar and his assistant sitar-teacher Shambhu Das for six weeks. The couple stayed in the Taj Mahal Palace hotel in Bombay (now Mumbai) under the alias "Mr. and Mrs. Sam Wells," and George grew a mustache in a failed disguise attempt. However, after George's identity was discovered and journalists mobbed him, he fled by rail to Jaipur, Delhi, Jodhpur, and Agra.

George and Pattie visiting the Ellora Caves; l. to r.: Kamala Chakravarty, Pattie, Ravi Shankar, George, Shambhu Das. Photo courtesy of Mani Biswas, daughter of Shambhu Das.

On the beach in India; l. to r.: Kamala Chakravarty, George, Shambhu Das. Photo courtesy of Mani Biswas, daughter of Shambhu Das.

George and Shambhu Das taking an old-fashioned selfie with a fish-eye camera lens. Photo courtesy of Mani Biswas, daughter of Shambhu Das.

Pattie said, "We had a long trip with Ravi. He took us to visit ancient caves and meet holy men."[179]

George recalled, "It was a fantastic time. I would go out and look at temples."[180]

They visited the Ellora Caves and the Taj Mahal.[181] Shambhu Das took them to the cremation *ghats* on the Ganges River in Benares (now Varanasi). They met holy men and Ravi introduced them to his guru, Tat Baba Maharaj, who was age 145, but looked forty.[182] Ravi expressed, "As a Hindu, I believe blessing of guru is the most priceless thing in life."[183]

Eventually George, Pattie, Ravi, his romantic partner Kamala Chakravarty, and Shambhu Das landed in the Himalayas and found anonymity and serenity on a houseboat on Dal Lake in Srinagar, Kashmir, for several weeks.

George playing sitar. © Colin Harrison-Avico Ltd.

Ravi Shankar teaching George Harrison on sitar in the 1960s. Courtesy of the Ravi Shankar Foundation.

Since mastering the sitar takes decades, there were limits to what George could learn during his brief stay. Ravi taught George that sitar was not just for entertainment. Indian ragas are like tuning forks, harmonizing and resetting everything into the proper rhythms of nature. From divine origins, cognized by ancient sages and preserved in the Vedic scriptures, they can elevate consciousness and influence people for good.[184]

Shambhu Das said, "Music is the easiest way to reach God. *Ahata* (struck sound) is hitting a string with a plectrum or bow. *Anahata* (unstruck sound) means the universal sound, like OM or AH. When an accomplished musician 'gets into' the music and reaches the climax, they are connected to unstruck sound—lost in that clear, wonderful aroma of environment, like floating on that. That is God! *Anandam*, full bliss."[185]

George's second wife, Olivia Harrison, said: "When George heard Indian music, that really was the trigger, like a bell that went off in his head. It not only awakened a desire to hear more music, but also to understand Indian philosophy."[186]

After meeting Ravi, he wanted "this quality that these people have."[187] "Ravi was my link into the Vedic world. Ravi plugged me into the whole of reality."[188]

Perhaps the greatest gifts Ravi and his brother Raju (Rajendra) gave George were spiritual books, including Yogananda's *Autobiography of a Yogi* and Vivekananda's *Raja Yoga*.

What Is Yoga, Anyway?

To understand George, it is essential to define the words *yoga* and *yogi*. Unfortunately, today the glorious, time-honored Yoga philosophy, one of the six major systems of Indian philosophy, has been sadly reduced to a "downward facing dog" gym exercise.

The word *yoga* derives from a Sanskrit root *yuj*, which means, "to yoke" or "to unite." But yoga is not uniting the nose with the knee or uniting the forehead with the floor. Yoga means integrating individual spirit with universal spirit—mystical union with God.

A *yogi* has attained this state of integrated awareness. So yoga is not an exercise. It is a state of higher consciousness. In 1982, George said, "The word yoga means union of the mind, body, and spirit. Yoga isn't lying on nails or standing on your head."[189]

There are many paths of yoga. The main paths revealed in the chief Hindu scripture, the Bhagavad Gita, are *Jnana Yoga* (Path of Wisdom), *Karma Yoga* (Path of Selfless Service), *Bhakti Yoga* (Path of Devotion to God), and *Raja Yoga* (Path of Meditation). None of these is taught in our local YMCA. There is a lot more to yoga than meets the eye, even if it is our third eye!

Yogananda

In the early twentieth century, few Indian spiritual masters had ever visited Europe or America. Paramahansa Yogananda was the first to settle in the US (from 1920 until his death in 1952). Founder of Self-Realization Fellowship/Yogoda Satsanga Society of India (SRF/YSS), he spread Kriya Yoga and was named "Father of Yoga in the West." During his lifetime, Yogananda established over one hundred SRF centers. Today, there are nearly eight hundred SRF/YSS temples and centers worldwide.

Published in 1946, Yogananda's *Autobiography of a Yogi*, with over four million copies sold, has probably left a deeper impression on spiritual seekers worldwide than any other book about Indian spirituality. Ravi Shankar related that George showed tremendous interest in Indian religion. *Autobiography of a Yogi* "changed his whole life and mind, and influenced his writing of beautiful songs like 'Within You Without You' and many others."[190] "I gave him this book and that did something very strong; he became so attracted and then he pursued a deeper study," Ravi said in 1996. "Even today he is hooked on our philosophy and religion."[191]

George's favorite book. Photo courtesy of Self-Realization Fellowship.

George said, "While I was in India with Ravi, I kept saying, 'I want to know about the yogis of the Himalayas.'" When George looked at the book cover, "Yogananda just zapped me with his eyes, and that was it—it was all over! Then I read it and it gave me goose bumps. With some things you read you think, 'Well, I'm not sure about *that*.' But with *Autobiography of a Yogi*, I was totally convinced about every word in the book; somehow his pureness and his heart just flow out of it."[192]

The book introduced George to the immortal ascended master Babaji, whom Yogananda dubbed the "Yogi-Christ." George was so impressed that he ordered the book by the case: "I keep stacks of *Autobiography of a Yogi* around the house, and I give it out constantly to people. When people need regrooving, I say read this, because it cuts to the heart of every religion."[193] George said that even though he never met Yogananda, "He's probably been the greatest inspiration [and] had such a terrific influence on me. A lot of my feelings are the result of what he taught, and is still teaching in his subtle state."[194]

On January 26, 1969, while the Beatles were composing "Let It Be," George spontaneously sang this verse: "Somewhere in the Himalayas lives a man named Babaji, singing words of wisdom, let it be." John answered with: "Somewhere out in Weybridge is the cat whose name is Babaji, singing words of wisdom, let it B-H-I-J-K."[195]

A little booklet that SRF has published for many years, "Light from the Great Ones," which features a quote from each of the gurus in the SRF/YSS lineage, was included in George's *All Things Must Pass 50th Anniversary Edition*.

Vivekananda

Disciple of renowned nineteenth-century holy man Ramakrishna Paramahansa, the charismatic Swami Vivekananda was the first spiritual master to introduce Indian philosophy to the West. Believing the path of Yoga was the surest way to world peace, he established the Vedanta Society in New York in 1894.

In his book *Meditation and Its Methods*, Vivekananda wrote: "What right has a man to say he has a soul if he does not feel it, or that there is a God if he does not see Him? If there is a God we must see Him, if there is a soul we must perceive it; otherwise it is better not to believe. It is better to be an outspoken atheist than a hypocrite."[196]

George commented, "Wow! Fantastic! At last I've found somebody who makes some sense."[197]

Swami Vivekananda, chief disciple of Ramakrishna Parmahansa.

In Vivekananda's book *Raja Yoga*, George learned the axiom *Tat Tvam Asi* ("I Am That"), which means divinity is within everyone. George also read *Yoga Sutras* by the sage Patanjali, which expounds Yoga Philosophy, and the Bhagavad Gita, which teaches Yoga through a dialogue between the Hindu deity Lord Krishna and his disciple Arjuna.[198]

George had been raised Catholic, but he believed many Christians were hypocrites who claimed to have a franchise on Christ but did not exemplify Christ's teachings. He felt Christians told him to blindly believe dogma rather than having direct experience.

Embracing Indian Culture

Vivekananda's words affected George deeply. Seeking a direct spiritual connection, he read books by holy men and mystics and wanted to meet them.[199] To this end, George visited Ramnagar, across the Ganges River from Benares (now Varanasi) during the Ram Leela festival. Rama's life story, as one of ten avatar (physical incarnations) of Lord Vishnu, is narrated in the sacred text the Ramayana and dramatized during this autumn gathering. The finale is burning giant effigies of the demon Ravana. *Ram Leela* means "play of Lord Rama."

Ravana burnt in effigy at Ram Leela.

For one month, thousands of colorful *sadhus* (holy renunciates) and pilgrims camped on a site of five hundred acres. George said, "I saw all kinds of groups of people, a lot of them chanting. It was a mixture of unbelievable things. It gave me a great buzz." George said these holy men would be arrested as vagrants in the West, but in India they roamed about with no name other than *sannyasi* (ascetic monk), and some of them looked like Christ: "There are also a lot of loonies who look like Allen Ginsberg—with the frizzy hair, and smoking little pipes called chillums, and smoking hashish."[200]

In 1967, George said, "Ravi's my musical guru. But then later I realized that this wasn't the real thing, this was only a little stepping stone, because through the music, you reach the spiritual part, [which] led me to become a Hindu."[201] George embraced Hinduism wholeheartedly. Carl Roles (Olivia Harrison's brother-in-law) told me that George wore a *navaratna* ("nine gemstones") ring, with each stone representing a planet in Hindu astrology. His reasoning: "I want every base covered just in case." George stated, "If you get a car and a telly and a house and even a lot of money, your life's still empty because it's still all on this gross level. And what we need isn't material; it's spiritual. We need some other form of peace and happiness."[202] "Through Hinduism I feel a better person. I just get happier and happier."[203]

Birth of the Song

Klaus Voormann, artist, session musician, and close friend of The Beatles since Hamburg, was the bass guitarist for rock group Manfred Mann and played on Beatles solo albums. He created the *Revolver* album cover and *Beatles Anthology* collages. After George returned from India, Klaus invited George, Pattie, and Tony King to a dinner party at his Hampstead, London, home.

Tony said the guests talked about "the wall of illusion and the love that flowed between us, but none of us knew what we were talking about. We all developed these groovy voices. It was a bit ridiculous, as if we were sages all of a sudden. We all felt as if we had glimpsed the meaning of the universe."[204]

There was a pedal harmonium in the house. George said, "I was doodling on it, playing to amuse myself, when 'Within You' started to come. The tune came first, and then I got the first sentence. It came out of what we'd been doing that evening—'We were talking.' That's as far as I got that night. I finished the rest of the words later at home."[205]

Pattie's sister Jenny Boyd recalled reading the book *Karma and Rebirth* by Christmas Humphreys. She came across this passage: "Life goes on within you and without you." "I read it again and again, marveling at the double meaning. It was so clever and so true. My first inclination was to call Pattie and George. George answered the phone. 'Listen to this,' I said, and then repeated the sentence. It inspired him to write 'Within You Without You.'"[206]

 Scan this code to read the lyrics.

The Lyrics

George said, "'Within You Without You' came after I had spent a bit of time in India and fallen under the spell of the country and its music."[207] That is why its lyrics convey a profound message of Indian philosophy: the absolute oneness and wholeness of infinite pure consciousness is the only reality. It is immeasurable and everywhere present: within and without, above and below, pervading everything. It is unmanifest, unbounded, nameless, formless, eternal, omnipresent, omniscient, omnipotent, complete, invincible, and everlasting—beyond space, time, and causation.

But we live in a dualistic world, where the infinite becomes finite, unmanifest becomes manifest, and absolute becomes relative. This manifest creation arises by placing boundaries on the infinite—boundaries known as *maya* (literally "to measure"). When we try to measure eternity, we create "time." When we try to measure omnipresence, we create "space." When we try to measure omniscience, we create "knowledge." When we try to measure "omnipotence," we create "power." When we try to measure "completeness," we create "desire." Maharishi Mahesh Yogi would often say, "'Time' is a concept to measure eternity."

The impossible paradox of maya splits the unsplittable absolute infinite wholeness, which in the Upanishads is described as "one and only one: one without a second." Oneness no longer retains its integrity when "one" becomes "two." Duality is born. Ignorance is born. The manifest creation is born out of illusion. The goal of the spiritual quest is to return to the oneness of infinite pure consciousness. In "Within You Without You," George asked us to realize the truth—that we are all one. Divine love is the balm that extinguishes the false self (our ego) and returns us to our true nature of wholeness (our higher Self). When we experience oneness, we find inner peace. And if many people would experience that, we would find world peace.

George's sister, Louise Harrison, said their father often quoted, "This above all, to thine own self be true." She remembered George saying, similarly, that the Creator is a "'massive, intelligent energy, and each of us has a drop of that energy, and that's what makes the soul within all of us. It is the life force within us."[208] George often quoted Vivekananda, who said, "Each soul is potentially divine. The goal is to manifest that divinity."[209] George elaborated, "There is the little 'i,' which is like a drop of the ocean. Get rid of that little 'i' by the drop becoming merged into the big 'I' (the ocean)."[210]

This song about oneness, annihilation of ego, the happiness of hippieness, personal responsibility, self-empowerment, and freedom from materialism, declared love is the power and love is the answer—before John Lennon's "All You Need Is Love."

The Music

In March 1967, George reached out to Asian Music Circle to hire musicians for a second time (the first for "Love You To").[211] However, hardly any well-trained Indian musicians lived in England, and none were professional. George spent weeks auditioning musicians who were not good enough, but he hired them anyway. Because they were amateurs, George recalled, "We spent hours just rehearsing and rehearsing."[212]

For the recording session on March 15, 1967, EMI Studio Two had been transformed into Little India. Throw rugs covered the hardwood floor for the Indian musicians. Recording engineer Geoff Emerick said, "The Abbey Road rugs were completely moth-eaten and dilapidated, but it was the thought that counted."[213] Burning joss sticks conveniently masked the cannabis odor. In this peaceful atmosphere, George felt relaxed for the first time during the *Sgt. Pepper* sessions. Paul showed some interest in the Indian instruments. John wandered about the studio aimlessly. Ringo played chess in the corner with Neil Aspinall.

George was the conductor. Having learned from Ravi how to write sheet music in Indian script, he gave the musicians notations on paper, but George Martin described, "To get them to play what he wanted, George would simply sing to the Indian musicians, or occasionally pick a few notes on the sitar."[214]

George said the melody was "based upon a piece of music of Ravi's that he'd recorded for All-India Radio. It was a very long piece—maybe thirty or forty minutes. I wrote a mini version of it."[215]

The Indian Instruments

Scan this code to watch a fascinating video of "Within You Without You" reproduced live with *dilruba*, sitar, tabla, and other authentic instruments as you read about how they are played in this song.

"Within You Without You" is arranged in a classical Hindustani structure. First, there is a wall of one note on tambura—a fretless drone instrument. Three or four musicians, including Neil Aspinall and George Harrison, played it. Up to five feet tall with four to six strings, tambura is tuned to the key of each piece and provides a tonic note so Hindustani vocalists can stay in key.

Dilruba plays the melody's introduction. This thirty-nine-inch instrument, with four main metal strings, twelve to fifteen sympathetic resonating strings, and twenty heavy metal frets, is played with a bow, like a cello. One glissando is played on an Indian zither known as *swarmandal*, with twenty-one to thirty-six strings. Two feet long and one or more feet wide, it is tuned to each specific piece.

The thumping, bending sound of tabla then enters. Consisting of bass and snare drum, it appears on "Love You To," "Within You Without You," and on George's *Brainwashed* album. Then eight violins and three cellos are played.

George Martin made careful notations on the sheet music and tutored musicians from London Symphony Orchestra to play Indian microtonal sliding notes bending and slurring into each other. Classical violinists and cellists struggled to master this challenge. The painstaking Martin and Harrison endured a harrowing night of recording.

In the middle instrumental section, the sitar plays a tiny role, echoing the dominant melody played on dilruba, violins, and cellos. The sitar has eighteen to twenty-one strings. Six or seven main strings that play the melody run over curved, raised, movable frets, and sympathetic strings run under the frets. These resonate with the main strings, played with a metal plectrum.

Mike Jones from the University of Liverpool and John Ball, a World Musician in Residence at the University of Sheffield's Department of Music, identified most of the Indian musicians on the track as Anna Joshi and Amrit Gajjar (both dilruba); Sikh temple musician Buddhadev Kansara (tambura); and Pandit Amiya Dasgupta and Natwar Soni (both tabla).[216] An unknown musician played *swarmandal.* A mystery Beatle played tambourine for a few bars. George Martin said some musicians were not paid because George Harrison never got their names.[217]

George overdubbed sitar, acoustic guitar, and vocals later in a marathon overnight session from April 3 to 4, 1967. It took many hours to record several difficult sitar fills. He finished recording by singing vocals in the requisite groovy atmosphere—lights dimmed with candles and incense burning.[218]

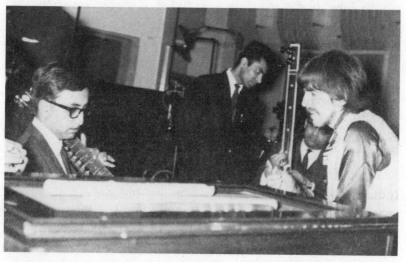

Musicians recording "Within You Without You": Amrit Gajjar playing dilruba on left. Buddhadev Kansara playing tambura and George on right. Dan Moss/Alamy Stock Photo.

Amiya Dasgupta at Abbey Road, recording "Within You Without You." Dan Moss/ Alamy Stock Photo.

More About the Musicians

Buddhadev Kansara commented, "George Harrison was passionate about Indian music. I only heard the music briefly and I didn't really think much of it, as it wasn't completed when I was working on it. It was only three to four years later when I finally heard the song in my shop and recognized it, that I thought, *This is excellent.*"[219]

Amiya Dasgupta was very close with George and stayed at his home while "Within You Without You" was being recorded. After visiting George, Amiya went on to Los Angeles to direct Ravi Shankar's music school. Amiya's student David Philipson told me: "Amiya was very modest and never would mention it, but if you asked him, he would softly confirm that he played on the track. I think he was embarrassed by the notoriety. George was composing the tune on the harmonium, and was kind of stuck on a line, and Amiya suggested 'Why don't you try this?'" Philipson further stated, "Amrit Gujjar, who played dilruba, was not a professional musician. Although he was very accomplished, he was a graphic artist by trade." Coincidentally, in 1963, Amiya Dasgupta had appeared on the LP record *Maharishi Mahesh Yogi—The Master Speaks*, released on World Pacific Records. The tracklist was Side A: "Love," and Side B: "The Untapped Source of Power Within." Dasgupta played sitar softly in the background behind Maharishi's discourse on the track "Love."

The Beatles Said

John said, "That is one of George's best songs, one of my favorites of his. I like the arrangement, the sound, and the words. George is responsible for Indian music getting over here. That song is a good example."[220]

Ringo said, "'Within You Without You' is brilliant. I love it!"[221]

It was a victory for George to get out from under John and Paul's shadow and compose something as meaningful as "Within You Without You." When he first previewed it in the studio, there was nothing but eye-rolling. Without a little help from his friends, George created a tour de force admired by all. Introducing Indian music to The Beatles increased George's standing within the band. But introducing Indian thought to the world made cosmic consciousness cool and made George venerated.

On November 6, 2006, George Martin and son Giles released an innovative mashup for the Las Vegas Cirque du Soleil production *Love*—combining "Tomorrow Never Knows" with "Within You Without You." The backward vocals of the Beatles track "Rain," with its drone baseline and Indian mood, capped off the track. "Rain" was the first song ever recorded with backward vocals.[222]

Sgt. Pepper's Lonely Hearts Club Band (album)

Written: November 19, 1966, to January 1967
Recorded: November 24, 1966 to April 21, 1967
Released: May 26, 1967

The Beatles released the iconic *Sgt. Pepper's Lonely Hearts Club Band* just in time for the 1967 "Summer of Love." Written at the height of John and Paul's psychedelic exploration and early days of George's spiritual searching, the album reflected The Beatles' deeper, self-reflective sentiments. John described their records as "diaries of their developing consciousness" and declared this evolution was also illustrated in their albums' photos and artwork.[223]

With George Martin's orchestrations of multiple layers of musical depth, the album took listeners on poetic journeys from nostalgic Liverpool to mind-bending psychedelic experiences through every musical genre. Martin said, "I'd been involved in a lot of avant-garde type recordings, and experimenting with electronic tracks and musique concrète. I introduced The Beatles to some new sounds and ideas; but [with] *Sgt. Pepper*, they wanted every trick brought out of the bag. Whatever I could find, they accepted."[224]

George recalled recording *Sgt. Pepper's Lonely Hearts Club Band* right after returning from India: "My heart was still out there. After what had happened in 1966, everything else seemed like hard work, a job I didn't really want to do, and I was losing interest in being 'fab' at that point."[225] George felt the trips to India had opened him spiritually. Spellbound by the music, the culture, the smells—free from the confines of the group, it was hard to return to the sessions, like going backwards. "Everybody else thought *Sgt. Pepper* was a revolutionary record—but I was growing out of that kind of thing."[226]

Album Cover

To create the Grammy-award-winning album cover, artists Jann Haworth and Peter Blake posed The Beatles in front of life-sized hand-colored black-and-white photographs pasted on hardboard. Among the celebrities represented, George's choices were Indian spiritual masters, in the Kriya Yoga lineage—Paramahansa Yogananda and his gurus.

 Please scan the code to see the album cover, and refer to the diagram below.

Now you can go on a treasure hunt to find the spiritual masters on the cover of *Sgt. Peppers Lonely Hearts Club Band*. By referring to the album cover, the numbered map, the list below that refers to the numbers on the map, and the photos of the spiritual masters, you can identify them on the cover.

Top row:

(1) Sri Yukteswar Giri was Paramahansa Yogananda's guru and founder of Kriya Yoga meditation practice. Yukteswar, a strict, exacting master, put Yogananda through his paces and directed him to bring Kriya Yoga to the US. His story is detailed in Yogananda's *Autobiography of a Yogi*.

(7) Carl Gustav Jung, psychiatrist and psychedelic pioneer (see pages 62–63).

(15) Bob Dylan, singer/songwriter, psychedelic pioneer, Literature Nobel Prize winner, who turned on The Beatles to marijuana (see pages 31–33).

Second row:

(18) Aldous Huxley, author, psychedelic explorer, and New Age pioneer (see page 62).

(26) William S. Burroughs, Beat generation writer (see page 16).

(27) Sri Mahavatar Babaji, ascended master and immortal yogi, the guru of Lahiri Mahasaya. George Harrison often wore a pinback button depicting Babaji, whom he discovered in the book *Autobiography of a Yogi* (see pages 93, 108, 270, 360, 396, 423, 435, 436, and 440).

(33) Sri Paramahansa Yogananda, author of *Autobiography of a Yogi* and disciple of Sri Yukteswar, named "Father of Yoga in the West." (See pages 91-93, 180, 396, 257).

Third row:

(51) Sri Lahiri Mahasaya, guru of Sri Yukteswar and direct disciple of Babaji. In the book *Autobiography of a Yogi,* there is a story where he bilocates (appears in two places at the same time).

Props on the cover:

An idol of the Hindu goddess of Wealth Lakshmi dressed in red is front and center.

A hookah (water pipe for smoking hashish).

Yogananda.

Sri Yukteswar.

Lahiri Mahasaya.

Babaji.

Ravi Shankar and George, who is wearing a pinback button of the immortal saint Babaji on his shirt, which displays the sacred symbol *Om*: ॐ. © Clive Arrowsmith.

"Lucy in the Sky with Diamonds"

Written: February 1967
Recorded: March 1 and 2, 1967
Released: May 26, 1967: Sgt. Pepper's Lonely Hearts Club Band

John Lennon never hesitated to reveal which song lyrics were inspired by drugs, but strangely, the public still believes he covered up the meaning of "Lucy in the Sky with Diamonds." Every time John was confronted with the coding of the initials LSD in the title, he insisted it was unintentional. Yet the song is still considered the prime Beatles drug-related track.

In 1971 John told Dick Cavett, "This is the truth: My son came home with a drawing and showed me this strange-looking woman flying around. I said, 'What is it?' and he said, 'It's Lucy in the sky with diamonds,' and I thought, *That's beautiful.* I immediately wrote a song about it." After the album had been published, fans noticed the letters spelled out LSD, but John was not aware of it. After that, he checked all the other Beatles songs: "They didn't spell out anything. It wasn't about that at all, but nobody believes me."[227]

The girl in the painting, suspended in air among gold and red stars, was Julian Lennon's classmate Lucy O'Donnell at the Heath House nursery school in Weybridge. The painting adorns the cover of Julian's single "Lucy," released in 2009. Lucy was suffering from Lupus, and proceeds from the record benefitted the Lupus Foundation. Julian explained, "I don't know why I called it that or why it stood out from all my other drawings, but I obviously had an affection for Lucy at that age. I used to show dad everything I'd built or painted at school and this one sparked off the idea for a song."[228]

Despite The Beatles' repeated denials, "Lucy in the Sky with Diamonds" was banned by radio stations throughout the world. Even Lucy O'Donnell herself believed the song was about LSD.

 Scan this code to read the lyrics.

The Lyrics

It does not take much imagination to notice psychedelic connotations in the lyrical pictures painted by "Lucy in the Sky with Diamonds," from kaleidoscopic hallucinations and incredibly high-growing flowers to heads disappearing into clouds. John's favorite childhood books, *Alice's Adventures in Wonderland* and *Through the Looking Glass* by Lewis Carroll, informed the trippy lyrics. Carroll also inspired "White Rabbit" by Jefferson Airplane—the first song about psychedelics, which became *the* psychedelic anthem of the sixties.

Acidheads believed Carroll's stories mirrored LSD trips. Alice drank potions, ate mushrooms, visited other dimensions, encountered strange creatures, hallucinated, and her world altered dramatically with shifting perceptions. There is no evidence that the highly imaginative nineteenth century author ever ingested psychedelics. However, because Carroll suffered from "migraine aura," there is speculation he may have had temporal lobe epilepsy, in which consciousness is altered, and symptoms can resemble Alice's adventures.

Raga Rock Sound

George played tambura on "Lucy in the Sky with Diamonds." "Under normal circumstances, that wouldn't work on a Western song like 'Lucy,' which has chord changes and modulations," George said. "I liked the way the drone of the tambura could be fitted in."[229]

In India, *khayal* (improvisational vocalists) and sarangi (stringed, bowed, violin-like instrument) typically perform identical melodies in unison. The instrument that most resembles the human voice, sarangi can imitate *khayal* vocal ornaments, such as shaking and sliding movements. The term *sarangi* derives from two roots: *sau* ("hundred") and *rang* ("color"), because it evokes and expresses so many feelings.

George said, "For 'Lucy' I thought of trying that idea [of melody played in unison with voice], but because I'm not a sarangi player, I played it on guitar along with John's voice. I was trying to copy Indian classical music."[230] (See page 426 for a photo of a sarangi.)

Sound engineer Geoff Emerick said: "We decided to route George Harrison's guitar through a Leslie speaker during the choruses, [like] the 'Dalai Lama' vocal effect we had used on 'Tomorrow Never Knows.'"[231] The result was the haunting sound of "Lucy in the Sky with Diamonds."

CHAPTER 4

BUS TO BLISS

Magical Mystery Tour (song, album, and film)

Written: April 11 to May 3, 1967
Recorded: April 25, 26, 27, May 3, November 7, 1967
Released: November 27, 1967: Magical Mystery Tour:
US LP; December 8, 1967: UK EP
Television Premiere Date: December 26, 1967

For Jane Asher's twenty-first birthday, April 5, 1967, Paul McCartney visited his girlfriend in Denver during her American tour, performing Shakespeare with Bristol Old Vic. While Paul was making home movies of Jane walking amongst the trees at Civic Center Park, an idea for a television special dawned on him. On the flight back to England, he started writing lyrics and planning the plot for what would become *Magical Mystery Tour*.

From his childhood, Paul remembered "mystery tours" where travelers would pile into a bus. The thrill was guessing where they were going: "From Liverpool, it was inevitably Blackpool—'Oooo, it was Blackpool after all!' Rather romantic and slightly surreal! All these old dears with the blue rinses, off to mysterious places. Generally there's a crate of ale in the boot of the coach and you sing lots of songs."[232]

"Paul had proposed The Beatles simply travel around the English countryside with a bus load of fat ladies, dwarfs, and other groovy people, and film whatever happened to happen," recalled Pete Shotton, Paul's childhood friend.[233] The Beatles' *Magical Mystery Tour* bus embarked on its phantasmic trip from London on September 11, 1967.

Paul alongside his Magical Mystery Tour bus. Trinity Mirror/Mirrorpix/Alamy Stock Photo.

According to Paul McCartney biographer Barry Miles and childhood friend Pete Shotton, "*Magical Mystery Tour* was inspired by the freewheeling adventures of Ken Kesey's Merry Pranksters, as chronicled in Tom Wolfe's book *The Electric Kool-Aid Acid Test*."[234]

Den of Geek's Tony Sokol further explained, "Paul wanted to make 'a crazy roly-poly Sixties film' that captured the spirit of Ken Kesey's 'Merry Pranksters,' who traveled the country in a brightly colored bus in 1964 giving out the still legal LSD."[235]

Kesey's Magical Mystery Tour

Author of *One Flew Over the Cuckoo's Nest* (1962) and *Sometimes a Great Notion* (1964), psychedelic guru Ken Kesey formed a pivotal link between beatniks and hippies in the sixties. While on a Ford Foundation fellowship at Stanford University in 1960, he became a guinea pig for Project MKULTRA, a classified CIA-backed study at Menlo Park VA Hospital. Test subjects ingested LSD (lysergic acid diethylamide), AMT (alpha-Methyltryptamine), DMT (N,N-Dimethyltryptamine), mescaline, psilocybin, and cocaine, allegedly to research mental illness cures, but in reality as a military mind-control experiment.

Enthralled by Jack Kerouac's *On the Road* and John Steinbeck's *Travels with Charley: in Search of America*, Kesey and his Merry Band of Pranksters took a road-trip-cum-acid-trip in a neon-painted, psychedelic-fueled school bus named *Furthur*, which Kesey defined as a "philosophical concept." The tribe of acidheads (a.k.a. "heads") set out from La Honda, California, towards the New York World's Fair in June 1964.

The bus driver was the speed-freak (amphetamine addict) road-trip veteran Neal Cassady—the real-life Dean Moriarty character in Kerouac's *On the Road* and Ginsberg's poems. Cassady chattered and sang day and night, regurgitating a nonstop upchuck of ramblings about *kundalini* and other Indian buzzwords: "We are actually fourth dimensional beings in a third dimensional body inhabiting a second dimensional world."[236]

Kesey said, "We felt like we were going into the conscious soul, the mainframe of the nation, and readjusting something. Without it being readjusted, we were doom-bound. All we have to do is get that to spread out—positive young faces smiling and reverberating back."[237] Kesey believed changing consciousness could change the world. To the Pranksters, enlightenment was about "going with the flow." One of their mottos was "Nothing lasts."

Ken Kesey and the Pranksters aboard his bus *Furthur.* © Lisa Law.

When they arrived in New York, the Pranksters hooked up with Ginsberg and Kerouac and tripped at the World's Fair on June 29. Ginsberg then arranged for the Pranksters to visit Timothy Leary's four-thousand-acre estate outside Millbrook, New York—The International Foundation for Internal Freedom: IFIF. Kesey envisioned a great meeting of minds between the West and East Coast acidheads.

Harvard professor, psychologist, King Pooh-bah acidhead guru, and counterculture icon of the sixties, Leary had a "profound transcendent experience" in 1957 while taking hallucinogens in Mexico. He began experimenting on LSD, which he likened to a microscope that opened an unexplored invisible world.[238]

After being dismissed from Harvard for advocating drugs, Leary, with colleagues Richard Alpert and Ralph Metzner, moved into the Hitchcock estate in Millbrook in September 1963, supported by heirs to the Mellon fortune. There, Leary continued his prolific experiments and writing career. Labeled "The Most Dangerous Man in America" by President Richard Nixon, Leary served several prison sentences. Frequent FBI raids eventually drove him off the estate.[239]

In July 1964, the Pranksters arrived in their crazy tripped-out bus at IFIF in the posh upper-crust Hudson Valley. Everyone in the mansion took one look at them and fled. The flute-playing, fun-loving heads had apparently disturbed their curriculum.[240] Richard Alpert (later known as Ram Dass) was relegated as the welcoming committee. Cassady and Ginsberg were invited upstairs, where Cassady took DMT. But the IFIF sanitized, clinical atmosphere turned off Kesey and his freeform Pranksters. So off they went to gambol in a waterfall. Leary eventually came out of hiding and visited the bus with Cassady.

On the way back to California, the Pranksters stopped in Canada by a scenic lake, where they dropped the Rolls Royce of psychedelics—IT290. Ken Kesey likened his Pranksters to astronauts: "These drugs were opening the door to new landscapes. Once you look out all these windows onto new vistas, you become tremendously excited, and want to do what you can to explore it, because you could look around and [see] there weren't human footprints all over this landscape."[241] Cassady declared, "On acid, it's a door. It's a door to heaven."[242]

After their journey, Kesey hosted LSD gatherings ("Acid Tests") every weekend—multimedia performances featuring light shows, ecstatic dancing, trippy costumes, Day-Glo paint, black lights, and strobe lights. Homemade posters asked rhetorically, "Can You Pass the Acid Test???" Regular attendees included Allen Ginsberg,

Tom Wolfe, and Kesey's acidhead house band The Grateful Dead, named after The Tibetan Book of the Dead.

On January 6, 1965, when he was busted for marijuana possession, Kesey stated, "I feel like you only come for this movie once, and if you don't get something rewarding out of every minute you're sitting there, then you're blowing your ticket."[243] One of his mottos: "The '60s aren't over; they won't be over until the Fat Lady gets high."[244]

George's Mini Cooper painted with Tantric symbols of the subtle body and its seven chakras from the book *Tantra Art: Its Philosophy & Physics*. Heritage Image Partnership Ltd/Alamy Stock Photo.

Pattie and George's Magical Mystery Car

An Austin Cooper S, LGF 695D was built by Harold Radford Ltd. for each of the Beatles, painted in metallic black. In early 1967, Dutch artists Simon Posthuma and Marijke Koger (known collectively as "The Fool") decorated George's Mini Cooper with Indian Tantric symbols of deities called *yantra*. In the film *Magical Mystery*

Tour, George's Mini, along with John's psychedelically embellished 1965 Rolls Royce Phantom V and several other cars, chased the tour bus around and around RAF West Malling, a decommissioned World War II airfield in Kent.[245]

Actor Victor Spinetti, who had also appeared in *A Hard Day's Night* and *Help!*, said that while filming *Magical Mystery Tour*, The Beatles took a Transcendental Meditation break every afternoon. Victor asked John, "Why would you go to India to find enlightenment? There's nowhere to go. We're already here."

John retorted, "Piss off."[246] Later John insisted that Victor meet Maharishi Mahesh Yogi at the Plaza Hotel in New York. Victor described Maharishi sitting on a divan, giggling away, with all these women bringing him flowers and fruit. One woman asked, "Maharishi, how do we teach children the principles of Transcendental Meditation?"

Maharishi fell apart laughing and said, "Ah my dear lady, they invented it." Victor then decided Maharishi was okay.[247]

 Scan this code to read the lyrics.

The Lyrics

Because the song "Magical Mystery Tour" was written while The Beatles were experimenting with psychedelics, the "mystery tour" became a "magical" mystery tour. Paul explained it was "a little bit more surreal than the real ones."[248]

The term "Roll up!" was a double-entendre—both a circus barker's cry and reference to rolling a joint. Paul said they would often stick in veiled references to drugs and trips for their "in group" of friends. The mystery tour symbolized a psychedelic trip, and "dying" referred to The Tibetan Book of the Dead. Paul explained ordinary people would just see a bus taking a mystery tour. But if you were tripping on acid, "it's dying, it's the real magical mystery tour."[249] On this magical trip, listeners are transported from this mundane world into a different dimension, with a little help from LSD.

"It's All Too Much"

Written: May 1967
Recorded: May 25 and 26, June 1967
Released: January 13, 1969: Yellow Submarine

George Harrison composed "It's All Too Much" to celebrate LSD. In 1980 he stated the song "was written in a childlike manner from realizations that appeared during and after some LSD experiences, which were later confirmed in meditation."[250]

Climax of Yellow Submarine

Every moment of the cinematic delight *Yellow Submarine*, directed by George Dunning, is a masterpiece, with fantastic, whimsical characters conceived by Heinz Edelmann and brought to life by animation directors Robert Balser and Jack Stokes. The star of the film is the song "It's All Too Much," which boldly resounds at the climax. The highly creative psychedelic sequence magically conveys the LSD experience, while simultaneously expressing the movie's theme of peace, love, and Flower Power. *Yellow Submarine* epitomizes The Beatles' positive vibe and their core message, "All You Need Is Love"—even though the Fabs had little to do with the film's creation.

Scan this code to
read the lyrics.

The Lyrics

The lyrical poetry of "It's All Too Much" conveys the sensitivity and higher perception that George experienced on acid. Since he said his LSD experiences sparked the song, the line about the blond, blue-eyed woman (which George lifted from "Sorrow" by the McCoys) probably referred to Pattie Boyd, with whom he took acid. Under the drug's influence, his perception of love was heightened when looking into her eyes. During his first LSD trip in April 1965, George recalled, "I felt in love, not with anything or anybody in particular, but with everything."[251]

George told *Crawdaddy* magazine that individual love is a part of universal love—the ultimate love, the universal love or love of God: "Each of us must manifest our individual love, the divinity in us. All individual love between one person loving another, is all small parts of that one universal love. It's all God."[252]

The deeper George went into meditation, the more he could see (view with his "third eye"). Through the window of our two eyes and five senses, we perceive our magnificent world. But with a sixth, higher sense perception, we open the gateway to subtler realms. Through our third eye we can view an invisible world—multiple dimensions and alternate realities of indescribable wonders. This eye of illumination is seated in an energy plexus called *ajna chakra* in the middle of our brain, in the pineal gland. Through this portal of higher vision and wisdom, we can see marvels hidden from view, develop our intuition, and awaken higher awareness.

In the chorus, George sang of love shining around Pattie, which is "too much"—hippie vernacular from the sixties referring to exceptionally mind-blowing, "far out" experiences. Seeing light around people means perceiving their subtle body, known as their aura or energy field. The stream of life refers to reincarnation from each lifetime to the next, where the same souls meet repeatedly. The goal of yoga is moksha, realization of our true Self and freedom from the cycle of recurring birth and death—beyond limitations of space and time.

George explained to *Billboard* in 1999, "I just wanted to write a rock 'n' roll song about the whole psychedelic thing of the time. Because you'd trip out, on all this stuff, and then whoops! You'd just be back having your evening cup of tea!"[253]

The song refers to a teaching from the Tao Te Ching, Chapter 47: "The more you know, the less you understand." This is the same chapter George quoted in the song "The Inner Light." It means that wisdom does not come from learning facts. Wisdom is gained through direct experience.

A few months after writing this song, during a scary visit to Haight-Ashbury while high on acid, George rejected drugs as a spiritual path. (See pages 133–136.) He realized that to develop the third eye in a stable way, to experience the love that shines around us, and to attain liberation, traditional meditation methods are the best choice. He declared, "The buzz of all buzzes which is God— you've got to be straight to get it. Even if you get it [with drugs], you only get it however long your pill lasts. Be healthy, don't eat meat, keep away from those nightclubs, and meditate."[254]

In 1977, George said, "I can get high like the rest of them, but it's actually low. The more dope you take, the lower you get. Having done that, I can say that from experience. Whatever it is— you just need more, and the more you take the worse you get."[255]

Maharishi Mahesh Yogi, with whom George studied meditation in August 1967 and February to April 1968, likened LSD to being in a dark cellar when the door is flung open and light comes flooding in. But then the door slams shut, and once again we are in darkness. LSD can temporarily open portals of extrasensory perception, but is not sustained or integrated into awareness.

The Sound

In this raga-rock track, the Hammond organ, which produced a drone-like undercurrent, mimicked Indian music. The song's Eastern style and feeling demonstrated George's continued commitment to Indian music and philosophy. George expressed, "Real

Indian classical songs are so much different from the sort of Indian pop songs being turned out over here. They're just ordinary pop songs with a little bit of Indian background. I'm not sure about the ones I've written. From what I really want to do, I don't like what I've done so far. I always seem to be rushed. I see things afterwards that I should have done."[256]

"Baby, You're a Rich Man"

Written: May 1967
Recorded: May 11, 1967
Released: July 7, 1967: Single; November 27, 1967:
Magical Mystery Tour

Back in the sixties, we hippies derided materialistic values. We criticized superficial socialites whose lives centered on money, status, fashion, make-up, bodybuilding, and cosmetic surgery. With sarcasm, we labeled them "the beautiful people." However, strangely, the British believed West Coast hippies nicknamed *themselves* "the beautiful people." Being a West Coast hippie myself, I can attest that nothing was further from the truth!

On April 29, 1967, John Dunbar (a co-founder of Indica Gallery) and John Lennon attended the 14 Hour Technicolor Dream, an all-night multi-artist gathering of poets, artists, and "thirty top groups." This fundraiser for the underground paper *International Times* was held in the Great Hall of London's Alexandra Palace.

Barry Miles (co-founder of Indica Gallery) was one of the organizers, Pink Floyd was the headliner, and Yoko Ono was among dozens of performance artists. The poster promised, "Kaleidoscopic Colour, Beautiful People." Ian MacDonald, author of *Revolution in the Head*, called this "the first tribal gathering of the British 'beautiful people.'"[257] Shortly after attending the event, John Lennon wrote a song called "One of the Beautiful People," which later evolved into "Baby, You're a Rich Man."

 Scan this code to
read the lyrics.

The Lyrics

From the lyrics, we gather that John's definition for "beautiful people" was people on a path of self-discovery. Once they realize who they really are, they are free to make choices of self-determination and self-empowerment where all things are possible. They can travel anywhere, both internally and externally. These beautiful people have been there, done that, and seen all. I believe this refers to psychedelic exploration as a spiritual path—an inward journey to higher awareness. The beautiful people are happy in their own skin, playing their own melody, but there are many other pathways to explore and other songs to sing.

Paul McCartney related, "There was a lot of talk in the newspapers then about the beautiful people. That was what they called them."[258]

John said, "The point was, stop moaning. You're a rich man and we're all rich men, hey, hey, baby!"[259] However, the true rich man finds richness within, where all possibilities lie and all wisdom is available. Not by hoarding money in a bag.

The Sound

This was another Beatles raga-rock track. John Lennon played a clavioline on an oboe setting, which created the lovely, exotic, snake-charmer sound of an Indian *shehnai*, a conical wooden oboe. Clavioline was an electronic keyboard, a forerunner to the analog synthesizer.

"All You Need Is Love"

Written: June 1967
Recorded: June 14, 19, 23, 24, 25, 1967
Released: July 7, 1967: Single; November 27, 1967:
Magical Mystery Tour

In early 1967, when Brian Epstein made a rare appearance in the recording studio with "fantastic news" that The Beatles were "selected to represent England in a television program which, for the first time ever, will be transmitted live around the world via satellite," he expected a reaction of effusive glee.

Instead, he was met with yawns and a reluctant, blasé John: "Oh, okay. I'll do something for that.'"[260]

But what John did was monumental. He composed an anthem of universal love that reflected The Beatles' mission statement and also epitomized the "Summer of Love." Neil Aspinall said, "'All You Need Is Love' went straight to number one. I think it expressed the mood of the time, with Flower Power and all that whole movement. It really was 'all you need is love' time."[261]

The Event

On June 25, 1967, the European Broadcasting Union, along with the television services of eighteen nations, transmitted *Our World*, where, for the very first time, five continents linked up in a worldwide television broadcast that reached 350 million people."[262] The program was divided into sub-sections: "This Moment's World," "The Hungry World," "The Crowded World," "Physical Excellence," "The World Beyond," and The Beatles wrapped up the "Artistic Excellence" section. They transmitted live from EMI Studios while recording a song written for the occasion.

George Martin said, "Brian suddenly whirled in and said that we were to represent Britain in a round-the-world hook-up, and [we had] to write a song. It was a challenge. We had less than two weeks to get it together, and then we learnt there [would] be over

300 million people watching, which was for those days a phenomenal figure."[263]

Brian Epstein said, "About three weeks before the program, they sat down to write. The record was completed in ten days. This is an inspired song, because they really wanted to give the world a message. It could hardly have been a better message. It is a wonderful, beautiful, spine-chilling record."[264]

 Scan these codes to watch videos of the *Our World* broadcast.

The Broadcast

With EMI Studios swathed in flowers, balloons, and streamers, a large contingent of celebrities assembled in colorful psychedelic attire. Ringo said, "We decided to get some people in who looked like the 'love generation.'"[265] The Beatles were similarly outfitted. Paul sported a red rose over his left ear, anchored by his headphones.

Guests included Marianne Faithfull, Keith Moon, Pattie Boyd, Jane Asher, Mike Paul, Graham Nash, Gary Leeds, Hunter Davies, Terry Condon, Alistair Taylor, Brian Epstein, and Paul's brother Mike McGear. George Harrison recalled, "I know that Mick Jagger is there. But there's also an Eric Clapton, I believe, in full psychedelic regalia and permed hair."[266] Several celebrities, including Keith Richards, walked about wearing sandwich boards printed with "all you need is love" in various languages. "Whacky baccy" smoke pervaded the studio.

The Beatles sang brilliantly, despite John and Paul chewing wads of gum between the notes. Orchestral musicians played flawless piano, violins, saxophones, trumpets, trombones, accordion, and flugelhorn. After hours of rehearsal from midday until 9:30 p.m., musicians and technicians performed the most carefully and thoroughly rehearsed adlibbed concert ever.

Scan this code to
read the lyrics.

The Lyrics

In the deceptively simple lyrics of "All You Need Is Love," John affirmed profound universal truths that demonstrated his understanding of Indian philosophy. The lyrics tell us we create our own reality, we can do anything, all things are possible, and life is a game we play. We are always in the right place because every experience is meant to be. In time, we can learn to realize who we really are. Thereby we overcome previous conditioning and societal programming. We benefit not only ourselves. We become a blessing for everyone we touch. And it is easy. Just by experiencing love and being loving, all things are possible. We need nothing other than love.

"If we weren't in The Beatles we would have been in something else, not necessarily another rock 'n' roll band. Karma is: what you sow, you reap," George said, and further explained that we can only be where we are meant to be, "because you yourself have carved out your own destiny by your previous actions."[267] Paul described the Law of Karma in his own poetic way in the lyrics of "The End."

Beatles Comments About the Song

Paul said, "We'd be seen recording it by the whole world at the same time. So we had one message for the world—Love. We need more love in the world."[268]

George described, "We just thought, *Well, we'll just sing "All You Need Is Love," because it's a kind of subtle bit of PR for God.*"[269]

Ringo commented, "We were big enough to command an audience of that size, and it was for love and bloody peace. It was a fabulous time. I even get excited now when I realize that's what it was for: peace and love, people putting flowers in guns."[270]

John told *Village Voice* journalist Howard Smith, "I still believe all you need is love. But I don't believe that just saying it is going to do it. There's a lot of changes in society to come before we can get to a state of even realizing that love is what we need. We've got this gift of love, but love is like a precious plant. You've got to keep watering it. You've got to really look after it and nurture it."[271]

"Blue Jay Way"

Written: August 1, 1967
Recorded: September 6, 7 and October 6, 1967
Released: November 27, 1967: Magical Mystery Tour*:*
US LP; December 8, 1967: UK EP

George Harrison's moody, haunting "Blue Jay Way" sounds like mystical Indian music, though its theme is the most mundane of topics. George, Pattie Boyd, Neil Aspinall, and Alexis Mardas (a.k.a. "Magic Alex") flew from England to Los Angeles on August 1, 1967.[272] They planned to visit The Beatles' press officer Derek Taylor, who lived in Los Angeles, and attend a sitar performance by Ravi Shankar on August 4, 1967, at the Hollywood Bowl. To promote the concert, George held a press conference with Ravi on August 3.

 Scan this code to
read the lyrics.

Ravi Shankar at Monterey Pop Festival in California, June 18, 1967; l. to r.: Alla Rakha (tabla player), Ravi Shankar (sitar player), Kamala Chakravarty (tambura player), who lived and traveled with Ravi as his romantic partner from 1967 to 1981, while he was still married to surbahar maestro and mentor Annapurna Devi (sister of Ali Akbar Khan). © Lisa Law.

The Lyrics and Sound

When George and Pattie arrived, they rode from the airport to a house in the Hollywood Hills at 1567 Blue Jay Way, a four-thousand-square-foot U-shaped mid-century modern with a spectacular view of Los Angeles. It belonged to Ludwig Gerber (entertainment attorney, film producer, and Peggy Lee's manager), who was vacationing in Hawaii.

Derek Taylor and his wife Joan had promised to visit the Harrisons that night but were running late. When Derek asked George where Blue Jay Way was, he replied, "I don't know. Somewhere up in the hills." Derek told George, "Never mind. I'll ask a policeman. There are plenty of them around."[273]

George recalled, "So I waited and waited. I felt really knackered with the flight, but I didn't want to go to sleep until he came. There was a fog and it got later and later. To keep myself awake, just as a joke to pass the time, I wrote a song about waiting for him in Blue Jay Way. There was a little Hammond organ in the corner of this house which I hadn't noticed until then, so I messed around on it and the song came."[274]

The song described the incident and also captured the mood of heavy fog. The minor key and drone invoked the flavor of Indian raga without Indian instrumentation. The Hammond organ, cello, and drums replaced tambura, dilruba, and tabla. There was no guitar. Biographer Hunter Davies wrote, "When George came back home to England, he bought himself a little Hammond organ, painted it white, and perfected the song."[275]

The Psychedelic Revolution

During the time George visited Los Angeles in 1967, kids flocked to Haight-Ashbury, San Francisco, from all over the country. About a hundred thousand came from small-town America. Dressed outrageously, they arrived in psychedelic-painted VW bugs and buses. Living on the street, in hippie pads, or crashing in Golden Gate Park, they were into love and peace and getting high. Many were runaways or tourists, but they found utopia, even for just one "Summer of Love."

We who followed the hippie credo ostensibly adopted an alternative lifestyle: lived in peaceful, idealistic communes; loved everyone; handed out flowers to straights; and generally created an alternate universe.

Frequenting the Avalon Ballroom, Fillmore Auditorium, and Winterland in San Francisco decked in our grooviest garb, we danced in a wild frenzy to Janis Joplin's Big Brother and the Holding Company, the iconic Jimi Hendrix, Jefferson Airplane, Grateful Dead, The Who, Loving Spoonful, The Doors, and my favorite: Cream—the "cream" of rock 'n' roll music: Eric Clapton on guitar, Ginger Baker on drums, and Jack Bruce on bass. Light shows meant to replicate an acid trip heightened the spectacle. Globs of multi-colored mineral oil, sandwiched between large glass clock faces, pulsated in time to the music. Overhead projectors cast these liquid light displays onto the walls and ceilings. Slide shows of bizarre photos augmented the fantasy. Strobe lights completed the hypnotic effect.

Across the Bay in Berkeley, Carlos Santana presented free concerts at People's Park—a vacant lot owned by the University of California and appropriated by hippies and political activists in the Free Speech Movement. Bounded by Haste and Bowditch Streets and Dwight Way, that was where we mingled, lived the free-love lifestyle, and made love—not war.

Be-Ins and Happenings

We attended the first big flower-power happening, the "Human Be-In," on January 14, 1967, when twenty thousand of us wildly attired hippies descended on San Francisco's Golden Gate Park. Speakers included LSD advocate Timothy Leary, counterculture comedian Dick Gregory, and political activist Jerry Rubin. Gary Snyder (Pulitzer-Prize-winning Beat poet) blew a conch shell in an Indian call to worship. Allen Ginsberg led a chant of Hindu mantras and read his poetry. Michael McClure (my art college English teacher and famous Beat poet) strummed an autoharp while reciting his poetry.

 Scan this code to watch a documentary about the Human Be-In.

Gathering of the tribes for a "Human Be-In," Golden Gate Park, San Francisco; l. to r.: Gary Snyder, Michael McClure, Allen Ginsberg, Maretta Greer, Lenore Kandel. © Lisa Law.

Allen Ginsberg dancing to The Grateful Dead at "Human Be-In." © Lisa Law.

Timothy Leary on stage at the "Human Be-In." © Lisa Law.

At his first San Francisco appearance, Timothy Leary introduced his "Turn on, Tune in, Drop out" catchphrase. "Turn on" meant to drop acid—ingest LSD or other psychedelic drugs. "Tune in" meant to experience "altered states"—levels of consciousness beyond normal perception. "Drop out" meant to quit the "Establishment"—colleges, government, military, corporations, capitalism, and other conventional institutions.

In our one-day hippie Dionysian paradise, we frolicked on the grass, blew bubbles, distributed flowers, spread love, and danced with abandon to the music of Jefferson Airplane, Grateful Dead, and Quicksilver Messenger Service. "Underground chemist" Owsley Stanley distributed doses of "Owsley White Lightning" LSD.

The "Summer of Love"

On the heels of the "Happenings" and "Be-Ins" in Golden Gate Park came the "Summer of Love." Scott McKenzie reflected the mood with his ballad, "San Francisco (Be Sure to Wear Flowers in Your Hair)," and the Youngbloods encapsulated the times in their anthem "Get Together."

The Diggers, an anarchist guerilla street theater group, created "models of Free Association." Their slogans included "Do your own thing," and "Today is the first day of the rest of your life." They served free dinner for hundreds of hippies at 4:00 p.m. daily in Golden Gate Park behind a giant yellow picture frame, called the "Free Frame of Reference." People donated furniture and "threads" (clothing) to the Diggers' free stores, where hippies took whatever they needed.

A Good Trip Gone Bad

Jenny Boyd, Pattie Boyd's sister, arrived in San Francisco on March 7, 1967. She stayed with her friend Judy Wong ("Jewel-Eyed Judy"), and helped her set up her boutique, Passion Flower, on the corner of Grant and Vallejo. Enchanted by the hippie revolution, Jenny wrote to Pattie and George about it.

On August 2, Jenny flew down to Los Angeles to stay at Blue Jay Way and sightsee with George, Pattie, Alexis, and Neil for a week. They visited Ravi Shankar in his music school, where fifty students were studying sitar, and attended his concert at the Hollywood Bowl. On August 7, George, Pattie, Jenny, Alexis Mardas, Neil Aspinall, and Derek Taylor flew in a Learjet to San Francisco to witness what Jenny had been raving about—the hippie utopia in the Haight, with its creative acidheads, psychedelic music, love vibe, and free lifestyle.

George had high expectations after Jenny's glowing reports of an enlightened artistic alternative community: hippies emanating patchouli fragrance, making peace-sign gestures and strumming guitars; hip shops selling handmade jewelry, crafts, and tie-dyed clothing; beatnik bookshops like City Lights in North Beach; incense-filled "head shops" (for hookah pipes, Zig-Zag rolling papers, and so forth); and the psychedelic music scene at the Fillmore.

To prepare for their visit, George and his entourage took what they imagined the requisite LSD dose. They arrived in Haight-Ashbury in a limo, but their driver refused to drive on Haight Street, so they hopped out. Within seconds George was spotted. At first, the crowds kept their distance, as the entourage visited a few shops near the corner of Haight and Ashbury. But then fans began following George like the Pied Piper. Someone put a wreath of flowers on his head.

Neil Aspinall led them to "Hippie Hill" in the Panhandle at Golden Gate Park, where they sat on a grassy slope surrounded by starstruck hippies. A fan handed George a guitar. George suggested he play it himself, which he did, then handed it back, asking George to sing and play a few chords. Taking that suggestion literally, George strummed chords, saying, "This is G, this is C, and this is E." He then said, "Sorry, man, we've got to go now." George returned the guitar and walked away.[276]

As the entourage headed back to the limo, a fan tried to offer George STP. George answered, "No thanks. I'm cool, man."

The guy turned around and yelled to the crowd, "He turned me down."

The crowd yelled, "No!" and the vibe turned unfriendly. When someone yelled, "You're our leader," George replied, "You have to lead yourself."[277] With Beatlemania in full force, Neil and Derek staved off fans and urged the entourage to move along faster. The atmosphere switched from hero worship to devil curse as the mob bore down with an increasingly angry tone.

George playing a borrowed guitar on Hippie Hill in the Haight. (AP/Shutterstock.)

Just when the entourage became fearful this walk would never end, Neil and Derek managed to shove them into the limo. Fists banged on the roof, faces pressed against the windows, and the limo rocked as George and company fled to the airport, in silence and in shock, to return to Los Angeles. The next day they flew to England. Thus ubruptly ended their stay in utopia.[278]

George commented in 1967, "The hippies are a good idea. I love all these people, the ones who are honest and trying to find a bit of truth, I'm with them 100 percent. But when I see the bad side of it I'm not so happy. Everybody is potentially divine [quoting Vivekananda, as George often did]. It's just a matter of self-realization before it will all happen. The whole point of life is to harmonize with everything and every aspect of creation."[279]

Renouncing Drugs

Disillusioned that Haight-Ashbury had been overrun by drug addicts, dropouts, and ne'er-do-wells, George questioned whether gobbling up LSD like candy was really his path to enlightenment, and whether his behavior as a role model was negatively influencing the youth. He decided to quit LSD.[280] Upon returning to London, George shared his concern with John, who was also questioning LSD's benefits.[281]

George said in 1967, "The Beatles got all the material wealth we needed. That's not what it's all about. We are all living in the physical world, yet what we are all striving for isn't physical. LSD isn't a real answer either. It enables you to see possibilities you may not have noticed before, but it isn't the answer."[282]

Later that month, on August 24, 1967, The Beatles met Maharishi Mahesh Yogi at the London Hilton. Their life took a different trajectory. Meditation became their new way to get high.

"Hello Goodbye"

Written: August 1967
Recorded: October 2, 19, 20, 25 and November 2, 1967
Released: November 24, 1967: Single

Alistair Taylor, "Mr. Fix-It," was Brian Epstein's personal assistant and The Beatles' gofer and fixer. Alistair signed the original Beatles contract as a witness on January 24, 1962. After John, Paul, George, and Pete Best signed (Epstein never did sign!), Paul foretold, "I don't know if we're going to make it as a group but I'll tell you what, I'm going to make it as a star!"[283]

Alistair recalled that Paul would invite him to his place on Cavendish Avenue for Scotch and Coke. One time, Paul asked, "Do you know anything about writing music?"

Alistair replied, "Good God, no!" Paul said, "It's dead easy, there's nothing to it!"

Alistair described, "In Paul's dining room, he had this little church organ and he said, 'You get on that end, I'll get on this end and run down the keyboard. I'm going to shout out a word and you shout out the opposite and keep this noise going.' So we went bang, bang, bang, 'Yes!' 'No!' 'Hello!' 'Goodbye!' for half an hour.

Two months later he came waltzing in and he'd just cut 'Hello Goodbye' and I didn't dare say, 'Hey mate, I wrote that.'"[284]

 Scan this code to read the lyrics.

"There are Geminian influences here: the twins," Paul commented. "It's such a deep theme in the universe, duality—man woman, black white, ebony ivory, high low, right wrong, up down, hello goodbye—that it was a very easy song to write. It's just a song of duality, with me advocating the more positive side of the duality, and I still do to this day."[285]

Perhaps a secret to The Beatles' success laid in the polarity between the ever-positive Paul and the oft-joyless John, as in Paul singing, "It's getting better all the time," and John's rejoinder: "It can't get no worse" (with a drone created by George Martin striking piano strings and George Harrison playing tambura—creating an Indian mood and balancing the polarities in "Getting Better").

But the concept of duality is integral to Indian philosophy, which The Beatles began to embrace during the period. The relative world where we live, consisting of pairs of opposites, is a perishable finite existence. The ultimate goal of spiritual development is to experience the imperishable infinite oneness, beyond the pairs of opposites that comprise this relative field. In the same month that Alistair and Paul played with duality on an organ, Paul met Maharishi Mahesh Yogi and learned Transcendental Meditation. This was a way Paul could transcend duality and experience oneness.

PART III

WHY DON'T WE DO IT ON THE ROAD TO RISHIKESH?

CHAPTER 5

GIGGLING GURU

"The Fool on the Hill"

Written: March to September 1967
Recorded: September 25, 26, 27, October 20, 1967
Released: November 27, 1967: Magical Mystery Tour:
US LP; December 8, 1967: UK EP

Paul McCartney recorded "The Fool on the Hill" one month after he met Maharishi Mahesh Yogi and began practicing his method, Transcendental Meditation (known as TM). Paul recalled, "I think I was writing about someone like Maharishi. His detractors called him a fool. Because of his giggle he wasn't taken too seriously. It was this idea of a fool on the hill, a guru in a cave I was attracted to. I remember once hearing about a hermit who missed the Second World War because he'd been in a cave in Italy, and that always appealed to me."[286]

George explained that Paul wrote the song before ever hearing about Maharishi. "But that's the way it was from the very beginning. It was an idea in the air that was about to happen and for some reason we were in the middle of it."[287]

Paul described, "'The Fool on the Hill' is a very complimentary portrait and represents Maharishi as having the capacity to keep perfectly still in the midst of the hurly-burly. He's admirably self-contained and doesn't pay much attention to popular opinion.

He's open to ridicule because of his beliefs, but his beliefs may well be right."[288] "There were some good words in it, 'perfectly still,' I liked that, and the idea that everyone thinks he's stupid appealed to me, because they still do. Saviors or gurus are generally spat upon, so I thought for my generation I'd suggest that they weren't as stupid as they looked."[289]

 Scan this code to
read the lyrics.

Who Was Maharishi?

On April 27, 1958, carrying all his belongings in a carpet roll, a forty-year-old yogi from India flew from Calcutta (now Kolkata) to Rangoon, Burma (now Myanmar). He recalled, "It never came to my mind where I will stay and to whom I will talk and what will happen when I arrive there. I just started out."[290] When he arrived in Hawaii, the *Honolulu Star Bulletin* reported: "He has no money, he asks for nothing. His worldly possessions can be carried in one hand. Maharishi Mahesh Yogi is on a world odyssey. He carries a message that he says will rid the world of all unhappiness and discontent."[291]

In 1958, the words *mantra, ashram, yoga, karma,* and *guru* did not exist in the West. Within ten years, with a little help from Maharishi's friends, The Beatles, these terms became commonplace. His method, "Transcendental Meditation," a specific technique and brand name, became as generic as Kleenex. Maharishi was the most famous guru of the twentieth century. In the late 1960s and 1970s, he appeared on *The Tonight Show* and *The Merv Griffin Show* several times, and on the cover of every major magazine.

The Fool Was No Fool

Though Maharishi Mahesh Yogi's birthdate has been questioned, this photo of his passport, taken when I served on his personal staff for six years in Switzerland, Italy, Austria, Spain, and Mallorca during the 1970s, settles any questions that it was January 12, 1918.

The happiest person I have ever encountered, Maharishi fully embodied his favorite slogans: "Life is not a struggle; life is bliss; man was not born to suffer; man was born to enjoy." He frequently cracked jokes and laughed at himself. His joy was contagious. He embodied bliss in the flesh. The press dubbed him "the giggling guru." A reporter described his robust laugh as "an irresistible invitation to join him in a huge joke—even if one was not at all sure what the joke was, whether it springs from his understanding of some sublime, specific truths or from his recognition of the idiocy of mankind in general."[292]

In Maharishi's presence, everything assumed a golden glow. Fully absorbed in the moment, his unwavering focus was 100 percent present. Charismatic to the point of hypnotic, he exuded a spiritually charged magnetism—spellbinding and inebriating. With just his glance, whoever was nearby became the only person, and now became the only time. While in his presence, spiritual impulses swept over us, cascading in ecstatic waves of love and bliss. No wonder Maharishi enchanted The Beatles, as he captivated so many of us.

September 26, 1967, marked Maharishi's first appearance on Johnny Carson's *The Tonight Show*. From the moment the guru appeared, carrying flowers, removing his sandals, and sitting cross-legged on a deerskin, Carson raised his eyebrows, rolled his eyes, and sneered. Still, the show resulted in thousands of eager students queuing up to learn TM. On January 19, 1968, he returned to *The Tonight Show*. After that, mocking Maharishi became a recurrent theme of Carson's jokes.

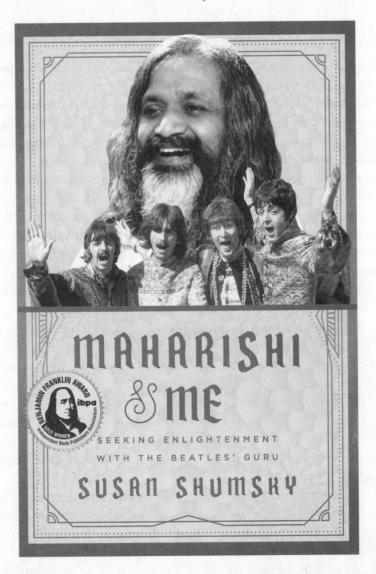

MAHARISHI & ME

SEEKING ENLIGHTENMENT

WITH THE BEATLES' GURU

SUSAN SHUMSKY

Maharishi demonstrated tremendous patience despite ridicule, especially during the beginning days of his mission. With his high-pitched voice, long stringy hair, and white silk robes, many considered him a fool. He was often mocked, derided, scorned, jeered, yelled at, or booed off the stage.

Plan or Premonition?

The Beatles' association with Maharishi began before they met him. Geoffrey Baker (later an art professor at Maharishi's university in Fairfield, Iowa) was a fellow student at the TM Teacher Training Course in India, which I attended in 1970. But in 1967, Geoffrey escorted Maharishi around England while the guru was teaching Transcendental Meditation.

While riding on a train, Maharishi suddenly asked Geoffrey, "How many are The Beatles?" Stunned that Maharishi knew of the rock stars, Geoffrey replied with uncertainty, "I believe there are four," as his interests skewed far afield from Beatlemania.[293] Maharishi then said he would autograph four copies of his book, *The Science of Being and Art of Living*—one for each Beatle, and Geoffrey should deliver the books to them.

Geoffrey could not fathom ever getting these books to the megastars. But later that year, Maharishi personally autographed and handed these books to The Beatles at his meditation retreat in North Wales. And the following year, Geoffrey and The Beatles meditated together with Maharishi in Rishikesh on the banks of the Ganges River.[294]

John in Bangor, North Wales, carrying his autographed copy of Maharishi's book. Trinity Mirror/ Mirrorpix/Alamy Stock Photo.

Hanging out by the Ganges in spring 1968; l. to r.: Richard Blakely (author of *The Secret of the Mantras*), Geoffrey Baker (art professor at Maharishi International University), Charlie Lutes (head of Maharishi's Spiritual Regeneration Movement). © Paul Mason.

"Across the Universe"

Written: October to December 1967
Recorded: February 4 and 8, 1968, April 1, 1970
Released: December 12, 1969: No One's Gonna Change Our World *charity album benefitting the World Wildlife Federation; May 8, 1970:* Let It Be

In February 1967, Pattie Boyd noticed a tiny classified ad in *The Times* of London, advertising Transcendental Meditation. Pattie and her friend, fashion model Marie-Lise Volpeliere-Pierrot, attended meetings at Caxton Hall held by Maharishi's "Spiritual Regeneration Movement" (SRM), and got initiated into TM. When Pattie told George how alert and energetic she felt, he declared, "I want my own mantra." One day David Wynne, sculptor of the royal family and of The Beatles, was talking with George about yogis. He showed George a photo of Maharishi's palm with its long life line and suggested he attend the guru's lecture in London on August 24, 1967.

Maharishi's organizers had planned an average hotel for the lecture. However, the yogi insisted on the newly built Park Lane Hilton, whose ballroom held over 1000 people. George got tickets for Pattie, her sister Jenny Boyd, John, his wife Cynthia, Paul, his girlfriend Jane Asher, and Paul's brother Mike McGear. Ringo could not make it. He was with his wife Maureen, who had just given birth to their son Jason five days earlier.

Beatles watching Maharishi's lecture at Park Lane Hilton hotel London; l. to r.: Paul, Mike McGear (Paul's brother), John, Cynthia Lennon, Pattie Boyd, George, Jenny Boyd. ANL/Shutterstock.

Pattie described Maharishi as "impressive," and herself as "spellbound." "That's the first time anybody has talked about these things in a way I understand," George recalled.[295] "I knew I needed a mantra—a password to get through into the other world."[296]

Paul, who thought Maharishi made a lot of sense, admitted they had been into drugs but were searching for more. He recognized that with Maharishi's "simple system of meditation, twenty minutes in the morning, twenty minutes in the evening, no big sort of crazy thing, you can improve the quality of your life and find some sort of meaning in doing so."[297] Paul remembered Maharishi appearing in 1960 on ITV Granada's *People and Places*, a Manchester-based current-affairs TV show.

Maharishi first meeting with The Beatles backstage at the Hilton. Trinity Mirror/Mirrorpix/Alamy Stock Photo.

After the lecture at the Hilton, Vincent Snell, MD, an orthopedic surgeon and the first Initiator (TM teacher) in Britain, introduced The Beatles to Maharishi backstage. The Beatles told the yogi, "Even from an early age we have been seeking a highly spiritual existence. We tried drugs and that didn't work."[298] George joked later: "We got backstage to see Maharishi and I said to him: 'Got any mantras?'"[299]

Maharishi told The Beatles, "You have created a magic attraction in your name, so you should do something for the youngsters."[300] When The Beatles asked what they could do, Maharishi advised them to learn TM in London and become TM teachers. However, the Fabs insisted on getting initiated by Maharishi himself, so he invited them as his guests to his ten-day retreat in Bangor, North Wales.

John recounted, "We met him and saw a good thing and went along with it. The youth of today are really looking for some answers—for proper answers the established church can't give them, their parents can't give them, material things can't give them."[301] Since The Beatles did everything together, they all decided to go for the retreat.

Blissed-out in Bangor

The Beatles boarded the train to Wales just as it pulled away from London's jam-packed Euston station on August 25, 1967—Friday on a bank holiday weekend. John bolted ahead of his wife Cynthia and left her to attend to the luggage. The police mistook her for a fan and blocked her. She got left behind on the platform, in tears.

This seemed an apt metaphor for her state of mind, with Yoko Ono quickly taking possession of John, often appearing at their private residence, conveniently leaving things behind. Cynthia recalled, "I knew in my heart, as I watched the people I loved fading into the hazy distance, that the loneliness I felt on that station platform would become permanent before long."[302]

Neil Aspinall drove Cynthia to Bangor in his car, but he did not attend the retreat. After the 269-mile journey from London, The Beatles and three hundred other course participants stayed in dorms at Normal College (now part of Bangor University), sharing bunk beds and eating dreadful canteen food. Attendees of the Bangor retreat included The Beatles, Cynthia Lennon, Pattie Boyd, Jenny Boyd, Jane Asher, singer Cilla Black, Mick Jagger, and his girlfriend, singer Marianne Faithfull. George recalled when they first arrived in Bangor, "we met all these meditators, and it's so obvious, just by seeing the people, that they give off this peace and happiness."[303]

Train to Bangor, North Wales: from front around circle clockwise: George, Hunter Davies (Beatles biographer), Paul, Ringo, John, Maharishi. Trinity Mirror/Mirrorpix/ Alamy Stock Photo.

George laughing with Maharishi on the train. Trinity Mirror/Mirrorpix/Alamy Stock Photo.

Beatles arrive in Bangor; l. to r.: Brahmachari Devendra, John, Maharishi, Paul, Ringo, George (carrying sitar). Trinity Mirror/Mirrorpix/Alamy Stock Photo.

Crowds greet The Beatles in Bangor: Top row l. to r.: Dr. Vincent Snell, Ringo, George, TM administrator Eileen Forrestal. Bottom row l. to r.: John, Maharishi, biographer Hunter Davies. David Thorpe/ANL/Shutterstock.

Beatles onstage with Maharishi in Bangor. Daily Mail/Shutterstock.

The Beatles carrying autographed copies of Maharishi's book, strolling on Normal College campus in Bangor, North Wales. Trinity Mirror/Mirrorpix/Alamy Stock Photo.

Meeting Maharishi was "one of those mind-altering moments of your life" for Ringo.[304] Impressed by the guru, who was always happy, laughing, and having a great time, he recounted, "For the first time, we were getting into Eastern philosophies—and that was another breakthrough."[305]

George said, "You can get control of yourself just by sitting quietly and by turning off from the external problems and go inside yourself where it's always calm and peaceful."[306]

John said that through meditation, "I could handle each day better than I could handle it before."[307]

Maharishi said, "Through this meditation, if [The Beatles] take it up, they could bring up the youth of today to a higher understanding of life."[308] "They are very important to me, because they are The Beatles. They can do a great deal for the whole of humanity, and particularly for the youth, which they can lead."[309]

George playing sitar for Maharishi in Bangor. Clockwise: Maharishi, Pattie Boyd, George, Jenny Boyd, Ringo, Paolo Ammassari, John. © Colin Harrison-Avico Ltd.

Maharishi initiated The Beatles into TM on Saturday, August 26. Since drug abstinence was prerequisite to learning TM, the musicians allegedly stopped taking drugs. Maharishi commented, "The interest of young minds in the use of drugs, even though misguided, indicates their genuine search for some form of spiritual experience."[310]

At the time, John said, "We've had enough acid. It's done all it can do for us. Meditation is much healthier. I like it better."[311] "Now we should be able to experience things first hand, instead of artificially with a wrong stepping-stone like drugs."[312]

Brian's Passing

Beatles manager Brian Epstein had planned to join the Beatles at the retreat, but an accidental drug overdose took his life on August 27 in London. Consequently, The Beatles only stayed the weekend. George said Maharishi was a great comfort when they lost Brian.[313] Yet Brian's relatives felt Maharishi spoke callously by telling the Beatles that death was not real, that Brian had gone on to his next stage of life, that they should not be overwhelmed with grief, and that their thoughts of Brian should be happy since those thoughts would travel to him wherever he was.[314]

John Lennon told journalist Ray Coleman, "We want to learn the meditation thing properly so we can sell the whole idea to everyone. This is how we plan to use our power now. We want to set up an academy in London and use all the power we've got to get it moving. It strengthens understanding, makes people relaxed, and it's much better than acid. This is the biggest thing in my life now and it's come when I need it most. Brian has died only in body. His spirit will always be working with us."[315] "His power and force will linger on."[316]

In December 1970, in his *Rolling Stone* magazine interview, John changed his tune and agreed with Epstein's relatives. He said Maharishi was "like an idiot," the way he told The Beatles to smile and be happy about Brian.

Tony Barrow, The Beatles' press secretary, said that even before Brian's funeral Paul called a meeting to discuss making the film *Magical Mystery Tour*. Paul was criticized as callous by resuming work so soon, but Paul had good reason: to keep the group together and working. He feared that in the wake of Brian's death, The Beatles would go off to India with Maharishi and "never come back together again as a working band."[317]

Maharishi met The Beatles at the home of his closest disciple Jemima Pitman, Albert Place, Kensington: Front row l. to r.: Paul, Jane Asher, John on floor, Maharishi. Back row: Dr. Vincent Snell, Pattie Boyd, Mike McGear, Ringo, Maureen Starkey, George. Mick Jagger and TM Initiator Hermione Cassell were also in attendance. Keystone Press/Alamy Stock Photo.

Love Letter to TM

Soon after John Lennon met Maharishi and learned to meditate, he wrote his love letter to TM—"Across the Universe." The Beatles finished recording it February 8, 1968, one week before flying to India to study with Maharishi at his Meditation Academy in Rishikesh. John evoked the meditation experience in the poetic verses. In the chorus, he sang a common expression in India, *Jai Guru Deva*, which means, "Glory to the divine preceptor," and tacked the syllable *Om* after it. *Om* is the holy primordial sound that is said to underlie and give rise to the universe. It is often chanted or repeated as a mantra in India, but not by Maharishi.

Whenever Maharishi greeted or parted with anyone, he would never shake hands or say "hello," "goodbye," or "have a nice day." Instead, he would place his palms together in front of his heart. This traditional Indian gesture, called *namaskar*, means: "I bow to God within you." With hands in this prayer-like position, Maharishi would exclaim *Jai Guru Dev* to hundreds of people every day, in tribute to his beloved guru, Swami Brahmananda Saraswati. From 1941 to 1953, the swami held the post of Shankaracharya of Jyotir Math, in the Himalayas, as one of four main Hindu religious leaders in India.

Maharishi often said that Guru Dev revived the lost wisdom of the Vedas by embodying omnipresence, the fullness of wisdom: "When thousands of people are living that, then this will be a world where angels will want to come. We want to leave a better world." In this way, Maharishi gave all credit to Guru Dev. He envisioned world peace, without suffering, and worked tirelessly toward fulfilling his "World Plan."

 Scan this code to read the lyrics.

The Lyrics

John's poetic lyrics capture the essence of the meditative state. He conveyed the experience of restless thoughts that wandered in and out of his mind. He sang of joy and sorrow, of dancing light, of laughter and love, shining with brilliance. These dreamy, inspirational, melodious descriptions evoke the cosmic, transcendent meditative experience in sensitive, perceptive ways.

In the chorus, he characterized the state of unbounded awareness experienced during TM as his own private, personal immersion into inner peace and heavenly bliss—unchangeable and absolute.

In 1970, John said these lyrics came first and then the music. "It's one of the best lyrics I've written—in fact it could be *the* best. It's good poetry. The ones I like are the ones that stand as words without melody. You can read them like a poem."[318] John recalled his wife Cynthia was mouthing off at him, which he found irritating. After she fell asleep, he kept hearing these words: "flowing like an endless stream." So he went downstairs and wrote a "cosmic song rather than an irritated song."[319]

Even though John was disappointed with the track's production, he stated, "the words stand, luckily, by themselves. They were purely inspirational and were given to me as *boom*! I don't know where it came from. Such an extraordinary meter and I can never repeat it! It's not a matter of craftsmanship; it wrote itself. It *drove* me out of bed. I didn't want to write it. It's like being *possessed*; like a *psychic* or a *medium*. It won't let you sleep, so you *have* to get up, *make* it into something, and then you're allowed to sleep. That's always in the middle of the bloody night when you're half awake or tired and your critical facilities are switched off."[320]

The Inner Genius

John's "aha moment" of spontaneous creativity was divine Spirit expressing in creative ways through him. Meditation helped him slip out of what he characterized as the "straitjacket of the mind."

He said, "to receive the 'wholly spirit,' i.e. creative inspiration, the main problem was emptying the mind. You can't paint a picture on dirty paper; you need a clean sheet."[321] The best way to awaken what I call our "inner genius" is through meditation. Here are some examples:

Pablo Picasso and Leonardo da Vinci stared at the blank canvas until a vision of their painting emerged. Michelangelo chipped away at the block of marble to free the figure hidden within. Brahms entered an altered state of awareness where he heard the music, and saw rhythms, chords, and notes. Mozart and Beethoven heard the music within and just transcribed it. Just before falling asleep, Robert Louis Stevenson gave what he called the "gremlins of his mind" a suggestion to produce a story.

Paul McCartney described his inspiration for "Let It Be," "Yesterday," and "Yellow Submarine" as arising from dreams and visions. While driving from London to Weybridge to compose with John Lennon, Paul would turn off the radio so the only music he would hear was what came into his head.[322] "Let It Be" might be Paul's most spiritual song. He wrote it after his deceased mother Mary appeared in a dream to reassure him during a troubling time. Similar to Maharishi, who often said, "Take it easy and take it as it comes," Mary told Paul, "It's gonna be okay. Just let it be." Paul expressed, "I felt so great. She gave me the positive word."[323]

Meditation Changes Your World

Paul remembered John discussing "Across the Universe" with Maharishi, who wanted more optimistic lyrics and suggested, "'Meditation will change your world." But John refused to change them because the original lyrics sounded better.[324]

Some commentators suggested that within the song's context, what will change John's world is "nothing"—meaning the nothingness or pure void of Buddhism: nirvana, or the absolute bliss consciousness of Hinduism: *satchitananda*.

Beamed to Polaris

Maharishi died on February 5, 2008. In an uncanny coincidence, on the same day, for the first time ever, NASA beamed a song into the universe, aimed into deep space towards Polaris, the North Star. It was "Across the Universe," recorded forty years previously, in February 1968. This event celebrated the fortieth anniversary of the song, the forty-fifth anniversary of the DSN (Deep Space Network), and fiftieth anniversary of NASA. As part of the celebration, people around the world simultaneously played the song while NASA transmitted it.

"Sour Milk Sea"

Written: February to April 1968
Recorded: June 24 to 26, 1968
Released: August 26, 1968: Single; August 6, 2021: All Things Must Pass: 50th Anniversary Box Set

"Sour Milk Sea" was recorded during the White Album demos but did not make the final cut. Instead, Jackie Lomax performed it, and the Apple record label released it. Written by George Harrison in ten minutes one evening in Rishikesh, the song promotes Transcendental Meditation as the way to overcome dissatisfaction and limitation and to bring illumination.

What Is the Sour Milk Sea?

In his memoir *I, Me, Mine*, George explained, "It's based on Vishvasara Tantra, from Tantric art ('what is here is elsewhere, what is not here is nowhere'): It's a picture, and the picture is called Sour Milk Sea—*Kalladadi Samudra* in Sanskrit—'the origin and growth of *Jambudvita* [correct spelling: *Jambudvipa*], the central continent, surrounded by fish symbols, according to the geological theory of the evolution of organic life on earth. The appearance of fishes marks the second stage.' I used Sour Milk Sea as the idea of—if you're in the shit, don't go around moaning about it: do something about it. Jai Guru Dev."[325]

Here is my interpretation of George's opaque explanation:

A famous saying of ancient India is usually attributed to its greatest scripture, the Mahabharata, but occasionally credited to a minor scripture, Vishvasara Tantra: "What is here is found elsewhere. But whatever is not here is nowhere else." The meaning of this is: "As above, so below." In other words, we are the unbounded being, present everywhere, and we mirror cosmic life.

Ancient Indian cosmology says the world is divided into seven concentric island continents, separated by seven encircling oceans, each double the size of the preceding one. The fifth from the center is a milk ocean, known as *Kshira Sagara*—the celestial abode of Lord Vishnu. Jambudvipa refers to a central mega-continent with Mount Meru (Earth's axis and abode of the gods) at its center.

The Sea of Milk also symbolizes the flood myth, found in nearly every culture. In India the belief is the universe repeats vast cycles of activity and rest, in which it is incessantly created, sustained, reabsorbed, and then recreated. This is similar to the big bang/big crunch theory.

Ancient Indian scriptures count twenty-four million Earth years as one day and night in the life of the creator, Lord Brahma. One year of Brahma is 360 of those days. After one hundred of those years, all elements get reabsorbed into primal matter and return to equilibrium in the *mahapralaya* ("great dissolution"). After another hundred years of Brahma, the universe emerges again. Both phases, creation and dissolution, are two facets of one reality—absolute consciousness, never changing, undiminished, and whole, just as a candle lit from another candle does not diminish the first candle's light.

The Sea of Milk symbolizes the dissolution, where Lord Vishnu is asleep, floating on the primal ocean, while the universe rests in absolute quietude. When Vishnu reawakens, duality begins. This is represented by *Samudra Manthana* ("churning of the milk ocean"), where forces of light and darkness (deities and demons) pool their resources to unearth the nectar of immortal life. During the thousand-year effort to bring up the nectar, a terrible poison appears, which threatens to destroy the universe.

Does your poisonous thinking sour the Milk Sea? As above, so below. Your individual life reflects this cosmic drama.

 Scan this code to read the lyrics.

The Lyrics

George claimed the lyrics of this song are "really about meditation."[326] Here is an explanation: The Law of Karma says we create our own destiny, and therefore we are responsible for our circumstances. We have the power to change our fate by changing our thoughts, words, and actions. If we have a bad attitude (sour milk is the metaphor), we can get back to finding inner truth through meditation.

A very simple process, Transcendental Meditation, quickly makes us more aware. This process allows us to get the most from everything we do. If we want to let go of limitations and get enlightened, trying different cults is just a waste of time. TM is the only method that gets results. We can get out of our sour milk sea of negative thinking by practicing TM.

The song is a blatant TM advertisement, and thus demonstrates how deeply George had been influenced by Maharishi, who hyped TM as the only true path to enlightenment and dismissed all other methods as worthless. In George's memoir *I, Me, Mine*, at the end of his explanation about this song, he exclaimed, "Jai Guru Dev" (Glory to Maharishi Mahesh Yogi's guru)—just in case we did not get the point that the song is about TM.

With a Little Help from His Friends: The Beatles

The Beatles were initiated into TM in late August 1967. Soon afterwards, they became highly vocal public advocates. They expressed enthusiasm and defended TM to skeptics in multiple interviews, including the *David Frost Programme* on September 29 and October 4, 1967, where John declared, "You just feel more energetic for doing work, or anything. You just come out of it and it's like (snaps fingers) Let's get going!"[327]

John told the *Daily Sketch*, "We've never felt like this about anything else."[328] He even suggested to his co-Beatles, "If we went round the world preaching about Transcendental Meditation, we could turn on millions of people."[329]

Once The Beatles became public supporters, Maharishi found himself all over the press and his following exploded to millions. Maharishi appeared in *Life* magazine three times: in 1967, posing with The Beatles in Bangor in "LIFE on the Newsfronts of the World"[330] and in "Invitation to Instant Bliss,"[331] and in February 1968 in "Year of the Guru."[332] *Time* magazine dubbed Maharishi "Soothsayer for Everyman."[333] The *New York Times Magazine* declared him "Chief Guru of the Western World."[334] In *Newsweek*, he was quoted: "Just as you water the roots of a tree, you have to water the mind through meditation."[335]

A 1968 cover article in *Look* magazine "The Non-Drug Turn-On Hits Campus" reported students learning TM at Harvard, Yale, and many other universities.[336] In the same issue, flautist and TM teacher Paul Horn quoted Maharishi: "Meditation we don't do for the sake of meditation. We want some positive effects in life—something that will make a man more dynamic in his field of activity." Paul Horn added, "Best of all, you can never have a 'bad trip' with meditation."[337]

Wonderwall Music (album)

Written: November 1967 to January 12, 1968
Recorded: November 1967 to February 1968
Released: November 1, 1968 UK; December 2, 1968 US

George Harrison was the first Beatle to release a solo album—*Wonderwall Music*, soundtrack to the 1968 trippy hippie movie *Wonderwall*, and the first album released on The Beatles' Apple record label. Joe Massot directed the film, which starred Jane Birkin, Jack MacGowran, and Iain Quarrier. It was about a lonely professor obsessed with watching his next-door neighbor, a young model and photographer, through a hole in the wall of his flat. George's haunting, innovative, avant-garde soundtrack, featuring Indian instruments, made the weird concept of this psychedelic film into something quite mesmerizing.

Although George told Joe Massot he did not compose film scores, Massot convinced him to create the soundtrack by promising he would use anything George gave him. *I'll give them an Indian music anthology, and who knows, maybe a few hippies will get turned on to Indian music,* George thought.[338]

John Barham, classically trained pianist and musical arranger, had studied composition with Ravi Shankar and met George in 1966. Barham recalled, "Ravi took me down to George's house in Esher, where he had asked Ravi to play a recital for a small gathering. A few months before recording began on *Wonderwall*, he asked me if I wanted to do some arranging, and so of course I agreed."[339]

Recording Wonderwall Music in London

In December 1967, sarod maestro Ustad Aashish Khan (son of Ustad Ali Akbar Khan) happened to be on tour in England with tabla doyen Pandit Mahapurush Mishra. George had befriended Aashish Khan in Benares, India, in 1966, while studying with Ravi.

Aashish accepted George's request to record at De Lane Lea Studios in London.[340]

Aashish Khan played the seventeen- to twenty-five-string lute-like fretless sarod, with polished steel plate, four to five main strings for playing melody, two *chikari* strings (drone strings), and nine to eleven sympathetic strings. It was played using the edge of the fingernails with one hand and a coconut-shell plectrum with the other.

Mahapurush Mishra played tabla (two hand-drums: treble and bass) and *pakhavaj* (double-headed barrel-shaped drum, beaten with both hands) on the track "Tabla and Pakavaj." Aashish and Mahapurush played together on "Gat Kirwani," based on "Raga Kirwani," a midnight raga popularized by Allauddin Khan and Ravi Shankar.

 Scan the code to watch the extraordinary Mahapurush Mishra play tabla with Ali Akbar Khan on sarod and his son Aashish Khan on tambura.

For the track "Love Scene," George needed romantic music. Barham recalled, "I knew a raga which had been created by Aashish's grandfather, Allauddin Khan, called 'Manjh Khamaj,' which I always thought was very romantic. So I suggested that to Aashish."[341] It is an evening raga, played up until midnight.

Though overdubbing had been unknown in India, George asked Aashish to double-track himself. Aashish recalled, "At first I was very confused, but then I started listening and found some spaces in between and started filling them, and he liked it very much."[342] Aashish later commented he was "thrilled" with the effect on "Love Scene," where the sarods "play to each other like two lovers in a romantic mood."[343]

George recorded rock musicians, including Eric Clapton and Ringo, on the track "Ski-ing." "Dream Scene" was a hodgepodge of

Indian music and vocals from Abbey Road's library collection, plus Barham on flugelhorn. Indian instruments included *tabla tarang*, *swarmandal* zither, and sitar. This dreamscape of backwards tape loops was recorded long before John Lennon's "Revolution 9." "On the Bed" featured a piano part from George, plus a sitar-like guitar part, based on a theme Barham had created.

Two sarod maestros: Ustad Aashish Khan with this father Ustad Ali Akbar Khan. Photo courtesy of Aashish Khan.

Aashish Khan on sarod and Zakir Hussain on tabla. Photo courtesy of Aashish Khan.

Pandit Mahapurush Mishra playing tabla. Photo courtesy of Anand Mishra, grandson of Mahapurush Mishra.

Musicians in London

Tabla master Pandit Mahapurush Mishra was the main accompanist for Ali Akbar Khan for three decades and professor at the Ali Akbar College of Music in Calcutta. He spent most of the late sixties in the USA, teaching, recording, and appearing widely in classical music concerts.

Sarod superstar Ustad Aashish Khan, son of Ustad Ali Akbar Khan and grandson of legendary Baba Allauddin Khan, is a Grammy-nominated musician, film and stage composer, and professor at several universities in California and at Ali Akbar College of Music in San Rafael. Khan played on film scores *Gandhi, The Man Who Would Be King, A Passage to India*, and many more.

In 1969, Aashish Khan formed the first World Music ensemble, an Indo-rock fusion group named Shanti ("inner peace") with tabla virtuoso Ustad Zakir Hussain (son of Alla Rakha). All the band members practiced Transcendental Meditation, and meditator Richard Bock produced their album. The group auditioned for Apple Records, but Ravi Shankar persuaded George Harrison not to sign them. Zakir recalled that Ravi "wanted Aashish and I to realize that we have this incredible gift that has been given by our forefathers, and we should not mess with it where it loses its identity."[344]

 Scan this code to watch this awesome group play.

George and musical arranger John Barham working on *East Meets West* for sarod player Aashish Khan in rear. Photo by Yogish Sahota, courtesy of Aashish Khan.

Aashish Khan's Missing Track Unearthed

On November 11, 2021, Indian journalist Suresh Joshi released a Hindu devotional rock song "Radhe Shaam." The track had been locked in Joshi's attic for fifty-three years and was restored by music producer Suraj Shinh. Though Joshi claimed he wrote and produced it, the song was actually composed and sung by Aashish Khan, arranged by John Barham, and played by musicians George Harrison, Eric Clapton, Billy Preston, Klaus Voormann, and Ringo Starr.

Aashish Khan had scored the music for a documentary film, *East Meets West*, produced by Suresh Joshi. While The Beatles were recording "Hey Jude" at Trident Studios in London, July 31 to August 1, 1968, Khan asked George Harrison to play guitar on a rock track called "Jai Siya Ram" (not Radhe Shaam) for the film score.

Joshi said, "The song revolves around the concept that we are all one, and that the world is our oyster—something that we have all realized during this pandemic. A song produced over fifty years ago could not have been more relevant today." Joshi claimed the proceeds from sales would go to charity.[345] [346]

 Scan this code to listen to the track.

Recording *Wonderwall Music* in India

In 1968, EMI/HMV had six recording studios in India, but Bombay was the movie and music recording hub. To find the best musicians for *Wonderwall*, George contacted Shambhu Das (head of Ravi Shankar's Kinnara School of Music in Bombay), who had assisted in George's sitar studies with Ravi in 1966.[347] George gave Das a list of instruments he wanted for the film score. Then Vijay Dubey, head of A&R for HMV Records in India, found the most accomplished musicians and hired them.[348] Thus, India's foremost classical musicians recorded *Wonderwall Music* and "The Inner Light."

The recording sessions took place at EMI's Bombay Studio from January 9 to 13, 1968. Bhaskar Menon (later head of EMI worldwide) lugged a huge two-track STEEDS stereo recorder all the way from Calcutta on a train, because HMV Bombay only had a mono machine.[349] Menon said George had a great ear for Indian musical instruments. "He was an incredibly hard worker and took this very seriously. It was a kind of immersion into the folk music of India."[350]

Every morning, George arrived at the studio early and listened to the musicians Dubey brought for the day. Each evening, George returned to his hotel and made notes about the instruments. The next day, George met with the musicians, who spoke no English, and played guitar or hummed tunes to convey what he wanted. He relied on Das and Dubey to translate. Das recalled, "George would convey to me what mood he needed, and the musicians improvised, and then he okayed for the recording."[351]

 Scan these codes to see George and the musicians recording in India.

George autographed this photo of George and Shambhu Das. Photo courtesy of Mani Biswas, daughter of Shambhu Das.

One month after recording *Wonderwall Music*, The Beatles would be in Rishikesh, studying with Maharishi Mahesh Yogi. Since Shambhu Das was George's close friend, Das was invited to join The Beatles there. He accepted the invitation and stayed at the ashram for four days, played sitar, and became close with Maharishi, who asked him to "do some special work." Shambhu found the guru's invitation confusing, since Ravi was not in tune with Maharishi's philosophy.[352]

Wonderwall musicians, January 11, 1968: Back row l. to r.: Masit Khan (sarangi), Rijram Desad's assistant (tambura), unknown, possibly Ghulam Dastigir Khan or Gyan Shankar Ghosh (sitar), possibly Shankar Ghosh (tabla), Chandrashekhar Naringrekar (sitar and surbahar). Middle row l. to r.: Shivkumar Sharma (santoor), George Harrison, Rijram Desad (harmonium). Front: Bengt Berger. Photo courtesy of Bengt Berger.

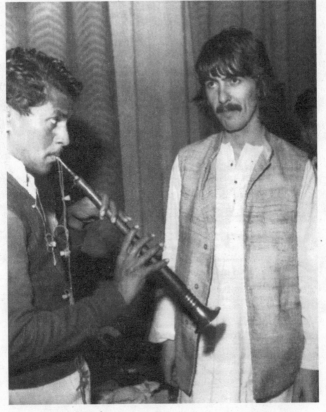

Hanuman Jadev playing shehnai for George on January 10, 1968.
AP/Shutterstock.

Musicians in India

George loved the exotic, moaning cry of the *shehnai*, a conical wooden oboe with a double reed at one end and metal or wooden flared bell at the other. Played by Sharad Kumar and Hanuman Jadev, it appeared on the tracks "Microbes" (based on raga "Darbari-Kanada") and "Guru Vandana."

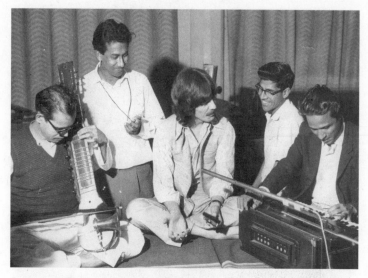

Recording *Wonderwall Music;* l. to r.: Vinayak Vora playing tar-shehnai, Shambhu Das (sitar player) holding stopwatch, George, unknown tambura player, and Rijram Desad on harmonium. Keystone Press/Alamy Stock Photo.

Vinayak Vora playing esraj. Photo courtesy of Uttank Vora.

Vinayak Vora playing his invention for his son Uttank, using a bow. A horn is attached to the sound board. Photo courtesy of Uttank Vora.

Pandit Vinayak Vora played *tar-shehnai*, a bowed stringed instrument known as *esraj*, but with an added amplifying gramophone-like metal horn attached to its sound board. The word *tar* means "stringed." *Tar-shehnai*, which sounds like a shehnai, appeared on the track "Fantasy Sequins" and was double-tracked on "Crying."

Vinayak's son Uttank Vora told me that at a flea market, his father found a broken two-stringed Japanese-fiddle-like instrument, added a sound box to its base, and played it with a bow. A small metal pin would touch the string and create a sharp wailing sound, like a shehnai. In a promotional brochure sent to me by Uttank, Ravi Shankar said, "Pandit Vinayak Vora's great contribution to Indian classical music is that he is the first to popularize the instrument *tar-shehnai* not only at home but far beyond our country."

"I remember my father saying that George Harrison was extremely studious for such a world-renowned celebrity," Uttank told me. "He loved his humility, modesty, dedication and overall respect for Indian classical music and musicians."

Chandrashekhar Naringrekar tutoring George in the hard-to-master, ginormous surbahar. Photo courtesy of Bengt Berger.

l. to r.: Aashish Khan on sarod, Ustad Zakir Hussain on tabla, Indranil Bhattacharya on sitar. Photo courtesy of Ali Akbar Khan Foundation.

Chandrashekhar Naringrekar playing surbahar, Maruti V. Kurdekar playing pakhavaj drum, and unknown tambura player.

Pandit Shankar Ghosh, who was credited with playing tabla on *Wonderwall*, with his son Bickram Ghosh, who played tabla on *Chants of India* and "Brainwashed/Namah Parvati." Photo courtesy of Bickram Ghosh by Greg Plachta.

Shambhu Das and Indranil Bhattacharya played sitar, and Chandrashekhar Naringrekar played *surbahar*, a bass sitar. Indranil studied with the celebrated Annapurna Devi (see pages 390–391).

These musicians are heard on several tracks and featured on "Glass Box," where sitar and surbahar played octaves in unison. The renowned tabla maestro and educator Pandit Shankar Ghosh is credited with playing tabla, and Bombay musician Gyan Shankar Ghosh possibly played sitar. *Ghunghroo* bells, sounding like tambourine, were heard on "Fantasy Sequins."

Pandit Shivkumar Sharma playing santoor in 1968. Don Douglas/Alamy Stock Photo.

Using walnut sticks, Pandit Shivkumar Sharma played *santoor*, a trapezoid-shaped hammered dulcimer with 116 strings. Santoor was heard on "In the Park," as was surbahar. Sharma recalled, "George Harrison—he loved India. He loved Indian music. He loved Indian spirituality. So this thing pushed Indian classical music on the top. Fusion we can call it. Western and Indian classical music, and that was the biggest fusion ever happened."[353]

Rijram Desad played *tabla tarang* (seven or more treble tabla drums tuned to different notes that play melodies: see photo, page 432) on "In the Park." He also played double-headed cylindrical drum *dholak* on "Glass Box," and harmonium, drone instrument on Indian tracks and on "Greasy Legs." Shridhar R. Kenkare played *bansuri* (bamboo flute) on "Singing Om."

Pandit Ramesh Prem played the vichitra veena on "In the Park." This huge, double-gourded rare stringed instrument, played with a spherical slide, takes ten to fifteen years of single-minded devotion to learn (see a photo of the instrument on page 431). A devotee of Paramahansa Yogananda (founder of Yogoda Satsanga Society of India: YSS and author of *Autobiography of a Yogi*), Ramesh Prem composed devotional songs and played his veena to celebrate the centenary of Yogananda's birth, January 5, 1993. Recorded by members of the Mumbai YSS, the songs were later released on the CD *Guru Sharanam* ("to seek refuge at the feet of the Guru").[354] Prem said his guru Yogananda "freed him of his agonies."[355]

Wonderwall and World Music

Bob Gill designed the *Wonderwall* album cover—a surrealistic image of a brick wall, separating a Magritte-like man in an overcoat and bowler hat from an Indian-miniature style view of naked ladies bathing in a lotus pond—representing Lord Krishna's delightful consorts known as *gopi*.

Through inspiration, dedication, and exacting precision, George completed the monumental task of scoring the *Wonderwall* soundtrack. Like so many "firsts" credited to John, Paul, George, and Ringo, this was the first album we would now classify as "World Music." In the *Guardian* in March 2017, Graeme Thomson called *Wonderwall Music* "a world music crossover before such a notion even existed."[356]

"The Inner Light"

Written: November 1967 to January 12, 1968
Recorded: January 12, February 6 and 8, 1968
Released: March 15, 1968: Single

George Harrison played a primary role in bringing Eastern music and religion to the West. Under his guidance, Indian musicians played on three Beatles songs: "Love You To," "Within You Without You," and "The Inner Light." George played sitar on "Norwegian Wood," *swarmandal* on "Strawberry Fields Forever," and tambura on "Tomorrow Never Knows," "Getting Better," and "Lucy in the Sky with Diamonds." The most "Eastern" Beatles song, "The Inner Light" was recorded in India using solely Indian instruments. Its lyrics quoted verbatim the Tao Te Ching ("The Great Book of the Way of Virtue")—a beloved ancient Chinese scripture.

The Way

Tao Te Ching, the foundation of Taoist philosophy, advocates a simple, peaceful life of moderation. The goal is to follow the Way (*Tao*) of the universe and live in harmony with the rhythm of natural and supernatural worlds, in tune with natural law. Tao Te Ching is attributed to Lao Tzu (circa 604–531 BC), founder of Taoism, known as Tao-chia ("School of the Way"). Said to be immortal, he keeps his identity secret to test his disciples. "Lao Tzu" simply means "old master." His home is the magical, fertile mountain Hua Shan, also called Western Mountain or Flower Mountain. Near its summit is his temple and great furnace, where he purportedly created the pill of immortality. Pilgrims visit this sacred mountain, hoping to meet the master or gain his blessing. Mushrooms growing on this mountain are believed to grant immortality.

Meeting Mascaró

On the British television show *The Frost Programme*, David Frost interviewed Maharishi Mahesh Yogi, John Lennon, and George Harrison about Transcendental Meditation on September 29, 1967, at Wembley Studios, North London. The show was so popular that Frost invited the Beatles back for his next episode, October 4, where intellectuals and religious leaders questioned the merits of TM while John and George defended it.

One of the panelists, Cambridge Sanskrit professor Juan Mascaró, wrote to George on November 16, 1967: "Two friends from abroad gave me the recording of your song 'Within You Without You.' I am very happy, it is a moving song and may it move the souls of millions, and there is more to come, as you are only beginning on the great journey."[357] Juan also enclosed his book *Lamps of Fire: From the Scriptures and Wisdom of the World*, a compilation of worldwide spiritual wisdom, which, on page 66, quoted a passage from the Tao Te Ching in a section titled "The Inner Light." The Tao Te Ching is divided into eighty-one brief "chapters," and Juan suggested that George use chapter 47 as lyrics for a song. The chapter poetically described the benefits of meditation.[358]

In *I, Me, Mine*, George related, "The song was written especially for Juan Mascaró, because he sent me the book and is a sweet old man. It was nice, the words said everything. Amen."[359]

 Scan this code to read the lyrics.

The Lyrics

Deep within our being is the source of all knowledge, both temporal and divine. We can tap that source by closing our eyes, getting quiet and still, and experiencing our higher Self in meditation. There we can see all, know all, receive answers to any question, and attain higher consciousness. We do not need anything external. Every treasure lies within. A life of simplicity brings greatest happiness. We need not go anywhere. Since our higher Self is unbounded, without limitations of time or space, we can be anywhere or everywhere at any time. We are one with everything. Therefore, we encompass the entire universe.

When our attention is directed outwards, overshadowed by sensory delights, we are out of touch with our true nature. The more we hanker after materialistic goals, the less we know real peace, which can only be found within. By turning 180 degrees away from the outer world, and diving inward, we can realize the ultimate truth, attain spiritual awakening, and find permanent contentment.

In 1967, Ringo said, "The four of us have got almost anything money can buy. But the things you buy mean nothing after a time. You look for something else, for a new experience. We have found something now which fills the gap. Since meeting Maharishi, I feel great."[360]

Paul said, "I think by 1968 we were all a bit exhausted, spiritually. Generally there was a feeling of: 'Yeah, well, it's great to be famous [and] rich—but what's it all for?' So we were enquiring into all sorts of things. After we met Maharishi and thought about it all, we went out to Rishikesh."[361]

In 1968 in Rishikesh, George told photographer and filmmaker Paul Saltzman, "Like we're The Beatles, aren't we? We can have anything that money can buy. And all the fame we could dream of. And then what? It isn't love. It isn't health. It isn't peace inside. Meditation and Maharishi have made the inner life rich for me. I get higher than I ever did with drugs. It's my way of connecting with God."[362]

On December 2, 1968, John said, "They spend all that time getting to the Moon and they don't know what's going on in their heads. This is the time of people discovering that it's all in your head and Venus is in your bloody head and so is the Moon, and you don't need a rocket to get there. And Man can do anything. And Jesus never came down in disguise as God any more than any of us did. We're all Jesus and we're all God, and he's inside all of us. And as soon as you start realizing that potential in everyone, then you can change it."[363]

In 1982, George said, "Everybody's looking for something and we are it. We don't have to look anywhere—it's right there within ourselves."[364]

One of Maharishi's go-to expressions was: "Do less and accomplish more. Do nothing and accomplish everything." We can see all, know all, and do all without doing anything. He believed meditation is the key to realizing our goals. He often used an analogy of archery, where we first draw back the arrow on the bow to gain maximum momentum and then hit the target. Drawing back the bow is a metaphor for deep meditation. Hitting the target is analogous to successful activity.

Maharishi often declared, "We can enjoy 200 percent of life, both worldly and divine," meaning both material and spiritual riches can be ours through meditation. He often said, "Just as we water the roots of a tree, we have to water the mind through meditation. Water the root to enjoy the fruit." By meditating daily, we get energy infusions that make it easy to joyously fulfill our aspirations.

Maharishi said frequently, "We cannot solve a problem on the level of the problem. We cannot bring light into a dark room by stumbling around in the dark. Instead, just flip a switch and turn on the light." His way of switching on the light was meditation.

This song is not a fortune cookie. The *Tao* literally translates as "the Way." It is a way of life and practical advice for everyday life.

Hariprasad Chaurasia playing bansuri. Photo from hariprasadchaurasia.com.

Recording the Song

George booked five days at HMV studios in Bombay to record the *Wonderwall* soundtrack—January 9 to 13, 1968. On January 12, the *Wonderwall* project was nearly complete, so George recorded instrumentals for future Beatles recordings with the same musicians. One became "The Inner Light," featuring Hariprasad Chaurasia (*bansuri* flute), Hanuman Jadev (shehnai), and Rijram Desad (harmonium, *dholak*, and tabla tarang). Another became a bonus track on the CD reissue of *Wonderwall Music*: "Almost Shankara." Ustad Masit Khan played sarangi and Shridhar Kenkare played bansuri on the track. A third track was "Don's Song," a composition by Donovan.

The instrumental track of "The Inner Light" was recorded January 12, 1968 (coincidentally, Maharishi's fiftieth birthday). The instrument playing the melody was identified at georgeharrison.com as *bulbul tarang*, known as Punjabi banjo or Indian banjo (player unknown).[365] Similar to Japanese *taishogoto*, *bulbul tarang* ("waves of nightingales") employs both drone and melody strings. Six to ten total strings run the length of a plate or fretboard on a long narrow hollow box. Typewriter-like keys or chord bars, when depressed, fret the strings to raise their pitch. The instrument is tuned to the key of the song. Keys are operated with the left hand and bow or plectrum with the right.

 Scan this code to see this rare instrument played.

The song begins with a harmonium drone followed by a riff played on bulbul tarang. The *dholak* drum starts the beat along with tar-shehnai playing the lead melody—a snake-charmer-like, high-pitched moan. The bulbul tarang (sounding like banjo) answers with a melody. Then tar-shehnai plays in unison with bulbul tarang. The harmonium drone segues into George's gentle, meditative vocals, accompanied by bansuri flute and harmonium. The bulbul tarang responds to each line of vocals. Faint taps of tabla tarang accompany the vocals. Bulbul tarang and tar-shehnai, accompanied by brisk dholak drumbeats, play the high-energy instrumental sections. Near the end, the tar-shehnai and dholak respond to George, Paul, and John's harmonies, and the tar-shehnai and harmonium close out the instrumental.

At EMI Studios in London on February 6, 1968, The Beatles recorded the vocal overdub. Tape operator Jerry Boys remembered: "George had this big thing about not wanting to sing it because he didn't feel confident that he could do the song justice. I remember Paul saying 'You must have a go, don't worry about it, it's *good*.'"[366] Sound engineer Geoff Emerick recalled that Mal Evans lit candles and incense to "create a vibe for George." With encouragement from Paul, George sang brilliantly.[367] "The Inner Light" was George Harrison's first original single (as the B-side to "Lady Madonna").

"Here, There and Everywhere"

Written: June 1966
Recorded: June 16 and 17, 1966
Released: August 5, 1966: Revolver

In the mid-1960s, Maharishi Mahesh Yogi, whom The Beatles studied with from August 1967 to April 1968, spoke the following:

> "'Love of God', someone said, 'is an abstract concept.' Yes it is abstract. It takes the experience of life to make it concrete. In its most infant state, love finds an expression on the lap of mother. In the sweetness of the mother's eye. It grows in toys and playfields, in the sweetness of friends and folks of society. It grows in the sweetness of husband and wife. With age and experience, the tree of love grows. It grows with the growth of life and evolution, and finds its fulfillment in the eternal love of the omnipresent God, which fills the heart and overthrows the darkness of ignorance.
>
> "And then, in the illumination of universal love, the abstract love of God finds concrete expression in everything. All becomes divine radiance of eternal love. Life finds its meaning in the living presence of God. Every phase of life then saturated with love breathes the living presence of God: Here, there, and everywhere, in this, that, and everything."[368]

Maharishi would often characterize God as being "Here, there, and everywhere." This quote is from *Love and God*, originally published on January 1, 1965, in Oslo by SRM Press. Since Paul McCartney spent his nights rifling through esoteric books at the Indica Bookstore starting in late 1965, we might wonder whether he read this book before writing "Here, There and Everywhere."

 Scan this code to
read the lyrics.

Yellow Submarine (song, album, and film)

Written: March to April 1966
Recorded: May 26, June 1, 1966
Released: August 5, 1966: Revolver; January 13, 1969:
Yellow Submarine
Film Released: July 17, 1968: UK; November 13, 1968: US

"Yellow Submarine" was not only the title track of the animated film of the same name; it was also the only British Beatles single with Ringo as lead vocalist. Paul remembered lying in bed in the Asher family home garret, where he lived from 1963 to 1965 with his girlfriend Jane Asher. Drifting in the twilight zone, in what he called "this little limbo-land just before you slip into sleep," Paul thought of a children's song. "The color yellow came to me, and a submarine came to me, and I thought, *Well, that's kind of nice, like a toy, very childish yellow submarine.*"[369]

Paul imagined it would be a song for Ringo, so he wrote it for the drummer's vocal range. "I just made up a little tune in my head, then started making a story."[370] It was about an ancient mariner telling kids about living in a yellow submarine that was both surrealistic and childlike. With Ringo so good with children, Paul liked the idea of giving him a children's song rather than a serious song: "I knew it would get connotations, but it was just a children's song."[371] "Kids get it straight away. I just loved the idea of kids singing it.'"[372]

 Scan this code to see
a trailer for the movie
"Yellow Submarine," which
introduces some of the
characters discussed here.

The Meaningful Film

The animated feature *Yellow Submarine* was conceived in 1967, during the year of "Flower Power" and the "Summer of Love." This avant-garde, surrealistic, artistically brilliant masterpiece is as fresh and current today as it was in the sixties. Its message is timeless. The Beatles wanted nothing to do with the project because they hated the Canadian animated cartoon and assumed the film would use those characters. But when they saw the sophisticated psychedelic artwork of the genius Heinz Edelmann, they regretted their decision. By then, it was too late for anything other than a cameo appearance at the end.

The theme of the film is love as the cohesive force that can overcome all negativity and create worldwide harmony. Its songs "All You Need Is Love" and "It's All Too Much" express that beautifully. The movie is rich with symbolism, which can be very personal and touch people in different ways.

I believe the unearthly paradise of Pepperland, eighty thousand leagues beneath the sea, deeper than the subconscious mind, represents the field of paradise within—our higher Self, beyond the relative world of duality. In India, it is called *satchitananda*: absolute bliss consciousness. The dualistic, relative nature of creation is explored repeatedly by The Beatles, in "There's a Place," "Hello Goodbye," "Within You Without You," "Circles," "Sour Milk Sea," and "Old Brown Shoe." This universe is built of pairs of opposites: yin/yang, male/female, black/white, up/down, yes/no.

The Blue Meanies, lacking love, shoot anti-music missiles that turn everything gray and colorless. They only take *NO* for an answer. The Blue Meanies, Nowhere Man, and Eleanor Rigby represent "all the lonely people" who are "blue," harboring a negative attitude. In contrast, the shaking hands, the words *LOVE, YES, OK*, and *KNOW* (clipped to *NO* by Blue Meanies) are symbols of positivism.

The yellow submarine, which represents the sun (illumination), perches atop a pyramid, just as the "Eye of Providence" tops the pyramid on the reverse side of the US one-dollar bill. It symbolizes the "third eye," our sixth sense, through which we see wonders hidden from view. John's "sign of the horns" is not a demonic sign—quite the opposite. It is an ancient Buddhist gesture that expels negative energies.

When John asks what day it is, Ringo answers, "Sitar-day." John follows with, "Then George will be here." When John opens the door to George's world, the opening glissando of "Love You To" plays, while a shimmering scene with two blue oxen pulling a plow appear—sacred cows of India. George stands on a mountaintop with wind blowing his hair, like "The Fool on the Hill."

When George's car keeps changing colors, confounding Ringo, George declares, "It's all in the mind"—a line repeated throughout the film.

Wallace Greenslade, announcer of the British radio comedy *The Goon Show*, ended episodes with "It's all in the mind, y'know." But that saying has deeper meaning; namely, that the world is a projection of the mind, which is central to Indian philosophy. According to ancient seers, we create our own destiny, moment by moment, through our thoughts. Buddha said, "All that we are is the result of what we have thought."[373] Ramakrishna Paramahansa said, "Bondage and liberation are of the mind alone."[374]

When the yellow submarine reaches the Sea of Time, John quips, "In my humble opinion, we've become involved in Einstein's time space continuum theory, relatively speaking, that is." The submarine becomes a time machine and takes them backwards and forwards in time. Parallel universes with duplicate submarines and duplicate Beatles appear.

In the Sea of Monsters, the yellow submarine encounters the Vacuum Flask, a black hole that swallows everything, even itself. What remains is the void, which is emptiness (*shunyata*), the state of nirvana ("burning out of flame of desire"), where seeds of desire (*samskara*) cannot sprout. In the void, The Beatles encounter the Nowhere Man, who is nobody: Jeremy Hillary Boob, PhD. This character represents the empty void of pure potential. Nothing and everything are contained therein. The Beatles tell him the world is at his command, for he can become anything.

The Beatles then enter the Foothills of the Headlands with psychedelic designs in people's brains, where "Lucy in the Sky with Diamonds" appears. In the sixties, a "head" meant an acidhead, who often tripped on LSD. The imagery of that song, inspired by Lewis Carroll, evokes the psychedelic experience.

Then the Sea of Holes appears, with its psychedelic op-art sequence. After finally reaching Pepperland, The Beatles find everything gray and devoid of music. They don *Sgt. Pepper's Lonely Hearts Club Band* uniforms and play music, which restores color to everyone and everything.

The blue Glove represents the iron fist of despotism. But it cannot overcome Love and its power of positivity. John takes the word *Glove*, drops the *G*, and it becomes *Love*. The Glove's finger keeps getting stuck on the *o* in *Love* until Glove is obliterated by "All You Need Is Love."

Armed with Flower Power, the inhabitants chase away the Meanies and restore Pepperland. *NO* turns to *NOW* and then *KNOW*. Sgt. Pepper's Lonely Hearts Club Band, which was trapped in a glass sphere, reanimates and sings, "Now that you know who you are, what do you want to be?" from "Baby You're a Rich Man." The Blue Meanies' weapons can no longer shoot bullets—only flowers. Words like *YES* and *OK* keep popping up.

Ringo frees Jeremy Boob, who had been held captive. Boob makes flowers bloom all over the chief Meanie. Then Ringo says, "First time I saw that Nowhere Man, that nobody, I knew he was somebody."

John replies, "You're right." He then invites the Meanies: "Won't you join us? Hook up and otherwise comingle."

When Blue Meanie says, "Yes," Boob says, "Ah YES is a word with a glorious ring, a true universal euphonious thing, engenders embracing and chasing of blues, the very best word for the whole world to use."

Blue Meanie says, "Yes, let us mix, Max. I never admitted it before, but my cousin is the bluebird of happiness."

The song "It's All Too Much" lifts Boob into the sky as he pirouettes constantly on psychedelic flowers that repeatedly unfold. Then all of Pepperland's inhabitants appear in love and harmony in psychedelic sequences. The Beatles cameo finally appears at the end singing "All Together Now" with a message of peace and unity. Those words are spelled out in many languages.

Thank you, Lee Minoff and Al Brodax, for writing a screenplay that reflects The Beatles' understanding of universal ancient wisdom. And to hundreds of nameless art students in London who were bussed after class to volunteer all night in the animation studio to create this timeless masterpiece.

CHAPTER 6

REMNANTS OF THE RAJ

"The Continuing Story of Bungalow Bill"

Written: March to May 1968
Recorded: October 8, 1968
Released: November 22, 1968: The Beatles

In the early 1960s, the popularity of Transcendental Meditation was rising quickly in England, Canada, Europe, and South America, but in the US, Maharishi Mahesh Yogi's students amounted to a small enclave of Los Angeles socialites and the Theosophy set.

The "Fashion Ambassadress"

Socialite Nancy Jackson (a.k.a. Nancy Cooke de Herrera) was among those TM trailblazers. Like so many spiritual seekers, she discovered Indian philosophy through Paramahansa Yogananda's *Autobiography of a Yogi.* B. K. Nehru, Indian ambassador to the US, gave her a copy. In 1962, she landed in India wearing four-inch heels during her twelve-year stint as official US "Ambassadress to Fashion." (See her photo on page 267.)

Nancy journeyed to "Hippie Hill" in Almora to meet Lama Govinda, guru to the Beat Generation (see pages 63–64). She met the Dalai Lama in Dharamshala and Swami Sivananda in Rishikesh, who suggested she study with Maharishi. Though his ashram was right across the Ganges River, Maharishi was in California at the time.[375] As luck would have it, Nancy returned to Los Angeles, learned TM on July 30, 1962, and met Maharishi at a TM retreat on Catalina Island.

With Nancy as Maharishi's event planner and publicist, Southern California became the first area in the States where TM got a foothold. As a TM Initiator, her students included health food author Gayelord Hauser; his lover, who was Hollywood icon Greta Garbo; pop stars Madonna, Sheryl Crow, Santigold, and Lenny Kravitz; and comedian Rosie O'Donnell.

Early TM meditators included flautist Paul Horn; gossip columnist Cobina Wright; eccentric American Tobacco Company heiress Doris Duke; and TV star on *77 Sunset Strip* and *The F.B.I.*, Efram Zimbalist, Jr. Duke, a former practitioner of Yogananda's Kriya Yoga, donated $100,000 to Maharishi, which financed building his Meditation Academy in Rishikesh, India. Zimbalist arranged for Maharishi's appearance on *The Steve Allen Show*. However, Maharishi's high-pitched voice, giggle, and long stringy hair did not play well.

All that changed when, in the late 1960s, a passel of rock stars and Hollywood celebrities learned TM, including The Beatles, The Doors, Mick Jagger, and Marianne Faithfull. Then came The Moody Blues, The Beach Boys, Donovan Leitch, The Grateful Dead, Jim Henson (creator of The Muppets), Andy Kaufman (Latka Gravas in the sitcom *Taxi*), Doug Henning (superstar magician), Richard Beymer (ardent TM devotee and star of *West Side Story* and *Twin Peaks*), film superstars Mia Farrow and Shirley MacLaine, and many more.

On the Way to Rishikesh

On January 22, 1968, Maharishi lectured to a sold-out crowd in Sanders Theatre at the Harvard Law School Forum in Cambridge. There he met Mia Farrow and her sister Prudence, who traveled with him on January 24 from New York to London, Paris, Bombay, and New Delhi, on their way to Rishikesh, India. Maharishi covered first class airline, hotel, taxi, and sightseeing expenses for the Farrow sisters.

Maharishi meets Mia Farrow in Cambridge. AP/Shutterstock.

Mia and Maharishi deplaning at Heathrow Airport on their way to India. PictureLux/The Hollywood Archive/ Alamy Stock Photo.

Mia and Prudence at Heathrow Airport. Howard/ANL/Shutterstock.

Seventy TM Teacher Training Course students from twenty countries waited for Maharishi one week at the spartan New Delhi YMCA at their own expense, while he held an ill-fated "World Peace Conference" where he was heckled and booed off the stage. Meanwhile, Mia and Prudence enjoyed a suite at the five-star Hotel Oberoi and indulged in shopping and sightseeing in Delhi, Agra, and Vrindavan—on Maharishi's tab.

Finally, on January 31 at 9:00 a.m., the students assembled in a dozen taxis and one rickety bus at the YMCA to leave for Rishikesh—all except Mia and Prudence, that is. Six hours later, the Farrows finally showed up, and at 3:00 p.m. the procession began.

The entourage reached Rishikesh too late to catch the ferry across the Ganges River. Both young and elderly teetered across the wobbly bridge over freezing rapids in the dark and hiked two miles to the Meditation Academy. They arrived at about 11:00 p.m. and, in the frigid night air, settled into their primitive barracks and climbed into their icy beds with hot water bottles.

The Meditation Academy

The students were housed in single-story U-shaped cinder-block-and-concrete barracks, called *puri*, with ten rooms per structure. A front porch lined the U. Its roof extended overhead, braced by slender pillars. The rooms were scantily furnished with a cot, bedding, chair, table, shelving, and an electric heater that blew fuses regularly. Dirt paths lined with whitewashed Ganges River rocks connected the buildings.

Students rose early, used an outdoor toilet and communal wash-basin, took a cold or lukewarm outdoor shower, and meditated all day, wrapped in blankets. Laundry was washed by beating it on rocks at the river. Clothes returned smelling like dirt, stretched out of shape, and filled with sand—but neatly pressed!

The vegetarian diet consisted of porridge, cereal, toast, marmalade, water buffalo milk, yogurt, rice, beans, *chapati* (whole-wheat flat bread), salad, and bland, overcooked, spiceless vegetables (unlike exotic delicacies in Indian restaurants). Drinks included hot buffalo milk, hot tea with milk, and Ganges water (pumped up from the river).

Maharishi lectured once or twice daily at 3:30 and 8:30 p.m. in a high-ceilinged hall with whitewashed walls, concrete floor covered with mats, stage decorated with potted plants and flowers, high recessed windows where birds nested on the ledges and flew to and fro, and concrete "caves" in the basement, for bearable meditations during hot weather. Maharishi sat cross-legged on his deerskin-and-white-sheet-covered stuffed slipper chair on the stage below Guru Dev's picture. His microphone and flower vase rested on a white wooden coffee table. A handful of white-robed *brahmacharyas* (celibate disciples) assembled cross-legged on the carpet that covered the stage.

Meditating in this holy place, the students drifted gently and placidly into a paradise of the mind—peaceful, deep, and euphoric. Cares vanished. Tranquility abounded. They meandered around pastoral surroundings, dazed and intoxicated. Fragrant flowers, lush foliage, exotic scenery, and charming creatures made the landscape all the more ambrosial.

In the roaring river and clamoring jungle, the mysterious echo of seekers of enlightenment throughout generations pulsated throughout these holy lands for as long as India has existed. Now these students were part of it.

The Star of the Show

Mia Farrow's impression of the ashram in Rishikesh: "It was a strange and colorless place. We moved as if in a dream and spoke only where necessary, in the respectful, hushed tones of visitors to a graveyard."[376]

Maharishi assigned Nancy Jackson to look after Mia, who became the first Westerner to adopt *salwar chemise* outfits sewn by the "ashram couturier"—a tailor who created fashion statements sitting cross-legged on a mat on the ground at an antique sewing machine, hand-operated by spinning a wheel. Mia's impressions of Nancy: "A self-important, middle-aged American woman, moving a mountain of luggage into the brand-new private bungalow next to Maharishi's along with her son, a bland young man."[377]

The vivacious, luminous Mia became Maharishi's center of attention. He acted starstruck over her and catered to her every whim. Nearly every afternoon, he invited her to his bungalow for a private talk and a mango snack. When Maharishi was warned that his coddling might backfire, he insisted, "An international star like Mia can bring such good publicity. We must treat her special."[378]

Maharishi singled out Mia during lectures, asking her questions that embarrassed her. He appeared oblivious to her feelings and continued to pile it on thick. "Maharishi is really bugging me," Mia complained. "He calls me over to his house all the time. I know I should feel flattered by the special attention, but I did come here to meditate."[379]

The more Maharishi showered favor on Mia, the more hostile she became. Finally, disgusted with the guru's apparent sycophancy, Mia dictated a cable intended for her husband Frank Sinatra (who deemed meditation "pagan"): "Fed up with meditation. Am leaving ashram. Will phone from Delhi."[380] The cable was never sent. Instead, Nancy invited Mia on a wild animal safari. Regardless of her opinion of Nancy, Mia accepted her offer of a change in scenery.

Mia's Safari

Today, in the twenty-first century, a "safari" is a jeep ride where tourists view animals in the wild. In 1968, a safari was a hunt to kill animals and bring home taxidermy trophies. Nancy's Indian tour guide Avinash "Avi" Kohli led Nancy and Mia, along with the Burkes (a couple who paid $7,000 to hunt for one month), to ride out on elephants in search of wild game—to no avail. The Burkes' smoking, drinking, and coughing scared off the prey. Nancy said, "We experienced the thrill of the hunt without the kill."[381] Mia was relieved, as she did not approve of animal slaughter for sport.

After Nancy and Mia returned, Maharishi assigned Nancy to decorate The Beatles' quarters for their arrival and to look after them. She remarked, "It was great fun taking The Beatles shopping. Nobody knew who they were. The tailor made clothes for The Beatles that changed fashion more than Givenchy or Dior." [382]

But Nancy's safari days were not over yet.

Scan this code to read the lyrics.

Rik's Safari

John Lennon's "The Continuing Story of Bungalow Bill" is a blow-by-blow account of Nancy's second jungle safari led by Avi Kohli, which occurred while Richard ("Rik") A. Cooke III (age twenty-seven) was visiting his mother Nancy Jackson in Rishikesh. Rik explained, "I didn't go to India to go to the ashram. I went to India to go hunting with a white hunter friend of our family." [383] For this purpose, Rik brought his rifle.

The Burkes, previously on safari with Nancy and Mia, had been hunting for a month. Avi gave the couple an extra complimentary week, and Rik and Nancy joined them. The hunt took place in Sitabani Forest, about three hours from Rishikesh. Mia described Nancy and her son Rik: "People fled this newcomer. No one was sorry when she left the ashram after a short time to go tiger hunting, unaware that their presence had inspired a new Beatles' song—'Bungalow Bill.'" [384]

Avi justified tiger hunting as culling dangerous elephant-killing beasts. With that noble pretext, Rik and his mother mounted the lead elephant with a shikari (professional hunter) and a mahout (elephant boy). Rik faced backwards to snap photographs of the seven other elephants following them. Avi and the Burkes lay in wait atop machans (high watchtowers in trees). The shikari, following animal tracks (pugmarks), would lead the elephants into a semi-circle, and "beaters" would make noise to drive the tiger towards the kill zone.

Suddenly the elephants encountered a tiger. That spooked them and they stampeded. Rik yelled to the mahouts, "Go back, you chicken shits, let's get that tiger!"[385] After some harrowing moments, the lead elephant got caught in a tree branch. That ended the stampede.

When the lead elephant reached the Burkes' machan, the couple traded places with Rik and Nancy, who stepped onto the platform. Rik whispered, "I have a feeling we're going to see that tiger again, Mom."

Nancy replied, "Yes, and you will shoot it just as though it were a deer on Molokai."[386]

Rik, waiting in anticipation, suddenly heard elephants banging in the bushes. Monkeys, mongooses, and other small animals appeared in front of them. "That was because the tiger was coming," Rik explained.[387]

Then Nancy saw a flash of yellow and black and let out a scream. Rik recalled, "The tiger did come out in a flash and I remember shooting. I can still remember just the color of the tiger through the [telescopic lens]. It turns out Avi, who was quite a ways away, we had both shot at the same time. So we never knew who shot the tiger."[388] The tiger lay dead at the foot of the ladder to the machan.

Nancy declared, "Rik, I'm so proud of you!"[389] But the Burkes claimed the tiger skin, insisting it was just a fluke that they were not on the machan at that time.

After the tiger hunt: Rik on left and guide Avi on right. Photo courtesy of Richard Alexander Cooke III.

Posing with the tiger: Rik on left and his mother Nancy on right. Photo courtesy of Richard Alexander Cooke III.

After the Kill

After their safari, Rik and Nancy headed straight for Maharishi's bungalow. John, Paul, George, and Jane Asher happened to be present as the hunters described their tiger kill in graphic detail, while Maharishi glared silently at Nancy. She was bursting to spill the entire gory story to the orthodox Hindu vegetarian pacifist yogi whose main platform was to create peace on earth. Surprisingly, she seemed to believe Maharishi would react differently than he did.

Rik recalled, "My mother is a very vocal person and she was talking excitedly about killing the tiger and Maharishi looked pretty aghast that his followers could actually go out and do something like this. It was the only time I ever saw him almost angry."[390]

Maharishi asked Rik, "You had a desire and now you have satisfied it and will no longer have the desire?"[391]

Rik answered with regret, "I don't think I'll ever kill an animal again." He then asked Maharishi, "Am I just a part, an agent of change? Am I just part of this bigger dance?"[392]

John, who coincidentally had recently spotted a tiger stalking Maharishi's bungalow, sneered, "But wouldn't you call that slightly life-destructive?"[393]

Nancy retorted, "Well, John, it was either the tiger or us. The tiger was right where we were."[394]

Paul then piped in, "Tell us the details, man—what an experience."[395]

Rik then asked Maharishi, "Was that bad karma for me, Maharishi? Was it a sin?"[396] [397]

"John Lennon was just horrified at this story," Rik recalled. "I remember Maharishi, incredibly cold. About one of the only times I've ever seen Maharishi with a really cold demeanor, saying, 'Life destruction is life destruction. End of story.'"[398]

Nancy alleged that the poor tiger, trapped between pointed guns and elephants, was really a threat. However, Rik did not see it that way: "[Mother's] version of the story and my version of the story are probably a little different. Her phrase was 'It was us or him.' But the tiger never saw us. To her, it was charging us. I could see it was just trying to get away."[399]

Life-Supportive and Life-Destructive Actions

One of Maharishi's main tenets, which John referred to in his scathing comment to Rik, is the idea of life-supportive or life-destructive actions. Maharishi often affirmed that we create our reality, moment by moment, through our thoughts, words, and deeds. That is the Law of Karma. Everything we think, say, and do has consequences. Our actions are either in tune with the Laws of Nature, or not.

Maharishi often said Almighty Nature supports us when we do "life-supporting" deeds, but Nature does not support when our actions are "life-damaging." To get Mother Nature's support, we must act in accord with Natural Law. One of his favorite expressions, "Nature supports," means a meditator's life is easy and effortless, as energies, people, and coincidences conspire to support in fulfilling his or her desires. Whenever a coincidence or positive outcome occurred, TM meditators would chime, "Nature supports!" When anything negative happened, they would blame it on "unstressing" (stress-release during meditation). Maharishi claimed Transcendental Meditation makes us in tune with Natural Law automatically.

When John called Rik's actions "life-destructive," he was parroting Maharishi's oft-repeated expression. John's comment reflected how much he was under Maharishi's influence at the time.

The Birth of Bungalow Bill

John Lennon answered Nancy's paltry excuse ("it was either the tiger or us") with "The Continuing Story of Bungalow Bill," which he described as "written about a guy in Maharishi's meditation camp who took a short break to go shoot a few poor tigers, and then came back to commune with God. There used to be a character called Jungle Jim, and I combined him with Buffalo Bill. It's sort of a teenage social-comment song and a bit of a joke."[400]

In the song, John, who never cared for snooty blue bloods, mocked the British Raj and its royals, the "great white hunters," white Anglo-Saxon gun-toting American heroes, male phallocentric firearm fanatics, and heroes of comic-book culture, such as Captain Marvel—The World's Mightiest Mortal.

Paul said, "This is another of [John's] great songs and it's one of my favorites to this day because it stands for a lot of what I stand for now. 'Did you really have to shoot that tiger' is its message. 'Aren't you a big guy? Aren't you a brave man?' I think John put it very well."[401]

Rik recalled, "The other Beatles were always real nice to me but John was always aloof. They epitomized the counterculture and I was the classic good American boy and college athlete. There wasn't a whole bunch that we got to connect on."[402] "I guess [the song] describes me as white Anglo-Saxon bullet-headed son with my mother—definitely a very strong mother. Total antithesis to everything that The Beatles represented at that time. So I became Bungalow Bill in their eyes. It's kind of a catchy tune."[403]

Nancy recalled The Beatles were friendly except John, whom she called "a genius," but disdainful towards her and her clean-cut son. Nancy and Rik maintained friendly relations with George until his death in 2001.

This event ended Rik's hunting career. In 2008, his wife Bronwyn told *Mojo* magazine that Rik has not owned a gun or shot anything since—except photographs.[404] He became a freelance photographer for The National Geographic Society. Rik said he found shooting photographs of animals far more challenging.[405]

The Great White Hunter

In the early 1900s, there were 40,000 tigers in India. At the time of this book's publication, there are less than 1,800. Humans are the tigers' greatest predator. Now an endangered species, the majority of the world's tigers live in captivity. During India's British Raj, tiger hunting was a manly, courageous feat that brought prestige, and trophies symbolized valor. British royalty photographed with tiger carcasses signified their imperial conquest of India. At that time, tigers were a perceived threat to human life, so tiger hunters were considered heroes.

"Mother Nature's Son"

Written: February to May 1968
Recorded: August 9 and 20, 1968
Released: November 22, 1968: The Beatles

Paul McCartney said a lecture about nature by Maharishi inspired "Mother Nature's Son." A notebook where Paul jotted down songs at Maharishi's ashram in India, labeled "Spring Songs Rishikesh 1968," contained the song's first two verses. The third verse was written at Rembrandt, a five-bedroom house Paul bought for his father in Heswall, Cheshire, about fifteen miles from Liverpool.

What Paul loved most about growing up in the postwar Speke Housing Estate at 72 Western Avenue, and later at 12 Ardwick Road, was its close proximity to the countryside and the River Mersey. He would trek into the deep woods brimming with rhododendron bushes, blossoming from March to June. Paul, his brother Mike, and friends would squeeze into the middle of the bushes, where the blooms were less concentrated, and make dens: "I've never seen that many rhododendrons since."[406] One of the greatest displays of rhododendrons in England is the magnificent Speke Hall Garden and Estate, where there is also a hedge maze—one and a half miles from Paul's family home.

Sometimes Paul would go bird watching alone, with S. Vere Benson's *Observer's Book of Birds* in his pocket. Barry Miles described, "He would wander down Dungeon Lane to the lighthouse on a nature ramble or climb over the fence and go walking in the fields."[407]

Paul said, "'Mother Nature's Son' was basically a heartfelt song about my child-of-nature leanings. I'd always loved nature, and when Linda and I got together, we discovered we had this deep love of nature in common."[408]

 Scan this code to read the lyrics.

Maharishi and Mother Nature

Maharishi often spoke about Mother Nature, Almighty Nature, Laws of Nature, and support of Nature. He claimed TM made people more attuned to Natural Law, which he defined as "the ultimate source of order and harmony displayed throughout creation."

In 1992, Maharishi founded the "Natural Law Party" (NLP), a political party with candidates that ran for US President and other governmental positions in various countries. The party proposed that problems could be solved through alignment with the "unified field of all the laws of nature" through TM.[409] One journalist declared, "This is not a party of the far left or far right—more of the far out!"[410]

George Harrison staged a concert in London with Ringo and Eric Clapton to benefit NLP. Soon afterward, George phoned Paul, giggling: "Maharishi would like you, me, and Ringo to stand as Members of Parliament for Liverpool. We'll win!"

Paul's response: "A week before the election! You've gotta be kidding!"[411]

Maharishi's favorite phrases included: "Nature Supports," "Support of Almighty Nature," "Mother Nature," "Life-Supporting Actions," Life-Destructive Actions," and "Life-Damaging Actions." In a 1968 lecture, Maharishi said: "In nature everything is born, it grows and dies, and this keeps on happening. All these different processes are being carried out on the level of eternal Being. When the mind makes conscious contact with that level, then such a mind befriends the ultimate basis of all creation. All the Laws of Nature functioning from that level become sympathetic to such a mind.

"This is why the moment you start to meditate and dive into Being, you feel you have become the cherished, adopted son of Almighty Nature. Nature begins to help you, begins to support all the aspirations of a mind which is in tune with Being. Nature seems to be supporting, everything is more harmonious, life becomes lighter and ceases to be heavy. It is only necessary to get familiar with that ultimate reality. You don't have to try to win the support of nature."[412]

"Child of Nature"

Written: February to April 1968
Recorded: May 1968
Released: November 9, 2018: The Beatles 50th Anniversary Edition

In 1980, John Lennon said the idea for Paul's "Mother Nature's Son" came from a lecture Maharishi gave about nature, and his own song, "I'm Just a Child of Nature," was also "inspired from the same lecture of Maharishi."[413]

 Scan this code to read the lyrics.

The last week of May 1968, John Lennon taped a demo of "Child of Nature" at Kinfauns—George Harrison's home in Esher, Surrey—for possible inclusion in the White Album. The track did not make the cut. On January 2, 1969, John demoed the song again to his bandmates during the "Get Back/Let It Be" sessions. He changed the opening line to "On the road to Marrakesh." Twenty-five seconds of that version appeared on a bonus disc included with early copies of *Let It Be... Naked*, issued November 17, 2003. That demo appeared on Peter Jackson's *The Beatles: Get Back* documentary, released November 25, 2021.

The Beatles chose not to include "Child of Nature" in the *Anthology* collections, probably because "Jealous Guy" was the same melody, included on John's album *Imagine*, September 9, 1971. "Child of Nature" was finally released as a Kinfauns demo on some White Album 50th anniversary reissues. Without doubt, the lyrics of "Child of Nature" are measurably more inspiring than "Jealous Guy," but the melody remains another John Lennon masterpiece.

"Why Don't We Do It in the Road?"

Written: February to March 1968
Recorded: October 9, 1968
Released: November 22, 1968: The Beatles

At Maharishi's ashram, in the arms of Mother Nature, The Beatles found peaceful respite from Beatlemania. In the jungle-covered Himalayan foothills, Maharishi's fourteen-acre Meditation Academy, "Shankaracharya Nagar," built on a 150-foot cliff on Manikoot hill, overlooked the Ganges from its eastern bank. Across the river downstream stood Rishikesh, a holy place of pilgrimage and haven of yogis, ascetics, devotees, and beggars. *Hrishikesha* ("Lord of the Senses") is an appellation for the Hindu Lord Vishnu.

John Lennon, known for nicknaming everyone and everything, called Maharishi's ashram "the Butlin's of Bliss," referring to the World War II army barracks converted into holiday camps for the British working class. When Ringo left the ashram, he told the press the ashram reminded him of Butlin's Holiday Camp.

In 1961, Maharishi leased the parcel for twenty years from Uttar Pradesh state forest department. In 1963, tobacco heiress Doris Duke financed the ashram's construction anonymously. But when an Indian swami asked for the same grant as Maharishi, Doris knew her privacy had been violated. She disavowed all association with Maharishi and TM.

The land was flanked on the north and east by a dense, dusty teak forest interspersed with evergreen rosewood (*sheesham*) and inhabited by rhesus macaque monkeys, elephants, tigers, crows, peacocks, parrots, vultures, chipmunks, pythons, and cobras. Further north, jagged Himalayan peaks touched the sky. To the south, a gravel road cut through the forest and crossed the river towards Haridwar. The western view revealed the river below and the tiny holy village of Rishikesh on the opposite bank, untouched by modern life. In this strict Hindu area, no meat or eggs were allowed.

A few huts comprised Shankaracharya Nagar, housing Maharishi's brahmacharyas (disciples) and staff, post office, commissary, and laundry. Upstream to the north, sculptures of Hindu deities and colorful murals illustrating the Hindu scripture Srimad Bhagavatam delightfully decorated Swarg Ashram and Gita Bhavan. Across the river resided a small Shiva temple and Sivananda Ashram: Divine Life Forest Academy. Distant chanting and tinkling temple bells wafted across the river.

Maharishi's ashram comprised a maze of dirt paths, streams, waterfalls, trees, flower gardens, and whitewashed cement buildings. Under continual construction, the place buzzed with scrawny men in dust-covered dhotis (cotton robes), wearing grimy turbans to absorb the sweat. Squeaky, rusty wheelbarrows filled with bricks or cement competed with animals crying in the jungle and the constant commotion of Hindi.

Monkeys bounced and made a racket on the barracks. Peacocks screeched and displayed feathers. Crows cawed with deafening shrieks. Skinny water buffaloes and mangy dogs snoozed in inconvenient spots on the paths. Centipedes, scorpions, spiders, and snakes invaded sleeping quarters and inhabited meditation caves.

The ashram was a menagerie of "All Creatures Great and Small." The song "Why Don't We Do It in the Road" is about some of them—specifically monkeys.

Scan this code to
read the lyrics.

Maharishi on the roof of his bungalow, enjoying the view of the Ganges. Trinity
Mirror/Mirrorpix/Alamy Stock Photo.

How the Song Came Together

The inspiration for "Why Don't We Do It in the Road" came while Paul McCartney was meditating on the flat roof of The Beatles' bungalow at the ashram. He had seen a troop of monkeys in the jungle, "and a male just hopped on to the back of this female and gave her one, as they say in the vernacular. Within two or three seconds he hopped off again, and looked around as if to say, 'It wasn't me,' and she looked around as if there had been some mild disturbance but thought, *Huh, I must have imagined it,* and she wandered off."[414]

Paul realized the act of procreation consisted of just hopping on and off. No muss no fuss. They simply got the urge and did it. He commented, "We have horrendous problems with it, and yet animals don't. 'Why Don't We Do It in the Road' could have applied to either fucking or shitting, to put it roughly. Why don't we do either of them in the road? Well, the answer is we're civilized and we don't. 'Why Don't We Do It in the Road' was a primitive statement to do with sex or to do with freedom. It's just so outrageous that I like it."[415]

The Candid McCartney

Though John and George were known for copious sexual conquests, Paul was the most uninhibited Beatle when talking and singing about sex. Not only did he compose "Why Don't We Do It in the Road?" he also wrote "Eat at Home," "Girl's School," "Come on to Me," "We Got Married," "I Saw Her Standing There," "Please Please Me," "Penny Lane," "I'm Down," "Day Tripper," "Fluid," and the banned "Hi, Hi, Hi."

When John and George left Maharishi's ashram in a self-righteous huff due to the guru's sexual improprieties, Paul commented, "It's really funny, John's reaction to this sexual thing. It seemed a little prudish to me."[416]

In 2018 Paul unabashedly admitted to *GQ* that, as a kid, he engaged in group-masturbation with John Lennon and three other friends, while they shouted out names of celebrities, from Brigitte Bardot to Winston Churchill (which smart-ass John yelled to spoil the mood).[417] Sort of gives the song "Come Together" a whole new layer of meaning!

When George Harrison lost his virginity in Hamburg in one of the bunk beds the band was sleeping in, Paul said that after George had finished, the other Beatles applauded and cheered. George recalled, "At least they kept quiet whilst I was doing it."[418]

The sixties was the era of freedom on every level: free love, free expression, war protest, anarchist political ideas, communal living, and breaking social norms. The Beatles were leaders in this revolution. John and Yoko fueled that bandwagon by releasing their album *Unfinished Music No. 1: Two Virgins* (November 11, 1968). The album cover photo featured the couple dressed only in a smile, an amulet, a foreskin, some nipples, buttocks, and masses of black fluffy pubic hair. Paul commented: "Our mothers and fathers had to get naked to conceive us, yet we're still very prudish about nudity. But John and Yoko were looking at nudity as artists."[419]

The Beatles managed to get five songs banned by the BBC: "Come Together," "A Day in the Life," "I am the Walrus," "Lucy in the Sky with Diamonds," and "Back in the U.S.S.R." Yet Paul and Ringo were dubbed Knights of the British Empire. Paul led the way in writing songs that break uptight ideas of polite social etiquette. One example was his ditty "Fuh You" from *Egypt Station*. You sort of wonder how he gets away with it. Maybe it's because he is, after all, Paul McCartney.

"Wild Honey Pie"

Written: February to March 1968
Recorded: August 20, 1968
Released: November 22, 1968; The Beatles

Paul wrote "Wild Honey Pie" in Rishikesh while The Beatles were studying with Maharishi. He recalled, "It was just a fragment of an instrumental, which we were not sure about, but Pattie [Boyd] liked it very much, so we decided to leave it on the album. The track emerged from a spontaneous sing-along in Rishikesh."[420] Paul said the song was "a reference to the other song I had written called 'Honey Pie.' It was a little experimental piece."[421]

The Sing-along

During The Beatles' stay in Rishikesh, the group of seventy students spent nearly all their time meditating in their rooms. However, on a few occasions Maharishi allowed some diversions. These included visits by holy men, torchlight processions, singalongs on the riverbank, traveling cinema-in-a-truck, smearing each other with paint to celebrate the Hindu festival "Holi," and trips to Dehradun—the closest large town. One full-moon night, Maharishi arranged two barges to cruise on the Ganges. Pandits chanted the Vedas, The Beatles sang Donovan songs, Mike Love and Donovan sang Beatles songs, and Paul Horn played flute.

Singalong march to the Ganges River; l. to r.: Paul playing guitar, Maharishi's favorite student Jemima Pitman wearing sari behind Paul, close devotee Walter Koch, Maharishi, John playing guitar, Geoffrey Baker in rear in sunglasses. © Colin Harrison-Avico Ltd.

On February 28, the happy meditators walked down the steep footpath through the forest to the Ganges River, while singing and playing acoustic guitars to the apropos "When the Saints Go Marching In." Once they arrived at the riverbank, loud crows cawed. They spread out plaid wool blankets and sat close to the shore. Mia and other participants took photos. Paul buried his feet in the sand.

While The Beatles strummed guitars, Maharishi remarked, "Now you can sing. Look at the song. Enjoy! Fathom the infinity. Dive in the Ganges. Fathom the ocean…. Ha Ha Ha…"

Then George said, "We don't even exist."

And Maharishi answered, "Right, right, right."

The Beatles played and sang "O Sole Mio," "It's Now or Never," "You Are My Sunshine," and "Jingle Bells," as sweet, melodic birds joined the chorus and monkeys hopped about, presiding over the proceedings.

Beatles singalong on the Ganges riverbank; l. to r.: Richard Blakely, Mia Farrow, Terry Gustafson, Donovan, George, Mike Love, Maharishi, John, Cynthia Lennon, Paul, Jane Asher. Front of Donovan: Pattie Boyd. © Colin Harrison-Avico Ltd.

Halfway through a singalong of "Comin' Round the Mountain," the group changed the lyrics to "Jai Guru Deva, Jai Guru Deva, Jai Guru Deva as she comes." Someone played a guitar instrumental, possibly George's "Dehradun" or Donovan's "Hurdy Gurdy Man." He later told *Billboard*, "I related the hurdy gurdy man in the song to the teacher Maharishi, who brings us songs of love."[422] The recorded song featured a tambura given to Donovan by George, who wrote a verse that did not make the final cut: "When the truth gets buried deep, Beneath the thousand years of sleep, Time demands a turnaround, And once again the truth is found."[423] This referred to Maharishi's claim that TM was a revival of lost ancient Vedic wisdom.

Then all sang Dylan's "Blowin' in the Wind," Donovan's "Happiness Runs" (known to be about Transcendental Meditation), "Hare Krishna," and finally, "Catch the Wind." They approached the river, stepped into the water with bare feet, and splashed water over their heads to receive Mother Ganga's blessings.

Scan this code to relive these moments on film, which include George, John, Paul, Pattie, Maureen, Jane, Jenny, Donovan, Mia Farrow, John Charles Villiers-Farrow, Mike Love, Geoffrey Baker, Maharishi's brahmacharyas (disciples), and other course participants.

Donovan and Paul playing music in the "silence zone." © Colin Harrison-Avico Ltd.

The dilapidated lecture hall in Rishikesh: thirty-three
years after Maharishi met The Beatles there.

The interior of Maharishi's lecture hall in Rishikesh. Photo taken in 2001.

PART IV

A PEACE OF
MAHARISHI'S MIND

CHAPTER 7

ROCKIN' IN RISHIKESH

"Revolution"

Written: February to May 30th, 1968
Recorded: May 30, 31, June 4, 21, 1968.
Re-Recorded: July 10, 11, 13, 1968
Released: August 26, 1968: Single. November 22, 1968: The Beatles

In the cover article of the *Saturday Evening Post*, May 4, 1968, Maharishi Mahesh Yogi was quoted: "If one person in every thousand meditated, there would be peace for a thousand generations."[424] This key statement expressed Maharishi's unwavering message and mission since he began teaching meditation in 1955—to establish peace on earth through meditation. He often declared, "For the forest to be green, the trees must be green. For the world to be at peace, the individuals must be at peace." This always struck me as a most sensible idea. For how could a world inhabited by angry, warring, conflicted people ever be peaceful?

I was born soon after the first atomic bombs dropped on Japan and grew up during the Cold War, under the perceived threat of nuclear war and the epidemic of bomb-shelter-building madness. Even as a child, whenever I wished on a birthday cake, wishing well, or falling star, my only wish was "world peace." That is why Maharishi's message appealed to me, and why it appealed to The Beatles and others of my generation.

It is inconceivable to imagine The Beatles' lives, growing up in Britain during World War II. Beatles fan Robert Bartel, who interviewed Louise Harrison, told me that many people in England died during the blitzkrieg, when Nazi bombs rained over Britain, driving citizens into air raid shelters. Liverpool was bombed into rubble. But somehow, the wee babes George, John, Paul, and Ringo survived. Louise often carried her baby brother George in her arms to protect him. She believes divine intervention saved these lads for a reason.

Bombs would drop on Liverpool overnight. The next day, Louise would read casualty lists at the town hall. Three or four friends were on the list every day: "But we developed an attitude about that. You'd read the casualty list and the joke became, 'I'm not on it so I guess I'll have to go to work after all.' As long as you can laugh about things, you can weather those storms."[425]

Although there was no report of air raids in Liverpool on John's birth date, October 9, 1940, his aunt Mimi said she held John right after he was born, when a parachute-borne landmine fell directly outside the hospital. John's mother Julia Lennon stayed in bed, and baby John was placed beneath it for protection.[426]

 Scan this code to read the lyrics for "Revolution."

"The Maharishi Effect"

John's "Revolution" is about the political atmosphere of the sixties. But more precisely, it originates from "The Maharishi Effect,"— the guru's theory about how his grassroots approach could create world peace. Maharishi believed peace could never be attained through politics, treaties, wars, or revolutions, but could be realized with even a small percentage of the population meditating—especially in large groups. His mission was to create a peaceful atmosphere through waves of peace radiating from meditators. That is why, during his lifetime, Maharishi trained forty thousand TM Initiators who taught six million people to meditate.

Maharishi demonstrated the validity of The Maharishi Effect through scientific studies. He would send hundreds or thousands of meditators to war-torn or crime-ridden areas. Then scientists published statistical studies that revealed the crime rate plunged or wars subsided during the time meditators practiced TM together in large groups. Published scientific research showed social indicators improved, conflict diminished, violent death lessened, quality of life increased, political violence and tension reduced, crime rate fell, and terrorism and international conflict decreased. These findings were consistent across a large number of replications in different geographic and conflict situations.[427]

In one study in June 1993, the crime rate in Washington D.C. plunged 23.3 percent. In experiments conducted during the Israel/Lebanon war in the eighties, violence dropped by about 80 percent.[428] Considering the bloodbaths of the twentieth-century world wars, where over one hundred million people were slaughtered in battle, as compared to today's world, I would venture to say that we are now closer to Maharishi's vision of world peace. If we would become more peaceful individuals, we could make and maintain a more peaceful world.

What John Said

Brian Epstein always wanted the Fab Four presented in the best light. He warned them to avoid controversial issues that might alienate some fans. But by 1966, The Beatles had already begun to express their views candidly, much to Brian's dismay. After Brian's untimely death in 1967, all bets were off.

In 1969, John declared, "The only way to ensure a lasting peace of any kind is to change people's minds. The Government can do it with propaganda, Coca-Cola can do it with propaganda—why can't we? We are the hip generation."[429]

In 1970, John expressed to *Rolling Stone* that in "Revolution" he wanted to talk about the Vietnam War: "I had been thinking about it up in the hills in India. I still had this 'God will save us' feeling about it, that it's going to be all right."[430]

John further declared in 1970: "If you want peace, you won't get it with violence. Please tell me one militant revolution that worked." In 1971 he elaborated: "All we're trying to do is make people aware that they have the power themselves, and the violent way of revolution doesn't justify the ends."[431]

In September 1980, John stated, "Count me out if it's for violence. Don't expect me on the barricades unless it's with flowers. As far as overthrowing something, I want to know what you're going to do *after* you've knocked it down. If you want to change the system, change the system. It's no good shooting people."[432]

On December 5, 1980, three days before his death, John said, "It's easier to shout 'Revolution' and 'Power to the people' than it is to look at yourself and try to find out what's real inside you and what isn't, when you're pulling the wool over your own eyes."[433]

What Other Beatles Said

Paul revealed, "They were very political times, obviously, with the Vietnam war going on, Chairman Mao and the Little Red Book, and all the demonstrations with people going through the streets shouting 'Ho, Ho Ho Chi Minh!' I think [John] meant we all want to change the world Maharishi-style, because 'Across The Universe' also had the change-the-world theme."[434]

Ringo told journalist Derek Boltwood, "If everyone in the world started meditating, then the world would be a much happier place, and there would be less wars."[435]

George said governments and people run around the planet chasing after a big illusion. "If you can live by an inner rule and become centered on some kind of cosmic law, you don't need governments or policemen or anybody laying down rules."[436]

"Blackbird"

Written: April 1968
Recorded: June 11, 1968
Released: November 22, 1968: The Beatles

"Blackbird" is one of Paul McCartney's most beautiful, poignant songs in both melody and lyrics. Paul said he wrote the melody in Rishikesh, based on Johann Sebastian Bach's Bourrée in E minor, and the lyrics at High Park Farm in Kintyre, Scotland. This tender song is deeply meaningful, encouraging, and empowering for anyone with a broken wing. We are all broken to some extent. We need to learn to see, to fly, and to be free. We need to find the courage to be ourselves.

 Scan this code to read the lyrics.

For decades there has been controversy about the song's meaning. Author Steve Turner wrote: "One story simply says that Paul woke up early one morning in Rishikesh to hear a blackbird singing, picked up his guitar to transcribe the bird song and came up with an album track."[437]

Ian MacDonald maintained "Blackbird" was inspired by Paul "being woken by a blackbird bursting into song before sunrise."[438]

William J. Dowlding mentioned that one of Paul's "most cherished moments as a songwriter was when he woke one morning to the sound of a blackbird singing the tune of his song."[439] However, in an obscure bootleg recording, Paul tells a different story.

Bootleg 1968 Recording

The Beatles LP album (the White Album) was released on November 22, 1968. On that very day, Paul McCartney and Donovan Leitch were at Mary Hopkin's *Post Card* album recording session at Abbey Road EMI studios. Paul and Donovan played acoustic guitars on Mary's album (released on Apple Records label February 21, 1969).

Below is a partial transcript of Paul and Donovan talking before the *Post Card* session began. On the "No. 3 Abbey Road N.W. 8" bootleg CD, you can hear what is written in the transcript below, which begins after Paul sings "Blackbird."[440]

Donovan: You've seen how there are so many black birds now.

(Paul stops playing.)

Paul: I sang it to Diana Ross the other night. She took offense. Not really.

(Everyone laughs.)

Paul: But I did mean it like that originally.

Donovan: Really?

Paul: Yeah, I remember...I'd just read something in the paper about riots and then (Paul quickly sings the rest of "Blackbird")

Donovan: That's funny, 'cause when you were just singing I was saying 'What a way to color a blackbird.' There are so many beautiful colors to lift a blackbird into people's eyes.

On April 30, 2016, at a concert in Little Rock, McCartney introduced "Blackbird" to the audience, saying, "In the sixties, there was a lot of trouble going on over civil rights, particularly in Little Rock. We would notice this on the news back in England.

We would sympathize with the people going through those troubles, and it made me want to write a song that might just help them."[441] Paul told *GQ* in 2018, "So, I wrote 'Blackbird.' And in England, a 'bird' is a girl, so I was thinking of a black girl going through this, you know, now is your time to arise, set yourself free, and take these broken wings."[442]

Beatles Stood Up to Injustice

On September 11, 1964, The Beatles were set to play in Jacksonville, Florida's Gator Bowl. When told the audience would be segregated, the Fabs refused to perform. The Civil Rights Act of 1964 prohibited discrimination on the basis of race, color, religion, sex, or national origin. It was passed on July 2, 1964, but ignored in Jacksonville. The Beatles, who had great respect for African American music, found the idea of segregation indefensible. John said, "We never play to segregated audiences, and we aren't going to start now. I'd sooner lose our appearance money." Five days before the show, The Beatles issued this statement: "We will not appear unless Negroes are allowed to sit anywhere."[443]

Despite wind gusts of forty-five miles per hour on the heels of Hurricane Dora, the concert was integrated, and the Beatles played.

"Back in the U.S.S.R."

Written: March 1968
Recorded: August 22 and 23, 1968
Released: November 22, 1968: The Beatles

Paul McCartney wrote "Back in the U.S.S.R." during The Beatles' stay in Rishikesh—one of the fifteen songs he wrote during his month at the retreat. According to author Ian MacDonald, the concept for "Back in the U.S.S.R." originated with "I'm Backing Britain." On December 29, 1967, five secretaries from a London suburb volunteered to work an extra half-hour each day without pay to boost productivity and invited others to follow suit. "I'm Backing Britain" became a nationwide movement within a week. Paul's song, originally called "I'm Backing the UK," morphed into "I'm Backing the U.S.S.R.," and finally landed on "Back in the U.S.S.R."

Paul said his inspiration was Chuck Berry's 1959 hit "Back in the USA," about a soldier returning from overseas, singing about things he missed while abroad: skyscrapers, freeways, drive-ins, corner cafés, hamburgers, jukeboxes, and records. Paul noticed American tourists typically complain about missing their dough-nuts, Howard Johnsons, laundromats, and more TV channels—how much better it was at home. So he decided to spoof that: "This'll be someone who hasn't got a lot but they'll still be every bit as proud as an American would be. It's tongue in cheek. This is a traveling Russkie who has just flown in from Miami Beach."[444]

In 1968, Paul explained the song was about a spy who had lived in America a long time, but returned to the U.S.S.R., saying, "'Leave it till tomorrow, honey, disconnect the phone,' and all that. And 'Come here honey,' but with Russian women. It concerns the attributes of Russian women."[445]

Paul recalled in 1984 (before the Soviet Union collapse in December 1991), "I liked the idea of Georgia girls, and talking about places like the Ukraine as if they were California. It was also hands-across-the-water. 'Cuz they like us out there, even though the bosses in the Kremlin may not. The kids do. He can't wait to get back to the Georgian mountains: 'Georgia's always on my mind.' It's a jokey song, but it's also become a bit of an anthem."[446]

How the Beach Boys Met Maharishi

One reason for the song's popularity is its undeniable Beach Boys sound. In autumn 1967, Beach Boys lead singer Mike Love attended a TM lecture at Santa Monica Convention Center pre-sented by Jerry Jarvis, head of Students International Meditation

Society (SIMS). Mike tried to learn TM, but the Westwood center sent him away because SIMS was for students only.

The Beach Boys appeared at a UNICEF Variety Gala in Paris in December 1967. On their way, they performed in London. Maharishi had asked The Beatles to find people who could influence the American youth, since TM was not taking hold there.[447] So John and George surprised rhythm guitarist Al Jardine by knocking on his Hilton hotel room door to tell the Beach Boys about TM. The next day, on December 15, at the UNICEF rehearsal at Palais De Chaillot in Paris, John and George introduced the Beach Boys to Maharishi. Though scheduled to perform, Maharishi got cut from the lineup.

Maharishi, George, and TM official Charlie Lutes behind John at UNICEF benefit. Keystone Press/Alamy Stock Photo.

Dennis Wilson described, "All of a sudden, I felt this weirdness, this presence this guy had. Like out of left field. First thing he ever said to me was 'Live your life to the fullest.'"[448] Dennis arranged a private lecture with Maharishi at the George V hotel for The Beach Boys and their wives. On December 16, 1967, Dennis Wilson, Carl Wilson, Al Jardine, and Mike Love learned TM. In 1968, Brian Wilson met Maharishi in the USA and also started meditating.

Mike described, "I wasn't dreaming. But the state itself was deeper than the deepest sleep. It was neither dark nor light." "I had found a place of infinite peace, of profound rest." "This is so easy that anyone could do it, and if everyone did it, it would be an entirely different world."[449]

In January 1968, Mike attended Maharishi's lectures at the Plaza Hotel in New York and Harvard Law Forum in Cambridge, with Mia Farrow sitting nearby. When Mike phoned Maharishi's hotel, the guru unexpectedly answered the phone and invited The Beach Boys to Rishikesh for a meditation retreat.

The Lyrics

Mike Love arrived in Rishikesh on February 26, 1968. He came with jazz flautist Paul Horn, who had learned TM in 1966. Mike described, "I was sitting at the breakfast table and McCartney came down with his acoustic guitar and he was playing 'Back in the U.S.S.R.' I told him what you ought to do is talk about the girls all around Russia. He was plenty creative not to need any lyrical help from me but I gave him the idea for that little section. I think it was light-hearted and humorous of them to do a take on the Beach Boys."[450]

Upon Mike's suggestion, Paul mentioned girls from Moscow, Ukraine, and Georgia in the chorus—a nod to "California Girls," where The Beach Boys mentioned "East coast girls," "Southern girls," "Mid-West farmers' daughters," and "Northern girls." A tribute to The Beach Boys, the song's harmonies emulated their hits "Fun, Fun, Fun" and "Surfin' USA."

Coincidentally, when Paul McCartney flew to India to take Maharishi's retreat, it was on BOAC: British Overseas Airways Corporation, which later merged with BEA to form British Airways. Moscow was also one of the cities on BOAC's routes.

 Scan this code to read the lyrics for "Back in the U.S.S.R."

 Scan this code to read the lyrics for "California Girls."

The Maharishi Tour

Mike Love planned a tour and television show featuring Maharishi and The Beach Boys. Paul McCartney, sniffing disaster, attempted to dissuade Maharishi from the hapless tour, albeit unsuccessfully. On May 3, 1968, Maharishi appeared in Washington, DC, as The Beach Boys' opening act. But the auditorium was half-empty, and hostile Beach Boys fans booed him off the stage. The "Maharishi Tour" folded in less than a week.

In 1968, The Beach Boys recorded their album *Friends*. "Transcendental Meditation" was one of the tracks. Mike and Al became Initiators in 1972. Maharishi advised Mike he would do more good spreading positive messages through music rather than teaching TM full-time: "Live your own life, but stay in the group."[451] Mike, who has remained a TM devotee, admitted, "My addiction, if it's an addiction, is to meditation."[452]

"Cosmically Conscious"

Written: February to March 1968
Recorded: September 1991 to June 30, 1992
Released: February 2, 1993: Off the Ground album; April 19, 1993:
Single; January 3, 2011: Off the Ground: The Complete Works

Paul McCartney wrote "Cosmically Conscious" in Rishikesh in 1968, but it was not released until 1993 as the B-side of his single "Off the Ground." An excerpt also appears as the last track on the album *Off the Ground.* This song was played live only once—during the "Change Begins Within" benefit concert in April 2009 (with Ringo on drums), which raised three million dollars for the David Lynch Foundation, which promotes and supports Transcendental Meditation.

 Scan this code to read the lyrics.

Just like "Everyone's Got Something to Hide Except Me and My Monkey" (see page 338), the lyrics of "Cosmically Conscious" consist of Maharishi's favorite expressions. The guru lectured frequently about attaining "cosmic consciousness." He also often exclaimed, "It's such a joy." The lyrics of this song comprise these phrases, repeated throughout.

Cosmic Consciousness

Maharishi spoke of seven states of consciousness: 1) Deep Sleep State, 2) Dream State, 3) Waking State, 4) Transcendental Consciousness, 5) Cosmic Consciousness, 6) God Consciousness, and 7) Unity Consciousness. Our everyday life consists of the first three states. However, in deep meditation, a fourth state is experienced as inner peace, oneness, fulfillment, and unbounded awareness. Maharishi described this as "restful alertness," where our body is deeply relaxed yet the mind is fully awake.

Gradually, with regular meditation, we can remain in that fourth state permanently, while simultaneously engaging in all activities. That permanent state of wholeness, "Cosmic Consciousness," is the fifth state, where we recognize who we really are—our higher Self, which is eternal beingness, known as *atman*. Then we no longer identify ourselves as our transitory ego, mind, body, history, family ties, profession, bank account, beliefs, or aspirations.

"Birthday"

Written: September 18, 1968
Recorded: September 18, 1968
Released: November 22, 1968: The Beatles

In a 1980 interview, when asked whether "Birthday" was written in India, John Lennon replied, "No. 'Birthday' was written in the studio. Just made up on the spot. I think Paul wanted to write a song like 'Happy Birthday Baby,' the old fifties hit."[453]

Having worked on Maharishi's personal staff for six years, I can say with certainty that the guru made a huge deal of birthdays. The birthdays witnessed by The Beatles in India were no exception. I like to think that somewhere in Paul's mind, those celebrations influenced his song.

George Harrison's Birthday

In Rishikesh on George's twenty-fifth birthday, February 25, 1968, The Beatles' foreheads were smeared with red *kumkum* and yellow sandalwood paste—considered a blessing in India. Course participants placed garlands around George's neck until he was engulfed with marigolds.

George celebrates his birthday onstage with Maharishi, Ringo, and Pattie. PictureLux/The Hollywood Archive/Alamy Stock Photo.

Maharishi presents to George a booklet with his left hand and a globe with his right hand. Rue des Archives/GRANGER.

The birthday boy played the sitar for twenty minutes. A seven-pound, fifteen-by-fifteen-inch sheet cake was served, covered with white icing and pink roses made of frosting, topped with gold letters saying "Jai Guru Deva." There was a recitation by a local pandit (scholar) and songs by Mike Love and Donovan.

The proprietor of Pratap Music House in nearby Dehradun, Ajit Singh, and his "Doon gang" from the elite Doon School, gave a recital, with Deshpande on vocals and Shrivastava on tabla. George was pleased that they played Raag Jog, a forty-minute piece upon which "Within You Without You" was based. The Sikh turbaned musician Ajit Singh played a vichitra veena. This rare stringed instrument, played with a spherical slide, comprises a broad, fretless, horizontal crossbar (dand), three feet long and six inches wide, with two gigantic resonating gourds (tumba) inlaid with ivory and attached beneath the crossbar at both ends (see a photo on page 431).

As Maharishi presented George with a booklet in Hindi about Guru Dev and a plastic globe of earth oriented with the Southern Hemisphere on top, he declared, "This is what the world is like today: upside down. It is rotating in tension and agony. The world waits for its release and to be put right. Transcendental Meditation can do so. George, this globe I am giving you symbolizes the world today. I hope you will help us all in the task of putting it right."[454]

George turned the globe right side up, saying, "I've done it!" The crowd cheered. Then fireworks brightened the sky.[455]

Mike Love's Birthday

Lead singer of The Beach Boys, Mike Love, celebrated his twenty-seventh birthday on March 15. The Beatles and Donovan sang a birthday song about Maharishi's Spiritual Regeneration Movement (SRM) organization. It was patterned after The Beach Boys' "Fun, Fun, Fun." The lead singer was John Lennon. Here are the lyrics (without repetition):

We'd like to thank you Guru Dev cause your children couldn't thank you enough

Spiritual Regeneration World Wide Foundation

We'd like to thank you Guru Dev just for being our guiding light

We'd like to thank you Guru Dev just for seeing us through the night

A B C D E F G H I Jai Guru Dev

Spiritual Regeneration World Wide Foundation Yeeaaah!

Happy birthday Michael Love, happy birthday Michael Love Love Love

Happy birthday Michael Love, happy birthday Michael Michael Michael Love

Spiritual Regeneration World Wide Foundation (of India)

Happy Birthday

 Scan this code to listen to "Spiritual Regeneration."

Jai means "hail" or "glory." *Guru Dev* (divine teacher) is what Indians call their spiritual master. This specifically referred to Maharishi's master, with whom he studied for thirteen years. "Spiritual Regeneration Movement," or SRM, was the name of Maharishi's organization.

George Harrison gifted a painting of Guru Dev to Mike for his birthday. John presented a handmade circular card scrawled with a nude self-portrait and farewell message, since Mike left for the USA shortly afterward, April 7, 1968, in time for his concert tour.[456]

Mike Love's birthday celebration; l. to r.: Mike Love, Maharishi, Brahmachari Shankar Lal. A painting of Guru Dev rests above Love's head. © Colin Harrison-Avico Ltd.

Later that night in his basement cave, Maharishi performed a private birthday *puja* (Hindu ceremony) for Mike, who expressed: "At the end of the puja, Maharishi bowed toward Guru Dev. I bowed as well. After about a minute, I sensed Maharishi rising, so I lifted myself, except I couldn't. I fell back down, dazed. My heart was overwhelming me. Maharishi reached over and patted me on my neck three times, and I'll never forget what he said. 'You will always be with me.'"[457]

Pattie Boyd's and Paul Horn's Birthday

March 17 was Pattie Boyd's twenty-fourth and Paul Horn's twenty-eighth birthday, celebrated with a birthday cake and ragas played by George. Then Paul played tambura while George played sitar on "God Save the Queen." Ajit Singh traveled from Dehradun to present Pattie a beautiful dilruba (Indian cello), with a bird's head engraved at the neck—a birthday gift from George. John drew a picture of The Beatles and their wives meditating and wrote "Happy Birthday Pattie love from John and Cyn." Cynthia gave her a handmade painting.[458]

Paul Horn received a *kurta* (Indian shirt) from Paul and Jane with the word "Paul" hand-painted on the front and "Jai Guru Dev" on the back. The evening ended with a magician's performance and fireworks display.

Maharishi performs a birthday puja for Paul Horn and Pattie Boyd; l. to r.: Maharishi, Paul Horn, Pattie, George. © Colin Harrison-Avico Ltd.

Ajit Singh from Dehradun delivers a dilruba to Pattie for her birthday; l. to r.: George, Pattie, John, Nicholas Nugent (schoolteacher from the renowned Doon School in Dehradun who carried the birthday cake), Ajit Singh, Steve Browne (also a Doon School teacher who carried the dilruba). Photographer Ram Panjabi.

Ajit Singh said, "[The Beatles] had visited our store and ordered a customized pedal harmonium. It was white with flowers painted on its sides."[459] John and George invited Ajit to play for them in the ashram several times, and on one occasion Ajit took John's acoustic guitar to his shop for repair.

CHAPTER 8

COSMIC CRIES

"Dear Prudence"

Written: March 1968
Recorded: August 28, 29, and 30, 1968
Released: November 22, 1968: The Beatles

Out of more than thirty Beatles songs written in India, one of the most popular is about Prudence Farrow. Mia and her sister Prudence were among seven children of Irish American film actress Maureen O'Sullivan ("Jane" in the *Tarzan* movies) and Australian American Oscar-winning screenwriter, director, and producer John Farrow. Though Maureen wanted all her children to become actors (like the Barrymores), only one took that path—Mia, who became a Golden Globe-winning film star.

A Chaotic Upbringing

Prudence described in her memoir *Dear Prudence* that it was harrowing to lose her brother as a child, her father as a teenager, and to live in the shadow of a superstar mother and sister. With her parents constantly traveling, she was raised by nuns and housekeepers. At her boarding school in England, the nuns saw her bad behavior as a cry for attention. One of her pranks was to emulate sainthood by scraping her skin with nettle leaves until welts appeared.

In high school, Mia blossomed into a stunning, charismatic charmer. Comparing herself to her magnetic sister, Prudence's poor self-image drove her to years of reckless, defiant, self-destructive behavior. She lost herself in alcohol, Dexedrine, and codeine, and attended school inebriated most days. Because drug users took over the family home and left chaos in their wake, in spring 1964 the police informed Prudence's mother that her children could no longer stay in Connecticut unsupervised. After getting expelled from a couple of boarding schools, Prudence landed in her mother's apartment on Central Park West in Manhattan.

When her mother's Broadway show headed on the road, Prudence ditched school and hid in her room. She chain-smoked pot with three siblings and slipped into paranoia, depression, and drug-induced delusions. In 1965, Prudence took LSD and suffered horrifying apparitions of merging with the devil in hell for eternity. This recurred in flashbacks, causing paralyzing fear. Ordinary tasks like washing dishes became monumental feats.

How TM Found Prudence

Motivated by immense dread, Prudence made the effort to attend school and, with support from new friends, by spring of 1966, she turned her life around. She read about meditation, became a vegetarian, and prayed to commit her life to God. She received a mescaline-induced prediction that in two months she would meet a spiritual master.

While visiting her brother Patrick and his wife in Malibu, Prudence met Patrick's friend Peter Wallace right on time—two months after her premonition. When she told Peter she was reading about meditation, he replied, "I know just the right thing for you."[460] Peter had just returned from India, where an Indian female saint Anandamayi Ma had referred him to Maharishi Mahesh Yogi. He was now practicing Maharishi's simple method of tapping a reservoir of inner bliss.

Prudence recalled, "I felt it was more than just someone telling me about something that I had been looking for—it was actually what I was looking for."[461] Peter introduced Prudence to TM Initiator Jerry Jarvis (head of Students International Meditation Society: SIMS), from whom she took a six-week course, with thirty fellow aspirants, in a classroom at UCLA. She knew this was the answer to her prayers. Though she applied to Maharishi's January 1967 TM Teacher Training Course in India, at age nineteen she was too young to qualify. (See page 323 for a photo of Jerry Jarvis and Prudence Farrow.)

Prudence's mother warned her that escaping life through her obsession with meditation and God was more dangerous than LSD. One day, as Prudence was meditating, her mother poured an entire bucket of water over her head. A psychiatrist threatened Prudence that unless she stopped this dangerous, damaging meditation nonsense, she would become a zombie.

Though Prudence entered a psychiatric hospital, she refused to stop meditation and refused to take medication. After a period of great distress, she was released with Mia's help. Prudence then studied with Swami Satchidananda, who was teaching yoga in Manhattan. She began teaching classes and opened a yoga school in Boston.

Meeting Maharishi

When Mia married Frank Sinatra in 1966 and became a leading Hollywood actress, Prudence felt overshadowed, as if her life had been stolen by her sister's fame. Rude people remarked, "Why aren't you successful like Mia?"[462]

Mia became interested in studying with Maharishi in India. So Jerry Jarvis arranged for her to speak with Maharishi, who invited the actress to meet him in Cambridge and travel with him to India in January 1968. Prudence became jealous, as she had implored Jerry for over a year to let her attend the India course. Finally, Maharishi consented to meet Prudence in Cambridge.

She recalled, "When I first met Maharishi, it was like meeting a category 5 hurricane. The amount of bliss he lived and exuded was just devastating to me."[463] "The peace emanating from him, from my estimate at the time, was 300 times what I had encountered with [Swami Satchidananda]."[464] "I just fell on the ground and wept."[465]

During Maharishi's extensive interview with Prudence, she poured out her heart. Finally, he extended his arm, made a fist, and declared, "You are mine!"[466]

Beatles Buddy Group

On Maharishi's meditation retreats, the attendees paired off with "buddies" to discuss experiences and check on each other. Maharishi placed Prudence in a buddy group with John Lennon and George Harrison. "We talked about the things we were all going through," Prudence said. "We were questioning reality, asking questions about who we were and what was going on."[467]

In their discussion group, George shared that a major shift was happening in collective consciousness, and he needed to be a part of it: "Our generation is breaking new ground, heralding a new time, just the beginning of a more powerful wave that will follow, and I want to help."[468]

Prudence said she liked The Beatles because they were on her same wavelength in many ways. "They were very real, all four of them. John and George, they were very much up my alley. They were musicians; they had other interests—whereas I really only had one interest, which was to get the maximum I could from that time. I was so much more extreme."[469] When Maharishi asked Prudence which Beatle she liked most, she said George had the most in common with her. Maharishi replied that was because he was most Indian.

Maharishi's Purposeful Button-Pushing

Mia had left the ashram on February 10 and was waiting in New Delhi for her brother John Charles Villiers-Farrow to arrive so they could travel to Goa. But on February 15, Maharishi asked Prudence to pick up Mia in New Delhi and bring her back to Rishikesh. Prudence, who resented breaking her long meditations for her privileged sister, resolved to meditate in the taxi and continue meditating all night. At 3:00 a.m., the phone rang in the sisters' hotel room. Maharishi was calling for Prudence: "Stop meditating! It's time to rest now."[470]

When Mia and Prudence discovered The Beatles were slated to arrive the same day as their brother, Mia asked their taxi driver to swing by the airport, where she bolted from their taxi and made a beeline toward John Lennon, deserting Prudence, who tried to follow but got separated in the crowd. From afar, Prudence watched Mia, their brother John Villiers-Farrow, and John and Cynthia Lennon enter taxicabs and ride off.

Prudence rode back to Rishikesh alone. Upon her return, Maharishi called her to his bungalow and asked, "Do you know your sister is a great person?"

Startled, Prudence replied, "No, I don't think she's a great person."

Maharishi laughed and asked, "Doesn't she want to do good?"

"Yes," Prudence said.

Maharishi said, "Tell me all about what good she wants to do."

"What kind of guru are you?" Prudence yelled. "Why don't you just go to Hollywood, where you can meet lots of stars and ask them these questions yourself?"

Maharishi replied, "Now go and rest."[471]

Prudence had presence of mind to understand Maharishi's method: "By praising my sister, Maharishi awakened me to the potency and danger of my hidden stress created from recent years of living in the shadow of Mia's famed existence. Lacking confidence in myself had exacerbated the situation, increasing repressed feelings of anger and inadequacy."[472]

Trying to Get Cosmic First

"Being on the course was a dream come true," Prudence said. "More important to me than anything in the world."[473] She wanted to meditate as much as possible, so she could become an Initiator. However, due to past drug use, she would first go through a dark night of the soul. Maharishi explained that past memories and trauma make a deep impression on the nervous system. With prolonged meditation, deep stresses, which he called "stones" or "icebergs," would dissipate. Concerned about drug flashbacks, Prudence told Maharishi about her past experiences. He assured her meditation would dissolve stones in her heart and fears would disappear.

Aspiring to release these stresses, Prudence always rushed straight back to her room after lectures and meals to meditate, whereas "John, George and Paul would want to sit around jamming and having a good time."[474] Prudence disliked the noisy music and celebrity circus around her. She asked Maharishi to move her from The Beatles' *puri*, but the ashram was full.

Course participants gradually increased their meditation time while continuing to come out for meals and lectures; however, Prudence took meditation to the extreme and refused to leave her room. Ringo recalled: "We saw her twice in the two weeks I was there. Everyone would be banging on the door: 'Are you still alive?'"[475]

Paul said, "Prudence got an attack of the horrors, paranoia, what you'd call these days an identity crisis, and wouldn't come out of her Butlins chalet. We all got a little bit worried about her so we went up there and knocked. 'Hi, Prudence, we all love you. You're wonderful!' But nobody could persuade her out."[476]

John said Prudence went slightly "barmy" locked in her room: "They selected me and George to try and bring her out because she would trust us. She'd been locked in for three weeks."[477] "All the people around her were very worried, because she was going insane. So we sang to her."[478] Prudence remembered John and

George bursting into her room, once singing "Sgt. Pepper's Lonely Hearts Club Band," and another time "Ob-La-Di, Ob-La-Da." She was grateful and thought they were sweet, but she just wanted them to disappear so she could meditate.

John said, "She was trying to find God quicker than anyone else. That was the competition in Maharishi's camp: who was going to get cosmic first. What I didn't know was that I was already cosmic."[479]

Meditation Meltdown

Eventually, Maharishi asked all the course participants to stay inside their rooms for five days. Prudence said others were sleeping, sunbathing, and taking walks, but "I was one of many just maybe a little more extreme."[480] Prudence sat in silent meditation, motionless, in full lotus position, for five days straight. She did not drink, eat, sleep, or wash. On the fifth day of her marathon, Prudence suffered a hellish LSD flashback and screamed, "Get Maharishi! I need him. Only he can help!" John Lennon fetched Maharishi and Prudence cried, "I am in hell again! It has come back! Please help me!" Maharishi managed to calm her down.[481]

One night in late March, George Harrison and another student, Richard Blakely (See his photo on page 148), chatted with Prudence in the garden. Her withdrawn demeanor prompted Richard to ask, "Prudence, are you okay?" Staring down at her clenched fists, she expressed she was afraid, but could not say of what.[482]

The men tried to assure her it was just a knot of stress releasing. They offered to take her to Maharishi. She refused. They asked if she wanted to be left alone. She answered, "Then I would be alone with all my fright."[483] George gently touched her knee. She jumped in fear and began sobbing. They helped her out of her chair and George led her back to her room.

Jenny Boyd, whose room was just opposite Prudence's, recalled, "The following morning nobody could rouse her out of a trance. We knew she'd been doing extensive meditations, non-stop, and wondered if she'd gone too far." Each of them walked into Prudence's room, trying to stir her. But she just sat bolt upright on her bed cross-legged, staring into oblivion. They tried to sing or play music to her, in vain. "Prudence looked as though she was locked inside herself."[484]

The following night, Prudence started screaming and throwing things around her room. She woke up everyone within earshot. She was led to Maharishi's bungalow, where he tried to comfort her. Finally, the doctor injected her with a sedative.

The next afternoon, Prudence was escorted to newly built quarters. On the porch before one of the rooms, an enclosure was constructed out of bamboo bars. The previous occupant, Richard Blakely, had been relocated. That night in the lecture hall, students asked Maharishi what had happened to Prudence. He replied that drugs had damaged her nervous system; she had hit a huge "iceberg" during long meditations, and it was good it happened here, because healing would be rapid.[485]

Soon afterward, Maharishi hired a massage therapist and instructed students to get massages, and never meditate more than thirty minutes without breaking for asanas (yoga postures) and pranayama (breathing exercises).

Ena Mahabir from Trinidad, a nurse trained in handling mental illness, volunteered to move next door to Prudence. Two nurses summoned from Delhi took turns sleeping inside her room. Volunteers took shifts sitting outside her door. Nancy Jackson related that Prudence could no longer feed herself or recognize anyone. Screams emanated from her room at all hours.[486] American flautist Paul Horn remembered, "She didn't even recognize her own brother, who was on the course with her. The only person she showed any slight recognition towards was Maharishi. We were all very concerned about her."[487]

Nancy Jackson begged Maharishi to send Prudence to a hospital, but he refused: "How can I send her away? She is in no condition to travel. This is the price I have to pay for wanting publicity from her sister Mia. If I send her to a hospital, they will just put her on drugs and give her more shock treatment. That way she will never recover. This is what she's afraid of and pleads against. I will work with her."[488]

Each day, Prudence was escorted to Maharishi's bungalow, where he directed her to practice yoga postures in the corner of his meeting room. If her mind wandered, he tapped on his coffee table with a pen to get her attention and said, "Continue, continue."[489]

Miracle Healing

After three weeks of daily sessions with a massage therapist and daily visits with Maharishi, Prudence returned from the abyss. One afternoon, she suddenly appeared at the dining area, drinking tea, smiling, laughing, and engaging in conversation with a responsive, positive attitude. One of the students, Mike Dolan, commented: "As the course neared its completion, Prudence became a glowing beautiful woman, self-confident and alert, a tribute to the restorative powers of TM."[490]

Maharishi said the stones in her heart had been healed and she would never have flashbacks again. It was true. Prudence and I both attended the Rishikesh course in 1970, where she was happy and healthy. She told *Rolling Stone*, "Right from the start, all I cared about was getting the job done, clearing out whatever darkness I had inside me, and becoming healthy and being able to live a real life. I knew meditation could do it for me."[491]

Prudence Farrow in 1970.

 Scan this code to read the
lyrics for "Dear Prudence."

The Song

On April 10, just as the Beatles were leaving Rishikesh, George gave
Prudence a message that John had written a song about her. She
was concerned about John's knack for mocking people. However,
when Prudence heard it, she breathed a sigh of relief. She thought it
was beautiful. Prudence told *Rolling Stone*, "It epitomized what the
sixties were about in many ways. What it's saying is very beautiful;
it's very positive. I think it's an important song. I feel that it does

capture that essence of the course, that slightly exotic part of being in India where we went through that silence and meditation.[492]

Prudence feels The Beatles were not only great musicians, they were "saying what we were all feeling, so they were kind of a voice [for] a lot of us." With young kids now interested in The Beatles, it means their voice is "still resonating and still being heard."[493]

Prudence overcame her self-destructive tendencies, earned a PhD from UC Berkeley, and became a successful author, journalist, film producer, Sanskrit scholar, and meditation and yoga teacher.

"Yer Blues"

Written: February to August 14th, 1968
Recorded: August 13, 14 and 20, 1968
Released: November 22, 1968: The Beatles

The purpose of the TM Teacher Training Course in Rishikesh was for students to gain deep experience of what Maharishi called "transcendental awareness" and become Initiators. As the course progressed, students gradually increased time spent in meditation. After a few weeks, Maharishi announced, "Now go to your rooms and meditate as long as you can. For the time being we will cancel all lessons, but remember one thing is important—if you want to talk to me about anything, come to me, even in the middle of the night."[494]

Unwinding Heavy Stress

The road to bliss was rocky at times. During periods of deepest silence, with students meditating all day, some developed psychological distress. To resolve the crisis, Maharishi convened an emergency meeting where he explained "unwinding" (a.k.a. "unstressing"). He likened past stresses to icebergs—small on the surface but massive below. As deep-seated traumas dissolved, students might feel discomfort.

On TM retreats, stress release usually resulted in dramatic improvements in health, wellbeing, and physical appearance. Chronic aches and pains disappeared. Psychological hang-ups lessened. Maharishi would say, "Something good is happening, hmm?" However, when I was involved with TM from 1967 to 1989, some students underwent emotional disturbances. Sometimes Maharishi assigned me to look after people with involuntary movements, spasms, facial distortions, verbalizations, hallucinations, or unusual behavior. Maharishi called them "heavy unstressers" and arranged for them to meditate together in a separate room.

Sometimes unstressing resulted in acute mental health issues and even death. During courses in Mallorca while I was on Maharishi's International Staff, one unfortunate man languished for months in a Spanish psychiatric hospital. Another person's lifeless body was found on the beach. After that, Maharishi moved "heavy unstressers" to the first floor to prevent suicide from hotel balconies.

During The Beatles' course in India, positive outcomes of stress release included miracle cures of Prudence Farrow, Mike Love, and Michael Tyne-Corbold from Australia. Mike Love had a terrific phobia of knives. While meditating, he felt an intense pain in his thigh, as though he were being stabbed. He continued meditating until the pain stopped. His fear of blades disappeared forever.[495] Childhood polio victim Michael Tyne-Corbold walked with a cane and leg braces. During a group meditation, he felt the sensation of an imagined snake wrapped around his leg and pain crushing his lower limbs. Once the pain subsided, he was healed. After one week, his leg braces were discarded.[496]

Lennon Sings the Blues

In "Yer Blues," John portrayed his irrational thoughts that arose during meditation. Although he was meditating eight hours a day, he recalled, "I was writing the most miserable songs on earth. In 'Yer Blues,' when I wrote, 'I'm so lonely I want to die,' I'm not kidding. That's how I felt. Up there trying to reach God and feeling suicidal."[497]

In the mid-sixties, several British bands (notably, The Rolling Stones, The Animals, and The Yardbirds) became enchanted with American blues and gained great success tackling the genre. "Yer Blues" is John's masterful endeavor. Though John felt inadequate and self-conscious about singing the blues, he managed to do it with aplomb as he poured out his feelings with candor.

 Scan this code to read the lyrics for "Yer Blues."

The Lyrics

In "Yer Blues" John referred to "Mr. Jones," from Bob Dylan's "Ballad of a Thin Man." Mr. Jones symbolized one of many reporters that covered Dylan's concerts. He was what beatniks called "square" or "straight"—part of the conformist "establishment"—viewed as an outsider by countercultural nonconformists.

We hippies were called "freaks" or "acid freaks" by the straights. But in "Ballad of a Thin Man," Dylan called out the square reporter as a freak who never could or would "grok in the fullness" of the Beat message. Dylan refused to cooperate with reporters, frequently belittling and insulting them with scathing tongue-lashings.

While in Rishikesh, John underwent an existential crisis similar to that of Mr. Jones. "Yer Blues" expressed his internal frustrations and conflicts. Trapped alone in a room, meditating all day, going through mental hell, he had to confront his demons, just as Mr. Jones cried out in Dylan's song.

There is no doubt Yoko was the "girl" in the lyrics. John described the experience of meditation, which is expansion of consciousness—a feeling of belonging to "the universe," rather than our earthly material existence of "earth" or "sky."

For John, the Rishikesh trip marked a major turning point. He would embark on a serious relationship with a new love and abandon his wife Cynthia and child Julian. He was going through the hell of guilt, shame, and all other emotions attendant to that transition. No wonder he was singin' the blues!

 Scan this code to read the lyrics for "Ballad of a Thin Man."

"I'm So Tired"

Written: March 1968
Recorded: October 8, 1968
Released: November 22, 1968: The Beatles

In the daily meetings at the retreat in Rishikesh, course members reported to Maharishi how many hours they meditated. The Beatles and their wives competed over who was "getting it," who was not, and "who was going to get cosmic first."[498] "Getting cosmic" was John Lennon's nickname for attaining Cosmic Consciousness, which Maharishi often lectured about (see page 232–233).

George said the main goal was to plug into divine energy and achieve higher consciousness. "All those things, like walking on water and dematerializing your body at will, are just the sort of things that happen along the way."[499] "There's high, and there's *high*, and to get really high—I mean so high you can walk on water, *that* high—that's where I'm going. The answer's not pot, but yoga and meditation, and working and discipline, working out your karma."[500]

John commented, "The way George is going, he will be flying on a magic carpet by the time he is forty."[501]

John and George meditated eight hours per day. Pattie Boyd reached seven hours. George disapproved when Pattie swam in the Ganges, shopped at Tibetan trading posts, or ate non-vegetarian food in nearby Dehradun or Mussoorie.

Five Days of Silence

A few weeks into the course, Maharishi suggested students stay inside their rooms for five days in deep silence. If they wished, they could mark food choices on menus, tack them to their doors, and meals would be delivered. Many students, including John and George, stayed in their rooms during this period, meditating all day.

Though John said Prudence had gone "barmy," she was not the only one. John wrote the song "I'm So Tired" when, as he recalled, "I was hallucinating like crazy.[502] "I was in a room for five days meditating."[503] "I'd been meditating all day and then I couldn't sleep at night. We were not supposed to leave the room because of this thing about staying in one room for five days. So I was so tired I couldn't get to sleep." [504]

 Scan this code to read the lyrics.

The Lyrics

In "I'm So Tired," John sang about the misery of persistent insomnia, hallucinations, and avalanches of churning thoughts continually flooding his mind due to so many hours of meditation, which drove him round the bend. At that point, he would have done anything to just get some peace. Insomnia was typical during Maharishi's long meditation courses. Meditating up to twenty hours per day, we became so energized that sometimes we could not sleep at night. John also sang about drinking alcohol, but his three "no's" might refer to alcohol being forbidden at the ashram. In fact, no meat, eggs, drugs, or alcohol are allowed in the entire strictly Hindu area of Rishikesh and Haridwar, along the sacred Ganges River.

Cynthia Lennon hoped for a second honeymoon with John in India; however, two weeks into their stay, John moved into separate quarters, where he was free to revel in secret telegrams and letters from Yoko Ono.[505] John recalled, "She would write things like, 'I am a cloud. Watch for me in the sky.' I would get so excited about her letters."[506] John ignored Cynthia nearly their entire stay in Rishikesh. She was heartbroken.

John referred to his obsession with Yoko in the song. His mind was fixated on her, especially after he had tried to bed her and she would have none of it. He considered calling her but did not, since he felt Yoko would not take him seriously. The truth was she already had him wound tightly around her finger. Even the intuitive, sensitive Cynthia recognized Yoko as a kindred spirit for John who might fill the hole in his heart resulting from losing his mother at age seventeen: "When I first set eyes on Yoko, I knew she was the one for John. The chemistry was right and the mental aura that surrounded them was almost identical."[507]

Regarding "Sir Walter Raleigh," he introduced tobacco to England. The term "get" refers to a Scouse (Liverpudlian slang) pronunciation of a British insult "git" (contemptible individual). Though agitated by insomnia, John could still crack a joke by blaming the purveror of tobacco for his misery.

"Long, Long, Long"

Written: August 1968
Recorded: October 7, 8 and 9, 1968
Released: November 22, 1968: The Beatles

George began writing "Long, Long, Long" in Maharishi's ashram in Rishikesh. People might assume it is about George's love affair

Susan Shumsky, D.D.

with Pattie Boyd, or perhaps just one of those "silly love songs." But it is really about tears shed in losing and finding God. George was seeking a genuine experience of God. This song was his heart-rending love letter.

 Scan this code to read the lyrics.

The Lyrics

The biggest clue to the song's true meaning lies here: "See you, be you." According to Indian beliefs, when we attain God realization, not only do we love God; not only do we see God; we actually *merge* with God. That is what Maharishi defined as "Unity Consciousness," where we release the false ego and realize the higher Self as pure consciousness—the nameless, formless, beginningless, endless, eternal absolute. George described himself this way: "I play a little guitar, write a few tunes, make a few movies, but none of that's really me. The real me is something else."[508]

Self-realization, higher states of consciousness, Cosmic Consciousness, God Consciousness, and Unity Consciousness are Hindu concepts—not Christian. Long before George wrote this song, he had moved past his Catholic background and embraced Hinduism. At age twenty-four, he wrote this letter to his mother: "I want to be self-realized. I want to find God. I'm not interested in material things, this world, fame—I'm going for the real goal. And I hope you don't worry about me, mum."[509]

During a 1966 BBC Radio World Service interview, while George was in India studying with Ravi Shankar, he revealed his predilection for Indian religion: "The difference is their religion is every second and every minute of their lives and it *is* them—how they act, and how they conduct themselves and how they think."[510] In May 1967, George further explained, "Religion is a day-to-day experience. You find it all around. You live it. Religion is here and now. Not just something that comes on Sundays!"[511]

The song refers to a past connection with God that had been lost and asks how we could ever lose that connection. For God is never lost. God hides in plain sight. If we develop our inner eye (third eye), we can see, feel, hear, and eventually unify with God. However, this can take lifetimes—thus a long, long time. The soul has been cut off from God not only in this lifetime; it also sheds tears for many past lives. But reuniting with God brings jubilation.

The longing for God is the most potent kind of love. It brings devotees to their knees and inspires the noblest acts. The great Sufi mystic Jalāl al-Dīn Rūmī wrote, "Listen to the moan of a dog for its master. That whining is the connection. There are love dogs no one knows the names of. Give your life to be one of them."[512]

Paramahansa Yogananda, author of *Autobiography of a Yogi*, George's favorite book, said, "You cannot summon God by a little cry; it must be unceasing." "Why shouldn't you cry for the Lord until the skies are shaken with your prayers? Remember, as long as you are making the effort, God will never let you down!"[513]

In case you have any doubts about the song's meaning, here is what George wrote in his memoir *I, Me, Mine*: "The '*you*' in 'Long, Long, Long' is God."[514] But George's recurring complaint was, "If you say the word God or Lord, it makes some people's hair curl! They feel threatened when you talk about something that isn't just 'Be-Bop-A-Lula,' and then their only way out of that is to say, 'You're lecturing us or you're preaching.' They just can't come to terms with the idea that there may just be something else going on apart from their individual egos."[515]

"Circles"

Written: February to April 1968
Recorded: May 5 to August 27, 1982
Released: November 5, 1982: Gone Troppo

George wrote "Circles" during his stay at Maharishi's ashram in Rishikesh. It was considered for the White Album, among other "Harrisongs" recorded as demos that never saw the light of day at the time. It was finally released in 1982. Along with "The Inner Light" and "Within You Without You," this is an example of George's role in bringing the wisdom of the Far East to the masses.

 Scan this code to read the lyrics.

The Lyrics

The themes of this song are duality, the ephemeral nature of the physical world, and freedom (moksha) from the "wheel of karma" (samsara)—the rounds of birth and death in perpetual reincarnation.

In Rishikesh, The Beatles learned about two aspects of life—absolute and relative. The absolute unmanifest Being is infinite oneness and perfection. The relative, dualistic, material world exists in contrasts: male/female, yin/yang, up/down, black/white, yes/no, good/bad, hot/cold, friends/enemies, happiness/sadness, poverty/abundance, loss/gain.

This song describes the fickle dualistic mind, subject to emotional swings of love and hate, acceptance and rejection. In India, it is believed the human mind in ignorance remains trapped in duality on the karmic wheel, in endless cycles of birth and death that circle repeatedly—that is, until it wakes up.

"He who knows does not speak; He who speaks does not know": Here George quotes verbatim from chapter 56 of the Tao

Te Ching by Lao Tzu. In the Eastern tradition, those who know the Tao ("The Way") live and breathe that reality quietly. They are unassuming and unpretentious. Those who do not know the Tao might boast and crow about what they think they know. The next line in chapter 56 states "Close the mouth; shut the doors." This refers to meditation—shutting out the outer world and diving into silence, turning away from the external and toward the internal.

Perpetual reincarnation characterizes life in ignorance—like a wheel circling endlessly. Once we are permanently established in higher consciousness, in a state of contented fullness, our mind is no longer shaken by loss or gain. Though we still face challenges, our mind remains steadfast in evenness—free from stings and slings of emotional swings. Our seeds of desire no longer sprout; we dwell in everlasting contentment; and we no longer need to reincarnate. These lyrics summarize teachings of the ancient Hindu scripture Bhagavad Gita.

"Dehradun"

Written: February to April 1968
Recorded: May to October 1970
Released: August 6, 2021: All Things Must Pass: 50th Anniversary Box Set

George Harrison wrote "Dehradun" in Rishikesh in early 1968 during his stay at Maharishi's ashram. Though recorded during the 1968 White Album Esher sessions and again during the *All Things Must Pass* sessions, it was never released. George performed the song on ukulele for the 1995 TV broadcast of *The Beatles Anthology.*

 Scan this code to read the lyrics.

The Lyrics

The song refers to Dehradun, the closest large town to the Rishikesh ashram—twenty-eight miles away. The road to Dehradun is a metaphor for the pathway towards (or away from) enlightenment. Many roads can take you to higher consciousness. One road takes days. Others take years, even lifetimes. Maharishi often compared TM to other meditation methods but touted TM as the fastest path to enlightenment.

George criticized students on the TM Teacher Training Course (especially his wife Pattie) who wandered away from the ashram. Since meat and eggs are prohibited in the sacred Hindu area of Rishikesh and Haridwar, course members sometimes procured these items while shopping in Dehradun. Many students walked down the path to swim in the Ganges River.

The goldmine is George's metaphor for TM, which Maharishi claimed to be the fast track to enlightenment. Yet students wasted time running away to Dehradun, far from the spiritual riches right there at Maharishi's ashram. George said, "Look inside. That's the answer. Meditation is the key to get from darkness into the light, from suffering into pleasure, from ignorance into wisdom. It doesn't matter if you're a beggar, you can still find God."[516]

Jenny Boyd commented, "It was about [George] seeing people leaving the ashram for a day's visit to the Taj Mahal or a town near Rishikesh called Dehradun. He couldn't understand having come all this way to be in meditation why anyone would want to go 'shopping for eggs' as he saw it, in Dehradun."[517]

PART V

THE LONG AND WINDING ROAD TO DISILLUSION

BEHIND THE CURTAIN

"Sexy Sadie"

Written: April 10 thru May 29, 1968
Recorded: August 13 and 21, 1968
Released: November 22, 1968: The Beatles

"Sexy Sadie" is not about a woman named Sadie. In fact, it is not about a woman at all. John Lennon wrote it, sitting at breakfast in Rishikesh, while waiting for a taxi to extract him from Maharishi's Meditation Academy on April 10, 1968.

The convoluted story that led John to write this song unfolded as shock waves hitting Rishikesh reverberated around the world. The planet paused for a moment, then changed orbit when The Beatles, Mia Farrow, Paul Horn, Mike Love, and Donovan visited Maharishi's ashram in early 1968. Here is how the drama began:

Sexy Sadie: A Play in Eight Acts

Act 1:

The Honeymoon

Stage curtain opens. Ladies and gentlemen, The Beatles!

On February 16, 1968, at New Delhi airport, Brahmachari Satyanand (direct disciple of Maharishi's guru) and Mal Evans welcomed John and Cynthia Lennon, George Harrison, and Pattie and Jenny Boyd to India. They then rode in Ambassador taxicabs, circa 1955 vintage, on the bumpy ride to Maharishi's ashram.

When The Beatles first alighted in Rishikesh, Geoffrey Baker (see pages 147–148) asked George, "Are you going to become Initiators? The four of you?" George said he could not speak for the others, but as for himself, "Sure, why not?"[518]

Paul McCartney and his fiancée, British actress Jane Asher, along with Ringo Starr and his wife, Maureen, arrived on February 20. During their flight to India, Ringo and Paul decided to become lacto-ovo-vegetarians.

In New Delhi, Ringo told the *Hindustan Times*, "We became his disciples at first sight. It came out of our hearts. If Maharishi wants us to be teachers, we will certainly obey. I am very much attracted to India, where there is peace of mind far from the world of materialism. Our guru Maharishi belongs to this land. It is our spiritual home."[519]

Red Carpet Treatment

Though struggling to keep his sparsely constructed ashram solvent, Maharishi upgraded Block 6, The Beatles' *puri*, with a few Western comforts, including four-poster beds, foam mattresses, bedspreads, carpeting, mirrors, and tiled ensuite bathrooms. However, the water was usually cold. Maharishi offered the Fabs a private dining room, but they elected to eat with other students outdoors under a creeper-covered trellis. Monkeys often dropped by to snatch a piece of toast or two. Near the dining area, a sign warned, "Beware of Monkey Attack."

Above the entrance to The Beatles' quarters, a Sanskrit sign said "Maharshi Dhyan Vidyaapeeth." The English translation: "Maharishi's Seat of Learning for Meditation."

The Beatles' quarters in Rishikesh, fifty years later. Photo courtesy of Ellie Quinn—The Wandering Quinn Travel Blog.

Maharishi's bungalow rooftop where he met The Beatles (at abandoned ashram in 2001).

Beatles meeting with Maharishi in Rishikesh. Pictorial Press Ltd/Alamy Stock Photo.

Maharishi asked that students respect The Beatles' privacy and treat them like everyone else, yet he failed to take his own advice. He proffered preferential treatment on them, as he had done with Mia Farrow. He held private lessons on the flat roof of his bungalow or inside his meeting room, where The Beatles sat cross-legged on the carpet, propped on pillows. Meanwhile, the other seventy participants wondered where Maharishi was.

The Beatles Impressions

Cynthia Lennon, who found Maharishi to be a wonderful, humorous, and enlightening teacher, said, "John and George threw themselves totally into Maharishi's teachings, were relaxed, and above all had found peace of mind that had been denied them for so long."[520]

John described, "It was a recluse holiday camp right at the foot of the Himalayas, with baboons stealing your breakfast and everybody flowing round in robes and sitting in their rooms for hours meditating."[521]

Ringo said, "We were in this really spiritual place, and we were meditating a lot, having seminars by Maharishi. It was pretty far out."[522] "If you're going to learn something, you might as well learn it from the boss man, and he's the guv'nor."[523]

George declared, "It's the only place to be. It's a quest to find the answer to 'Why are we here? Who am I? Where did I come from? Where am I going?' That became the only important thing in my life."[524]

Nancy and Beatles with Maharishi; l. to r.: Socialite Nancy Jackson, John, Paul, Maharishi, George, Mia Farrow, Mia's brother John Farrow, Donovan Leitch. Keystone Press/Alamy Stock Photo.

The Beatles Meditate

"Maharishi shows you that, through meditation, you achieve a sort of inner peace," said Ringo. "I've found it works, anyway. So have the others. We all feel so much better for it."[525] He told journalist Derek Boltwood, "Meditation is my cup of tea. I'm far more relaxed now than I ever have been."[526]

John recounted, "One of the happiest times was in India, in some kind of pit. Happily mentally and physically y'know, because it was just such a groove, such a pure thing! It was really some trip, like acid was nowhere. Just sitting there, muttering some word in a room was the biggest trip I ever had in me life."[527]

Paul recalled a blissful meditation: "It appeared to me that I was like a feather over a hot-air pipe. I was just suspended by this hot air. And I thought, *Well, hell, that's great, I couldn't buy that anywhere.* That was the most pleasant, the most relaxed I ever got, for a few minutes I really felt so light, so floating, so complete.'"[528] "I reported that to Maharishi, and he giggled, 'Yes, this is good! Just enjoy!'"[529]

"I felt the power of the enormous silence. I became aware that on a very subtle level past the senses, everything was more liquid. I could feel this during and right after meditation," George described.[530] "The only reason to be living is to have complete, full knowledge of bliss consciousness—to transcend from this relative state of consciousness to an absolute state of consciousness."[531]

Yet, during one tedious lecture, George stood up and complained it was unbearably boring. All laughed uproariously, including Maharishi.

Ravindra Damodara Swami, one of Maharishi's brahmacharyas, noted in his diary Maharishi's impressions of The Beatles: "Ringo is always in meditation and goes by feeling and heart, but as for the other Beatles, too much brain is in the way. Of all the Beatles, George is the most advanced, and this is his last life. John has many more [lifetimes] to go and must not give in to his weakness for women or it will ruin him."[532]

During their stay in India, Maharishi prophetically warned The Beatles: "If you don't continue your meditation practice, your singing group will break up."

Ringo Left Early

Ringo Starr and wife Maureen stayed in Rishikesh only nine days. Terrified of insects, Maureen demanded "Ritchie" kill them all and discard the carcasses. Ringo had to fight off scorpions and tarantulas to take a bath: "You'd start shouting, 'Oh yes, well, I think I'll be having a bath now' and banging your feet. Then you'd get out of the bath, get dry, and get out of the room before all the insects came back in."[533]

Paul said a single fly over the door once trapped Maureen inside a room. When Ringo complained of flies, Maharishi said, "For people traveling in the realm of pure consciousness, flies no longer matter very much."

Starr retorted, "Yes, but that doesn't zap the flies, does it?"[534]

The food was impossible for Ringo due to childhood peritonitis and allergies. He recalled, "I took two suitcases with me, one of clothes and the other full of Heinz beans (there's a plug for you)." One morning, the cooks offered Ringo eggs, secretly smuggled in by Mal Evans. When eggs appeared again the following day, Ringo thought, *Oh yeah, great—things are looking up.* However, Ringo caught the staff burying the eggshells—the first of several incidents that disillusioned him: "You weren't supposed to have eggs inside this religious and spiritual ashram. I thought: *What do you mean, you're burying the shells? Can't God see that too?*"[535]

"We came home because we missed the children [three-year-old Zak and six-month old Jason]," Ringo recalled. "I wouldn't want anyone to think we didn't like it there. It was a good experience—it just didn't last as long for me as it did for them."[536]

Pattie Boyd said, "Ringo looked so sad when they left, but I think they missed their children, who were very young—and he was probably tired of baked beans."[537]

Maharishi tried to convince Ringo to stay or return later. "He wanted us to stay because he's helping us," Ringo said.[538] But after nine days, on February 29, Ringo and Maureen left with Donovan's associate Gypsy Dave. Mal Evans left one week later, on March 8.

On March 16, 1968, Ringo told *Melody Maker* that meditation "calmed me and made me more relaxed, although I still have the same emotions as anyone else. This eases your mind and no problem seems as big as you make it out to be." Ringo said Maharishi was "a long way ahead from where I am. There's something about him. I can't tell you what it is really. You just know, there's a great man. He's put me on the road. Now it's up to me whether I follow or get off."[539]

On March 5, 1988, Ringo told Michael Aspel on his British TV talk show, "I still thank Maharishi for what he said, but in the end I felt he was telling me stories."[540]

Back of an Elephant

Kumbh Mela is a religious festival held every twelve years where thousands of ascetics and millions of pilgrims bathe in the Ganges River at auspicious astrological times. George wanted to attend the fair in Haridwar, thirteen miles south of Rishikesh. Maharishi insisted The Beatles ride in on elephants on the main bathing date, April 13. George argued, "Being a Beatle is already seeing life from the back of an elephant. We want to mix with the crowds. Maybe I'll find Babaji sitting under a tree."[541] (Babaji is a legendary immortal saint pictured on the Sgt. Pepper album and described in Yogananda's *Autobiography of a Yogi*. See page 106.)

Police would not authorize the planned procession with The Beatles, for fear it would cause a stampede.[542] In the end, The Beatles never made it to Kumbh Mela.

Act 2:
Maharishi and Mia

Now we welcome to our stage…the lovely Mia Farrow! When Maharishi and the Farrow sisters flew to India from the US, at their stopover at a beach hotel in Bombay, Maharishi initiated Mia into TM. As a new meditator, Mia was not practicing marathon meditations like others at the ashram. She often wandered off to read by the Ganges or shop in Rishikesh. Concerned for her safety, Maharishi sent a brahmacharya after her. Mia was simply "bored out of her skull," trying to occupy herself.[543] During one outing, she adopted a puppy and Maharishi named it Arjuna (after Lord Krishna's disciple).

Fed up with Maharishi's overly solicitous behavior, Mia threatened to leave. But he convinced her to go on safari with Nancy Jackson. Mia promised to return by February 9, her birthday.

Pass From a Puja

Upon Mia's return, Maharishi held an elaborate birthday celebration. Lavish flowers, pennants, and balloons festooned the hall. Maharishi directed Mia to sit cross-legged before him onstage. He placed a silver paper crown on her head. Every student presented a gift, furnished by Maharishi. Smiling on cue, Mia accepted each trinket, billing and cooing in her baby-like voice and wide-eyed expression, exclaiming variations on the theme of "Oh wow! Just look at that!" A decorated candlelit carrot sheet cake appeared, and fireworks brightened the sky. Maharishi's devotees felt Mia had been granted a great honor.

Mia's birthday celebration. © Colin Harrison-Avico Ltd.

Later that night, Mia vented uncensored, hostile feelings during her private after-party: "I'm so fucking mad! Have you ever seen anything like it? I felt like an idiot up on that stage, with everyone bowing down to me!" She demanded a ride to Delhi from her safari guide, Avi Kohli: "When you leave tomorrow, I'm going with you. That is final." She raised a glass of champagne. "To the last night in this holy place. Hah. That's a laugh. Maharishi's no saint. He made a pass at me when I was over at his house before dinner."[544]

The shocked Nancy Jackson asked how she could say such a thing. Mia insisted, "Look, I'm no fucking dumbbell. I know a pass when I see one." Confronted by incredulous onlookers, Mia laughed with contempt. "He asked me down into his private puja room, saying he would perform a birthday puja for me. Big deal. But what could I say?"[545]

She described how Maharishi made her kneel on a small carpet, performed the ceremony, and placed a flower garland around her neck. Then he made the pass. When asked what he did, Mia replied, "He started to stroke my hair." The listeners tried to convince Mia it was a blessing and she had misconstrued his intentions. But Mia insisted, "Listen, I know a pass from a puja."[546]

 Scan this code to watch a video of Maharishi performing the puja ceremony.

Group photo in Rishikesh: Top row l. to r.: Walter Koch, Maharishi, Benjamin Lange, Dr. Ute Otter. Bottom row l. to r.: Mia Farrow holding puppy Arjuna, Gerd Hegendörfer, Georg Meier-Siems. © Colin Harrison-Avico Ltd.

The following morning, during a group photograph, Maharishi placed Mia front and center, wearing her silver crown. Still infuriated over Maharishi's behavior, Mia feigned a happy face and promised to return after traveling with her brother John Charles Villiers-Farrow to Kathmandu and Goa, where a colony of European hippies camped out.[547]

Nancy hoped Mia would not return.[548]

Mia's Return

On February 27, Maharishi sent Nancy Jackson to pick up Mia and her brother John at New Delhi airport. Mia returned with rekindled enthusiasm. She began meditating six hours a day and exclaimed, "Good to be back, believe me."[549] All smiles, she seemed to overlook Maharishi's previous indiscretion.

Because of her role in the movie *Secret Ceremony* with Elizabeth Taylor, Mia left the ashram on March 7. She told Maharishi, "I hate to leave you and all this knowledge, but I will be back to join you in Kashmir."[550]

Upon Mia's arrival in England, she told the press, "It's been the most rewarding experience of my life." She explained how meditation "helps your general well-being because you go right to the source of thought, the source of creativity, the source of happiness."[551]

When asked by a reporter whether she was "absolutely happy in your own mind that you're not being conned," she nodded and replied, "Yes."[552]

At the time, the prevailing belief was that The Beatles left Rishikesh because of Maharishi's advances towards Mia Farrow. Pattie Boyd recounted that Mia told John Lennon about Maharishi's inappropriate behavior.[553] However, this did not cause The Beatles' departure, since John and George stayed in Rishikesh until April 10, more than one month after Mia left.

Mia's Memoir

In her 1997 memoir, Mia described that Maharishi said, "Now we will meditate in my cave." They meditated twenty minutes before a flowered, sandalwood-scented shrine to Guru Dev in his basement. After they stood up, she recalled, "I was blinking at his beard when suddenly I became aware of two surprisingly male, hairy arms going around me."[554] She panicked and bolted up the stairs, apologizing as she went.

Mia raced to her sister Prudence, who responded, "It's an honor to be touched by a holy man after meditation, a tradition." But Mia quickly packed some essentials and rushed out the ashram gates—frightened when Maharishi's brahmacharyas followed her. [555]

Ned Wynn was the son of film actor Keenan Wynn, grandson of comedic actor Ed Wynn, and a childhood friend of Mia. After I first got involved with TM, Ned became my lover. Years later, we both served on Maharishi's staff.

Ned was one of Maharishi's "skin-boys." These doorkeepers/personal assistants spent every waking moment with the guru and lived in the room next to him. They carried Maharishi's deerskin and placed it wherever he would sit. At any given time, two skin-boys took shifts guarding his door, greeting visitors, screening phone calls, and doing Maharishi's bidding on three to four hours' sleep per night.

In the early 1970s, Mia told Ned Wynn and Nini White Winquist (another of my close friends) that Maharishi clearly wanted her to lie down and have sex with him. Ned did not believe Mia at first, but then, as he described in his memoir, *We Will Always Live in Beverly Hills*, "The former Mrs. Frank Sinatra turns to me. 'Ned,' she says with great patience, 'don't you think I know when a man wants to fuck me?'"[556]

Act 3:
Not-So-Magic Alex

Enter stage right, Johan Alexis "Magic Alex" Mardas, who shared a flat with Marianne Faithfull's estranged husband, Indica Art Gallery proprietor John Dunbar. On an acid trip in 1966, Dunbar introduced John Lennon to the Greek ersatz-inventor Alexis, who possessed Marconi's and Edison's genius combined. He told them so himself.

Impossible Inventions

After John introduced Alexis to his Beatle-mates as "my new guru 'Magic Alex,'" the Greek seemed to surgically attach himself to John's hip.[557] Alarmed at his Svengali-like influence over her husband, Cynthia declared that Alexis "made her skin crawl."[558]

Paul McCartney contended that to wheedle his way into position as head of Apple Electronics, "Magic Alex" convinced The Beatles he could invent wallpaper doubling as stereo speakers, car enamel changing colors with a switch, an anti-gravity levitating recording studio that dampens vibrations, and dozens more gadgets.[559] Alexis's harebrained schemes included drilling The Beatles' skulls at their foreheads ("trepanation") to open their third eye and "get cosmic" instantly.[560]

Dazzled by the Greek's self-professed genius, John tied a bow around his priceless Italian Iso sportscar for Alexis's birthday. In turn, Alexis gave John a "Nothing Box" with eight Christmas lights that blinked on and off until they blinked out.[561] John gazed at it for hours (until the LSD wore off). The Greek did not originate it, though he claimed to. The *New Yorker* reported that a retired engineer invented the box to amuse his wife. She brought it to the president of Hammacher Schlemmer, who released it for the 1962 Christmas season. Dwight Eisenhower even bought one.[562]

Magic Alex Makes the Money Vanish

Perhaps Magic Alex's greatest prestidigitation involved casting his spell on The Beatles to back his flights of fancy. At his workshop, 34 Boston Place, Marylebone, Alexis wasted an estimated £300,000 in Apple funds dreaming up "inventions." Of one hundred filings by EMI's patent attorneys for Alexis, every one was declined as previously submitted.[563]

Alexis in his workshop with picture of Hindu goddess Durga on the wall. Sampson/ANL/Shutterstock.

Alexis urged Apple Corps Ltd. to purchase enormous computers from British Aerospace at £20,000 each, but no one could decipher how they worked or what they did.[564] They became mouse nests in Ringo's barn.[565] Alexis asked for engines from George's Ferrari Berlinetta and John's Rolls Royce to build a flying saucer.[566] They nearly agreed to the mad scheme.

Alexis assembled the Apple Corps' recording studio at 3 Savile Row, termed by George "the biggest disaster of all time."[567] When The Beatles tried a take, the playback consisted of hum and hiss. All the equipment was sold for scrap.

When it came to Alexis, George characterized The Beatles as "naïve to the teeth" and "daft buggers." Alexis would "pick up on the latest inventions, show them to us, and we'd think he'd invented them."[568] Paul McCartney and George Martin figured Alexis had a subscription to *Popular Science*, so he wowed them with common knowledge.[569] John summed it up: "And then I brought in Magic Alex and it just went from bad to worse."[570] By summer 1969, with Apple Corps hemorrhaging money at an alarming rate, Beatles manager Allen Klein shut down Apple electronics.

Reality check—Alexis was a TV repairman.

Act 4

The Beatles Disappear by Magic

The curtain opens on the next act: Magic Alex arrives in Rishikesh and performs his vanishing trick. He makes everyone disappear. The Greek landed at the ashram five weeks after The Beatles, on March 27, 1968. When he left on April 10, John and George left with him.

In August 1967, Alexis told The Beatles that he knew all about TM and had attended Maharishi's lecture at the University of Athens several years before.[571] Maharishi did visit Greece in 1961, when he was interviewed by BBC television at the Acropolis.[572] [573]

In December 1967, Alexis confronted Maharishi when meeting him at the UNICEF Variety Gala in Paris with John, George, and Pete Shotton (see page 229): "I know I've met you. Only you didn't call yourself Maharishi then. You were traveling under another name, doing something completely different." Maharishi replied that he had never visited Greece. Afterwards, Alexis told John, "I'm positive I've met him. He's not what you think he is. He's just an ordinary hustler—only in it for the money."[574]

In 1968, Pattie's sister Jenny Boyd had been sharing a flat with Alexis in Pimlico, Westminster, London. The night before the Beatles left for India, John visited the flat, where Alexis urged John to cancel his trip. Jenny figured Alexis was "jealous of John's trust and loyalty to Maharishi."[575]

Alexis claimed John summoned him to Rishikesh to build an apparatus the size of a trash can lid that would power a radio station to broadcast Maharishi's message worldwide—plus provide electricity to the entire region. This improbable device would consist of electronic parts from the Rishikesh RadioShack (as if such thing existed in 1968 rural India—or even today). Jenny believed Alexis came to Rishikesh "because he didn't approve of The Beatles' meditating, and he wanted John back."[576]

Alexis and Rosalyn

Alexis described the ashram students as "second-rate American actresses," "mentally ill Swedish old ladies who had left their money to Maharishi, and a bunch of lost, pretty girls."[577] [578] Yet he had no qualms about taking up with the prettiest—a shorthaired blond schoolteacher from Brooklyn in her late twenties, Rosalyn Bonas, who resembled actresses Jean Seberg and Mia Farrow.

At The Beatles' quarters in Rishikesh: Back row l. to r.: Sarah Sadowski, Jenny Boyd, Donovan Leitch, Wendy Winkler, Joe Lysowski. Front row l. to r.: Edna Linnell, Rosalyn Bonas, John Lennon, Sundar Singh, Mike Dolan. © BeatlesPhotos.de.

Rosalyn learned TM one year before traveling to India. At that time, there was only one TM Initiator in New York City, Dr. Harold Bloomfield, with nowhere to teach. So she volunteered her apartment in Brooklyn as a TM Center.

Rosalyn wanted to take the Teacher Training Course to become a better schoolteacher, spread TM to the world, and get near Maharishi to absorb his vibrations. She felt her meditations had deepened after meeting him at his lecture in New York. In order to finance the trip to Rishikesh, Rosalyn sold her baby grand piano. She flew to India on the plane with Maharishi, Mia, and Prudence.

Hollywood film and television actor Tom Simcox, who was also at the ashram, had an affair with Rosalyn during the summer of 1967, while they were studying at the TM Center in Westwood, California. Their relationship reignited briefly in Rishikesh, until Tom decided to focus solely on meditation.[579]

Mike Dolan, Rosalyn's next-door neighbor at the ashram, described her: "perkily attractive, very funny, and at times combative. She would interrupt Maharishi with pointedly uncosmic questions during his lectures."[580] Maharishi told Rosalyn to socialize less and meditate more, and then after long meditation, socializing would be more enjoyable. Rosalyn found Maharishi's advice was true. She dedicated herself to her practice. Then, after emerging from long meditation, she felt more alive and in touch with things around her. She looked and felt more radiant.[581]

Maharishi claimed TM was a relaxation technique and not religious. But Mike Dolan said, "It seemed to hit [Rosalyn] all of a sudden that this technique was more of a greater Hindu tradition than she expected. I believe she felt deceived by the movement."[582] As a result, Rosalyn was still friendly, but she became increasingly hostile towards meditation. She stopped attending Maharishi's lectures and wanted to go home. Tom Simcox also affirmed her discontent. She turned to him increasingly for emotional support, and also wrote her father about how unhappy she was. She told Tom she was losing her enthusiasm for meditation and felt depressed and homesick.

But Rosalyn later denied that: "I believed every word Maharishi said, and I was determined to make a difference in the world by teaching his meditation. I might have missed a few lectures because I found Alex an interesting character, but other than that I was a devoted student meditating several days at a time, taping every lecture sitting at the feet of Maharishi, studying and reading daily."[583]

Tom saw how starstruck Rosalyn was over Alexis and warned her to not get involved with him. Rosalyn replied that Alexis was "very nice," "really into meditation," "knows all about" tantra, and they had been practicing tantric yoga and then meditating with a black candle.[584]

Tom recalled, "She was getting into a more sexual type of meditation. She started talking to me about [tantra], and I told her I thought it was strange." When she laughed and said, "Oh, it's just a bit of fun," Tom cautioned, "You should stay away from that, Rosalyn. That's on the other side."[585]

Mike Dolan said he overheard Alexis and Rosalyn next door, practicing the Kama Sutra late at night. Whiffs of a distinct herb wafted from her room, and bottles of fermented brews came and went.[586] Beatles manager Peter Brown said Alexis was smuggling wine into the ashram and drinking with Cynthia, Pattie, and some Americans. John and George did not partake.

However, Rosalyn later said no happy weed was allowed or smoked at the ashram.

Maharishi's assistant Brahmachari Raghvendra told Mike the couple's behavior was causing a rift in the ashram's tranquility, and Rosalyn would be asked to leave. Mike reported that the night before The Beatles left, a messenger arrived at Rosalyn's door to take her to Maharishi's bungalow.[587] Rosalyn simply affirmed, "I left the ashram the day after I was totally disillusioned with my guru."[588]

In early April, Alexis told John Lennon that Rosalyn [whom Maharishi nicknamed 'Rose'] had visited Maharishi's bungalow for private counseling, and the guru made sexual advances. Alexis accused Maharishi of being a phony sexual predator and a secret proponent of black magic. John dismissed the allegations, demanding to hear it straight from Rosalyn. After she confirmed the story, Alexis proposed that John and George hide in the bushes and spy the next time Rosalyn would return to Maharishi's bungalow. However, John refused the plan as childish behavior and beneath him.[589]

Pattie reported, "We stayed on but the next night I had a horrid dream about Maharishi, and when George woke me the next morning, I said, 'Come on, we're leaving.'"[590]

Pattie's sister Jenny recalled, "It was all very sudden. Alex's companion [Rosalyn] alleged that Maharishi had made an inappropriate advance. When Pattie told George she'd had a dream that night depicting Maharishi in the same light, it confirmed their decision."[591]

What Happened Behind the Curtain

One of Maharishi's skin-boys gave me this statement:

"When Maharishi was presenting a lecture in New York, he invited Rosalyn to the course in Rishikesh. Rosalyn was unaware of his hidden agenda. She was simply intent on becoming a TM Initiator.

"One night in Rishikesh, Maharishi sent a brahmacharya to Rosalyn's room at about 9:30 p.m. She told him it was too late and she wanted to go to bed. The brahmacharya insisted she get dressed and come to Maharishi's house. When she arrived, Maharishi took her downstairs to his basement cave, where they meditated together for twenty minutes. Then he took her up to his bedroom. He started hugging her, and she could feel his erection. Maharishi sat on his bed and patted the bed for her to come over and get in. Rosalyn got the impression that Maharishi did this a lot. She totally freaked out and told him she had to go say goodnight to a friend. She ran out of his house. Maharishi told her to come back later and he would leave the door open.

"After this, Rosalyn no longer felt comfortable on the course because Maharishi was on the make for her. She told Alexis what had happened, and he told John and George."

Fact, Fiction, or Fate

In 2010, Alexis Mardas reported to *The New York Times* that, "After I had arrived at the retreat, we were attending a lecture given by Maharishi. Also present was an American teacher, whose name I now know to have been Rosalyn Bonas. I remember Maharishi saying this lady had an 'iceberg' in her brain and was unable to understand what he was saying. In the presence of everyone there, he told her that she should come to his villa after the lecture for private tuition."[592]

Alexis further reported that one or two days after that lecture, Rosalyn told Alexis and John that Maharishi had made sexual advances and invited her to return. Alexis also alleged that the following night John, George, and Alexis hid outside Maharishi's bungalow, where they spied Maharishi trying to hug Rosalyn (both fully clothed) and were very upset by what they saw.[593] However, if Alexis ever hid near the bungalow, he was there alone, since John and George refused to participate.

On the night of April 9 into 10, Alexis spent hours debating with the Beatles about the allegations. George did not believe it and was furious. But Alexis swore it was true and insisted they leave immediately. Finally, when George started to believe Alexis, John thought, *Well, it must be true; because if George started thinking it might be true, there must be something in it.*[594]

In the wee hours of the morning of April 10, Cynthia, clearly distressed, knocked on Tom's door and woke him. She said John insisted they all leave, and she implored Tom to try to change John's mind. When Tom suggested to John they go talk with Maharishi, John glared at Tom and retorted, "Cynthia was alone with [Maharishi] many times, you know. How would you feel if your wife was alone with him, and you knew he'd hit on some of the other girls? Let's get the fuck out of here!"[595]

Pattie Boyd, who felt John was seeking an excuse to return to Yoko Ono, said, "John threw a hissy fit" when he discovered Maharishi had behaved improperly. Alexis seemed convinced Maharishi was evil and wanted to get John away from Rishikesh. He kept repeating, "It's black magic."[596]

Later, when Maharishi's SRM organization president Charlie Lutes heard about sexual allegations contributing to The Beatles' sudden departure, he confronted Maharishi, who replied, "But Charlie, I am a lifetime celibate; I don't know anything about sensual desires."[597]

Act 5:
The Film Deal Goes South

Now, as he comes onstage, let us greet Charles F. Lutes, whom John Lennon dubbed "Captain Kundalini." Magic Alex had sewn seeds for The Beatles' departure, but these seeds did not sprout until a film deal imploded, via the Captain. (See Charlie's photo on pages 148, 229, and 287.)

During The Beatles' stay in Rishikesh, Maharishi promised exclusive rights for The Beatles' Apple Corps Ltd. to produce a film about the TM Movement and about Maharishi's guru, Swami Brahmananda Saraswati. The movie would star Maharishi, The Beatles, and Mia Farrow. Mia's brother John would be the director. (See John Farrow's photo on pages 267 and 315.)

Apple Film Project

In late March, Neil Aspinall (manager, Apple Corps) and Denis O'Dell (producer, *A Hard Day's Night*) arrived in Rishikesh to negotiate the film contract. However, Aspinall's agenda was to thwart the project, since the Fabs were under contract with United Artists for a third film (the first two being *A Hard Day's Night* and *Help!*).

During the meeting in Maharishi's bungalow, Aspinall realized this little holy man in white robes started haggling about his 2.5 percent. *Wait a minute*, Neil thought, *Maharishi knows more about making deals than I do.*[598]

Denis O'Dell had his own agenda—to produce *The Lord of the Rings*, starring The Beatles. United Artists was onboard with making the film, but J.R.R. Tolkien did not trust four acidheads to adapt his life's work. Ultimately, the United Artists commitment was met by *Yellow Submarine*—but not before the film rights promised by Maharishi to The Beatles went south.

Paul Goes Home

On March 23, Aspinall left India, along with Paul McCartney and Jane Asher, and after a stop in Tehran, the couple arrived in London on March 26, in time for Jane's theatrical commitment. Paul had resolved to stay in Rishikesh only a month and was anxious to return to Apple Corps. When he left, Paul thanked Maharishi and said his stay at the ashram had changed him for the better in ways he had not anticipated or thought possible:[599] "Maharishi, you will never fathom what these days have meant to us. To have the unbroken peace and quiet and all your loving attention—only a Beatle could know the value of this. You protected us from the press and all outsiders. This has been the ultimate luxury. We will never forget you."[600]

When a reporter asked Paul if he felt better after five weeks of meditation, he answered, "I feel a lot better. The meditation is great. You sit down. You relax, and then you repeat a sound to yourself. It's just a system of relaxation. We meditated about five hours a day in all. The rest of the time, we slept, ate, sunbathed, and had fun."[601]

Paul and Jane in Rishikesh. © Colin Harrison-Avico Ltd.

John and George, the two remaining Beatles, suggested to Maharishi a musical event in New Delhi with sitarist Ravi Shankar, Donovan, and The Beach Boys. On March 27, Joe Massot, director of *Wonderwall*, arrived at the ashram after George invited him to film in Rishikesh. Then John and George cabled Neil Aspinall to return to Rishikesh with a crew and equipment to start shooting the Apple Corps film.

However, Maharishi had already granted those film rights to someone else!

Captain Kundalini's Film

Knowing that Maharishi had agreed to a prior contract, Nancy Jackson cabled Charles F. Lutes, president of Maharishi's Spiritual Regeneration Movement (SRM), in Los Angeles: "Charlie, a film deal with The Beatles' Apple Films is on the table right now."[602]

Nancy then reminded Maharishi that in August 1967, Charlie Lutes had granted permission to meditator and filmmaker Alan

Waite to film Maharishi and The Beatles in Rishikesh (without The Beatles' consent). David Charnay of Four Star Productions of Hollywood contracted those rights, brokered by Paul Horn. Despite obvious legal conflicts of interest, Maharishi paid no mind and declared, "If Charlie has a contract, then they can all work together for the glory of Guru Dev. There will be enough work for all."[603] Nancy warned Maharishi that contracts did not work that way.[604]

On April 3, 1968, Charlie Lutes arrived in Rishikesh with a Four Star Productions lawyer and a signed contract—granting exclusive rights to film Maharishi for the next five years! The short-sighted Charlie failed to perceive that a movie produced by The Beatles (the biggest act since Moses parted the Red Sea) might have just a tad more potential to help Maharishi's mission than Charlie's "Bliss Productions."

Maharishi walking with leaders of his US organization; l. to r.: Charlie Lutes carrying the deerskin, Debby Jarvis, Jerry Jarvis, Maharishi, unknown. Keystone Press/ Alamy Stock Photo.

The two conflicting film deals reflected the schism in the TM Movement. One camp was Charlie Lute's old guard SRM, straight-laced mature meditators who had supported Maharishi since the beginning. With the advent of The Beatles, SRMers were pushed aside for the other camp—Jerry Jarvis's fledgling SIMS organization of hippies and college students.

Perhaps Charlie felt like the jilted lover. He wanted Maharishi back, his SRM organization back, The Beatles and their dirty hippie fans out, and his own movie made. After Charlie arrived, endless meetings began. Heated verbal exchanges collided as warring factions argued far into the night.

Four Star Crew Arrives

In early April, Gene Corman, executive producer of Charlie's Four Star film, finally arrived in Rishikesh and met with Maharishi, John, George, and *Wonderwall* director Joe Massot. Corman's film crew was waiting in Delhi with director Earl Barton (a choreographer/producer who had never made a film) and a highly respected cameraman, Néstor Almendros. Realizing Almendros had been hired, Massot figured he was cut out of the deal. He took the only taxicab available back to New Delhi and checked into the Hotel Oberoi.[605]

Then the Four Star advance film crew arrived at the ashram. At dawn, the bed-headed, bleary-eyed, half-asleep Lennon opened the door of his bungalow. In the courtyard before him, a cameraman pointed a camera at him, and a director yelled "Action."[606] John and George were furious. In this bizarre turn of events, the Beatles had become unwitting two-bit players in Charlie's "Bliss Productions" Four Star film. The irate Beatles avoided the lecture hall, installed with lights and cameras, and refused to leave their rooms.

Using The Beatles?

Once the film crew arrived, John and George suspected Maharishi had been exploiting The Beatles for publicity, starting with the 1967 reissue of the LP record, *Maharishi Mahesh Yogi: The Master Speaks*, on World Pacific Records (founded in 1958 by TM meditators John Siamas and Richard Bock). The record sleeve displayed the guru's photo. The reverse showed a psychedelic op-art photo of roses and the following words, never authorized by The Beatles: "Maharishi Mahesh Yogi, The Beatles' spiritual teacher, speaks to the youth of the world on Love and the untapped source of Power that lies within."

Maharishi also repeatedly promised ABC network that The Beatles would appear with him on a television special. Peter Brown (an Apple Corps founder and board member) told ABC this would not happen and told Maharishi to quit making that promise. This did not deter the yogi, however. He simply reconfirmed The Beatles' appearance with ABC.

Paul, Maharishi, and George in Falsterbo, Sweden. © Ewa Säfwenberg.

Finally, on October 14, 1967, Peter Brown and Denis O'Dell traveled to Sweden with Paul and George to confront Maharishi in Falsterbo, a seaside resort near Malmö. After the Beatles asked Maharishi to stop, the guru backed off. However, when they insisted that he quit using The Beatles for self-promotion, he simply giggled. Afterwards, George defended Maharishi, saying he was "not a modern man and just doesn't understand these things."[607]

Before The Beatles arrived in Rishikesh, Maharishi had sent a telegram to the Prime Minister of India, Indira Gandhi. He asked that she invite The Beatles to her residence upon their arrival, and, without asking The Beatles' permission, Maharishi claimed a documentary film would be made for worldwide release.

Maharishi's draft of a telegram sent to Indira Gandhi. © Judith Bourque.

When The Beatles were asked to deposit 10 to 25 percent of their income into a Swiss bank account to benefit Maharishi's organization, Mal Evans noted John Lennon's reaction: "Over my dead body."[608] However, Peter Brown said John did not oppose paying the tithe until Alexis intervened. When Maharishi was ridiculed as "Veririchi Lotsamoney Yogi Bear," John defended him: "So what if he's commercial? We're the most commercial group in the world!"[609]

But later Cynthia Lennon said John "had begun to feel disenchanted with Maharishi's behavior. He felt that, for a spiritual man, Maharishi had too much interest in public recognition, celebrities and money."[610]

However, when Nancy Jackson asked Maharishi how much The Beatles were paying to take the Rishikesh course, he replied, "Nothing. Just by being meditators they will bring the world to us. In their own way they will repay for all this happiness they are now experiencing."[611]

Mike Dolan said when the Four Star film crew arrived, John and George "were more than a little pissed"[612] and made a point of staying out of sight. Paul Horn and Nancy Jackson believed the Four Star deal and appearance of the film crew incited John and George's premature departure from Rishikesh.[613]

Contentious Conclave

Early morning April 10, Alan Waite and Paul Horn were discussing the Four Star film with Maharishi in his meeting room. When John and George appeared, Maharishi took them into his adjacent bedroom. Twenty minutes later, the Beatles reemerged, moody and quiet. They shook hands with Waite and Horn, and said, "Nice to have met you guys! See you another time." Then walked off to get in their taxicabs.[614]

According to John and George, here is how the meeting went:
John announced to Maharishi, "We're leaving."
Maharishi asked, "Why?"

George, who had already made a commitment to make a documentary film titled *Raga* with sitarist Ravi Shankar in Madras (now Chennai), said, "Look, I told you I was going. I'm going to the South of India."[615]

Maharishi, not buying George's explanation, asked, "What's wrong?"

Since Charlie Lutes often told stories about Maharishi's miracles, John responded sarcastically: "Well, if you're so cosmic, you'll know why."[616]

Maharishi responded, "I don't know why. You must tell me."[617]

John answered, "Well, you're supposed to be the mystic. You should know."[618]

Then Maharishi shot John an intense, piercing glare. John described, "He gave me a look like, 'I'll kill you, you bastard,' and he gave me such a look. I knew then. I had called his bluff and I was a bit rough to him."[619] Maharishi then told the Beatles the truth was like an iceberg with only 10 percent visible.

John considered Maharishi's scorching look to be an epiphany. Yet Maharishi never claimed to be a mind reader or to possess supernormal powers. When John described this incident to Jann Wenner of *Rolling Stone*, Yoko Ono commented, "You expected too much from him."

John reacted, "I always do, I always expect too much. I was always expecting my mother and never got her. Or some parent."[620]

Alexis had his own version of the incident. He said that when John asked Maharishi to explain himself, the guru replied, "I am only human."[621] John returned to his bungalow. In defiance, he ripped his poster of Maharishi in half and tossed it, face down, onto the cement floor.

Alexis urged the group to leave immediately, warning Maharishi might curse them with black magic. Since pilgrims traveling to and from the nearby Kumbh Mela festival had engaged all available taxis, Alexis scrambled to find taxis in Dehradun to speed the group to the airport before The Beatles could change their minds.

Dismal Departure

With jangled nerves, the distraught Beatles entourage ate breakfast in whispers, surrounded by a ghostly mist blanketing the early morning air, while faint chants of mantras and a tinkling of bells wafted across the river from the Sivananda ashram on the far riverbank.

John took out vengeance by writing a song: "Maharishi, you little twat. Who the fuck do you think you are? Who the fuck do you think you are? Oh, you cunt."[622] When George complained the lyrics were ridiculous, John changed them. The sexy sadhu known as "Sexy Sadie" was born and christened by George. She became the seductress.[623]

John said he wrote the song while waiting for taxis that never seemed to arrive: "We thought: *They're deliberately keeping the taxi back so as we can't escape from this madman's camp.* And we had the mad Greek with us who was paranoid as hell. He kept saying, 'It's black magic, black magic. They're gonna keep you here forever.'"[624]

Maharishi's robed form, clouded by fog, emerged like a specter from the gloom, seating itself silently about one hundred yards from the dining area. Jerry Jarvis approached the Beatles and pleaded on behalf of the guru "to talk things over properly." He said that Maharishi is "very sad and wants desperately to put things right."[625]

The Beatles denied his request. Instead, John, Cynthia, George, Pattie, Jenny, Rosalyn, Alexis, and Tom filed past Maharishi to the taxis without making a sound. Maharishi called out to them, "Why are you leaving? Don't go. Wait! Please talk to me!"[626]

Cynthia said, "It was so sad. Maharishi was sitting alone in a small shelter made of wood with a dried grass roof. He looked very biblical and isolated in his faith. To me he was a man with a quest, a dream for a better world and here were we, a group of people who had the power to influence the youth of the world, possibly squashing all the good work he had done."[627] "I felt ashamed that we had turned our backs on him without giving him a chance. Once John was running away, I had little choice but to run with him."[628]

Final Farewell

As George was loading his taxi, Nancy Jackson and her son Rik appeared. George told Nancy they were just in time for a fast farewell. Nancy said, "What do you mean? Where are you going?"

Pattie Boyd, teary-eyed and distressed, joined George and said, "We have to leave because of a misunderstanding."

Nancy responded, "But only a few nights ago we were discussing your plans for making the movie of Maharishi's life. You had definitely decided to go to Kashmir with the group and finish the course. Will you still meet us there?"

Then John, angry as hell, walked up: "We're not going to join Maharishi there or anywhere—we've 'ad it. If you want to know why, ask your fuckin' precious guru!" His face was tight and eyes full of fury. He yelled, "Cyn, get your ass out here! I want to get out of this bloody place *now*, for Christ sakes!"

The befuddled Nancy asked Pattie and Cynthia, "What has happened? You were all fine this morning. Does Maharishi know you're leaving?"

John then snapped, "Does he know we're leaving? That's the laugh of the day!"

Cynthia spoke with anguish as she was hustled into the taxi after Pattie: "We are so unhappy. I can't explain what happened. It is all a big mistake, but the boys insist on leaving."[629] With a final farewell from Nancy and Rik, The Beatles' entourage vanished in a cloud of Himalayan dust.

Grieving Guru

After watching the taxis depart, Nancy visited Maharishi in his bungalow. Appearing sad and defeated, he mentioned celebrities' fragile nervous systems and icebergs coming to the surface. He suggested they not talk about negative things.[630]

Mike Dolan told me, "What has never been reported was the dramatic effect that The Beatles leaving had on Maharishi. His brilliant, beautiful yogic radiance was reduced to grey and ashen. He became physically sick when the course moved to Kashmir on Dal Lake."

At the end of the course, each graduate met privately with Maharishi to be made an Initiator. Mike described that Maharishi "looked visibly frail and without that effervescence." During the interview, Maharishi asked Mike if he was from England. He answered, "Yes, from Liverpool."

Maharishi asked, "Do you know The Beatles?"

Mike answered, "Yes" (misunderstanding his meaning).

Maharishi then said, "When you see them, please ask them to come back to me."

Mike described: "It was so sad my eyes welled up, and I never spoke to Maharishi again."

Act 6:
Awkward Aftermath

The Beatles arrived in New Delhi after a harrowing journey. The Lennons' taxi got a flat tire, the driver abandoned them, and they were forced to hitchhike in the pitch-black wilds of rural India. They speculated Maharishi had put a curse on them.[631] John exclaimed, "God, Cyn. I won't feel safe until we're back in England."[632]

John and George were extremely bitter and disappointed. Their concern was what to say to the press. John asked the group, "Should we tell the world that The Beatles made a mistake? [Maharishi] isn't what's happening at all."[633] They were worried that if they told the story, it would reflect poorly on them, and they also did not want to disillusion fans who had relinquished drugs for meditation.[634] Ultimately, they decided to say nothing. John simply told reporters they had urgent business in London and did not want to appear in Maharishi's film.[635]

Repercussions of observing this policy of silence still echo today. In later years, eyewitnesses avoided embarrassing questions by agreeing with the official TM Movement's position; namely, that nothing happened. Even Mia Farrow, in her 1997 memoir, backpedaled, stating, "At my level of consciousness, if Jesus Christ Himself had embraced me, I would have misinterpreted it."[636]

Tom Simcox, riddled with guilt and feeling strangely responsible for what had happened, asked John and George to meet him in the Oberoi hotel lobby. Tom tried to convince them to return, talk with Maharishi, and find out what really happened: "This is going to destroy Maharishi."

John snapped back, "You know, you're crazy," and walked away with Alexis.

George then said, "It'll be alright," and asked Tom to wait for a few minutes until he got back. Shattered with emotion, Tom broke down in tears. Finally, George returned with his sitar and gave it to Tom, who started weeping again. George put his hand on Tom's shoulder and said, "Don't worry. You didn't do this. It'll be fine. We already are whatever it is we would like to be."[637]

The Beatles ran into Massot at the hotel. Then Corman arrived, declaring his film project was "dead as a doornail." He pleaded with Massot to persuade John and George to participate in the Four Star film. Massot retorted that Corman could always film the lepers. Afterwards, Massot and the Beatles howled with laughter.[638]

Alexis, insistent the Lennons fly to London immediately to avoid Maharishi's alleged black magic, booked the first plane out of New Delhi, where (ironically) John confessed to Cynthia his infidelities, saying "Do you know something, Cyn, you are really naïve!"[639] Incredibly, she never dreamed John had been unfaithful.

George, feeling betrayed and devastated, traveled south to Madras (now Chennai). He spent a couple of days in private with Ravi until he calmed down.[640] To ward off spells that George believed Maharishi had cast to cause him dysentery, Ravi Shankar gave George amulets and a puja ceremony of protection. George recovered.[641] Then George, Pattie, and Jenny toured around India with Ravi.

Paul Was Shocked—But Not About Maharishi

John stormed back to England, outraged that "Maharishi had tried to get off with one of the chicks"—the American Mia Farrow looka-like. When Paul asked what was wrong with that, John answered, "He's just a bloody old letch just like everybody else. What the fuck, we can't go following that!"[642]

Paul was shocked at John's righteous indignation. Paul expected a reaction more like, "Hey, we thought he was better than that." Paul felt John acted prudish and overreactive—even if they found Maharishi in bed, was that a justifiable reason to leave? Paul recalled, "It became public that we didn't like Maharishi, but I never felt that way."[643]

Paul argued with John, "But he never said he was a god. In fact very much the opposite, he said, 'Don't treat me like a god, I'm just a meditation teacher.'" Paul realized John had been seeking a god and found Maharishi was just a guy. Whereas Paul found a guy who said, "I'm only giving you a system of meditation." Paul believed, "There was no deal about 'you mustn't touch women,' was there? There was no vow of chastity involved."[644]

But Maharishi actually did claim to be a monk. He called himself *Bal Brahmachari* (life celibate) Mahesh Yogi, even on his passport (see page 144). Since Maharishi initiated several of my personal friends into brahmacharya vows, they branded him a hypocrite. They were required to maintain celibacy, while, as they said, "Mahesh was getting all the action."

Press Clippings

Soon after John and George bolted from Rishikesh, Maharishi diplomatically told the press, "The Beatles did extremely well in meditation. But they are not among the forty I have selected from the seventy devotees to graduate as guides."[645]

In May 1968, John declared on New York's PBS Channel 13 that The Beatles' association with Maharishi was a mistake, though meditation was not a mistake.[646] The same night, John stated on *The Tonight Show*, "We believe in meditation, but not Maharishi and his scene. Meditation is good and does what they say. It's like exercise or cleaning your teeth. It works."[647]

In June 1968, Paul declared, "We thought there was more to [Maharishi] than there was. He's human."[648]

In 1970, when asked by *Rolling Stone* about "Sexy Sadie," John replied: "That's about Maharishi, yes. Now it can be told, Fab Listeners. There was a big hullaballoo about him trying to rape Mia Farrow or somebody and trying to get off with a few other women."[649]

When reporters asked Maharishi about The Beatles' allegations, he replied, "I think I would love them, whatever they say." When asked why The Beatles would make such a statement, Maharishi replied, "I'm unaware, completely, why. I only extend my love to them."[650]

Despite the dramatic falling out between The Beatles and Maharishi, that did not dent the exponential growth of Maharishi's following, which continued a meteoric rise.

He's Cracked, You Know

Charlie Lutes said Alexis admitted to him in Rishikesh, "I came to India to get the boys out of India, away from Maharishi." When Charlie asked, "Why do you want to do this?" Alexis answered, "We don't want Maharishi to have this much control over the boys." However, Alexis told *The New York Times*, "Quite the contrary: I was pleased with the influence that Maharishi had over The Beatles, because he managed to wean them off drug addiction."[651]

Yet Beatles biographer Barry Miles wrote, "Alex had been introduced to the others as John's guru, and he could see his position was about to be usurped by Maharishi, particularly if John gave up drugs permanently."[652]

Jenny Boyd, who shared a flat (platonically) with "Magic Alex" in London in 1968, called him "Not very magic at all."[653]

John Lennon commented, "He was just another guy who comes and goes around people like us. He's cracked, you know."[654]

Act 7:
How Sexy Was Sadie?

Let us now peek behind Maharishi's proscenium curtain. I personally know fifteen women who have said Maharishi made sexual overtures towards them. Some liaisons lasted months or years. I have seen photos and videos of a woman asserted to be Maharishi's grown daughter, who bears an uncanny resemblance to him. Maharishi's doorkeepers often witnessed women coming and going from his private chambers early in the morning or late at night. They jokingly nicknamed the women "girlfriends," while unaware they actually *were* girlfriends. I have known these women and skin-boys since the late sixties or early seventies, and I was in Maharishi's inner circle when these encounters occurred. No, Maharishi never made a pass at me.

The Early Days

Maharishi began soliciting females long before meeting Mia Farrow. One of my closest friends in the TM organization described to me details of a highly inappropriate overture he made towards her in those early days.

Joyce Collin-Smith, author of *Call No Man Master*, was a personal assistant to Maharishi for many years in Britain, starting in 1960. She said, "When we first knew him, he ate little, slept little, wore little clothing against the cold, had few possessions. He did not touch us, we did not touch him. He was as unsexy as a young child."[655]

After The Beatles' rebuff became public, Joyce and others in his inner circle looked back at "when he first began locking his door in the afternoons, closeted alone with one young woman or another. We thought him to be giving 'special tuition' to chosen devotees—

we now realized something different. We saw something he had intended to conceal."[656]

Joyce believed that Maharishi psychically controlled The Beatles and sowed the seeds for Brian Epstein's death. She claimed that Brian, The Beatles' father figure, did not approve of Maharishi and was therefore a "decided nuisance." Brian's death removed the major obstacle to the guru's plans. After Brian died under what Joyce considered suspicious circumstances, Maharishi told The Beatles, "Now you will be able to come to India with me."[657]

Along with Mick Jagger, Marianne Faithfull was with Maharishi at the time of Epstein's death. She reported being "appalled" at his behavior: "It was a dreadful moment, and Maharishi acted so badly and inappropriately: 'There was a death in the family. There are many families. There is one family. Brian Epstein has moved on. He doesn't need you anymore, and you don't need him. He was like a father to you, but now he is gone and I am your father. I'll look after you all now.'"[658]

Maharishi spoke of The Beatles' departure from India this way: "They were too unstable, and they weren't prepared to end their Beatledom for meditation.[659] But as long as they go on meditating, they will be mine."[660]

Though Joyce's claims appear far-fetched, here is an anecdote I witnessed firsthand: M.P. Uniyal was a Vedic astrologer and Maharishi's close friend as teenagers. Uniyal's father had been the astrologer for Maharishi's guru: Swami Brahmananda Saraswati. I met Uniyal several times in his home at Monrovia, California, where he was practicing astrology in his later years. I was shocked when Uniyal confided to me that while they were in college, Maharishi asked Uniyal for a mantra by which he could control people. Uniyal told me he did impart that mantra to Maharishi.

"Gunilla"

Richard Blakely's memoir, *The Secret of the Mantras*, recalls his time in Rishikesh during The Beatles' stay. There, Richard fell in love with "Gunilla," a tall, slender, attractive Swede. (See photos of Richard on pages 148 and 315.) Gunilla's devotion to Maharishi was significantly more than Richard's, which made him uneasy. Early one morning, she excused herself to "go visit Maharishi and give him a flower." Upon her return, she recounted that she talked with Maharishi for an hour or more. Richard asked, "Just the two of you?"

Gunilla answered, "Ja, and it was so beautiful! I came away flying!"[661] But Richard suspected something else had happened.

On April 28, 1968, after the TM Teacher Training Course had moved to the Lodhi Hotel in New Delhi, course participants waited for private meetings with Maharishi to become TM Initiators. (See a photo of these students on page 315.) While eating breakfast with Geoffrey Baker and photographer Larry Kurland, Richard learned that Maharishi had been "fooling around with one of the girls on the course," and when Alexis told John that Maharishi made a pass at Rosalyn, The Beatles left in anger.[662]

Geoffrey, incensed by this accusation, marched away in a huff. Richard asked Larry, "What do you think?"

Larry shrugged and replied, "He's only human. He never said he was a god."

Richard asked, "So you think it's true?" Larry replied he was *sure* it was true because he had talked with Tom Simcox on April 10, the morning he and Rosalyn had fled the ashram along with The Beatles' entourage. Though Tom was no longer Rosalyn's boyfriend, he was still close with Rosalyn and Alexis, and was "really pissed."[663]

Richard then returned to his hotel room, where he finally approached Gunilla about her encounter with Maharishi in Rishikesh. She recounted reluctantly that because Maharishi had invited students to see him anytime, she visited him in early mornings, whenever the spirit moved her. Always happy to greet her, Maharishi would often send other guests away. Understanding and forgiving, he was like the father she had lost. But that morning was different.

The meeting began like any other. But after a long silence, Maharishi asked her to shut the door. Then he asked if she would do something for him. She agreed, and he asked her to take off her blouse. After a few seconds hesitation, she removed it and exposed her breasts, rationalizing she should never be ashamed of her body.

Maharishi laughed, waved his head side to side, and said, "You are so beautiful." Gunilla felt both excited and ashamed. He asked her to move closer, then closer. Then he reached out and jiggled her breasts back and forth. It was so strange and silly that she burst out laughing. Maharishi stopped, leaned back, declared he was tired, removed his shawl, and lay on his back. After a while, Gunilla put on her blouse, said goodbye, and left.[664]

Richard pitied Maharishi's inept attempts at seducing a woman, yet he worried the guru might try again. Sure enough, during Gunilla's private meeting to become an Initiator, Maharishi invited her to come to Rishikesh and stay with him.

Gunilla told Richard tearfully, "It was so awful! I could see he was embarrassed. I could tell what he was really asking me. He didn't have the nerve. He didn't dare say it right out because he's such a coward! Rikard, I don't want to sleep with a fat, 50-year-old man, even if he's the greatest guru in the world."[665]

In 2021 Richard confirmed: "I am certain that Maharishi groped Rosalyn in his bungalow (because she told me about it, in lurid detail), and he also did the same thing to the woman on the course that I was 'seeing' at the time, and eventually married [Gunilla]. All the time preaching celibacy to any men on the course who might invade his territory."

Linda Williams Pearce

On my TM Teacher Training Course in Rishikesh in early January 1970, a twenty-two-year-old British woman approached me unexpectedly with a confused, troubled look in her eyes. Linda Williams (later Linda Pearce) said something happened, she was freaked out, and she could not talk about it. Yet she blurted out that Maharishi had hugged her. Then she confessed, "But that wasn't all. We did a lot more than that."

In August 1981, Linda told UK journalist David Mertens that Maharishi seduced her while professing celibacy. "I was a virgin and knew nothing about sex. He said he loved me and that I was the only one. 'You make my life so good,' he told me. When I asked about his celibacy he said, 'There are exceptions to every rule.' He was a brilliant manipulator. I just couldn't see that he was a dirty old man. We made love regularly. At one stage I even thought I was pregnant by him. And I don't think I was the only girl."[666]

Strolling through the ashram in Rishikesh; l. to r. Maharishi's secretary Marguerite Causley, Maharishi, Linda Williams.

In January 1969, at her TM Teacher Training Course in Rishikesh, their sexual union began. She returned to India for Christmas 1969 and the liaison resumed for a couple of weeks. By then, she thought it was "wrong and immoral." But "Maharishi just laughed that off."[667]

At a TM retreat in Spain, Linda met her South African husband, Peter Pearce. But Linda recalled, "I really thought I was going mad. Maharishi still had a mental hold over me." Because Maharishi insisted celibacy was required for spiritual progress, Linda believed she must stay celibate. She could not stand being kissed or touched. When the couple traveled to Switzerland to ask Maharishi for help, "All he did was roar with laughter and tell me to go on more courses."[668]

Judith Bourque

Judith Bourque, whom I have known since 1970, shared her experience: "From 1970 to 1972 I was involved with the 'celibate' monk Maharishi Mahesh Yogi in an intimate love affair. He told me not to tell anyone. I waited until he passed to write my book *Robes of Silk, Feet of Clay*, which tells the story of my travels to India in the hopes of having a deeply spiritual experience. I had a very human one instead.

"I followed Maharishi around the world for two years, working as a member of his inner circle. In the beginning my intention was to be devoted to him for the rest of my life, living publicly as a kind of nun and then secretly as a lover/wife. Two things changed my mind: firstly, the realization that he was meeting with other young Western women, and secondly the insight that I had become highly dependent upon his moods and the way he treated me. Today I am infinitely grateful that I had that insight. Had I remained in the TM Movement, I would have led a miserable life.

"It has always disturbed me that Mia Farrow's description of Maharishi making a pass at her in Rishikesh has been ridiculed and denied both in the media and in internet gossip, once even by Beatle George himself (but never by John). Equally upsetting has been the portrayal of another young American woman linked to The Beatles and 'Magic Alex.' I have met this woman personally and she has told me her story many times. Due to my own experiences with Maharishi, I believe she is absolutely telling the truth about what happened in Maharishi's bungalow so many years ago.

Judith Bourque and Maharishi at the ashram in Rishikesh. © Judith Bourque.

"Susan Shumsky accurately uses the word 'convoluted' to describe all of the theories, stories, and gossip surrounding The Beatles' departure from Rishikesh. There is a reason it's all such a mess: personal and organizational agendas. The TM Movement, for example, is highly protective of their guru's image as a celibate monk, and has thousands of active devotees who comment, compose and describe the 'truth' on social media and the internet in the way they want the rest of the world to see it. I know, because I have been called 'schizophrenic,' 'mentally out of balance,' and 'wacko' by TM leadership and devotees since I released my book in 2010.

"The continued attempts to discredit these women who have done nothing more than tell some friends or acquaintances about what happened to them at Maharishi's bungalow in Rishikesh is so out of date! Isn't it time to #MeToo this fifty-year-old past once and for all? I feel that there is only one person to blame for The Beatles leaving Rishikesh so abruptly and that is Maharishi Mahesh Yogi himself."

Ned Wynn

In the early 1970s, Mia Farrow revealed to Ned Wynn her story of Maharishi's inappropriate behavior. Judith Bourque and "Belinda," who both had liaisons with Maharishi, visited Ned in Santa Monica in the early 1970s. Ned recalled, "These girls told me (and Jane Goe, my former wife) the stories personally. 'Belinda' felt Maharishi used his power and his aura to take advantage of her. Once the blinders were off, she felt abused and cheated, as if she had been fucked while in a stupor. I was amazed by the distaste with which Belinda referred to her sex with Maharishi.[669]

"The girls were very explicit; there was no coy innuendo. They did not sound like women making anything up or embellishing on a look they got. There was no doubting anything they told me. They were not rumor mongering or trying to self-aggrandize. I made sure to ask whether they actually had complete sex. They said 'Yes,' though it was less than thrilling for Belinda."[670]

Maintaining the Mythos

The TM Movement's official position is Maharishi was a life celibate. TM devotees discard reports of Maharishi's dalliances as lies, dreams, or fantasies. The saddest case is a woman who told me she would literally fear for her life if she were to reveal her experience, even anonymously.

We who served on Maharishi's personal staff steadfastly believed his claim of life celibacy and followed his directive to remain celibate ourselves. Yet one time in Switzerland, Maharishi revealed to a small group of us staff members, "I thought I had to be a monk and live the lonely life. But I was wrong."

In 1969 on BBC, Maharishi declared to reporter Leslie Smith, "I had the idea that I must renounce the world in order to be really a spiritual man, a *yogi*. But, what I found out is that this spiritual life is not dependent on the renunciation of the world. It's only solely dependent on morning and evening practice of meditation."[671]

Act 8:
Requests for Reconciliation

John Lennon

John never saw Maharishi again. In December 1969, twenty months after John left India in a huff, Maharishi was meeting a handful of devotees, including one of my friends, in his bungalow in Rishikesh. Maharishi's secretary suddenly burst into the room and announced, "Maharishi, I have a very important telegram for you."

Maharishi replied, "Yes, who it is from?"

She said, "It's from John Lennon. He is in New Delhi, and he's asking if he can come and see you."

Maharishi looked at her and his response was, "Who?"

She replied, "John Lennon, Maharishi, who was one of The Beatles who were here."

Again, Maharishi asked, "Who?"

She replied, "Maharishi, it's John Lennon from The Beatles. He flew into Delhi, by himself, and he very much wants to come and see you."

Maharishi turned away from her, and declared, with derision: "I do not know a John Lennon."

George Harrison

One of Maharishi's skin-boys in Sweden and in Seelisberg, Switzerland, Conny Larsson, author of *The Beatles, Maharishi och jag* ("The Beatles, Maharishi and I"), told me that Maharishi rode roughshod over people for whom he no longer had use, including George Harrison. Conny acted as George's go-between with Maharishi in the mid-seventies.

Conny said the first time George phoned was late night in early autumn 1973 at the Külm Hotel (European headquarters of the TM Movement) in Seelisberg, Switzerland. Maharishi refused to speak with George but asked Conny why he called. Conny answered, "George wants to apologize for all the trouble The Beatles and the whole other bunch of people caused Maharishi and the TM organization." Maharishi motioned to Conny from his bed to just hang up the phone.

The second time George called, Maharishi asked Conny to tell George to come back after doing some *tapas* (austerities). Maharishi said to Conny, "Tell him we don't need him, tell him to meditate regularly for a year and then come back to me."[672]

Conny said that Maharishi "was not at all satisfied with learning that George had joined the Krishna organization. George wanted always to be forgiven for his actions and especially for the damage John Lennon had caused. Maharishi was stone hard, and there was never any talk between them. During my time [as Maharishi's skin-boy], George called him four times as I recalled. Maharishi's message was always the same: 'I don't need The Beatles. The TM organization is moving on, not looking back. Past is past.'"

When George offered repeatedly to serve Maharishi in any way he could, Maharishi would not accept his offers. Conny said, "George followed up and that call came much later when I was back on duty [in the late seventies]. Still Maharishi didn't talk to him. Later, after George being diagnosed with cancer, I came to know that [spiritual author] Deepak Chopra connected them and finally Maharishi gave in to talk to him."

Conny also attested to Maharishi's late-night escapades with his favorite women, to whom Conny delivered Maharishi's bedroom key. Conny said, "I was puzzled why I had to leave the key to them after massaging Maharishi's legs [due to poor circulation] around 3:00 or 4:30 every morning, instead of leaving it to John Gray, who was my co-secretary at the time." (John Gray, one of Maharishi's skin-boys, later wrote *Men Are from Mars, Women Are from Venus*.)

Deepak's Story

In the 1980s, Maharishi was grooming Deepak Chopra to become his successor, to spread TM and Ayurveda worldwide. In 1988, George Harrison attended a two-week yoga therapy program at Maharishi Ayurveda Health Center in Lancaster, Massachusetts, where Deepak was the director.[673] In 1993, Deepak had a falling-out with Maharishi and became persona non grata in the TM organization.

On February 15, 2006, Deepak reported to the *Times of India* that in September 1991, George asked Deepak to set up a private meeting with Maharishi. Deepak said they flew to Vlodrop, Netherlands, to meet the guru at his residence.

Deepak claimed that George first gave Maharishi a rose. This was followed by a long silence. Then Maharishi asked, "How have you been?"

George replied, "Some good things (have happened), some bad things." Then he added, "You must know about John being assassinated."

Maharishi replied, "I was very sorry to hear about it."

After some time, George said, "I came to apologize."

Maharishi asked, "For what?"

George replied, "You know for what."

Maharishi said, "Tell Deepak the real story."

George said, "I don't know about it 100 percent, but here's what I know transpired."

George then narrated that Maharishi asked The Beatles to leave Rishikesh because they were using drugs during the meditation course. But Maharishi refused to reveal this to the public because it would humiliate The Beatles.

The topic then turned to The Beatles' appearance on *The Ed Sullivan Show*, when it was reported no crime occurred in the US for that one hour. Maharishi told George and Deepak, "When I heard this, I knew The Beatles were angels on earth. They created such beautiful music for the world. It doesn't matter what John Lennon said or did, I could never be upset with angels."

On hearing that, George broke down and wept. There was another long silence. Then George told Maharishi, "I love you" and Maharishi responded, "I love you too."

After this meeting, George phoned Deepak and told him, "A huge karmic baggage has been lifted from me, because I didn't want to lie."[674]

In a second *Times of India* article published the same day, Deepak reported: "The Beatles—along with their entourage, which included Mia Farrow—were doing drugs, taking LSD, at Maharishi's ashram, and he lost his temper with them. He asked them to leave, and they did in a huff." Deepak continued, "I'm sure there was never any truth to John Lennon's allegations. In fact, the rumor was that Maharishi had misbehaved with Mia Farrow, but I met Mia years later at the airport while taking a flight to India, and she asked me to tell Maharishi that she still loved him."[675]

Mia Contradicts Deepak

In June 2006, four months after Deepak's report, Jeff Dawson interviewed Mia Farrow for *The Times Magazine*. Dawson said that on the meditation retreat, "relations with Maharishi soured when the yogi got a bit fresh with Farrow. The story was recently contradicted by self-styled guru Deepak Chopra, who claimed it was rather Maharishi who had evicted The Beatles for dropping acid in his ashram."

Mia became agitated and snapped back, "Deepak Chopra should talk about what he knows. *I* was there. There were no drugs at the ashram; those guys were not kicked out. Ringo left because of the flies [she laughs], I left for my own reasons, and the other guys left eventually because they just got bored. George stuck it pretty close to the end along with Prudence."[676]

Mia's "own reasons" that she left the ashram on March 7, 1968, were due to a film acting commitment in London. No mystery there. But her account did contradict Deepak's.

George and Paul Weigh In

In the *Beatles Anthology*, George stated there were nasty rumors and stories about how Maharishi was not on the level, but that was just jealousy: "I don't know what goes through these people's minds, but this whole piece of bullshit was invented. It's probably even in the history books that Maharishi 'tried to attack Mia Farrow'—but it's total bullshit. Just go and ask Mia Farrow. There were a lot of flakes there; the whole place was full of flaky people. Some of them were us."[677]

George said John wanted to leave anyway, so this situation gave him a good excuse to get out. "Now, historically, there's the story that something went on that shouldn't have done—but nothing did."[678]

Paul concurred, "I think George was right. It was Magic Alex who made the original accusation and I think that it was completely untrue."[679] "He didn't seem like the kind of guy who would [make a pass]. I've since wondered, 'How would a maharishi go about making a pass?' It's not so easy. I don't think any of that happened."[680]

These statements from Paul and George are characterized as proof that Maharishi never made a pass at anyone. But Mike Dolan, Rosalyn's next-door neighbor at the ashram, commented that, in the twentieth century, "there was a knee-jerk reaction to disbelieve the woman, to stab her with her own sexuality."[681] Even today, fifty years later, with #MeToo boosting women's courage to reveal embarrassing situations where they felt powerless, the fifteen women I know are still reticent to speak out—except for Judith Bourque, who bravely published her story.

 Scan this code to read the lyrics for "Sexy Sadie."

"Sexy Sadie:" The Lyrics and Recording

In this song, John expressed that Maharishi made a fool of The Beatles by using them for publicity and by promising film rights to two companies simultaneously. John was furious that Maharishi broke the rules by making sexual advances while claiming to be a monk—thus the moniker "Sexy" Sadie.

In the sixties, we hippie flower children were seeking higher consciousness. Along came the bearded, white-robed Maharishi, looking like a hippie/holy man and handing out flowers to everyone. John commented about meeting Maharishi: "We thought, *What a nice man*, and we were looking for that. I mean, everyone's looking for it, but we were all looking for it that day."[682]

"Laid it down" and "for all to see" might refer to Maharishi having sex. It might also refer to Alexis's claim that he spied on Maharishi hugging Rosalyn. What John did not know was that at least four women said Maharishi made sexual advances towards them during The Beatles' stay in Rishikesh: Rosalyn, Gunilla, Mia, and one of my British friends.

John believed Maharishi was behind Charlie Lutes spreading tales claiming the guru's supernormal powers, so John wanted to take Maharishi down a few notches. However, in reality, Maharishi opposed anyone ascribing him such abilities. When devotees tried the traditional *pranama* (bowing down) and *charan sparsh* (touching feet), Maharishi would catch their arms and stop them.

About The Beatles giving Maharishi "everything they owned," that was simply false. John told *Playboy* in 1980: "All the stuff on the White Album was written in India while we were supposedly giving money to Maharishi, which we never did."[683]

Ringo declared, "We never did anything for him. We never paid him one penny."[684]

George wrote to his mother: "He's not phony. He's not taking any of our money. All he's doing is teaching us how to contact God."[685] The Beatles were Maharishi's invited guests in Bangor and Rishikesh. Their entire entourage received free lodging, board, and instruction for months.

John's lyrics referred to Maharishi's charismatic, jovial, magnetic personality. He transmitted love to all and made them feel they were the most important person in the world. His smile lit up everyone around him. However, because John came to believe Maharishi was an egomaniac, he sarcastically called him "latest and greatest," and threatened karmic payback for his inappropriate actions.

Perhaps John's resentment sprang from excessively unrealistic expectations—placing Maharishi up there at the right hand of God itself, in contrast to the reality that Maharishi was a human being with sexual urges just as John was.

The Beatles took a total of twenty-six hours to record "Sexy Sadie," spread over four days.[686] On take number 117, they finally finished—the highest number of takes to record any Beatles song. John spent much of that time cussing his way through the sessions, still angry and hurt after concluding Maharishi was not the holy man he had anticipated.[687]

In 1987, when George was asked whether he had qualms about including 'Sexy Sadie,' John's diatribe against Maharishi, on the White Album, he answered, "Not at all. In fact, *I* titled it 'Sexy Sadie.' I was saying 'Well, John, wouldn't it be more subtle to call it, say, something like 'Sexy Sadie'? It's a bit *obvious*—'Maharishi.' No, I didn't mind, because I like that tune. The words, that was

John's concept of what happened to him. But even John was wrong some of the time."[688]

John's Final Words on Sexy Sadie

Five months before his death in 1980, John told David Sheff of *Playboy*: "I wrote it when we had our bags packed and were leaving India. I just called him, '*Sexy Sadie*,' instead of 'Maharishi.' I was just using the situation to write a song, rather calculatingly but also to express what I felt. I was leaving Maharishi with a bad taste. It seems that my partings are always not as nice as I'd like them to be. At first I was bitter about Maharishi being human and about Janov being human. Well, I'm not bitter anymore. They're human and I'm only thinking what a dummy I am. Although I meditate and I cry."[689]

"The Maharishi Song/Blues Vibration"

Written: May 1968
Recorded: May 1968
Released: 2019: Unofficial Release: The Lost Album II *(Bootleg)*

In May 1968, one month after John and George left Maharishi's ashram in a huff, John and Yoko recorded a demo expressing John's continued bitterness towards the guru. This mostly-spoken, partly-sung proto-rap duet was recorded at John's home in Kenwood.

Please visit *genius.com/John-lennon-the-maharishi-song-lyrics* and refer to specific lyrics as you read the detailed commentary below.

 Also, you can hear the song by scanning this code.

Verses 1 and 2:

Most of the students at the TM Teacher Training Course in Rishikesh were mature adults, compared to the fab twenty-something Beatles and their ravishing fashion model-actress wives and girlfriends. The Beatles dwelt in the rarified air of the mod British Invasion/James Bond culture of sixties London. The humdrum meditators schlepping around the ashram wrapped in plaid woolen blankets, without makeup, perhaps did not look so attractive to the most famous pop god in the world, John Lennon.

Verse 3:

The younger course participants often trekked down the steep footpath to the Ganges River to swim. Here John referred to those students who followed down to the river for a look-see at the bikini-clad hotties, when they should be in their rooms, meditating.

Course participants bathing at the Ganges; l. to r.: TM teacher Colin Harrison, author Richard Blakely, his girlfriend "Gunilla," actor Jerry Stovin, Jenny Boyd, photographer Larry Kurland, Mia Farrow's brother John Villiers-Farrow, Geoffrey Baker, Pattie Boyd. © Paul Mason.

Verses 4 and 5:

Tom Simcox, a course participant in Rishikesh, was a film and television actor from New Jersey, known for roles in *Shenandoah* (1965), *Simon & Simon* (1981), and *Piranha* (1972). He often appeared in TV Westerns, including *Death Valley Days*, *Wagon Train*, *Bonanza*, and *Gunsmoke*. Other TV appearances included *Naked City*, *Ben Casey*, *Perry Mason*, *General Hospital*, *The Alfred Hitchcock Hour*, *Ironside*, *Columbo*, *Charlie's Angels*, *Dragnet*, and more. Simcox owned the Riverbottom Bar & Grill on Olive Avenue, just outside Warner Bros. studio lot in Burbank, frequented by cowboy actors such as Clint Eastwood (who, like Tom, also practiced TM).

After the retreat, seeking to divorce Cynthia, John accused her of adultery: "You're no innocent flower. What about that Yankee cowboy in India?" [Referring to Simcox]. Cynthia could not believe her ears. The accusation was preposterous. John continued, "When he left Rishikesh, that cowboy gave George a letter to pass on to you, but instead he gave it to me. He was being loyal." When Cynthia asked John about the mysterious letter, he snapped, "We can do that through the lawyers."[690]

Simcox admitted being romantically attracted to Cynthia ("She had such wonderful cheek bones and a wonderful smile") and made friends with her in Rishikesh. They would have tea and he became her confidant during a time of great strain in her marriage. But Cynthia said, "Tom had never even hinted at anything untoward between us, apart from once asking me, very sweetly, if I had a twin sister."[691]

Verse 6:

"We got our mantra, we sat in the mountains eating lousy vegetarian food and writing all those songs," John recalled.[692] "I wrote hundreds of songs." He described "having dreams where you could smell. I'd do a few hours and then trip off; you could go on amazing trips."[693]

John reported to Maharishi, "Whenever I meditate, there's a big brass band in me head."[694] "When I'm deep in meditation, I start writing songs. What should I do?"

Maharishi replied, "When you are deep in meditation, and you feel a song, come out of meditation, write down the song. After you have written the song, go back to the meditation."

John asked, "You mean that simple?"

Maharishi answered, "That simple."[695]

Paul said he wrote quite a few songs and John came up with creative stuff, but George told him off for trying to think of the next album: "We're not fucking here to do the next album, we're here to meditate!"

Paul replied, "Ohh, excuse me for breathing!"[696]

Ironically, soon afterwards, George began playing music for elderly female course members and those on meditation melt-

down.[697] On the lecture hall roof, he played an organ in a daily mini-rock-festival for twenty-somethings, who envisioned a TM hippie revolution, without course fee, Initiation ceremony, or drug ban. The group pleaded their case to Maharishi, who responded with his usual evasive giggles.[698]

George playing organ on lecture hall roof. © Colin Harrison-Avico Ltd.

Richard Blakely told me that George converted a hut overlooking the Ganges into a music room, lined with carpets, cushions, and Indian musical instruments. He extended an invitation for anyone to listen or learn to play. Pattie Boyd practiced the dilruba that she had received on her birthday. Ringo played tabla drums. Maharishi hired musicians from Jammu, Vachaspati Sharma (sitar player) and Shri Rajinder Kumar Raina (tabla player), to instruct Donovan and George.

Flautist Paul Horn said, "Look how prolific [The Beatles] were in such a relatively short time. They were in the Himalayas away from the pressures and the telephone. When you get too involved with life, it suppresses your creativity. When you're able to be quiet, it starts coming up."[699]

John said, "Regardless of what I was supposed to be doing, I did write some of my best songs while I was there. It was a nice scene. Nice and secure and everyone was always smiling. The experience was worth it if only for the songs that came out."[700]

Verse 7:

Maharishi was an extraordinarily charismatic, charming, loving, joyful, and playful person. He expressed endless effusive enthusiasm about everything, everyone, and every situation. His contagious perpetual optimism made every moment glow. We were entirely captivated by the spiritual emanation radiating from his sparkling, magnetic, ebony eyes, the headiness of his hypnotic aura, and his inscrutable air of mystery. His beguiling presence was at once impenetrably enigmatic and entirely irresistible.

John described that when he was about to leave Rishikesh, "Even then, [Maharishi] sent out so much power that he was like a magnet, drawing me back to him. Suddenly I didn't want to go at all, but I forced meself to carry on before it was too late."[701]

Verse 8:

On the way to Maharishi's ashram, George Harrison told reporter Don Short, "A lot of people think we've gone off our heads. Well, they can think that—or anything they like. We've discovered a new way of living."[702]

Reporters' requests to interview or photograph The Beatles in Rishikesh ended in frustration: "They do not want publicity, fans or press. They want to be left alone to meditate."[703] Desperate reporters broke through the ashram gates and stormed The Beatles' quarters. Maharishi's brahmacharyas bodily removed them. Maharishi enlisted Gurkhas to guard the gates round the clock and dislodge photographers from the trees.

Growing angrier daily, the press fabricated creative headlines: "Wild Orgies in Ashram," "Beatles Wife Raped at Ashram," "Cartons of Whiskey Delivered to Maharishi's Guests at Ashram." John Lennon tried to defend Maharishi, declaring: "They had to kill Christ before they proved He was Jesus Christ."[704]

Maharishi tried to quell journalistic passion with press-conferences-cum-TM-advertisements, just outside the ashram gates. Most questions, particularly those about wealthy disciples, the ashram's alleged luxury, celebrities, or planned airstrip for a twin-engine Beechcraft, remained unanswered, as Maharishi responded with evasive rejoinders, punctuated by giggles. He could never be pinned down.

Finally, one day in late February, the press had something to photograph. A helicopter, in its noise and fury, made a ruckus on the Ganges riverbank below the ashram—loaned by Bombay transportation magnate, Kershi S. Cambata (one of Maharishi's followers), president of Cambata Aviation.

Paul recalled the whole line of devotees bouncing down the trail to the Ganges River, singing like Hare Krishnas. When the helicopter landed, they asked if anyone wanted a quick ride with Maharishi. "John jumped up. 'Yea, yea, yeah, yeah!' John got there first, and there was only room for one."[705]

John's helicopter ride with Maharishi.

Afterwards, Paul asked John why he was so keen to ride with Maharishi. John answered he was thinking, "Maybe if I go up with him in the helicopter, he may slip me *the answer* on me own."[706] John naïvely believed there was some secret to get—then he could just go home. He suspected Maharishi's devotees knew the secret but were holding out on him. Paul thought that was revealing: "I suppose everyone is always looking for the Holy Grail. I think John thought he might find it. I think it shows an innocence, a naïvety. It's quite touching really."[707]

Maharishi took a spin in the copter with John, and photos circulated worldwide. But no earth-shattering secrets were revealed to John (or to any reporters) that day.

Verses 9 and 10:

Charles F. Lutes was the president of Maharishi's Spiritual Regeneration Movement (SRM) in the US, and a cement salesman. The rumor was he had been in the CIA (John Lennon believed so, anyway). Charlie often related notable memories about Maharishi.

One time, when fog obscured the runway in Calgary, a pilot was worried they could not land. When Maharishi looked up at the sky, an amazing corridor of clear air suddenly appeared. This tunnel led straight to the landing strip, and they landed safely. The pilot never saw such a bizarre weather phenomenon.

Another time, Charlie was speeding Maharishi to the ferry to Vancouver Island. Maharishi told him not to worry but just keep driving fast—over 100 mph. When they arrived late, the purser said it was their lucky day. The captain, never failing to sail on time in eighteen years, had not cast off yet because he was "standing on the bridge like he was in a trance."[708]

Maharishi frequently detained disciples in his meeting room long past scheduled departure times, yet their plane or train was inevitably and conveniently delayed. Even the train transporting The Beatles and Maharishi to North Wales on August 25, 1967, was handily suspended for six minutes until the late-arriving Beatles boarded.

Spiritual author Deepak Chopra and wife Rita attended Maharishi's Ayurveda conference in Washington, DC, in 1985. The couple stole out of the lecture hall early to catch a plane. Suddenly, the meeting ended abruptly, and everyone spilled out of the hall. Maharishi made a beeline toward the couple, handed them flowers, and requested they meet him upstairs. After a two-hour meeting, the couple finally arrived at the airport—to find all planes on the Eastern seaboard had been delayed.

Another incident I personally witnessed: in August 1974, Maharishi was about to fly from Arosa to a course in Avoriaz, France. His pilot "Andrew" alerted him that they were grounded due to dense fog and zero visibility. Maharishi insisted, "We will fly. Go now and get your helicopter ready." About two hundred devotees gathered on the foggy mountaintop, waiting to send off Maharishi, who boarded the helicopter and motioned to Andrew to start the rotors. The rotors whirled but Andrew shook his head, indicating it was too dangerous to fly. Maharishi giggled and gestured to Andrew to take off. The helicopter rose about fifty feet. But Andrew brought it right back down.

Maharishi spun his finger around, indicating to keep the rotors running. Then he shook with laughter. Within a couple of minutes, the fog began lifting. At first there was a hole in the bank of clouds overhead, revealing a blue sky. Andrew and Maharishi laughed, and the helicopter took off. By the time they reached cruising altitude, the fog cleared entirely. As the sun shone, the crowd cheered and clapped.

Such happy "coincidences" were staple in Maharishi's world. However, as John perceived Maharishi in cahoots with Charlie and his Four Star movie deal, he discounted all such tales as fantastic lies. (See page 287–288.)

Verse 11:

The woman who resembled the Hollywood actress Jean Simmons (according to John) was Nadine Lewy, one of Maharishi's early disciples from Los Angeles, where his movement first emerged in the US.

Nadine was married to Henry Lewy, a German American Jewish sound engineer and record producer for Joni Mitchell, Leonard Cohen, The Monkees, Joe Cocker, Burt Bacharach, Neil Young, The Mamas and the Papas, Van Morrison, The Chipmunks, Johnny Rivers, Sérgio Mendes, Stephen Bishop, The Flying Burrito Brothers, Paul Horn, Judy Sill, and Crosby, Stills & Nash.

At age thirteen, Henry narrowly escaped Nazi internment by leaving Germany on the eve of Hitler's 1939 invasion of Poland. After Pearl Harbor, he was drafted and did multiple tours during World War II. He finally married a Jean Simmons lookalike in

Southern California, where he studied under Lou Adler and produced some of the seventies' best records.[709]

TM leaders at Squaw Valley Course 1969: Seated in front row l. to r.: Colin Harrison, Nadine Lewy, Brahmachari Satyanand (course teacher), Jerry Jarvis (TM Initiator and head of SIMS), Prudence Farrow.

Verse 12:

A tailor at Maharishi's ashram sewed custom ensembles for celebrity guests and their companions who bought rich fabrics in nearby Rishikesh or Dehradun. I assume John was referring to an assistant or companion of the tailor whom Maharishi favored and asked to sit near him. Perhaps the woman John described was more than just a disciple to Maharishi.

Verse 13:

It was never easy to get a private or semi-private audience with Maharishi. People often waited, sitting on the floor in hallways of hotels or on the porch of Maharishi's bungalow, for hours or days. Of course, The Beatles had no problem getting his attention. They received private lessons daily.

Wherever Maharishi walked, crowds of devotees inundated him, vying for attention. Throngs stood in a stifling double line, to his right and left, for the five-foot-tall yogi to pass through. With palms together in prayer position, holding flowers to offer Maharishi, poised to say *Jai Guru Dev* as he strolled by, our gaze trained intently on him. We were all hungry for a glance or a word. If he handed us a flower or said some words, we were overjoyed. We vied for his attention, seeking the divine love and energy felt in his proximity.

John recalled sarcastically: "Cut to Maharishi's health farm on the tip of the Himalayas. Eye-ing, eye-ing, eye-ing. He picked the right mantra for me. OK, he's a lot balder now than when I knew him. How come God picks on these holi-men? Ulcers, etc. 'He's taking on someone else's karma.' I bet that's what all the little sheep are bleating. He's got a nice smile, though. This is turning into *The Autobiography of a Yogurt*, but isn't everything? I ask myself. He made us live in separate huts from our wives. Can't say it was too much of a strain."[710]

Verse 14:

This statement about the million-dollar house is quite a fantasy, considering Maharishi's simple, modest bungalow of brick, concrete, and Ganges rocks—far from the "villa" or "air-conditioned mansion" described by the media, or "very rich-looking bungalow in the mountains"[711] professed by John in December 1970, though John had visited the simple quarters nearly every day for two months.

Maharishi's abandoned modest bungalow, forty years after The Beatles visited. flickr: Panoramio/by Achyut41.

Verse 15:

I suppose Maharishi looked holy. He had long wavy ebony hair, a snowy beard, and dressed like a brahmacharaya (a celibate monk). His dhoti (robes) consisted of two pieces of silk. His lungi (lower garment), about four meters of unsewn white silk, wrapped around his waist like a sarong. His *angavastram* (upper garment) draped about his shoulders like a shawl. Both of these were tucked into the waistband of his loincloth.

Maharishi's undyed *shahtoosh* shawl, or "ring shawl," could be pulled through a finger ring due to its fine material. Yet the shawl kept Maharishi so warm that he never wore a coat. These downy shawls have been illegal since 1977, due to the slaughter of Tibetan antelopes for their under-fleece.

Maharishi wore wooden foot-shaped sandals held on his feet by two-inch wide rust-colored rubber straps, and necklaces of 108 beads strung on silver wire: one of red coral and another of *rudraksha* (sacred seeds embodying Lord Shiva).

I would not describe Maharishi as a "sex maniac." I never saw him make sexual advances to anyone in public. In rare instances, he lightly touched the head of devotees in private. Other than that, he was strictly hands-off with thousands of devotees. However, there were many women I have personally known for fifty years who had sex with him or were bidden to. These women compared his sexual ineptness to an inexperienced teenage boy. So, as John Lennon answered Yoko in this song, "I couldn't say that."

Verse 16:

Maharishi was often called "His Holiness." However, whether he was "holy" would depend entirely on defining the word "holy." I do not know what "the true sense of the word" would be.

"The Rishi Kesh Song"

Written: 1980?
Recorded: 1980
Released: November 2, 1998: John Lennon Anthology

"The Rishi Kesh Song" is a satire about blind belief and a send-up of Maharishi and TM. After John and George parted ways with Maharishi in April 1968, The Beatles no longer advocated for him. That did not slow Maharishi's success, however. TM became increasingly popular in the 1970s. Thousands of devotees flocked to Maharishi's TM Teacher Training courses in Europe when I worked on his International Staff in Austria, Spain, Mallorca, Italy, Switzerland, and France.

This song was included in the *John Lennon Anthology* box set in 1998, issued by Yoko Ono. The coda was sometimes listed on bootlegs as "Something Is Wrong."

 Scan this QR code to listen to the full version.

 Scan this code to read the lyrics.

The Lyrics

The "Rishi Kesh Song" criticized Maharishi and his TM method. In the chorus, John ridiculed a little Sanskrit word called a mantra, used in TM meditation. However, there really *is* magic in the mantra—especially the way it is taught in TM. Mantras have been chanted for thousands of years. But Maharishi taught a way to repeat a mantra mentally that brings the mind to profound quietude and peace. So TM really *is* sort of magical.

By likening repeating a mantra to swallowing a pill, John derided the notion that a pill would deliver answers to all the mysteries of the universe. However, strangely, that was exactly what The Beatles expected. Maharishi never promised that, but the Fabs were a bit naïve.

John sitting at Maharishi's feet in Bangor. © Colin Harrison-Avico Ltd.

Before leaving for India, Paul expressed to Donovan Leitch that The Beatles hoped Maharishi would give them answers for both personal and global peace.[712] However, their towering expectations included the meaning of life, the secret of immortality, astral magic, supernormal powers, and universal peace—all in one month. Just a few days after arriving in India, George said, "I believe that I have already extended my life by twenty years. I believe there are bods up here in the Himalayas who have lived for centuries. There is one somewhere around who was born before Jesus Christ and is still living now."[713]

Paul asked Maharishi about the Indian rope trick: "Was that just a magic trick? Do they really levitate, Maharishi?" The yogi replied that yes, there are people who did it. Assuming Maharishi could invite a local fakir to demonstrate, Paul said, "Great. Give me one photograph and I'll have you on the *News at Ten* tonight, and you'll be a major source of interest to the world and your organization will swell its ranks."[714]

Others took a more sensible approach: Ringo said, "I'm quite happy to sit back and wait for whatever's coming next. I haven't found out the answer to the question: 'What's life all about?' and I don't suppose I ever shall. I do know that meditation is an important part of being a relaxed and sane human being."[715]

Donovan said, "Other people used to ask him for secrets like 'Can men really fly?' I asked him if I could have some more mango juice. Meditation doesn't mean you are going to get rid of all your pain so that you'll only feel joy all the time. It's just a way back to God."[716]

In the first verse, John sarcastically misquoted and thereby disparaged a famous saying of ancient India: "What is here is elsewhere, what is not here is nowhere" (meaning there is only one reality present everywhere, and whatever exists is that one ultimate omnipresent reality): "Here, there, and everywhere, within this, that, and everything," Maharishi would often say.

John sang that something was missing from this cosmic plan. The "plan" probably referred to Maharishi's "World Plan" to create peace on earth. John then criticized Maharishi for his sexual indiscretions. Maharishi advocated celibacy for his disciples, yet he did not follow his own advice. Perhaps something was missing in Maharishi's world. Maybe, as John suggested, he needed a woman. In Europe in the early seventies on a TM Teacher Training Course, a student boldly asked Maharishi about being a monk: "Don't you need women?" to which the guru quipped with a giggle, "I have goddesses."

In the final verse, John sang about feeling suicidal, referring to his long hours of meditation in Rishikesh. He concluded something must be amiss if TM made him feel suicidal. When I served on Maharishi's International Staff at his TM retreats in Europe, there were some meditation mishaps, psychotic breaks, and even suicides. Maharishi sometimes assigned me to attend to people who had gone over the edge as a result of long meditation practices.

CHAPTER 10

MYSTIC MEMORIES

"India, India"

Written: 1980
Recorded: 1980
Released: October 5, 2010: John Lennon Signature Box

John Lennon's beautiful song "India, India," recorded in 1980, is the polar opposite of "The Rishi Kesh Song." There is nothing cynical about this gentle love ballad dedicated to India and to Yoko Ono. Inspired by John's 1968 visit to Rishikesh, the song was written for a musical theater show named *Lennon*, directed by Don Scardino, which had a short run in New York and San Francisco in 2005.

 Scan this code to read the lyrics.

The Lyrics

In Rishikesh, John was searching for what he imagined was "the answer." Paul said, "John and George were going to Rishikesh with the idea that this might be some huge spiritual lift-off and they might never come back if Maharishi told them some really amazing thing."[717]

John and George on the Ganges riverbank in Rishikesh. AP/Shutterstock.

John and George were the two Beatles most dedicated to meditation. To say they had high expectations would be an understatement. Seeking ancient mysteries, they followed Maharishi's program with enthusiasm and waited by the Ganges River for "the answer." When their idealistic fantasy did not materialize, they became highly disillusioned and bitterly disappointed. They did not get the answers to all the mysteries of the universe or attain supreme enlightenment in one month. The astronomical hopes of their magical mystical quest were dashed.

However, the lyrics show a step towards self-awareness. John expressed a realization that answers could not be found in India or any other external place. They were found within himself, within his mind. John later declared, "There is no guru. You have to believe in yourself. You've got to get down to your own god in your own temple. It's all down to you, mate."[718]

The lyrics also referred to John following his heart and returning to Yoko Ono, whom he had wanted to bring to India with him. So when John became disillusioned with Maharishi, as Pattie Boyd said, "Perhaps John had been waiting for an excuse to leave—he wanted to be with Yoko. Whatever the truth, they left."[719]

Paul said, "They were scandalized. And I was quite shocked at them. I didn't think it was enough cause to leave the whole meditation center. And to tell the truth, I think they may have used it as an excuse to get out of there."[720]

"The Girl I Left Behind"

Cynthia Lennon remembered that in early February 1968, a few days before traveling to Rishikesh, The Beatles met Maharishi's financial administrator Eileen Forrestal (see her photo on page 153) in London to finalize their travel plans. Upon arriving at the Spiritual Regeneration Centre at 20 Grosvenor Place, London, The Beatles noticed Yoko Ono seated in a corner, dressed in black. She introduced herself to the group but remained silent throughout the meeting.

Afterwards, Les Anthony, the Lennons' six-foot-four former Welsh Guardsman chauffeur, opened the car door to their psychedelic-painted limousine. To everyone's astonishment, Yoko came out of nowhere and barged into the limousine ahead of John and Cynthia. John shrugged his shoulders, leaned into the limousine, and asked politely if they could give her a ride. Yoko answered, "Oh yes, please. Twenty-five Hanover Gate." John and Cynthia then climbed into the limousine. Not another word was spoken until they dropped her off, when Yoko said, "Goodbye."

Les Anthony, Lennons' chauffeur, standing next to the Lennons' decorated Rolls-Royce. Trinity Mirror/Mirrorpix/Alamy Stock Photo.

Cynthia exclaimed, "How bizarre. What was that all about?"

John, feigning innocence, replied, "Search me, Cyn." Obviously, John had invited Yoko to the meeting. In 1970, he admitted to *Rolling Stone*, "I lost me nerve because I was going to take me wife *and* Yoko, and I didn't know how to work it, so I didn't quite do it."[721]

Soon after the incident, when Cynthia confronted John about letters from Yoko amongst John's fan mail, John replied, "She's crackers, just a weirdo artist who wants me to sponsor her. Another nutter wanting money for all that avant-garde bullshit. It's not important."[722]

India's Memories of Tennessee

John had originally written the music for "India, India" in approximately 1975, as an ode to the playwright Tennessee Williams: "Tennessee." It was then reimagined as a beautiful, poetic demo, "Memories," also written in 1975 and revised in 1980.[723]

"India"

Written: Unknown
Recorded: November 29, 2002
Released: December 16, 2002: "Secret Website Show" unreleased song accessed through Back in The US DVD website;
2015: The Space Within Us - Ultimate Archive Collection: Disc 3

Paul McCartney performed his haunting song "India" on his Back in the World Tour in 2003. This love letter to India was never officially released. However, you can listen to this inspiring anthem by scanning this QR code.

There is no doubt that India profoundly influenced The Beatles. But The Beatles influenced India in equal measure. Once the Fab Four landed at Maharishi's ashram, the obscure hamlet of Rishikesh became the center of the world. Fifty years later, Maharishi's Meditation Academy was renamed "The Beatles Ashram" and tourism in Rishikesh has skyrocketed. When the

Liverpudlians became enamored with Indian philosophy and Indian music, the world shifted to a new paradigm. Now Indian music is known throughout the world, and yoga and meditation classes are available everywhere. All because of The Beatles.

Paul's India Experience

On April 3, 2009, Paul commented on what he gained from traveling to Rishikesh: "Getting a mantra from Maharishi and then learning how to use it was the most important aspect of the trip; the rest was great fun."[724] He described Maharishi as "a very spiritual and intelligent man, but what made him so endearing to me was his infectious sense of humor."[725]

Paul recalled, "We wrote quite a few songs in Rishikesh. We had some good inspiration. In the times when we weren't meditating, we had our guitars with us. So we would do quite a bit of writing. It was inspirational."[726] "I think meditation offers a moment in your day to be at peace with yourself and therefore the universe, which once was thought of as a slightly silly hippie idea, but now it's much more accepted and even fits with some of the most advanced scientific thinking."[727]

After Maharishi's death on February 5, 2008, Paul released a statement: "Whilst I am deeply saddened by his passing, my memories of him will only be joyful ones. He was a great man who worked tirelessly for the people of the world and the cause of unity. I will never forget the dedication that he wrote inside a book he once gave me, which read, 'Radiate bliss consciousness,' and that to me says it all. I will miss him but will always think of him with a smile."[728]

Scan this code to read the lyrics.

The Lyrics

The simple song lyrics consist of Paul's plea to return to India. He begins with gibberish sounds meant to evoke the Hindi language—not very effectively. However, when he begins the heartfelt lyrics and beautiful music, we feel transported to the mystic land of Rishikesh. We can imagine the Ganges River running swiftly below the high cliff where the ashram was perched. We can climb to the roof of Maharishi's bungalow overlooking the river. We can hear the faint sounds of temple bells and the chanting of monks from nearby ashrams. We can smell the fragrance of incense and hear the cries of peacocks, crows, and monkeys.

I believe that India indeed stayed in Paul's heart "forever and ever," and that he does long to return somehow to those simple halcyon days at the ashram. That is the message of this ardent song.

A Supernatural Event

The day Maharishi died, there was a tremendous storm in Rishikesh. The water from the Ganges came whirling up and showered into Maharishi's bungalow. Devotees who visited the ashram that day to pay their respects were amazed by this unprecedented supernatural occurrence. It is said the power of Maharishi brought the Ganges onto the top of the 150-foot cliff on Manikoot hill.[729]

"Not Guilty"

Written: August 1968
Recorded: March to October 1978
Released: February 23, 1979: George Harrison

George wrote "Not Guilty" in 1968, after The Beatles returned from Rishikesh. It was recorded during the White Album sessions, but not released until 1979. "It was me getting pissed off at Lennon and McCartney for the grief I was catching during the making of the White Album," George told *Musician* in 1987.[730] George had been severely crushed and disheartened by The Beatles' split with Maharishi. To make matters worse, his Beatle-mates accused him of introducing them to Maharishi and dragging them to India.

 Scan this code to read the lyrics.

The Lyrics

In the song, George asserted that he was not guilty of getting in the way of the career of the Lennon/McCartney songwriting team, or of leading them astray. He declared, "I was sticking up for myself."[731]

After The Beatles returned from India on a sour note, George was blamed for dressing in freaky India-inspired clothing and for associating with Indians, for example, those who follow Sikhism—a monotheistic religion that originated in the Punjab state of northern India. Mandalay is in Myanmar—not India, but George could not rhyme "Rishikesh" with "astray." Though John felt angry and victimized by Maharishi, George refused to be vilified for that.

It was always difficult for George to get his songs recorded by The Beatles. The Lennon/McCartney team took priority in songwriting and therefore received the lion's share of royalties. Justifiably, George felt cheated. When he returned to London from India, he was horrified to see that without Brian Epstein's guidance, the Beatles' new enterprise Apple Corps had become a free-for-all for any hippie freeloader ne'er-do-well to get a blank check for specious projects: "[Epstein] had taken care of everything, and it was chaos after that."[732] But George decided not to interfere and catch even more grief from his Beatle-mates. He would not upset the "Apple" cart.

"Everybody's Got Something to Hide Except Me and My Monkey"

Written: May 1968
Recorded: June 27, July 1, 23, 1968
Released: November 22, 1968: The Beatles

It might be surprising to learn that in the entire Beatles catalog, "Everybody's Got Something to Hide Except Me and My Monkey" is one of the top three where Maharishi's influence is most obvious. However, John Lennon never admitted that—probably because he remained bitter towards Maharishi for the remainder of his life and did not want to attribute anything to his ex-guru. But anyone who knew Maharishi as I did recognizes immediately the lyrics of this song consist of catchphrases that he used every day.

 Scan this code to read the lyrics.

Come, Come

Any time Maharishi wanted someone to approach him, walk with him, meet with him, or join him in his private meeting room, he would say in his tenor melodic voice, "Come, come," or "Come on." Those of us on his staff lived for those words. Being near Maharishi was everything. While in his immediate presence, we would feel waves of ecstasy pouring into our open minds, sounds of laughter inviting us, and love and bliss shining around us, as John eloquently described in "Across the Universe."

Maharishi would smile mischievously and zap us with a loving glance that infused us with rapturous energy. This gift of grace, the spiritual vibration transference from guru to *chela* (master to disciple), is known as *shakti-sanchara*. The closer the proximity to

Maharishi's presence, the more intense and powerful that wave of bliss. Because we craved that love-energy, we staff members would compete fiercely to get near him.

Just Enjoy

Some of Maharishi's primary philosophical tenets included "Life is not a struggle. Life is bliss!" "Man is not born to suffer. He is born to enjoy!" Maharishi often said to his followers, "Enjoy" or "Just enjoy." He autographed his books with the word "Enjoy!" And to express his enthusiastic delight about anything, which he did many times daily, he would say, "It's such a joy!"

In 1999, the *Boston Globe* reported that during Paul McCartney's four-hour visit with Maharishi in Vlodrop, Holland, his daughter Stella recorded some video. She said, "Okay, Maharishi, what have you got to say for the camera, then?"

Maharishi said, "Enjoy!"

Paul then recalled, "That happened to be the same message from thirty years ago that he wrote in my book. So he's consistent at least. And you know what? That is actually awfully good advice."[733] "Now I say to my own kids, 'Go and get a mantra, because then if you ever want to meditate, you'll know how to do it.'"[734]

Take It Easy

Maharishi often said that meditation should be easy and effortless. He contended that effort and strain would only result in a headache and would not take anyone to transcendental consciousness. Maharishi touted Transcendental Meditation as a simple, natural technique. Other forms of meditation required effort, concentration, renunciation, celibacy, difficult exercises, contemplation, or hypnotic suggestion. But TM required none of these. Maharishi said if you could think a thought, you could practice TM. It was as easy as sitting comfortably, closing your eyes, and mentally repeating a word.

Maharishi's instructions for meditation were simple: "Take it easy. Take it as it comes." This was also his primary philosophy. Often, when someone would come with a problem, his answer would be that simple phrase. Along with "It's such a joy," it was his most often repeated phrase. In a *Life* magazine article in November 1968, "Invitation to Instant Bliss," Maharishi stated, "It's so very simple. They keep telling me I must make it complicated so that people will think I'm saying something important."[735]

Going Deep and Flying High

It takes no stretch of imagination to realize that John was referring to meditation when he sang about going deep and flying high. Though some might attribute these lyrics to drug culture, these references are definitively about meditation, written while John was off drugs, meditating in an ashram.

Maharishi often used a metaphor of diving deep into meditation. In fact, when he first started teaching meditation in 1955, his method was called "Deep Meditation." In 1960 he changed the name to "Transcendental Deep Meditation" and eventually to "Transcendental Meditation."

The Monkey

In a 1980 interview, John described the title as a nice line about Yoko and him that he made into a song: "Everybody seemed to be paranoid except for us two, who were in the glow of love. Everything is clear and open when you're in love. Everybody was, sort of, tense around us. You know, 'What is SHE doing here at the session? Why is she with him?' All that sort of madness is going on around us because we just happened to want to be together all the time."[736]

Paul had a different interpretation. "Monkey on your back" was a mid-twentieth century beatnik phrase denoting heroin addiction. Paul said that John started "talking about fixes and monkeys and it was a harder terminology which the rest of us weren't into. We were disappointed that he was getting into heroin. We just hoped it wouldn't go too far. He did end up clean."[737]

John told David Sheff in 1980, "They're always arresting smugglers or kids with a few joints in their pocket. They never face the reality."[738] John felt we should instead try to discover the cause of the drug problem and ask why people take drugs and what they are escaping from.

What George Said

The only Beatle who admitted the lyrics came from Maharishi, George said, "Come on it's such a joy" was one of Maharishi's favorite sayings as was the song's title, "apart from the bit about the monkey, that was just what Maharishi used to always say."[739] However, unlike George, I have never heard Maharishi use the phrase, "Everybody's got something to hide." Perhaps he said it to The Beatles in Rishikesh. The reality is that Maharishi was the one with something to hide (see pages 299–307).

"While My Guitar Gently Weeps"

Written: April to September 1968
Recorded: September 5 and 6, 1968
Released: November 22, 1968: The Beatles

"While My Guitar Gently Weeps" is George Harrison's most beloved song, listed as number ten in *Rolling Stone*'s "The Beatles 100 Greatest Songs" special edition. The self-effacing Beatle admitted, "I knew the song was pretty good."[740]

In 1968, after the Fabs returned from India, George visited his parents' home in Warrington, North England, a bungalow named Sevenoaks that was located in Appleton Thorn, which he had bought for them in 1965 to escape Liverpool's Beatlemania. During this visit in April or May 1968, the concept for the song emerged.

Meant to Be

An ancient Chinese oracle book called *I Ching: The Book of Changes* was popular in the sixties among us flower children. The book employs "cleromancy," a divination method. Yarrow stalks or coins are cast, and the resulting formula points to specific passages in the book that provide cosmic advice and predictions.

The idea of divination is that life is not accidental. Our destiny is tied to cosmic forces that guide us purposefully and meaningfully. George believed there are no coincidences, and everything happens according to cosmic plan. So he wanted to try an experiment: "I was thinking about the Chinese *I Ching*, ("The Book of Changes"). In the West we think of coincidence as being something that just happens. But the Eastern concept is that whatever happens is all meant to be, and that there's no such thing as coincidence—every little item that's going down has a purpose."[741]

George decided to open a random book to a random page and write a song based on the first thing he read—"as it would be relative to that moment, at *that* time. I picked up a book at random, opened it, saw 'gently weeps', then laid the book down again and started the song."[742] Some writers have conjectured the phrase came from an 1849 poem by Coates Kinney that appears in many poetry anthologies: "Rain on the Roof," which states, "And the melancholy darkness, Gently weeps in rainy tears."

 Scan this code to read the lyrics.

The Sound and Lyrics

The bent, distorted notes, played by Eric Clapton, sound like the guitar is literally weeping, not so much about the state of humanity, but specifically about John and Paul. George felt the spiritual force of divine love was asleep within his compatriots. They had not learned how to unfold or express this force; therefore, they did not know how to love. George viewed John and Paul entranced by the material world, where superficial values of money, glamour, fame, and ego rule.

Hopefully, they would learn from their mistakes and break out of their ignorance. But they were diverted from their purpose, perverted by false beliefs, and inverted from who they really were. George resented Yoko Ono's presence during the White Album recording sessions—a major distraction from The Beatles' purpose. He also felt marginalized and belittled by Paul. And no one was elated about John taking heroin.

The following lyrics did not make the final cut: "I look at the trouble and hate that is raging," "I look from the wings at the play you are staging," "As I'm sitting here, doing nothing but ageing." These lines reflected George's dissatisfaction about his songs not appearing on Beatles albums and about the gross mismanagement of Apple Corps.

George went so far as to say, "I had no confidence in myself as a guitar player, having spent so many years with Paul McCartney. He ruined me as a guitar player. I rated Eric [Clapton] as a guitar player and he treated me like a human."[743]

"Old Brown Shoe"

Written: November 1968 through January 26, 1969
Recorded: April 16 and 18, 1969
Released: May 30, 1969: Single

On March 12, 1969, Sgt. Norman Pilcher (an aggressive narc who was notorious for framing pop stars) raided George and Pattie Harrison's home "Kinfauns," where a drug-sniffing dog named Yogi (presumably to mock Maharishi) and a dozen police personnel "found" a chunk of hashish in George's shoe—the last place he would keep hashish. One month later, George, who claimed the drug had been planted, recorded "Old Brown Shoe."[744]

The Beatles often used objects as metaphors in their lyrics. The "Old Brown Shoe" represented old constructs binding us to the material world. George was keen to transcend that dualistic world and attain higher consciousness, beyond waking, dreaming, and deep sleep. He was seeking samadhi—transcendental awareness beyond space, time, and causality.

The metaphor of sloughing off an old shoe and walking into a future with a new lover symbolized something deeper—letting go of his past and seeking a new goal, God's love. As he kicked off his worn-out shoe, he began walking in the footsteps of divine love. He trod a new pathway, leading him to the ultimate goal of life— the realization of who he really is.

 Scan the code to read the lyrics for "Old Brown Shoe."

The Lyrics

George Harrison described the birth of "Old Brown Shoe" this way: "I started the chord sequences on the piano, and then began writing ideas for the words from various opposites. Again, it's the duality of things."[745]

In early 1968, George had spent two months in Rishikesh with Maharishi. Though departing highly disenchanted, his spiritual quest did not diminish. He continued seeking the meaning of life. Author Steve Turner explained, "The lyric had its origins in George's religious view that we must free ourselves from the material world, as it is illusory. Once absorbed into the divine consciousness, there would be no right versus wrong, body versus soul, spirit versus matter."[746]

Though the theme of duality had been explored in "Hello Goodbye," the metaphors in "Old Brown Shoe" strode a step further than Paul's wordplay. George used contrasts of right/wrong, short/long, up/down, smile/frown, love/hate, early/late, to illustrate the relative world and its ever-changing transience. Author Bruce Spizer described the lyrics as "a rocking extension of the Eastern Philosophy of yin-yang."[747]

Bhagavad Gita

In India, The Beatles learned that all activity in creation consists of the interplay of three gunas (modes of operation): sattva, rajas, and tamas, born of unmanifest cosmic energy. Rajas creates the spur of activity. Sattva directs movement towards peace, harmony, and expansion, and tamas directs movement towards dissolution, inertia, and contraction.

There are two aspects of life—perishable and imperishable. The perishable is relative, manifest, finite existence, under the sway of the three gunas. Beyond all activity is the imperishable, absolute, unmanifest infinite consciousness.

In the Bhagavad Gita 2:45, Lord Krishna teaches, "Be without the three gunas, O Arjuna, freed from duality, ever firm in purity, independent of possessions, possessed of the Self."[748]

No guna can exist without the other two. So Lord Krishna asked Arjuna to be entirely free from all these three forces. In meditation, we go beyond the relative field and experience the bliss of absolute pure consciousness, our higher Self. No longer possessed by the relative world, we stand steadfast in the perfection of absolute being. We are then "possessed of the Self." That is moksha: spiritual liberation.

The Sound

After George stopped trying to master sitar and returned to guitar, the Indian-inspired microtonal slide became his signature sound for the remainder of his career. In "Old Brown Shoe," a hint of that bottleneck sound is evident in the recurring Bob Dylan-"Highway 61 Revisited"-style riff, though no actual slide was used.

PART VI

HARRY B. KRISHNA, LT. IT. B.

CHAPTER 11

CALLING KRISHNA

"Hare Krishna Mantra"

Written: Traditional
Recorded: July 1969
Released: August 22, 1969: US: Single; August 29, 1969:
UK: Single; May 21, 1971: The Radha Krsna Temple

In 1965, the remarkable Indian spiritual master A. C. Bhaktivedanta Swami Prabhupada arrived in America. The following year, he founded ISKCON (International Society of Krishna Consciousness, a.k.a. the Hare Krishna Movement). On July 13, 1966, his first temple opened at 26 Second Avenue, New York City.

In the sixties, ISKCON devotees, nicknamed "Hare Krishnas," gained attention as saffron-robed shaved-headed youngsters chanting and dancing in the streets, distributing leaflets, soliciting donations, and offering flowers, candy, and books at airports.

Bhaktivedanta Swami Prabhupada with Hindu deity Jagannatha in Golden Gate Park, February 1967.

Worship of Krishna

Prabhupada's mission was to propagate Gaudiya Vaishnava ("worship of Vishnu"), a Hindu religious movement founded by an illustrious Bengali saint of the fifteenth century, Chaitanya Mahaprabhu. This sect's focus is devotion to Lord Krishna and his consort Radha.

Hindus worship a trinity of three gods: Brahma (creator), Vishnu (maintainer), and Shiva (destroyer). Krishna and Rama are two of the ten avatar ("incarnations in the flesh") of Lord Vishnu. *Krishna* means "all-attractive," and *Rama* means "delightful." *Haraa* is Lord Krishna's consort or supremely potent energy, Radha, and *Hari* is Lord Vishnu. *Hare* is the vocative form for both. The main scriptures of Gaudiya Vaishnava are the Bhagavad Gita and the Bhagavata Purana (a.k.a. the Srimad Bhagavatam).

The Gaudiya Vaishnava meditation practice comprises two basic forms: individual (*japa*) and congregational (*kirtana*). The *japa* practice consists of reciting repeatedly the Hare Krishna Maha-Mantra ("great mantra"). From an ancient scripture, the Kali-Santarana Upanishad, the mantra comprises names of gods/goddesses. Practitioners use a *mala* (string of 108 prayer beads) to count the number of repetitions:

Hare Krishna, Hare Krishna;
Krishna Krishna, Hare Hare.

Hare Rama, Hare Rama;
Rama Rama, Hare Hare.

In the congregational (*kirtana*) practice, musical instruments are played and the mantra is sung in a group rather than recited. Invoking deities by chanting their names is said to further spiritual evolution and cleanse mental impurities.

 Scan this code to watch a music video for "Hare Krishna Mantra."

Gaudiya Vaishnavas are expected to follow a strict vegetarian diet and abstain from ingesting animals, fish, eggs, onions, garlic, caffeine, alcohol, and drugs. They believe celibacy is the ideal lifestyle. Sexual relations are only for procreation.

Beatnik poet Allen Ginsberg met Prabhupada in New York, learned the Maha-Mantra, and helped the swami extend his USA visa. Ginsberg often led group chanting, playing harmonium. During a *kirtana* gathering with Prabhupada at Tomkin's Square Park in New York City in October 1966, Ginsberg told the *New York Times* the mantra "brings a state of ecstasy."[749] In December 1966, Ginsberg loaned his harmonium to the swami so he could record his first album, *Krishna Consciousness.* A few months later, The Beatles ordered one hundred copies.

Prabhupada's arrival in San Francisco with Allen Ginsberg, January 17, 1967 ; l. to r.: unknown woman, Allen Ginsberg, unknown man, Harsharani Devi Dasa, A.C. Bhaktivedanta Swami (a.k.a. Srila Prabhupada), and Mukunda Das. "Das" and "Dasa" mean "servant," and "Prabhu" means master. When Hare Krishna devotees say "Prabhu" to each other, that signifies serving each other. "Das anu das" is the principal to serve each other, which devotees believe can save the world.

Mantra Rock Dance

In 1967, Prabhupada's early disciples Mukunda Dasa Goswami (a jazz musician born Michael Grant) and his wife Janaki Devi Dasi (Jak Raymen) opened the West Coast ISKCON center in a Haight-Ashbury storefront, with help from college friend Sam Speerstra and his girlfriend Melanie Nagel. To raise funds for the temple, the couples organized the "Mantra Rock Dance" fundraiser, held on January 29, 1967, at the Avalon Ballroom (compliments of music producer Chet Helms), which I personally attended.

Speerstra and Nagel convinced The Grateful Dead, Moby Grape, Jefferson Airplane, Quicksilver Messenger Service, and Big Brother and the Holding Company (Janis Joplin's band) to play for minimum wage. In attendance were psychedelic guru Timothy Leary; LSD curator and sound engineer Augustus Owsley Stanley III; and Swami Kriyananda (disciple of Paramahansa Yogananda and founder of Ananda), carrying a tambura.[750]

At 10:00 p.m., Prabhupada arrived. Allen Ginsberg led "Hare Krishna" chanting, playing his harmonium. Prabhupada stood up, lifted his arms, and led devotional dance. Lightshow producers Ben Van Meter and Roger Hillyard projected onto the walls pictures of Krishna, words of the Maha-Mantra, dancing globs of paint, and strobe lights. Incense filled the air. Rock musicians accompanied sitar, tambura, and drums, as chanting and dancing continued for over an hour.

This unlikely confluence of stoned hippies and celibate monks was deemed the "ultimate high" and "major spiritual event of the San Francisco hippie era."[751] This gathering put Prabhupada on the map in the underground sixties culture. Though he began his mission at age seventy, Prabhupada wrote over sixty books, and his organization established 108 temples throughout the world.

Prabhupada initiated Speerstra and Nagel and gave them spiritual names Shyamasundar Das Adhikari and Malati Devi Dasi. They volunteered in the temple, cooked free vegetarian "love

feasts," and distributed *prasad* (food blessed by Krishna) to the hippie community.

George's Devotion to Krishna

Before ever meeting Prabhupada, George Harrison bought his
record *Krishna Consciousness* in New York and often listened to it
with John. While sailing through the Greek isles with Alexis Mardas
("Magic Alex") in summer 1967, John and George played ukulele
and chanted the Maha-Mantra for six hours, until their jaws ached
(and the LSD wore off). Another time, George chanted the mantra
nonstop while driving twenty-three hours from France to Portugal.

George expressed, "I always felt at home with Krishna. It was
already a part of me. I think it's something that's been with me
from my previous birth." He defined *mantra* as "mystical energy
encased in a sound structure," where "each mantra contains within
its vibrations a certain power." He asserted the Hare Krishna
Maha-Mantra "has been prescribed as the easiest and surest way for
attaining God Realization in this present age." He claimed chanting brings "a much higher taste than any happiness found here in
the material world. The more you do it, the more you don't want
to stop, because it feels so nice and peaceful."[752] "It's really the same
as meditation, but it has quicker effect, because music is such a
powerful force. It's like God likes me when I work, but loves me
when I sing."[753]

George was flying in a private plane from Los Angeles to New
York to organize the Bangladesh concert. When lightning struck
the plane three times, George started chanting the Hare Krishna
Maha-Mantra. A Boeing 707 flew over, missing the plane by
inches. For about two hours, the small plane thrashed about, dropping hundreds of feet at a time in severe turbulence. The lights
went out and there were several explosions. George pressed his feet
against the seat in front of him, clenched his seatbelt for dear life,
and shouted the Maha-Mantra at the top of his lungs. The plane
leveled out just before hitting the ground. George commented, "I

know for me, the difference between making it and not making it was chanting the mantra."754

George Supported ISKCON

In 1968, Prabhupada sent three couples to London to establish ISKCON in Britain. Malati Devi Dasi, her husband Shyamasundar, their infant daughter Saraswati, Mukunda and Janaki, and Gurudas and Yamuna endured many hardships. Malati recalled, "Often we would go hungry. [We had] hardly any possessions, no money, no protection. It often got very cold. We had nothing. All we had was love for Shrila Prabhupada."755

The seven ISKCON pioneers; Front row l. to r.: Yamuna Devi Dasi, Janaki Devi Dasi, baby Saraswati, and Malati Devi Dasi. Back row: Mukunda Das, Shyamasundar Das, Gurudas. Photo by Gurudas a.k.a. Roger Siegel.

The pioneer devotees had talked about meeting The Beatles even before leaving San Francisco. Shyamasundar got the brainstorm of inspiring The Beatles to record the Hare Krishna mantra. Trying to get noticed by Peter Asher (head of A&R for Apple

Records), the Krishna devotees sent an amateur demo of Hindu prayers, arranged and composed by Mukunda. Receiving no reply, they sent photos, articles, stories, paintings, handbills, and wrote the Hare Krishna mantra in gold paint on the back of a wind-up, walking apple toy.

Malati recounted, "We chanted and got arrested in front of the Apple Studio. We ultimately got their attention by making and sending in apple pies to the studio."[756] Gurudas said they cut letters of the Maha-Mantra in the top crust of an apple pie and brought the fresh, steaming Maha-pie to Apple Records to deliver to Peter Asher—without luck. Finally, Chris O'Dell, George Harrison's assistant, a Los Angelite who was happy to see Americans, gave the pie to George. [757]

In December 1968, upon first laying eyes on Shyamasundar in the crowded reception area of Apple Records, George made a beeline towards him and said, "Hare Krishna! I've been waiting to meet you!"[758]

Shyamasundar recalled, "It seemed like we were taking up a conversation we'd started yesterday. We understood each other immediately. It was a kinship of the soul."[759]

Soon after that, George chanted and dined with the Hare Krishnas at their Temple and lodgings—two floors in a warehouse at 22 Betterton Street in Covent Garden, headquarters of the *International Times* newspaper (see page 122), an unheated cold-water building where bundles of old newspapers served as furniture.[760]

During his visit, George asked, "Is Krishna the only name for God?"

Gurudas answered, "There are many names for God. If someone chants with devotion any bona fide name of God, it is the same as chanting Krishna. Krishna and His name are nondifferent. When we say Krishna, He is actually dancing on our tongue. It is a transcendental sound vibration."

George asked, "Why is the Hare Krishna mantra called the Maha, or great, Mantra?"

Yamuna answered, "Because Lord Chaitanya has made it easy and available for everyone."[761]

Soon afterwards, the devotees gathered at George Harrison's home, "Kinfauns" in Surrey, to chant kirtana. Just before they left, George exclaimed, "I love this chanting. You all sound so great! I want Apple to record you guys chanting the Hare Krishna mantra, if it's all right with you." George and Pattie invited Malati and Shyamasundar to live with them at Kinfauns for awhile.[762] From then on, whenever Krishna devotees popped in to Abbey Road studios with a shaved head and Indian garb, the Fab Three would just say, in Beatle-esque fashion, "Oh yeah. They're with George."[763] On January 2 and 6, 1969, during The Beatles' "Get Back" sessions at Twickenham Studios, Shyamasundar Das and Mukunda Goswami brought *prasadam* (blessed food and flowers), and chanted mantras in the corner (at George's request) as The Fabs rehearsed.[764]

Prabhupada in front of Radha Krishna Temple, 7 Bury Place, Bloomsbury. Photo by Gurudas a.k.a. Roger Siegel.

George Harrison and Mukunda Goswami at Bhaktivedanta Manor

In 1969, George co-signed the lease for the building to house the Radha-Krishna Temple at 7 Bury Place near the British Museum in Bloomsbury. In February 1973, George purchased a mansion that became Yoga Bhaktivedanta Manor in Letchmore Heath, Watford, Hertfordshire—the largest British ISKCON center. George envisaged the Manor would guide seekers toward Krishna Consciousness—"a place where people could get a taste of the splendor of devotional service to the Supreme Lord."[765]

In March 1970, George financed the publication of *Krsna: The Supreme Personality of the Godhead*—Prabhupada's translation of the tenth canto of the Hindu scripture Srimad Bhagavatam. [766] George wrote its introduction, where he declared: "If there's a God, I want to see Him. It's pointless to believe in something without proof, and Krishna Consciousness and meditation are methods where you can actually obtain God perception. In that way you can see, hear, and play with God. Perhaps this may sound weird, but God is really there next to you."[767] This quote originated with Swami Vivekananda, the first spiritual master to bring Indian philosophy to the West, who famously said, "If there's a God, we must see him, and if there's a soul we must perceive it. Otherwise, it's better not to believe."

George's home altar includes pictures of Srila Prabhupada, of the Hindu trinity Shiva, Vishnu, and Brahma, and Lord Shiva with the Ganges River sprouting from his topknot. Prabhupada's record Krishna Consciousness is on the rack. Incense is burning. George is picking up a poster of the "Yogi-Christ" Babaji. Photo by Gurudas a.k.a. Roger Siegel.

George Produced the Hare Krishna Mantra

Prabhupada wanted The Beatles to record the Maha-Mantra.[768] But George Harrison produced the "Hare Krishna Mantra" record himself. Six devotees from the London Radha-Krisha Temple performed, and Apple Records released it.[769] Because George sought to spread Krishna Consciousness to millions, he kept the timing to three and a half minutes so it would be played on the radio.

The BBC television music show *Top of the Pops* featured the "Hare Krishna Chanters" five times. That was one of the "greatest thrills" of George's life and "a breath of fresh air," because of how hard it was to get on the show, which was only for the Top Twenty. George commented, "If everyone can go around the world on their holidays, there's no reason why a mantra can't go a few miles as well. So the idea was to try to spiritually infiltrate society, so to speak."[770] Lord Chaitanya himself predicted that one day, the chanting of the holy names of God will be heard in every town and village of the world.[771]

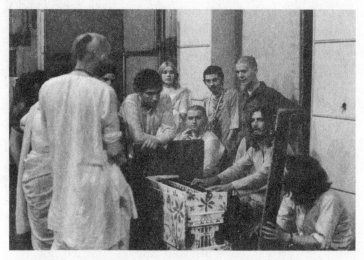

Hare Krishna chanters recording "Hare Krishna Mantra" at Abbey Road Studios, July 1969. Photo by Gurudas a.k.a. Roger Siegel.

George on guitar and Mukunda Das on piano playing "Hare Krishna Mantra," while Shyamasundar Das observes. Photo by Gurudas a.k.a. Roger Siegel.

The Recording Session

The "Hare Krishna Mantra" was recorded right before an *Abbey Road* album session at EMI studios. George recorded the harmonium and guitar track. Mukunda Das (former jazz musician) played piano. Yamuna and Shyamasundar sang the verses.[772] Other chanters repeated in chorus.[773] They kept time with Indian instruments mridangam (double-headed barrel-shaped drum—see page 433 for a photo) and *khartal* (wood clappers with sets of small cymbals). The devotees overdubbed the chorus four times to create forty-eight voices.[774] Malati Devi Dasi (Shyamasundar's wife) rang the closing gong at the song's final climax.[775]

Shyamasundar remembered, "We all watch George's face, but his eyes are closed. He is concentrating. It's finally happening like we imagined a year—lifetimes ago: George Harrison is playing and singing the Hare Krishna mantra with us."[776]

Paul McCartney, who directed and engineered the recording, brought his wife Linda along.[777] When Gurudas met them and reminded Linda they had attended high school together in Scarsdale, she replied, "I didn't think anyone from affluent Scarsdale would become a monk and renounce their wealth!"

Gurudas retorted, "Why not? Material wealth is only temporary, and besides, Krishna owns Scarsdale too. He is, after all, God!"

Linda seemed to understand, but her reply was surprising: "Paul is my God."[778]

Apple employees Mal Evans and Chris O'Dell also attended. Chris sang in the chorus at Shyamasundar's invitation. In her 2009 autobiography, she recalled feeling "physically and spiritually changed" after singing the mantra: "Chanting the words over and over again was almost hypnotic. There was a point of freedom where there was no effort at all, no criticism or judgment, just the sound generated from deep inside, like a flame that warmed us from the inside out."[779]

The B-Side

On the record's B-side, the Krishna devotees sang "Prayer to the Spiritual Masters."[780] The song praised gurus of the Gaudiya Vaishnava lineage, including Srila Prabhupada (founder of ISKCON), Bengali saint Chaitanya Mahaprabhu, and his disciples, the Six Goswami of Vrindavan (gurus from the fifteenth and sixteenth centuries, extolled for austerities in practicing Bhakti Yoga—devotion to God).

Paramahansa Yogananda playing the esraj—the instrument Shyamasundar played on the record. Photo courtesy of Self-Realization Fellowship.

Accompanying the Hare Krishna chanters were harmonium, percussion, and *esraj* (Indian bowed stringed instrument), commonly played by Shyamasundar during group chanting. The arrangement was credited to Mukunda Das.

During a promotional press conference, the media seemed shocked to hear George speak about the soul and God. George felt it was important to "come out of the closet and really tell them. Because once you realize something, then you can't pretend you don't know it."[781]

John, Yoko, and George first met Prabhupada on September 11, 1969, when the guru and eighteen close disciples stayed one month (in exchange for restoring the property and its grounds) in John's newly acquired Tittenhurst Park, Berkshire estate.[782] During his lengthy conversation with John and Yoko, Prabhupada used an analogy never uttered before—addiction to Krishna. He said we can love Krishna as addicts love their substances. The addict feels separation and is always longing, waiting, and thinking about gratification. But, while material relief is temporary, spiritual addiction (love of Krishna or God) is eternal bliss.[783] John Lennon later admitted that two days after this meeting with Prabhupada, his heroin addiction had caused vomiting for hours before (and nearly vomiting during) his Plastic Ono Band performance of "Cold Turkey" at the Toronto Rock and Roll Revival.[784]

Yamuna serving lunch to Pattie and George at the Lennons' estate in Tittenhurst. Photo by Gurudas a.k.a. Roger Siegel.

Janaki showing John how to play khartal (hand cymbals) at the Temple Room in Tittenhurst. Photo by Gurudas a.k.a. Roger Siegel.

Hare Krishna devotees dancing at Tittenhurst before Prabhupada, seated on platform at right. Photo by Gurudas a.k.a. Roger Siegel.

While staying at John's estate, Prabhupada held public lectures. A Temple Room was established, complete with a deity altar, framed pictures of Gaudiya Vaishnava masters, a large photo of Prabhupada above his elevated podium, and Hare Krishna devotees chanting and dancing.

Prabhupada and the Hare Krishna devotees left Tittenhurst when Yoko Ono's behavior became increasingly erratic. She asked them to leave one day, but then rescinded: "The only people I trust have shaved heads." As they departed for their newly built Radha Krishna temple in London, a freak storm emerged, and just minutes after they drove away, many of the prize trees on the property were ripped out of the ground by a violent, angry wind.[785]

"I Me Mine"

Written: January 7, 1969
Recorded: January 3, April 1, 1970
Released: May 8, 1970: Let It Be

As with many songs George Harrison wrote around this time, a spiritual meaning lay beneath its surface. George had learned there are two fields of life: absolute and relative. The absolute field is eternal, omnipresent, omniscient, omnipotent, and complete. That higher Self, or big "I," is universal consciousness (like an ocean). The relative field is this dualistic physical world and the lower self or ego, with whom we mistakenly identify (like a drop of water). When the drop realizes it is the ocean, spiritual enlightenment dawns.

In his autobiography *I, Me, Mine*, George explained that LSD was his biggest experience ever—like being catapulted out into space. After one dose of acid, George felt stuck in "relativity"—the dualistic material world: good/bad, yes/no, heaven/hell, and so on. He recalled, "Everything was relative to my ego—like, 'That's *my* piece of paper,' and 'That's *my* flannel,' or, 'Give it to *me*,' or '*I* am.' I hated my ego—it was false and impermanent. But later I [realized] there *is* somebody else in here apart from old blabbermouth."

George said once we realize whatever we experience through our five senses is not real, we can answer the question "Who am I?"[786]

Lord Krishna states in the Bhagavad Gita 2:54-65 and 71-72, "They are forever free who renounce all selfish desires and break away from the ego-cage of 'I,' 'me,' and 'mine' to be united with the Lord. Attain to this, and pass from death to immortality." George explained, "I kept coming across the words 'I, me and mine' in books about Yoga and stuff. And about the meaning of life and the difference between the ego and the soul, the real you and the 'you' that people mistake their identity to be."[787]

It seems ironic that when George first introduced *I Me Mine* to John on January 8, 1969, during the "Get Back" sessions, John replied with smug egotism: "Run along son, see you later," and patted George on the head. "We're a rock 'n' roll band you know. George, do you have any idea what we play?"[788]

On January 25, 1969, Paul was reminiscing how The Beatles had traveled to India and "sort of put our own personalities under for the sake of it." Though Paul and John said they did not regret traveling there, Paul admitted they had not been very truthful. He mocked John's reverence towards Maharishi, seeking "the answer" ("Tell me, Oh Master").

John then joked: "The 'word' is *Bagheera*" (the panther from Rudyard Kipling's *The Jungle Book*). Paul and John both agreed they should have been more themselves in India.

But George retorted disdainfully, "That is the biggest joke, to be yourselves. Because that was the purpose of going there—to try and find who your self really is. And if you were really yourself, you wouldn't be any of who we are now."[789]

 Scan this code to read the lyrics.

"Govinda"

Written: Traditional
Recorded: January 1970
Released: March 6, 1970: Single; May 21, 1971:
The Radha Krishna Temple

Govinda ("cowherd") and Gopala ("protector of cows") are names for the Hindu deity, the avatar Krishna (3228 b.c.–3102 b.c.), referencing Krishna's youth as a cowherd. Hindus believe the immortal soul of living beings continues after death and reincarnates repeatedly. In its long evolutionary path, each soul moves through tens of thousands of bodies, starting as microscopic organisms, then plants, animals, humans, angelic beings, and divine beings.

According to the caste (*varna*) system of India, Brahmins are born as priests, teachers, and intellectuals, Kshatriyas are warriors, kings, politicians, police, and administrators, Vaishyas are agriculturalists, merchants, and traders, and Shudras are artisans, laborers, and servants. Orthodox Hindus believe following their caste brings societal order and spiritual enlightenment. Deviation from that path results in an unstable, chaotic, suffering society.

Cattle are sacred in India because it is believed all cows become humans of Brahmin caste in their next life. If cows are slaughtered, their full development is impeded and they reincarnate as spiritually underdeveloped Brahmins. Therefore, to preserve the highest virtue of Brahmin priests and teachers, slaughtering cows is forbidden. Calling on Krishna as Govinda means praising him as the cowherd, the protector of the Brahmin caste.

Hare Krishna devotee Gurudas, whose wife, the accomplished Yamuna, sang lead on the record, said the song was "from the Satya Yuga or Golden Era of the universe and was passed down through the ages by a chain of self-realized gurus."[790]

Krishna devotees performing "Govinda"; Behind George: Yogeshwara Das; l. to r.: George Harrison, Shyamsundar Das, unknown, Tamal Krishna Das, Malati Devi Dasi, Dhananjaya Das, Hilavati Devi Dasi, Jotilla Devi Dasi, Jagannath Das, Yamuna Devi Dasi, Pritha Devi Dasi. Photo by Gurudas a.k.a. Roger Siegel.

 Scan this code to hear "Govinda" on The Radha Krishna Temple YouTube channel.

 Scan this code to follow along with the English translation.

Recording the Song

Recorded at Trident Studios in London, George Harrison played lead guitar and harmonium. Klaus Voormann played bass guitar and Ringo played drums, as he did on several of George's India-influenced records. Gurudas recalled Ringo asking about reincarnation and whether he could return next life as a cat. Gurudas asked, "Why a cat?"

Ringo replied, "Because I like cats," and laughed. Gurudas reflected about humans enduring so many animal births in order to reach human birth—but he kept that thought to himself.[791]

Shyamasundar played the stringed bowed Indian instrument *esraj*; Gurudas played *khartal* cymbals; and a Krishna devotee from Iran, Hari Vilas, played a fretless, lute-like oud. Billy Preston, Donovan, and Mary Hopkin joined the choruses.[792] Musicians from the London Philharmonic Orchestra overdubbed strings, harp, and tubular bells, arranged by John Barham, George's frequent collaborator who introduced much Indian music to the West.[793]

When Prabhupada first heard the record, he was moved to tears. He asked that it be played every morning during ISKCON worship service. "Govinda" continues to greet the deities daily at ISKCON temples around the world.[794] After the release of "Govinda," George accompanied Shyamasundar and other devotees to Paris to establish a temple.[795]

"My Sweet Lord"

Written: December 1969
Recorded: May to October 1970
Released: November 23, 1970: US: Single; January 15, 1971:
UK: Single; November 27, 1970: All Things Must Pass

"My Sweet Lord" was George Harrison's first single as a solo artist. It was his biggest hit, and the first number-one solo record for any Beatle. It remained number one—the bestselling UK single in 1971. In December 1970, John Lennon told Jann Wenner of *Rolling Stone*, "Every time I put the radio on, it's 'oh my Lord'— I'm beginning to think there must be a God!"[796]

In 1969, George picked up his guitar and started singing the word "Hallelujah" over a two-chord progression—inspired by the Edwin Hawkins Singers' version of the eighteenth-century hymn "Oh Happy Day." "It really just knocked me out, and I just felt a great feeling of the Lord. So, I thought, *I'll write another 'Oh Happy Day,'* which became 'My Sweet Lord.'"[797]

George said that in the pop world, no one was writing this type of music: "There was, I felt, a real need for that. So I thought, *Just do it. Nobody else is, and I'm sick of all these young people just boogying around, wasting their lives.*"[798]

Experiencing God Directly

George's mother was Catholic and would sometimes take him to church, where he was told Jesus is dead and unreachable. By the time he was age twelve, George decided the Catholic Church was "bullshit."[799] What impressed George about Indian religion was the promise of experiencing God directly. George said, "I believe in the saying, 'If there's a God, we must see him.' And I don't believe in the idea like, in most churches they say now, you're not gonna see him, he's way above you. Just believe what we tell you and shut up."[800]

George felt that through chanting and meditation, we could experience direct God realization: "But you don't get it in five minutes. It's something that takes a long time."[801] "You have to really struggle to see him but he can be seen. You have to practice."[802] "Once you get to the point where you're doing things for truth's sake, then nobody can ever touch you again, because you're harmonizing with a greater power."[803]

Harry Who?

George described, "'Hare' is the word that calls upon the energy that's around the Lord. Whichever Lord you like, really. But in this case it happens to be Krishna."[804] He further explained that Jesus's words became the Christian Bible, and Krishna's words became the Hindu Bible—the Bhagavad Gita.

George believed that by repeating the divine name, "It's the same if you were to go round chanting Christ, Christ, Christ, Christ. If you say it long enough, then you build up this identification. Whatever you identify with, you become one with it. So it's really a method of becoming one with God."[805]

Who is "My Sweet Lord"? George intended to create a non-sectarian anthem praising God, inclusive of all religions. George was an avid reader of both Eastern spirituality and alternative Christianity: the Gnostic gospels and Gospel of Thomas. George's signature on his letters included an *Om* symbol as well as a cross. He had a relationship with Christ as well as Krishna.[806] In 1969, George said, "I got to understand what Christ really was through Hinduism. Down through the ages there has always been the spiritual path, it's been passed on, it always will be, and if anybody ever wants it in any age it's always there."[807]

 Scan this code to read the lyrics.

The Sound, Lyrics, and Recording

"My Sweet Lord" is a love letter to God, in whatever form we believe—a universal prayer to the God of our personal understanding. George included both "Hallelujah" (praise to Christian God) and Hindu mantra "Hare Krishna" (praise to Hindu gods).

About mentioning "Lord" in the title, George said, "I thought a lot about whether to do that, because I would be committing myself publicly and I anticipated that a lot of people might get weird about it."[808]

In September 1982, George commented, "I wanted to show that 'Hallelujah' and 'Hare Krishna' are quite the same thing." The choral singers started chanting "Hallelujah" and then, half-way through the song, they switched to the Hare Krishna Maha-Mantra. He made that switch so "people would be chanting the Maha-Mantra before they knew what was going on." The song was meant as "a western pop equivalent of a mantra that repeats over and over again the holy names."[809]

George said, "'Hallelujah' is a joyous expression the Christians have, but 'Hare Krishna' has a mystical side to it. It's more than just glorifying God; it's asking to become His servant. And because of the mystic spiritual energy contained in those syllables, it's much closer to God than the way Christianity currently seems to be representing Him."[810]

The choral singers on the track also chanted Sanskrit words from the puja ceremony, which is sung during every TM Initiation, from the scripture the Guru Gita (Song of the Guru): *Gurur Brahma, Gurur Vishnur, Gurur Devo, Maheshwara. Gurur Sakshaat, Parabrahma. Tasmayi Shree Guruve Namah.*

During Maharishi's TM Teacher Training Course attended by The Beatles in Rishikesh, all course participants were required to memorize this verse. Here is the translation: "The guru is Brahma, Vishnu, and the great Lord Shiva. The guru is the eternal Brahman, the transcendental absolute. I bow to the supreme guru, adorned with glory."

 Scan this code to hear these Sanskrit words chanted at the beginning of this excerpt from Maharishi's puja ceremony.

George's iconic guitar riff, with its microtonal range vibrato, mimicked instruments such as dilruba and sarangi. This raga-rock element blended artfully with the gospel feeling and churchlike chorus. This slide guitar work, never heard previously on George's recordings, became his signature throughout his solo career.

Keyboard player Bobby Whitlock recalled, "All during the sessions, the door would pop open and in would spring three or four or five Hare Krishnas in their white robes and shaved heads with a ponytail coming out the top. They were all painted up [referring to white sandalwood paste and red kumkum on their foreheads], throwing rose petals and distributing peanut butter cookies."

The Song Lives On

Once "My Sweet Lord" was released, George received letters from fans worldwide, thanking him for validating their search for God.[811] Decades later, George said, "I still get letters from people, so I know by the Lord's grace I am a small part in the cosmic play."[812] "All I'm doing is acting out the part of Beatle George and we're all acting out our parts. You know, the world is a stage and the people are the players."[813] George declared he was only "pretending to be a Beatle," whereas his true purpose in life was to champion Indian music and Hinduism in the West.[814]

After George passed in 2001, "My Sweet Lord" was re-released in the UK, where it soared to number one again. Proceeds went to the Material World Charitable Foundation, which George established in 1973. Proceeds from the January 2002 US reissue of "My Sweet Lord" benefitted the Self-Realization Fellowship, which promotes teachings of Paramahansa Yogananda, author of *Autobiography of a Yogi*.

All Things Must Pass (album)

Written: 1966 to 1970
Recorded: May to October 1970
Released: November 27, 1970; August 6, 2021: All Things Must Pass: 50th Anniversary Box Set

After The Beatles' breakup, George Harrison launched the most successful solo career of all four Fabs. Although he had produced the instrumental *Wonderwall Music* (1968) and *Electronic Sound* (1969), he regarded *All Things Must Pass* (1970) as his first solo album. This triple album quickly soared to number one on the Billboard 200 album chart. And with "My Sweet Lord" topping the singles listings, George achieved a rare "Billboard Double."[815]

George had been stockpiling unreleased songs since 1966. When producer Phil Spector visited him at "Friar Park," Henley-on-Thames, Oxfordshire (his newly acquired palatial home and gardens), George said, "I have a few ditties for you to hear."

Phil commented, "It was endless! He had literally hundreds of songs and each one was better than the rest. He had all this emotion built up when it was released to me."[816]

Martin Scorsese, who produced the documentary *Living in the Material World*, remarked upon first hearing the album: "It was like walking into a cathedral. George was making spiritually awake music—we all heard and felt it—and I think that was the reason that he came to occupy a very special place in our lives."[817]

Here, a few songs from *All Things Must Pass* are illuminated.

"Isn't It a Pity"

Starting in 1965 with "Think for Yourself" and "If I Needed Someone," George's songs often conveyed a moral. In these *Rubber Soul* songs, George pointed blame by using the pronoun "you." However, in "Isn't It a Pity" George took personal responsibility by using "we." This song expressed regret about our blindness to the beauty around us, and remorse about our mistreating others and causing heartbreak.

George commented, "It was a chance to realize that if I felt somebody had let *me* down, then there's a good chance *I* was letting someone else down. We all tend to break each other's hearts, and not giving back—isn't it a pity."[818] "It's an observation of how society and myself were or are. We take each other for granted—and forget to give back."[819]

 Scan this code to read the lyrics.

"What Is Life"

Although we might consider this a teeny-bop love song, the title suggests something deeper. "What Is Life" is not a question love-struck teenagers would ask. At that time, George was no longer singing about teen crushes. He was crying out to God for the love that knows no boundaries. Without God's love, there is no life. Without walking beside God, life is meaningless.

 Scan this code to read the lyrics.

"Beware of Darkness"

Indian philosophy says our thoughts, words, and deeds determine our destiny. That Law of Karma is succinctly stated by Jesus, "It is done unto you as you believe" (Matthew 8:13), and "As you sow, so shall you reap" (2 Corinthians 9:6). The outcomes we envision will outpicture, manifesting our everyday experiences, whether positive or negative. We write our own script, we are the director, and we are the actor on our life's stage.

 Scan this code to read the lyrics.

The Lyrics

"Beware of Darkness" cautions us to eschew negative thoughts, embrace positive thoughts, disallow illusion from blocking our life purpose, and avoid harmful influences of conmen (shufflers), politicians (leaders), pop idols (swingers), and sad, hopeless thoughts.

The term *maya* is Sanskrit for "measure," though it is usually translated as "illusion," because we live in an illusory universe by virtue of maya, which impossibly divides wholeness into parts. Please read an explanation of how maya manifests this relative, dualistic, physical world on page 97–98. George said, "One by one, everybody's got to escape maya."[820]

Blue Atlas Cedars are strong, hearty trees, even under adverse conditions. The Beatles posed before these conifers during their final photo session in August 1969.

George composed the song in spring 1970, while devotees from the Radha Krishna Temple were staying at Friar Park and blessing it with a spiritually charged atmosphere while helping him renovate it.

"Awaiting on You All"

This track conveyed George's unapologetic feelings about chanting the Hare Krishna Maha-Mantra. In his autobiography *I, Me, Mine*, he stated the song was about *Japa Yoga* meditation—repeating mantras while counting 108 prayer beads on a *mala* (Indian rosary).

Ever since Ravi Shankar's brother Raju gave Vivekananda's book *Raja Yoga* to George in 1966, where he learned the saying *Tat Tvam Asi* ("I Am That"), George sought to realize God. He resonated with Hinduism, where God is within, in contrast to Catholicism, where God is unattainable. George affirmed, "Although Christ in my mind is an absolute yogi, I think many Christian teachers today are misrepresenting Christ. They're supposed to be representing Jesus, but they're not doing it very well. They're letting him down very badly, and that's a big turn off."[821]

 Scan this code to read the lyrics.

The Lyrics

In this song, George extolled direct experience of God and denounced trappings of organized religion (churches, temples, rosaries, books, the Pope); travel gear (passports, visas); symbols of hippies (horoscopes, love-ins); and John and Yoko's activism (bed-ins). George declared, "By chanting the names of the Lord, you'll be cleansed. You don't need a passport or visa to see Jesus. Just open your heart."[822]

George espoused Bhakti Yoga ("divine union through devotion to God"), one of four main paths of Yoga, which he had adopted since discovering Krishna. Prabhupada, founder of ISKCON, claimed chanting God's names is the direct path to moksha (liberation) in our Kali Age (the age of ignorance). The lyrics expressed that by addressing our own imperfections rather than trying to fix everyone else, human suffering could be averted.

George said, "The best thing you can give is God consciousness. Manifest your own divinity first. The truth is there. It's right within us all. Understand what you are. If people would just wake up to what's real, there would be no misery in the world. I guess chanting's a pretty good place to start."[823]

In accord with George's signature microtonal sound he adopted after giving up sitar, he played slide guitar on the track to achieve the glissando riffs, which imitate Indian instruments.

"Art of Dying"

There is an art of living and an art of dying. Both are identical. By realizing our true nature, we find contentment, fulfill our destiny, and achieve final liberation, known in Hinduism as moksha. This song, written in 1966, is about attaining that enlightened state, where we no longer need to reincarnate. Because spiritual enlightenment was a new concept in the West at the time, George asked twice during the song whether we believe him.

 Scan this code to read the lyrics.

In August 1966, George described his personal goal: "To do as well as I can do, whatever I attempt, and someday to die with a peaceful mind."[824] "You can't just at the end of your life start thinking about God. It's not something you just stumble upon—consciousness and self-realization. You have to work for it."[825] Carl Roles told me that George often said, "We know we're going to die but we don't believe it." He likened bodily death to taking off our suit when we get home. But we still have two other suits: the astral body made of light, and the causal body.[826]

The only reason we are in embodiment is because we are ignorant. We have already lived countless lifetimes as microscopic organisms, plants, animals, and humans. Unless we engage in sadhana (spiritual practice), we will live many more, climbing the slow ladder of evolution, becoming increasingly aware at each rung. At death, we enter a divine light and dwell in a heavenly realm for some time, until we return to a human womb chosen for our specific soul growth, then take birth again and again, repeatedly.

George told journalist Don Short, "I am sure I was with Paul, John and Ringo before. What were we doing? I've no idea but we couldn't have done all that good because we wouldn't be here now. We didn't make it."[827] George declared that the only way out of the karmic cycle of reincarnation is to follow a genuine spiritual practice, whereby we can realize our true nature and unify with supreme Spirit.[828]

No longer bound to the material word by "seeds of karma" (attachments known as samskara), we can choose to never take birth again. In that state of moksha (liberation), we can merge with the undifferentiated absolute *Brahman*, the supreme Godhead, and give up our individuality; or we can dwell in a celestial *loka* (realm) with the personal deity of our choice and maintain our individuality. (For a deeper explanation of seven possible choices human souls can make at death, please read my book *Ascension*.)

When The Beatles were studying in Rishikesh, Maharishi told one of his brahmacharyas, "Of all The Beatles, George is the most advanced, and this is his last life." George had achieved the art of living and the art of dying.

"Hear Me Lord"

A composition rejected by George's Beatle-mates in January 1969, "Hear Me Lord" was a personal prayer set to music. It was written January 4 to 5, when his wife Pattie Boyd left temporarily after learning of an affair between George and a French woman staying in their home. At the time, George got an idea that he should be like Lord Krishna, a spiritual being with a retinue of beautiful *gopi* (consorts) around him (including Ringo's wife Maureen), tending to his needs. At that time, George's wife Pattie became "almost suicidal" due to George's moody intensity and Krishna-mania about meditation and chanting.[829]

Scan this code to
read the lyrics.

In this song, George expressed regret and sought forgiveness and strength as he strove to raise his consciousness and release the pangs of desire (samskara) that bound him to the karmic wheel (samsara). He sang of God's nature, immanent and everywhere present. This was an appeal for God to hear his plea and a request for God's love, mercy, and compassion to forgive and transform him. George said, "Music should be used for the perception of God, not jitterbugging."[830] "I want to be God-conscious. That's really my only ambition, and everything else in life is incidental."[831] This obsessive fixation contributed to his split with Pattie, who confessed that even though she left George for Eric Clapton, George was always the love of her life.[832]

"All Things Must Pass"

The inspiration for "All Things Must Pass" came from Timothy Leary's book *Psychedelic Prayers after the Tao Te Ching*. Leary adapted "All Things Pass" from various translations of Chapter 16 of Lao Tzu's Tao Te Ching (see pages 181–182).

 Scan this code to read Timothy
Leary's poem "All Things Pass"
by scrolling down to I-5.

Scan this code to read
George Harrison's lyrics for
"All Things Must Pass."

The song's theme is the ever-changing, transient nature of the physical world. Nothing lasts. All things in relative manifest creation pass away. But the absolute infinite consciousness is eternal. In Taoism, that is called *Tao* (the Way). George's hopeful message is that negative experiences do not last. After every long night, the sun rises again.

On the track, the pedal steel guitar created George's signature sound of microtonal sliding notes that mimic an Indian dilruba or sarangi.

All Things Must Pass (50th Anniversary Edition)

The boxed set edition *All Things Must Pass*, released on August 6, 2021, included some of George's heretofore-unreleased tracks. Here is information about a few of them.

"Om Hare Om (Gopala Krishna)"

This lovely song written and chanted by George praises Krishna, his consort Radha, and other Hindu gods. The sweetness in his voice expresses his devotion.

Scan this code to see the lovely
kaleidoscopic video with lyrics.

The three main gods in Hinduism—Brahma (creator), Vishnu (maintainer), and Shiva (destroyer)—are lords over the modes of operation, the three gunas (rajas, sattva, and tamas), by which all things in this ever-changing universe are continually created, maintained, and transformed in each moment. Without these three functions, nothing could ever happen.

Krishna is one of the ten incarnations of the "maintainer" god Vishnu. Hare is the energy (shakti) of Krishna, embodied in his consort "Radha." The word Hare means "all-attractive." *Rama* is another of the ten incarnations of Vishnu. Rama's wife is "Sita." *Om* is the primordial sound that gives rise to the universe. *Govinda* means cowherd or keeper of the Veda (supreme truth), and *Gopala* means protector of cows and protector of the world. These are both epithets of Lord Krishna. Lord Shiva's consort is "Bala." Both *Jai* and *Jaya* mean "glory." So this song praises the gods Vishnu and Shiva, along with their consorts.

"Cosmic Empire"

This song is about visiting the celestial *loka* (worlds) of Lord Krishna and other deities of the Hindu religion, a heavenly place George was waiting in queue to experience. Rather than a material empire, this cosmic empire in subtle planes is experienced in meditation.

From an unbounded, omnipresent perspective, we can see beyond this physical realm. There, one truth shines clearly and brightly, which feels like light. This physical world disappears when we experience the brilliance of that heavenly realm. In that irresistible state of bliss, our souls fill with joy. That transcendental experience of divine love and light is our true nature—immortal and indestructible.

 Scan this code to see the exquisite Indian-themed psychedelic video with lyrics.

"Mother Divine"

George's widow Olivia Harrison said she ran across the lyrics to "Mother Divine" while compiling the 2017 revision of *I, Me, Mine*. Olivia believed George wrote the song in India during the late 1960s. She said, "It's a lovely sentiment, and something he did sing over the years, maybe as a mantra."[833]

 Scan this code to read the lyrics.

I believe Olivia was spot on about George writing this song during his time of involvement with Maharishi Mahesh Yogi, who often used the term "Mother Divine" to refer to the goddess. Each year, Maharishi went into silence and stayed inside his room for one week, starting at midnight New Year's Eve. When he came out of silence at midnight January 7 into 8, a handful of us closest disciples would enter his private meeting room. He would then reveal what Mother Divine had told him during silence. Each year on his birthday, January 12, he would then announce a new theme for the year during the lavish yearly celebration, flourishing with pomp and circumstance.

The Radha Krsna Temple [album]

Written: Traditional
Recorded: July 1969, January to March 1970
Released: May 21, 1971, US; May 28, 1971, UK

The Radha Krsna Temple is an album of Hindu *bhajan* (devotional songs) recorded by London Hare Krishna chanters. These eternal sounds of love take listeners beyond barriers of time and space to the ecstatic realm of Krishna consciousness, joyfully experienced as inner peace and awareness of God.

George said, "Everybody is looking for Krishna. Some don't realize that they are but they are. Krishna is GOD, the Source of all that exists, the Cause of all that is, was or ever will be. As God is unlimited, He has many names, Allah, Buddha, Jehovah, Rama: all are Krishna, all are ONE. God is not abstract; He has both the impersonal and the personal aspects to His personality. As a single drop of water has the same qualities as an ocean of water, so has our consciousness the qualities of GOD'S consciousness."[834]

In the Hare Krishna Movement, gathering in temples for kirtana (recitation) is central to their spiritual practice. This involves chanting devotional songs, music, and/or dancing. One or more leaders sing the verse; then the group repeats the verse in call-and-response chanting.

Released on the Apple label and produced by George Harrison, the album included two hit singles, "Hare Krishna Mantra" and "Govinda," as well as other Sanskrit mantras from the Gaudiya Vaishnava (Vishnu devotees) tradition. Mukunda Das created the musical arrangements.[835]

 Scan this code to listen to this entrancing, spiritual album.

George on guitar and Mukunda Das on harmonium arranging music. Photo by Gurudas a.k.a. Roger Siegel.

Vocals and Instruments

George played guitar and bass on the album. On the tracks "Sri Guruvastakam" and "Sri Isopanisad," he played a Dobro resonator guitar. Like a lap steel guitar, it is played on the lap with a pick and slide, mimicking microtonal sliding notes of Indian stringed instruments. Yamuna and other Krishna temple devotees sang vocals, and they played the harmonium, mridangam (double-headed drum), tambura (drone instrument), and *khartal* (cymbals).[836]

The *murti* (idols) of Krishna and Radha from the temple at Bury Place in London adorned the album cover. The inner sleeve displayed a print of Chaitanya Mahaprabhu. A photo of Prabhupada graced the back cover.

George recalled that recording the abum "was more fun than trying to make a pop hit record. It was the feeling of utilizing your skills to do some spiritual service for Krishna."[837] In 1973, Paul McCartney mentioned the *Radha Krsna Temple* album as "great stuff" and an example of a worthwhile project undertaken by Apple.[838]

Tracks on the Album

Tracks 1–7 per original release:
1. "Govinda"
2. "Sri Guruvastak"
3. "Bhaja Bhakata/Arotrika"
4. "Hare Krsna Mantra"
5. "Sri Isopanisad"
6. "Bhaja Hure Mana"
7. "Govinda Jai Jai"

Bonus tracks on the remastered album of 2010
8. "Prayer to the Spiritual Masters"
9. "Namaste Saraswati Devi"

The Concert for Bangladesh (album)

Recorded: August 1, 1971
Released: December 20, 1971: US; January 10, 1972: UK

In June 1971 in Los Angeles, when Ravi Shankar told George about the genocide of millions of Bengalis in East Pakistan during Operation Searchlight, George organized two fundraising concerts. He urged colleagues to join the first high-profile supergroup musical charity event ever. He composed "Bangla Desh" as a charity single and released it four days before the concerts.

On the B-side was "Deep Blue," about the death of George's mother. As Louise Harrison lay dying in July 1970, George read to her passages from the Bhagavad Gita and chanted softly in her ear. The serious atmosphere of "Deep Blue" made an appropriate accompaniment to the A-side about the Bangladesh crisis.[839]

The Concert for Bangladesh was a triple album, recorded live August 1, 1971, at Madison Square Garden, New York, and released on Apple records. In aid of homeless refugees of the Bangladesh Liberation War, this pioneering event set the precedent for future benefits such as Live Aid in 1985 and the Concert for

New York City in 2001. A total of forty thousand people attended the concerts, and the initial gate receipts raised nearly $250,000 for Bangladesh relief, administered by UNICEF.

 Scan this code to watch a short video about the concert.

The Concert for Bangladesh topped charts in several countries and won the Grammy for Album of the Year in March 1973. Reissued in 2005, sales continue to benefit the George Harrison Fund for UNICEF, which raised $1.2 million for children in the Horn of Africa to mark the album's fortieth anniversary.

The Musicians

The all-star cast of twenty-four musicians included rock musicians George Harrison, Ringo Starr, Bob Dylan, Eric Clapton, Billy Preston, Leon Russell, Badfinger, Klaus Voormann, and more, as well as classical Indian musicians Ravi Shankar (sitar), Ali Akbar Khan (sarod), Alla Rakha (tabla), and Kamala Chakravarty (tambura). This was the first time George and Ringo performed together in concert since 1966, and Dylan's first live appearance after a five-year hiatus.

Allarakha Quereshi (a.k.a. Ustad Alla Rakha) declared, "God sent me into this world as a tabla player." At age ten he ran away from home to study tabla. Formally adopted by a Punjabi musician, he began a strict regimen of rigorous practice in both tabla and vocals. In 1940, Rakha played the first ever tabla solo on All-India Radio. He composed music for two dozen Bollywood movies and played with the top classical musicians. Starting in 1959, as Ravi Shankar's accompanist for over three decades, Rakha introduced tabla to the Western world. Rakha said of Ravi, "He's a very good artist and is like a brother."[840] Rakha's sons have continued his legacy. (Use the QR code on page 73 to watch Alla Rakha play.)

Ustad Ali Akbar Khan playing sarod. Photo courtesy of Ali Akbar Khan Foundation.

Baba Allauddin Khan: exacting, demanding music teacher of Ravi Shankar and Ali Akbar Khan. Photo courtesy of Aashish Khan.

Starting at age three, renowned sarod player Ali Akbar Khan was tutored in vocal composition and many instruments by his father, the legendary Baba Allauddin Khan, a strict taskmaster who taught music until over age 100 and died at age 105. Allauddin said, "To a musician, music should be the Supreme Deity who will be worshipped with the eagerness of an undivided mind, and tears shall be his ritual ingredients."[841] Lessons for Ali Akbar and eventually his sister Annapurna Devi (who was trained on surbahar—bass sitar) would begin before dawn and continue for eighteen hours.

Ravi Shankar also studied with Allauddin Khan, and Annapurna Devi became Ravi's first wife in 1941 in an arranged marriage (he was twenty-one and she was fourteen). When the couple played concerts together, she received all the accolades. It was said she had inherited Allauddin's genius and neither Ravi nor Ali Akbar could match her ability. To try to save her marriage, Annapurna took a vow to never perform in public again. But in 1962, Ravi abandoned her for Kamala Chakravarty (sister-in-law of Ravi's brother Rajendra), who had been Ravi's companion since 1943. Ravi and Annapurna formally divorced in 1981. They both remarried. Their son Shubhendra ("Shubho") Shankar, who studied with his mother and played surbahar on *Shankar Family & Friends* (see his photo on page 418), died at age fifty in 1992.[842]

Allauddin Khan extolled his daughter as Saraswati (goddess of the arts). As tutor for some of the finest musicians of India, she was as strict and as venerated as her father. Her students swore that when she practiced surbahar late at night, her entire apartment emitted an inexplicable sandalwood fragrance. Allauddin told her this was how Saraswati made her presence known.[843]

In the seventies, when George Harrison was visiting India with violinist Yehudi Menuhin, the Indian Prime Minister Indira Gandhi offered them her assistance. Menuhin said he wanted something impossible. Could Mrs. Gandhi get Annapurna Devi to play for him? After much persuasion the reclusive maestro agreed, but not to give a performance. She would allow him to attend her early morning practice session. Because Menuhin had to rush back home due to a family illness, George became the lucky one to see her play.[844] (See Annapurna Devi's photo on page 425.)

Living in the Material World (album)

Recorded: February 1971, October 1972 to March 1973
Released: May 30, 1973

Living in the Material World, George's love letter to Lord Krishna, reflected his search for spiritual enlightenment amid a life of superstardom. Upon meeting ISKCON's founder in September 1969, George was impressed with his sincerity. Prabhupada declared himself "the humble servant of the servant of the servant" of Krishna, and advocated chanting God's name.[845]

George counts mantras with beads using his Japa Yoga prayer bag.

George embraced the practice passionately, counting prayer beads stored inside a cloth bag worn over his shoulder—a Japa Yoga prayer bag. However, he grew tired of people asking if he had injured his hand: "There was a period when I was heavy into chanting and I had my hand in my bead bag all the time. In the end I used to say, 'Yeah. Yeah. I had an accident,' because it was easier than explaining everything."[846]

Visiting Prabhupada

In 1969 George admitted that, visiting Prabhupada, "I get so nervous when I am around His Divine Grace." Humble and unassuming, George entered his room one time, fully prostrated, and offered prayers. Prabhupada smiled ear-to-ear. George sat back by the door, but Prabhupada beckoned him to come near, then greeted him and hugged him.

During their conversation, George asked if he should shave his head and live in the temple. Prabhupad said emphatically, "No! You have a great gift for the world in your music. Just continue your music and Krishna will be greatly pleased and He will bless you." "I will give you some ideas for your songs." Then Prabhupada recited a few songs from the Hare Krishna songbook. George came back daily for a week, along with Ravi Shankar, to meet him in the afternoons. Soon after this, George wrote "My Sweet Lord."[847]

At Bhaktivedanta Manor in summer 1973, Prabhupada told George: "You have given us this shelter, and Krishna will give *you* shelter—at his lotus feet."[848] Prabhupada later referred to George as ISKCON's "archangel" for his generosity.[849] In November 1977, on his deathbed at the Vrindavan, India temple, Prabhupada removed a ring from his finger and instructed his devotees to deliver it to George.[850]

George to the Extreme

Due to George's obsessions, Pattie and close friends wondered which George would appear at any point: "His Lectureship," pontificating about spirituality and dipping into his ever-present prayer bag (to count mantras); or dipping into the coke bag (to snort cocaine; or crashing his Mercedes into a roundabout at ninety miles an hour; or shagging Ringo's wife Maureen.[851]

George admitted, "I am an extreme person. I was always extremely up or extremely down, extremely spiritual or extremely drugged."[852] "Oh yeah. I'm living in it [the material world]. But people interpret it to mean money, cars, that sort of thing—although those are part of the material world. The material world is the physical world [manifest relative creation], as opposed to the spiritual [unmanifest transcendental realm]. For me, living in the material world just meant being in this physical body with all the things that go along with it."[853] "We're all conditioned, our consciousness has been so polluted by the material energy it's hard to pull it all away in order to really discover our true nature."[854]

While recording the album *Living in the Material World*, George created the atmosphere of Little India in the studio. Bass player Klaus Voormann described, "He put up joss sticks, made a nice smell, turned the lights down, a really nice surrounding. He played the song and then slowly we would start picking up the feel of the song. We could take our time, do what we wanted, make suggestions."

George included an insert in the album—a reproduction of a painting of Krishna driving his disciple Arjuna's horse-drawn chariot, taken from the cover of Prabhupada's edition of the Bhagavad Gita. George explained, "I wanted to give them all a chance to see Krishna, to know about him."[855]

The album's front cover, representing the spiritual world, showed a Kirlian photograph (aura photo) of George's right hand, taken in Thelma Moss's famed parapsychology laboratory at UCLA. He held a silver medallion of Baba Ramdev Pir on horseback, a ruler from the late fourteenth century with miraculous powers who opposed the strict caste system and championed the poor. Believed to be an incarnation of Lord Vishnu, Pir is worshipped in Rajasthan, India.

The back cover represented the material world with a Kirlian photograph of George's left hand holding three US coins.

"Give Me Love (Give Me Peace on Earth)"

This song is George's prayer to Krishna, as he sought to touch and reach the deity with his heart and soul. He pleaded with Krishna to take his hand and grant him love, world peace, hope, inner strength (to deal with the burden of human life), and moksha (liberation, freedom from reincarnation). George declared, "Everybody is worried about dying, but the cause of death is birth, so if you don't want to die, don't get born!"[856]

George chants the mantra *Om* in the song, which is the sound that is said to give rise to and underlie the universe. In his memoir *I, Me, Mine*, George explained, "This song is a prayer and personal statement between me, the Lord, and whoever likes it."[857]

 Scan this code to read the lyrics.

"The Light That Has Lighted the World"

This song is about the gap between spiritual seekers and those who do not understand them. Back in the sixties, we hippie flower children spurned our families, religions, backgrounds, and society at large. Our loved ones did not understand our discontent with the status quo. We were looking beyond the horizon to a new vision. We sought to change the world through raising our own consciousness as well as world consciousness.

Scan this code to
read the lyrics.

Beatles fans felt George had subscribed to a strange cult, the Hare Krishnas, considered the laughingstock of the time. Westerners dressed in Indian robes with partially shaved heads and ponytails were dancing in the streets, chanting Hindu mantras, handing out leaflets, distributing bizarre vegetarian food, and worshipping Hindu gods.

George was not the same fab Beatle his fans expected. They did not want him to change, and they did not want to change themselves. Those stuck in a hole could not experience their soul. They just wanted the old George back. But he said, "I'd rather be one of the devotees of God than one of the straight, so-called sane or normal people who just don't understand that man is a spiritual being, that he has a soul."[858]

However, even George had his limits. In a 1987 interview for *Guitar World*, Chris Willman recalled Hare Krishnas soliciting him at the airports in the seventies: "I'd be wearing a Beatles shirt and they'd come up and say, "Do you like George Harrison?""

George replied to Chris: "If their master [Srila Prabhupada] had known they were doing that, they would have got their behinds kicked. It's biting the hand that feeds you. I was trying to help them, and I'd find there'd be all that stuff going on behind my back, giving me a bad name. I've been associated and have friends in that, but I never joined 'em. I mean, I joined 'em in spirit, but not in that spirit of trying to rip people off at airports."[859]

In later years, George often spent time at Yogananda's Self Realization Fellowship retreat in Encinitas, California, overlooking the Pacific Ocean, only three miles from Ravi Shankar's home. Ravi had met Yogananda in the 1930s and gave his first US concert at the retreat in 1957. SRF strictly respects its members' privacy, which George appreciated after his notorious affiliation with Krishna devotees. He felt calmed by the quiet ambience of the SRF retreat and the organization's focus on achieving heightened awareness through the practice of Babaji's Kriya Yoga.[860]

Musician Gary Wright said the president of SRF, Sri Daya Mata, truly embodied her name—'mother of compassion.' "When George came to L.A. feeling a bit down spiritually, he would often ask me to arrange a meeting with her and we'd drive to Mother Center together. How touching it was to watch him *pranam* [bow down] when he first greeted her, as they do in India. In her presence we became like little boys, bathing in the love she exuded."[861]

"Living in the Material World"

The musical arrangement and lyrics in this song contrast material and spiritual goals in a playful, amusing way, by switching back and forth between rock and raga. George on sitar and Ustad Zakir Hussain on tabla appeared in the verses about spirituality, sweet memories, and prayers.

Ustad Zakir Hussain playing tabla.

Ustad Zakir Hussain, son of famed tabla maestro Ustad Alla Rakha, is a tabla superstar, composer, producer, and movie star. Tutoring Zakir in the barrel-shaped two-headed drum *pakhavaj* at age three, his father Alla Rakha woke him at 3:00 a.m. daily and they recited rhythms till 6:00 a.m. Zakir performed his first concert at age seven and was touring by age eleven. He moved to the San Francisco Bay Area to accompany famed sarod player Ali Akbar Khan on tabla. He plays 150 concert dates a year and has recorded Grammy-Award-winning albums.[862]

 Scan this code to read the lyrics.

The Lyrics

In this song, George expressed his search for salvation and escape from the misery of physical existence through Lord Krishna's grace. He underscored the illusory nature of human existence and the necessity of ending the cycle of reincarnation. The human body, the vehicle of physical existence, was likened to a car that wears out. He characterized worldly life as endless, engulfing, frustrating tidal waves of unfulfilled desires, and prayed he would not get lost in it.

George said that after writing the song, "I decided to call the foundation the Material World Foundation. Most people would think of the material world as representing purely money and greed and take offence. But in my view, it's the idea that if it is money and greed, then give the greedy money away in the material world."[863]

The publishing royalties for nearly all songs on *Living in the Material World* were assigned in perpetuity to the Material World Foundation, which encourages alternate and diverse forms of artistic expression, life views, and philosophies and also supports established charities and people with special needs.

"Be Here Now"

"Be Here Now" is one of George's most melodious spiritual songs. It was inspired by the book *Be Here Now* (1971), authored by psychedelic guru Richard Alpert (a.k.a. Ram Dass). In 1967, Dass became a disciple of Neem Karoli Baba, an exceptional Indian saint who inspired millions of spiritual devotees worldwide. Dass's book popularized yoga and Indian philosophy in the West.

 Scan this code to read the lyrics.

The Lyrics

The song advised us to dwell in the eternal now, because the only real thing is the infinite, beyond time and space. Time is an illusory way to measure eternity. The past is just a memory, and thus unreal. The future is unknown, also not real. It is impossible to identify a time called the "present," because it keeps disappearing each moment. "Now" is not a finite concept. But when we experience the transcendental infinite bliss within, we are present in the eternal Presence now and always. George sang about an unwise, wandering mind, dwelling in illusion and not focused on that Presence. Meditation is a way to experience the Presence.

"It's being here now that's important," George said. "There's no past and there's no future. Time is a very misleading thing. All there is ever, is the now. We can gain experience from the past, but we can't relive it; and we can hope for the future, but we don't know if there is one."[864]

Olivia Harrison recalled that sometimes Dhani [their son] would ask, "Well, what if this happens?"

George's reply would be "Be here now. Be here now."[865]

This hypnotic raga-rock track, with its beautifully sung Indian-style melody, is reminiscent of "Blue Jay Way." There is also a lovely Indian drone background—an organ imitating a tambura.

"The Lord Loves the One (That Loves the Lord)"

In 1982, George declared this song was about Srila Prabhupada, founder of the ISKCON movement: "I didn't realize it then, but I see now that because of him, the *mantra* has spread so far in the last sixteen years, more than it had in the last five centuries."[866]

 Scan this code to read the lyrics.

The Lyrics

The lyrics reflect Prabhupada's philosophy of placing the quest for Krishna Consciousness above all other endeavors, such as domination, conquest, fame, and wealth. The ancient Indian scripture Katha Upanishad 1.2.6 states, "Intoxicated, deluded by the glamour of riches, the childish do not see that they must pass away. They think, 'This is the world and there is no other.'"[867]

This song was George's object lesson about the Law of Karma, which states that as you give, you will receive. "As you sow, so shall you reap" (Galatians 6:7). The Sanskrit word *karma* means "action." Every action (thought, word, and deed) has consequences.

George's point was that we create our destiny moment by moment. Nothing ever happens to us. We only happen to ourselves. Therefore, we are responsible for ourselves and should not blame God for whatever pickle we find ourselves in. "The gods help those who help themselves" is an ancient Greek saying.

Calling politicians "big girl's blouse" is a British slur for a wimpy guy. However, George was equally hard on himself when he sang about name, fame, and fortune in the second verse.

"Try Some, Buy Some"

This love song to God expressed George's conversion from sex, drugs, and rock 'n' roll to devotion to God. The lyrics contrasted the life of a rock star (a diseased world of fleeting, seemingly glamorous pleasures found in drugs, and ending in loneliness, bitterness, and death) to the life of a devotee to God (a new world of love, happiness, peace, contentment, and eternal life). For anyone who has suffered drug addiction and found a way back to sobriety, this track strikes a chord.

 Scan this code to read the lyrics.

"That Is All"

George stated this last track on the album said everything he wanted to say. It was The Beatles' theme, as well as the theme of George's solo career: Love is all you need, love can save the world, love can heal you, love is all there is to live for, and love is in the silence—not in the words. God's love is all George wanted. He loved God, and that was enough.

 Scan this code to read the lyrics.

George told *Rolling Stone*, "I think all love is part of a universal love. When you love a woman, it's the God in her that you see. The only complete love is for God."[868] Other songs George wrote as love letters to God, or the God within women, include "Long, Long, Long," "What Is Life," "Don't Let Me Wait Too Long," and "Learning How to Love You."

George played his signature slide guitar on the track to again invoke the flavor of Indian instrumentation.

CHAPTER 12

CUTTING KARMIC CHORDS

"Give Peace a Chance"

Written: May 1969
Recorded: June 1, 1969
Released: July 4, 1969 Single UK; July 7, 1969 Single US

Though Maharishi Mahesh Yogi's essential mission was to create world peace, John Lennon might be remembered as the greatest peace advocate of the twentieth century. The powerful effect of "Give Peace a Chance" and "Imagine" cannot be overstated.

John spoke of Yoko, "When we met, and we discussed what we wanted to do together, what we wanted to do was carry on me in my 'love, love, love' and her in her 'peace, peace, peace'; put it together and that's how we came out with the bed-in."[869]

From March 25 to 31, 1969, while youngsters fought a pointless, unwinnable war in Vietnam, John and Yoko invited reporters to their first one-week "Bed-in for Peace" in room 902, the Presidential Suite at the Amsterdam Hilton, to celebrate their honeymoon. They conceived "bed-ins" as nonviolent war protests—like "sit-ins," where protesters sat in groups until their demands were met (or, more likely, they got arrested).

John and Yoko bed-in, Amsterdam Hilton, March 1969.

From their bedly-pulpit, dressed in pajamas, the couple preached peaceful alternatives to violence, "in the tradition of Gandhi—only with a sense of humor."[870] John said, "I'm selling peace, and Yoko and I are just one big advertising campaign. We're Mr. and Mrs. Peace." He thought this would make people laugh, but also make them think.[871]

John and Yoko at Schiphol airport leaving Amsterdam after their bed-in.

On May 26, 1969, John, Yoko, and Yoko's daughter Kyoko checked into the Queen Elizabeth Hotel in Montreal for another one-week bed-in. When a reporter confronted John about what he was trying to achieve, he replied spontaneously, "Just give peace a chance."[872]

The couple reserved several rooms, but their famous "Bed-in for Peace" occurred in Room 1742, where John wrote and recorded "Give Peace a Chance." Some Toronto Krishna devotees sang along, playing cymbals and drums, and the Hare Krishna Maha-Mantra (see page 351) made it onto the track.

Montreal Bed-in "Give Peace a Chance": John and Yoko in bed, Tommy Smothers playing guitar, Timothy Leary and wife Rosemary singing. Pictorial Press Ltd/Alamy Stock Photo.

This first solo record by John Lennon sold over two million copies and became an immediate anti-war anthem—sung by five hundred thousand demonstrators led by activist Pete Seeger in Washington, DC, on Vietnam Moratorium Day, November 15, 1969.

 Scan this code to read the lyrics for "Give Peace a Chance."

The Montreal Bed-in was made into a documentary film *Bed Peace*, which you can watch via the QR code below. Those who visited John and Yoko in bed included LSD advocates Timothy Leary and Rosemary Woodruff Leary; singer Petula Clark; comedian/activist Dick Gregory; Beat poet Allen Ginsberg; DJ/promoter Murray the K; CFOX DJs Charles P. Rodney Chandler and Roger Scott; Toronto rabbi Abraham Feinberg; Joseph Schwartz; Canadian politician Allan Rock; satirist Al Capp; journalist Ritchie Yorke; and comedian Tommy Smothers of the Smothers Brothers, who played acoustic guitar on the record.

 Scan this code to
watch *Bed Peace*.

"Instant Karma!"

Written: January 27, 1970
Recorded: January 27, 1970
Released: February 6, 1970: Single

John and Yoko celebrated the 1970 New Year in Aalborg, Denmark, with Yoko's ex-husband Tony Cox, Tony's girlfriend Melinda Kendall, and Yoko's six-year-old daughter Kyoko Chan Cox, who was living with Tony. During this visit, John, Yoko, Tony, and Melinda were discussing "karma." When they conceived a concept of karmic consequences occurring immediately rather than stretched over a lifetime, Melinda coined the phrase "instant karma."[873]

Two days after returning to England, on January 27, 1970, John woke up inspired with a song based on this idea. He wrote "Instant Karma!" on a piano in one hour and phoned George Harrison: "Come over to Apple quick, I've just written a monster."[874] George brought along Phil Spector to mix the record, and four musicians played: John on piano, George on guitar, Klaus Voormann on bass, and Alan White on drums.

An instant song in one day: "Instant Karma!"—an instant success, the first Beatles solo single to sell a million copies.

Lennon/Ono/Cox extended family; l. to r.: Yoko, John, Kyoko, Tony, Melinda.
Keystone Press/Alamy Stock Photo.

Instant Karma Struck

As fate would have it, John and Yoko had strange karma with Tony and Melinda and also Maharishi, who held a TM Teacher Training Course in Calas de Mallorca in 1971, where I was working on staff. On April 23, John and Yoko suddenly appeared at Hotel Samoa's front desk to "collect" Yoko's seven-year-old daughter Kyoko, while her father Tony Cox and his wife Melinda Kendall were meditating on the course. Cox had custody of Kyoko, but a battle raged over visitation rights.

Though John and Yoko wore dumb disguises, everyone recognized them, including the hotel manager, who called Maharishi's skin-boy "Gregory" to meet "Mr. and Mrs. Smith." When faced with John and Yoko, the gobsmacked Gregory was incapable of uttering a sound. Yet someone pointed the Lennons in the right direction, because they kidnapped Kyoko from daycare at 1:00 p.m. Cox reported the abduction to the Guardia Civil. By 5:00 p.m., Miguel Buñola from the Criminal Investigation Brigade arrested John and Yoko at Hotel Meliá Mallorca on Palma's Paseo Marítimo, where they were staying.

Outside the courthouse: Yoko, John, and Miguel Buñola on the right. Diario de Mallorca. Photographer Tortelló.

Kyoko is returned to Tony and Melinda. Diario de Mallorca. Photographer Tortelló.

Buñola recalled that John and Yoko acted with extreme polite-ness. As they left the police station, a journalist from *Diario de Mallorca* asked Buñola to take the couple for drinks so he could get the story. All four had coffee and milk at Formentor Bar then pro-ceeded to the Palace of Justice, in Plaza del Mercat, where newspa-per photographer Joan LLompart Torrelló took photos. For seven hours, Buñola tried to keep the beautiful seven-year-old girl calm.

Late that night, Kyoko was returned to her father. The Lennons received a parole discharge on the condition that they fly to Paris. The kidnapping charge was dropped. Buñola said he had met other famous personalities, but his coffee with the Lennons was his "most beautiful episode."[875]

After the Lennons were awarded custody of Kyoko later that year, Tony and Melinda abducted Kyoko and went into hiding. They joined a cult, "The Walk," and brainwashed Kyoko to believe John and Yoko personified evil. Sadly, Yoko did not reunite with her daughter Kyoko and granddaughter Emi until 1997. John never saw Kyoko again.

Karmic Law

The Law of Karma is widely misunderstood. The Sanskrit word *karma* means "action." It does not mean payback, retribution, reward, punishment, or predetermined fate. There are no past-life karmic debts that we must pay in future lives. Nor do karmic lords, courts, trials, or judges sentence us.

According to Karmic Law, we create our own destiny, moment by moment, through every thought, word, and deed. Whatever we think, say, or do produces consequences. When we drop a pebble into a small pond, ripples radiate outward. When these ripples reach the pond's edge, they converge back towards the center. In the same way, even imperceptible thoughts affect the universe profoundly. Every moment, we radiate either harmonious or inharmonious waves of thought energy. Positive feelings create an aura (vibrational field) that attracts good by the law of magnetic attraction. Whatever we project into the universe results in either happiness or suffering.

The sum total of all memories and experiences from this life and all past lives is called *sanchita karma* in Sanskrit. That is like a mountain of karma. Each time we incarnate, we break a chunk off the mountain. This chunk, *prarabdha karma*—based on our beliefs, habits, and goals—colors this lifetime's experiences. Free will, *agami karma*, conceives of creative solutions to karmic situations. Those choices are implemented by *kriyamani karma*: thoughts, words, and deeds created in the present, which can mitigate future events. We design our own destiny.

In mid-1973, John began an affair with May Fung Yee Pang, which continued until January 1975. From this experience, John learned that his relationship issues repeated: "You have to start again and you go through the same pattern with the next person anyway. And even presuming that I could ever get involved with some other woman, nine years later I'd be in the same place and face the same situation."[876]

 Scan this code to read the lyrics.

The Lyrics

Biographer Philip Norman wrote: "The idea was quintessential Lennon—the age-old law of cause and effect turned into something as modern and synthetic as instant coffee and, simultaneously, into a bogey under the stairs that can get you if you don't watch out."[877]

Despite the jokey lyrics about karma stalking and pouncing like a goblin, the song's message is about spreading love and light into the atmosphere rather than hatred, and about treating fellow humans with love and respect. But when it came to his family, John failed to take his own advice. In 1998, after Julian Lennon finally won a sixteen-year lawsuit against his father's estate, Julian commented, "Dad was a hypocrite. He could talk about peace and love to the world but he could never show it to his wife and son."[878] [879]

John urged us to take responsibility for our actions and make the most of this incarnation. He asked us to live in love rather than pain and fear, and to radiate love like cosmic bodies of light, because indeed we are all omnipresent beings. When a reporter said, "You say everybody is equal, but some people are more equal than others," John shot back: "But they are all infinite. They all have infinite possibilities, my friend."[880]

Because of the quarrelsome state of The Beatles at the time, John might have had Paul McCartney in mind with the "superstar" reference. Or John may have just been making a universal statement that indeed we are all superstars.

In 1980, John said, "It occurred to me that karma is instant, as well as it influences your past or future life. There really is a reaction to what you do now. Also, I'm fascinated by commercials and promotion as an art form. So, the idea of instant karma was like the idea of instant coffee: presenting something in a new form."[881]

On February 11, 1970, John performed "Instant Karma!" live on piano on BBC's *Top of the Pops*—the first Beatle to appear on the show since 1966. The ever-irreverent Yoko Ono sat in the background, crocheting a white garment while wearing a sanitary napkin as a blindfold![882]

"God"

Recorded: September 26 to October 9, 1970
Released: December 11, 1970: Lennon/Plastic Ono Band

Written while John Lennon was undergoing primal scream therapy with Dr. Arthur Janov, "God" was his declaration of independence from idolatry and his affirmation of self-empowerment. When John asked Janov about God, the therapist answered that people who have deep pain generally tend to believe in God with fervency. John replied, "Oh, you mean God is a concept by which we measure our pain."

Janov commented: "Just bang. I would go all around it and he was there, just like that. And that was John. John could take very profound philosophical concepts and make it simple."[883]

 Scan this code to read the lyrics.

The Lyrics

In this song, as well as in his tirade "I Found Out" (also released in 1970), John declared his rejection of idols, superstars, and cult heroes: Hitler, Kennedy, Elvis, Dylan, kings, The Beatles, and the Walrus. He also dismissed icons associated with Christianity and

Hinduism: Jesus, the Bible, mantra, Gita, yoga, Hare Krishna, and Buddha; and metaphysical symbols: magic, *I Ching*, and Tarot.

None of these was John's path to salvation. No external idol could show him the way. Nor could he show anyone else the way. We all have to find truth within and attain self-awareness. The illusory dream that the four lads had woven as "The Beatles" was over "Yesterday" (as a barb against Paul McCartney). Now he could chart a new future free from Beatledom, as just "John."

John said, "Beatles was the final thing because it's like I no longer believe in myth, and Beatles is another myth. I don't believe in it. The dream's over, and I have personally got to get down to so-called reality." "If there is a God, we're all it."[884]

"Imagine"

Recorded: May 27 to July 4, 1971
Released: October 1971: Single US; 1975:
Single UK; September 1971: Imagine

John Lennon's most beloved anthem, "Imagine" has stirred billions of hearts worldwide, including during Olympic Games ceremonies in Tokyo 2021, where the *Today* show's Savannah Guthrie commented, "If the Games were a song, 'Imagine' would be the song." It was also sung at the Olympics in Atlanta 1996, Turin 2006, London 2012, PyeongChang 2018, and Beijing 2022.

In 1980, three days before his death, John told *Rolling Stone*, "We're not the first to say 'Imagine no countries' or 'Give peace a chance,' but we're carrying that torch, like the Olympic torch, passing it hand to hand, to each other, to each country, to each generation, and that's our job."[885] John described the song as "anti-religious, anti-nationalistic, anti-conventional, anti-capitalistic, but because it is sugarcoated it is accepted. Now I understand what you have to do. Put your political message across with a little honey."[886]

Scan this code to
read the lyrics.

John and Yoko: visionary iconoclasts of their generation.

Yoko Ono, whose poetry inspired the song's concept, described the message of "Imagine" as "just what John believed: that we are all one country, one world, one people."[887] The spiritual concept of "we are all one" is a distinctly Indian idea. Hinduism teaches we are ultimately all part of one divine presence, and our highest attainment is to merge with God. Mystical union is the goal of all systems of Indian philosophy.

"Imagine" became John's bestselling solo single and *Imagine* his most commercially successful and critically acclaimed solo album. *Rolling Stone* declared "Imagine" was John's "greatest musical gift to the world."[888]

"Mind Games"

Written: 1969 to 1973
Recorded: July to August 1973
Released: October 29, 1973: Single US; November 16, 1973: Single UK; October 29, 1973 US, November 16, 1973 UK: Mind Games

On April 1, 1973, John and Yoko declared the birth of a conceptual country Nutopia, whose people are all ambassadors, without labels of race, religion, or politics; without land, boundaries, passports, or laws (other than cosmic laws of peace, justice, and harmony). As Nutopia ambassadors, John and Yoko asked for diplomatic immunity and recognition by the United Nations. This declaration was printed on the album sleeve for "Mind Games."

John wrote this song after reading *Mind Games: The Guide to Inner Space*, by human potential pioneers Robert Masters and his wife Jean Houston.[889] Their first book, *The Varieties of Psychedelic Experience*, published findings about altered mental states studied at the Foundation for Mind Research.

After the US government withdrew all licenses for LSD research, Masters and Houston wrote *Mind Games* as a training manual to develop imagination, inspiration, and self-exploration without drugs. John and Yoko bought many copies, played the games, and extolled the book. When Jean Houston ran into John at a Japanese restaurant in New York and introduced herself, John shot up, blushed, shook her hand, and said, "I am one of your fans. You wrote *Mind Games*."[890]

Mind Games groups became popular in the seventies and eighties, and Masters and Houston continued writing books and teaching self-help methods of trance, meditation, hypnosis, guided imagery, and active imagination. The goal of playing mind games is to become more imaginative and creative, to access capacities, and to use them productively.

Scan this code to
read the lyrics.

The Lyrics

In the spirit of the Flower Power generation, this song, originally titled "Make Love, Not War," advocated the hippie tribe's continued group effort in the cause of world peace. In 1980, John explained, "When this came out, in the early seventies, everybody was starting to say the sixties was a joke; it didn't mean anything, those love-and-peaceniks were idiots. And I was trying to say: 'No, just keep doin' it.'"[891]

Since 1968, when John wrote "Revolution" under Maharishi's influence, he campaigned to change the world by changing minds. Pushing the envelope of human consciousness and lifting the veil between the physical and spiritual planes, "mind guerillas" (guerrilla warfare metaphor) can change the future by using world peace as their mantra, and by projecting thoughts of love, peace, and positivism.

John declared, "If you speak, what you say doesn't end here. Vibrations go on and on and every action goes on and on infinitely and has its effect. Your attitudes to life have an effect on everyone—and thereby, the universe."[892] This concept that thoughts, words, and actions affect the entire cosmos originates in the ancient scriptures of India.

"Mind Games" is about consciousness expansion, visualization, and divine love. It is a call to action—using the power of our mind and soul, keeping our nose to the metaphoric grindstone of the "karmic wheel" in order to change our destiny, essentially John's endorsement of the "Law of Attraction"—thirty-three years before the release of *The Secret!*

"Watching the Wheels"

Written: 1980
Recorded: 1980
Released: March 13, 1981: US; March 27, 1981:
UK: Double Fantasy

This song answered fans who criticized John Lennon for becoming a recluse, starting with his "househusband" years after his son Sean was born. When asked about the song's meaning, he replied, "The whole universe is a wheel, right? Wheels go round and round. They're my own wheels, mainly, but, you know, watching meself is like watching everyone else. And I watch meself through my child, too."[893]

The illusion of "The Beatles" had ended with John's song "God." With "Watching the Wheels," he let go of playing the fantasy games of "John Lennon" and "John and Yoko." He referred to the karmic wheel: the wheel of birth and death that keeps us bound to the world illusion of samsara (the rounds of incarnation), and avidya (the illusion of ego individuation). Now, rather than taking the merry-go-round ride, it was time to jump off and witness the revolving wheel as an observer, and to let go of physical attachment.

On May 27, 1979, John and Yoko's open letter was published in *The New York Times,* describing their life as a work of art in progress: "Remember, we are writing in the sky instead of on paper—that's our song. Lift your eyes and look up in the sky. There's our message. Lift your eyes again and look around, and you will see that you are walking in the sky, which extends to the ground."[894] John and Yoko revealed their simple method: imagine drawing a halo around the head of anyone who is angry at us; thereby we begin to see them as angels. "The future of the earth is up to all of us."[895]

 Scan this code to read the lyrics.

CHAPTER 13

RAVIN' 'BOUT RAVI

Shankar Family & Friends (album)

Written: Spring 1973
Recorded: April 1973 to early 1974
Released: September 20, 1974

Shankar Family & Friends is an album composed by master sitar player and composer Ravi Shankar and produced by George Harrison on his Dark Horse label. This East-meets-West blend featured forty-three musicians, including these members of Ravi's family: Ravi's sister-in-law Lakshmi Shankar (vocalist); Ravi's son, Shubho Shankar (surbahar bass sitar); Ravi's romantic partner Kamala Chakravarty (backing vocals); and Ravi's nephew by marriage Dr. L. Subramaniam (violin).

Shubho Shankar on sitar and Aashish Khan on sarod. Photo courtesy of Aashish Khan.

Rare photo of Indian musicians; l. to r.: Vinayak Vora (tar-shehnai and vocalist), Lakshmi Shankar (vocalist), Alla Rakha (tabla), Ravi Shankar (sitar), seated: Viji Shankar (tambura). Lakshmi was Rajendra Shankar's wife and Viji Shankar's mother. Photo courtesy of Uttank Vora.

In addition, some of Ravi's "friends" played on the album, including: Alla Rakha (tabla); Aashish Khan (sarod); Shivkumar Sharma (*santoor*); Hariprasad Chaurasia, Sharad Kumar and G.S. Sachdev (bansuri); Jitendra Abhisheki (vocals); Harihar Rao (tabla and sitar); Nodu Mullick (*khartal*, tambura); Palghat R. Raghu (mridangam); the Hare Krishna Chanters; Tom Scott (saxophone and flute); Emil Richards (percussionist and TM meditator who visited Maharishi in Rishikesh: marimbas); Billy Preston, Ringo Starr, Klaus Voormann, and Jim Keltner (drums); David Bromberg (guitar); and Nicky Hopkins (piano).

Ravi's colleagues l. to r. Hariprasad Chaurasia (bansuri player), George, and Shivkumar Sharma (santoor player). Photo from hariprasadchaurasia.com.

Ravi's friends. Front row l. to r.: Alla Rakha, Ravi Shankar. Second row: unknown, unknown, Alla Rakha's companion behind him, Kamala Chakravarty behind Ravi. Third row: Jitendra Abhisheki, Lakshmi Shankar with long braid. Fourth row: Nodu Mullick standing, Misha Schreiber: student at Kinnara School in Los Angeles and Amiya Dasgupta's future wife, Sabri Khan far right. Don Douglas/Alamy Stock Photo.

Indian musicians in studio; l. to r.: Pandit Shivkumar Sharma (santoor), Nodu Mullick (Ravi Shankar's sitar craftsman and tambura player), Jitendra Abhisheki (vocalist, swarmandal), probably Mishkin Khan (tabla), Sabri Khan (sarangi). Edwin Sampson/ANL/Shutterstock.

The featured track is the devotional song "I Am Missing You." George called it "a love song to Krishna."[896] It was sung by Lakshmi Shankar, wife of Ravi's brother Rajendra, who introduced George to Indian philosophy during his studies with Ravi in 1966.

The first side of the album includes Krishna *bhajan* (Indian devotional songs), written by Ravi Shankar: "Kahān Gayelavā Shyām Saloné," (Where Has Lord Krishna Gone?), "Supané Mé Āyé Preetam Sainyā" (My Precious, Darling Beloved Came in My Dream), and a gospel-inspired take on a traditional folk song, "Jaya Jagadish Haré" (All Glories to Hari, Supreme Lord of the Universe). The second side features ingenious instrumental pieces, from Indian classical to avant-garde, with fascinating surrealistic Indian and Western chanting thrown in for good measure.

The combination of traditional Indian instruments, bhajan (devotional songs), and kirtana (call and response chanting), along with Western instruments, raga rock, pop, funk, choral, jazz, and even showtune influence, made for a highly original, exotic album.

Ravi Shankar commented, "The album contains almost every possible style that you can think of."[897]

Ravi Shankar's Music Festival from India (album)

Written: Traditional Classical
Recorded: August to September 1974
Released: February 6, 1976: US; March 1976: UK

Ravi Shankar was musical director for All India Radio from 1949 to 1956, when he composed an orchestral piece 'Nava Rasa Ranga.' When Ravi played it for George in Bombay in 1966, it rang something in George's head that sounded very familiar. He was so moved by the piece that it set him on a spiritual journey. He was determined to recreate it: "Until then I had not heard Indian classical music in any form other than solos or duets, and the beauty has haunted me for the past eight years and still haunts me today. I hope this music may help a little to nurture the wealth of the West. God only knows."[898]

In January 1974, on the banks of the Ganges River in Benares (now Varanasi), George attended a ceremony to bless Ravi's new home. After the ritual, George suggested that Ravi assemble a traditional classical Indian music orchestra to tour the West and make recordings for George's Dark Horse label. Ravi would be composer and conductor. The Music Festival was George's first project for his Material World Charitable Foundation, which aimed to "sponsor diverse forms of artistic expression and to encourage the exploration of alternative life views and philosophies."[899]

Ravi, George, and musicians, 1974. George is wearing his Babaji pinback button and his medallion of Baba Ramdev Pir (see page 393–394.) Shutterstock.

Musicians and Instruments

Ravi assembled an orchestra of superstar Indian musicians for the Music Festival. With great respect for Ravi, these legendary musicians, matchless in their field, agreed to join this collaboration. Olivia Harrison said, "Fifty years later, you look at these revered musicians. George at that age was bringing them together and Ravi hand-picked them. It was extraordinary if you know who those musicians are."[900] Each of the musicians in the photo is identified below, along with the instruments played.

Music Festival musicians. © Clive Arrowsmith

Front row l. to r.: Gopal Krishan (vichitra veena stick zither, vocals), Anant Lal (shehnai oboe), Rijram Desad (pakhavaj, dholki, madal-tarang, nagada, huduk, duff drums), Alla Rakha (tabla drums), Ravi Shankar (direction, arrangements, sitar), George Harrison, Shivkumar Sharma (santoor dulcimer, kanoon box zither, vocals), Hariprasad Chaurasia (bansuri flute), Ustad Sultan Khan (sarangi chordophone).

Back row l. to r.: Kamalesh Maitra (tabla tarang set of tabla, duggi tarang set of kettle drums, sarod lute, madal drum from Nepal, ektara one-stringed lute), Satyadev Pawar (North Indian violin), Harihar Rao (khartal and manjira finger cymbals, dholak two-headed hand drum, gubgubbi percussion chordophone, sitar, vocals), Viji Shankar (wife of L. Subramaniam and daughter of Lakshmi and Rajendra Shankar, who is elder brother of Ravi Shankar: tambura lute, vocals), Lakshmi Shankar (Ravi's sister-in-law: lead vocals, swarmandal table harp), Kamala Chakravarty (Lakshmi Shankar's sister: tambura lute, vocals), T.V. Gopalakrishnan (mridangam drum, khanjira tambourine, vocals), L. Subramaniam (Viji Shankar's husband: South Indian violin), Kartick Kumar (sitar), Kumar Shankar (Ravi Shankar's nephew: sound engineer).

Bansuri maestro Hariprasad Chaurasia, who studied with Annapurna Devi, daughter and disciple of Allauddin Khan. Photo from hariprasadchaurasia.com.

Pandit Hariparasad Chaurasia's family profession was wrestling, but he fell in love with the sound of bansuri flute. After three years of begging the reclusive, rigorous taskmaster Annapurna Devi (daughter of Allauddin Khan and first wife of Ravi Shankar), she finally accepted him as her disciple. Chaurasia said music is his spiritual pathway: "The flute is the symbol of spiritual call, the call of divine love. To play in tune, you must first tune yourself. All the beauty of music lies in between the notes."[901]

Chaurasia said, "George was a great human being. He treated everyone equally, irrespective of his or her race or nationality." He loved everything Indian: "So much that he wanted to be born in India in his next life. He used to go to the Lord Krishna temple at Mathura, with his face covered with a shawl to avoid recognition. He enjoyed going to the temple alone and collecting prasadam [offerings to the gods]. He loved listening to the dholak and the singing and dancing. His favorite place was Vrindavan and said he could never find such an environment anywhere else in the world."[902]

Ustad Sultan Khan playing sarangi. © Jack Vartoogian/Front Row Photos.

Ustad Sultan Khan's first sarangi performance for All-India Radio (AIR) was at age eleven. His numerous recordings and compositions for movie and television included the Oscar-winning film *Gandhi*. Zakir Hussain spoke of Khan: "It is thought among musicians in India that his sarangi literally sang. He was able to coax out of the instrument all the nuances of the vocal style of Indian music."[903]

Pandit Anant Lal playing shehnai. Photo courtesy of Ashwani Shankar.

For over two hundred years, Pandit Anant Lal's ancestors have
played the shehnai, an oboe-like instrument that produces an
exotic moaning sound. Starting at age nine, Lal studied with his
father and uncles. He also played the bamboo flute bansuri and was
a session musician for AIR. He was one of the leading exponents
of the shehnai, and his sons and grandson carry on the musical
tradition.

Dr. L. Subramaniam playing South Indian violin and his wife Viji Shankar playing tambura. Photo courtesy of Dr. L. Subramaniam Foundation.

From a renowned musical family, Dr. L. Subramaniam started studying music before age five. His first public performance was at age six. Having made two hundred recordings and composed for orchestras, ballets, and film scores, he declared, "Music is a vast ocean and no one can claim to know it all. The more you know, the more you realize how little you know. It is an eternal quest."[904] His daughter Gingger Shankar is the only woman in the world to play the double violin.

Sitarists Ravi Shankar with his disciple Kartick Kumar, after a concert at Shanmukhananda auditorium, Sion, Mumbai, in the 1980s. Photo courtesy of Kartick Kumar Archives.

One of Ravi Shankar's seniormost students, Kartick Kumar played with his guru for many film compositions, concerts, and recordings during their fifty-five-year association. Kumar described Ravi: "As a guru, Panditji was the king of kindness. He would give me constant training and even during meal times, when other musicians prefer not to be disturbed, he would ask me to practice the sitar before him."[905] Kumar accompanied the legendary vocalist Lata Makgeshkar for nearly four decades and played for many Bollywood composers. For one of his albums, he orchestrated a 31-sitar ensemble. His son Niladri Kumar invented the zitar, which combines sitar and guitar.[906]

Harihar Rao, disciple and lifelong associate of Ravi Shankar, playing sitar. Photo courtesy of Paula Rao, wife of Harihar Rao, of The Music Circle.

In California in 1973, Ravi Shankar and his main protégé and close friend Harihar Rao co-founded The Music Circle, which has presented hundreds of musical events and continues to promote Indian music in the West. Rao taught at several universities in Southern California and co-founded the Hindustani Jazz Sextet, a pioneer Indo jazz group. His album *Raga Rock*, released on June 10, 1966 on World Pacific, was the first pop LP starring the sitar.

Pandit Gopal Krishan Sharma playing vichitra veena. Photo courtesy of Pandit Shri Krishan Sharma (son and disciple).

Pandit Gopal Krishan's grandson Akshat Sharma told me he quit his MNC finance job to carry on his family's musical legacy. "My grandfather told me about the grand music tour organized by George Harrison—a joint collaboration with stalwarts of Indian classical music. Grandfather was a spiritual and saintly personality. People asked him for meditation classes, but he always told them music is the highest and easiest way to meet God. He used to practice late hours and said his music was dedicated to Lord Krishna. Many of his musical compositions were based on anecdotes from mythology. That's why Krishan was always in the middle name in the family."

Interestingly, George Harrison used slide guitar to imitate Indian music, and Gopal Krishan's son Pandit Shri Krishan Sharma plays entire ragas on Hindustani slide lap guitar.

 Scan this code to watch Pandit Gopal Krishan Sharma and his son playing together.

Kamalesh Maitra's favorite photo of his hand gesture offering his tabla tarang music. Photo courtesy of Laura Patchen.

In tabla tarang, each treble tabla drum is hand-tuned to play a separate note so melodies can be played. The term *tarang* means "waves," where rhythm, melody, and harmony weave into one flowing element. For two decades, Kamalesh Maitra was musical director for Ravi Shankar's brother Uday Shankar's dance troupe. Maitra's life partner Laura Patchen told me that as a child in East Bengal, he predicted he would live with the "white people" one day. He settled in Berlin in 1977 and formed the Ragatala Ensemble, fusing jazz with Indian and European classical music.

Dr. T.V. Gopalakrishnan playing mridangam. Photo courtesy of T.V. Gopalakrishnan.

Dr. Tripunithura Viswanathan Gopalakrishnan (Dr. TVG) started playing mridangam at age four and gave his first concert onstage at age nine. He is the first vocalist who performs with equal mastery both Carnatic and Hindustani classical music. Dr. TVG told me, "Every time I sit to perform, I get inside a bubble of *nada* (pure sound) and all that I experience is sheer ecstasy. One needs no external stimulus! I firmly believe that music gives the easiest access to peace and tranquility. Devotion (*bhakti*) through music crystallizes purity of thought, sound, rhythm, and sentiment. One does not need any extra effort other than listening. The rest follows!"

Recording Sessions and Live Tour

The rehearsals and recording sessions for *Ravi Shankar's Music Festival* took place in summer 1974 at George's home studio: F.P.S.H.O.T.—Friar Park Studio, Henley-on-Thames. Describing how Ravi composed improvisational music, George remarked: "It was amazing, because he'd sit there and say to one person, 'This is where you play,' and the next one, 'And you do this,' and 'You do that,' and they're all going, What? 'OK, one, two, three.' And you'd think, 'This is going to be a catastrophe,' and it would be the most amazing thing."[907]

Percussionist Kamalesh Maitra described to his partner Laura Patchen that rehearsals for the tour were long and intensive in George's Henley-on-Thames "castle," as Maitra called it. On tour, they flew around in a private plane with the *Om* symbol painted on its skin. Some seats remained for take-off and landing, but the rest were removed to create an area with carpets and pillows where the musicians could relax in Indian fashion during flight. George brought a cook along to prepare Indian food.

During the concerts, Maitra (tabla tarang) combined with Alla Rakha (tabla), T.V. Gopalakrishnan (mridangam) and Rijram Desad (*pakhavaj*) in extended, four-way drum soloing—the highlight of their set. For the finale of the Indian sets, they played with George's rock band.

Dr. TVG told me about the Music Festival: "Living in the company of George, his team, the maestro Ravi Shankar, and our group of super musicians day after day, month after month was spectacular! The tour program was mind-boggling. Playing and singing to thousands in most of the colosseums to palaces, and four continuous concerts at Madison Square Garden, was a kind of magic!"

On September 23, 1974, the Musical Festival ensemble opened at Royal Albert Hall. The skinny, mustached George ascended the stage wearing a yellow long-sleeved knit shirt with a large red *Om* symbol printed on the front. At his neck, front and center, he wore a pinback button of the immortal saint Babaji. George announced, "Let's hear it for the one and only blessing to the world, in the form of Ravi Shankar."[908] When Ravi ascended the stage, George hugged him with great affection.

 Scan this code to see a brief video of this introduction.

This first major tour in Europe by an Indian orchestra represented folk traditions from all over India. The program included traditional classical Indian music, ancient Vedic hymns, medieval, and modern. It explored devotional bhajan (chanting names of God) and romantic and erotic forms and ended with an earthy folk style.[909]

The European tour traveled to Paris, Brussels, Frankfurt, Munich, and Copenhagen, and ended in October. The ensemble then played Vancouver's Pacific Coliseum on November 2, 1974, and forty-five other appearances in North America. The tour was financially successful but unfavorably reviewed by *Rolling Stone*. Beatles fans wanted Beatles songs rather than Indian music.[910] When asked about a Beatles reunion, George told journalists he enjoyed playing with this band more than with The Beatles—and declared he would never play in a group with Paul McCartney.[911]

The album's release coincided with a concert by Ravi at the Cathedral of St. John the Divine in New York City—a dawn-to-dusk recital celebrating twenty years of Ravi's performances in the West.[912] The album's liner notes introduced and displayed the Indian musical instruments.

George Visits the White House

For twenty years, Chris Murray, proprietor of the Govinda Gallery in Washington, DC, was the exclusive US distributor for Genesis publications, which created *The Beatles Anthology* and distributed George Harrison's autobiography, *I, Me, Mine.*

Chris, author of *Illuminations from the Bhagavad Gita* (with artwork created under Prabhupada's direction), made a pinback button of Radha and Krishna from an illustration in his book, and musician Tom Scott gave the button to George the night before their meeting with US president Gerald Ford at the White House Oval Office on December 13, 1974.

George wearing the Radha Krishna button on top right, Krishna button on bottom right, Babaji button on left, and *Om* button on far left. Photo courtesy of Gerald R. Ford Presidential Library: David Hume Kennerly.

George visited President Ford at the invitation of Jack Ford, the president's son. The guests, including George's father Harold Harrison; George's future wife Olivia Arias; and Music Festival musicians Ravi Shankar, Billy Preston, and Tom Scott, dined in the solarium while George's newly released *Dark Horse* album played in the background. Jack and Susan Ford, the president's offspring, gave the guests a White House tour. Jack wore a shirt with the *Dark Horse* logo on the back, representing the Hindu seven-headed horse Uchchaisravas.

Jack Ford wearing Dark Horse shirt and George wearing a golden silk *Om* shirt.
Photo courtesy of Gerald R. Ford Presidential Library: David Hume Kennerly.

During the visit, the president gave George and the other guests WIN buttons (for Ford's Whip Inflation Now program). George teased him about it. His natural self in all situations, George never wore a mask to impress anyone, or to audition for anyone's approval—even the president of the United States.

Guest musicians having a laugh with President Ford. All are wearing WIN buttons received from the president. Photo courtesy of Gerald R. Ford Presidential Library: David Hume Kennerly.

Meeting in the Oval Office. The book *Autobiography of a Yogi* on the table is George's gift to Ford. Photo courtesy of Gerald R. Ford Presidential Library: David Hume Kennerly.

George pinned his *Om* button on the president's lapel. Photo courtesy of Gerald R. Ford Presidential Library: David Hume Kennerly.

George described the president: "He seemed very relaxed. He was much easier to meet than I would expect. You can imagine the number of things he's got on his plate." George declared he "felt good vibes about the White House."[913]

Dark Horse (album)

Recorded: November 1973, April 1974, August to October 1974
Released: December 9, 1974

Dark Horse was released right after the Ravi Shankar Music Festival's North American tour, which garnered poor reviews due to George Harrison's laryngitis and Ravi's Indian music dominating the program. Though the tour unfavorably impacted the album's success, Brian Harrigan of *Melody Maker* magazine lauded George for establishing "a new category in music—Country and Eastern" and commented, "Yep, the Sacred Cowboy has produced a good one."[914] George was himself a "dark horse," surpassing both John and Paul with his surprisingly successful solo career.

 Scan this code to view the *Dark Horse* album cover.

A nod to *Sgt. Pepper*, the album cover, designed by Tom Wilkes, shows students and teachers from the Liverpool Institute seated on a lotus, like Hindu gods. The lotus floats on a lake in a Himalayan landscape, with the immortal Indian master Babaji, grandfather of the Kriya Yoga lineage, floating above.

Schoolteachers wear colorful shirts adorned with emblems, such as Apple Records' logo. The disapproving headmaster sports the bull's-eye Capitol Records logo. The art teacher, whom George liked, dons the *Om* symbol. The Dark Horse Records logo portrays the seven-headed horse Uchchaisravas, one of the *ratna* (gems) that arose from churning the primordial ocean to unearth the *amrita* (nectar of immortality) by deities and demons at the beginning of creation (see page 162–163).

The boys in the front row wear yellow varsity sweaters with red letters. George Harrison, age thirteen, with blue skin, is top and center, just above the headmaster. (Lord Krishna is always depicted with blue skin.) The back cover of the album bears a dedication: "ॐ ALL GLORIES to SRI KRSNA"

"It Is 'He' (Jai Sri Krishna)"

This Hindu chant was inspired by George and Ravi's visit in January 1974 to Vrindavan—Lord Krishna's birthplace. George described, "The whole town is Krishna conscious—everyone, everywhere was chanting 'Hare Krishna.'" George and his companions slept overnight at one of the temples. There, he dreamed of "huge heavenly choirs" and experienced "the deepest sleep I had ever had in my life."[915]

After the morning puja (religious ceremony) at 4:00 a.m., their spiritual tour guide Sripad Maharaj, a holy ascetic, led a kirtana (call-and-response chant) for five hours, as George and his companions sang Maharaj's lines in response. Afterwards, Maharaj suggested that George record the bhajan as a song titled "It Is 'He' (Jai Sri Krishna)."

Later that morning, the group toured Seva Kunj, a park commemorating Krishna's dance with his *gopi* (cowherd girls), which represent the *lila* (playfulness of Krishna as he constantly creates the universe). George commented: "All the trees, which are so ancient, bow down and the branches touch the ground. Just to walk in that place is incredible."[916]

George and Ravi then spent a few days at the Sri Chaitanya Prema Samsthana ashram, on the banks of the Yamuna River. George, who also reunited with Prabhupada and ISKCON disciples Gurudas and Yamuna during the visit, described this Vrindavan pilgrimage as "my most fantastic experience."[917]

 Scan this code to read the lyrics.

The track offers praise to Krishna and his consort Radha, the female form of god/goddess. The Sanskrit words translate as: "All glories and praise to Lord Krishna; all glories and praise to goddess Radha." The English lyrics teach us that Krishna knows who we really are, even if we do not know ourselves. With just a glance, Krishna blesses us with his sweet smile. He is wholeness and the primary cause of everything.

A stringed Indian instrument, *gubgubbi*, and an Australian wobble board gave the music an Indian flavor.

"Maya Love"

This song, written as George and Pattie's marriage was breaking up, is about the illusory, fleeting, transient nature of human sexual relationships. According to Indian philosophy, we all live in a dream of unreality in this physical plane. Nothing lasts. The only eternal love is God's love.

George's wonderful signature slide guitar work dominates the track, hinting at an Indian sound that accompanies the toe-tapping funk vibe.

 Scan this code to read the lyrics.

"Ding Dong, Ding Dong"

This light-hearted holiday ditty, written by George in three minutes, is about letting go of the old year and bringing in the new. Nearly all the lyrics were inscriptions carved in woodwork or stone by the original owner of George's Friar Park mansion—Sir Frank Crisp. George was playing his guitar when he noticed "Ring out the old, Ring in the new" inscribed to the left of a fireplace. To the right was "Ring out the false, Ring in the true." The words for the song's middle eight were carved in stone around two matching windows in what George called "the garden building."[918]

 Scan this code to see the video of "Ding Dong, Ding Dong."

On the hilarious official video of this tongue-in-cheek rocking song, George, with his deadpan expression, dressed in several Beatles outfits (starting with his Hamburg Ton-up Boy leathers and ending with his *Om* shirt). He wore various wigs and played numerous guitars. He mocked the Lennon-Ono *Two Virgins* album by appearing naked (a guitar covered his privates). He also appeared as the "Pirate Bob" character, when George performed "The Pirate Song" in 1975 for a Christmas Special on *Rutland Weekend Television*.[919]

The song said goodbye to the old Beatle George and his previous wife Pattie and brought in the new George, the gardener at Friar Park, and his new girlfriend Olivia Arias, who appeared in the video and on the US side-A face label. Olivia was a disciple of the "boy guru" Maharaj Ji, founder of Elan Vital, the next iteration of his father's organization: the Divine Light Mission.

Some India references appeared in the "Ding Dong, Ding Dong" video, including a nine-headed mask of the demon Ravana from the Ramayana, who is burnt in effigy during the yearly Dussehra holiday; a life-size photo of Paramahansa Yogananda (author of *Autobiography of a Yogi*) with Yogananda's guru Sri Yukeshwar; and an Indian holding a sitar. Plus, George replaced a pirate flag with an *Om* flag. Lord Krishna's symbol, peacock feathers, embellished the set.

George commented, "Instead of getting stuck in a rut, everybody should try ringing out the old and ringing in the new. [People] sing about it, but they never apply it to their lives."[920] Thirteen days after this song was released, on December 19, George signed the "Beatles Agreement," which dissolved the band.

Chants of India (album)

Recorded: January to August 1996
Released: May 6, 1997: US; September 1, 1997: UK

Composed by Ravi Shankar and produced by George Harrison, *Chants of India* combined traditional Indian Sanskrit mantras, chants, and prayers with a Western choir and instrumentation. While maintaining the spiritual force and purity of the ancient hymns, Ravi wanted the album universally appealing.[921] In the extensive liner notes, he described the tracks as "prayers for the well-being of the universe, physical mental and spiritual selves of everyone, and for overall *shanti* (peace)."

George explained, "Vedic music really is spiritual music. It's like where you go inside to your own temple, to calm you down in order to clear the mind and be at peace."[922]

Ravi said, "The repetitive use of mantras invoke a special power within oneself and I have tried to imbibe this age-old tradition in this recording."[923]

Album Cover

Front and center on the album cover, we see the Sanskrit symbol *Om*: ॐ —the primordial sound believed in India to underlie and give rise to the universe. The Sanskrit letters running across the cover spell out (three times) the famous ancient Vedic hymn on Track 6: "Poornamadah" from Brihadaranyaka Upanishad, 3:5.1.

Here is the transliteration of the Sanskrit:

Om poornamadah poornamidam
poornaat poornamudachyate

Poornasya poornamaadaaya
poornamevaa vashishyate

Here is an English translation:

"That (the invisible, unmanifest being) is full, this (the visible, manifest being) is full. This fullness (visible being) proceeds from that fullness (invisible being). Upon taking the fullness from this fullness (visible being), that fullness (invisible being) remains."

Album Tracks

Track 1 includes the section of the "Guru Gita" ("song of the guru") that George sang in "My Sweet Lord" (see page 373). Other well-known hymns on the album:

Track 5, "Sahanaa Vavatu," is a hymn for world peace and brotherhood from the Taittiriya Upanishad. Track 7 is the Gayatri Mantra, a prayer for spiritual enlightenment from the Rig Veda 3:62; and Track 8, the Mrityunjaya Mantra, also known as Tryambakam Mantra, from the Taittiriya Upanishad, is an invocation for Lord Shiva to grant immortality.

Beatles statue at Pier Head Liverpool, UK.

Gayatri mantra on George's belt. Photo courtesy of Mark Ashworth.

In a statue of The Beatles in Liverpool, the Gayatri Mantra in Sanskrit is carved on George Harrison's belt. Here is the transliteration: *Om Bhur Bhuvah Swaha. Tat Savitur Varenyam. Bhargo Devasya Dheemahi. Dhiyo Yonah Prachodayaat.*

Here is a translation: "I meditate on that most adored Supreme Lord, the creator, like the sun, the source of all life, whose effulgence illumines all realms (physical, mental, and spiritual). May this divine light illumine my intellect."

 Scan this code to see the track list, read the liner notes, and read the lyrics for every song on the album.

The Power of Mantras

Laurence Juber was the lead guitarist for Paul McCartney and Wings. In April 1986, he was in the studio with George Harrison, working on the soundtrack for the movie *Shanghai Surprise*. His wife Hope had always wanted to meet George, but the night before she was scheduled to visit the studio, she went into labor with their daughter Ilsey. The next day the phone rang at the hospital. It was George, inviting Hope and the newborn to meet him! When she arrived, George gave Hope toys for her two babies and then lifted Ilsey out of the carrier, took her into the cavernous studio, and danced around, waltzing with her in his arms.

Hope described, "We just stood back and watched. It was very magical. At the end he touched her on the forehead and said a blessing in Sanskrit. When he handed her to me, I asked 'What did you say to her?' He replied, 'Well I was just dancing and enjoying the energy of this new life and at the end I decided I would like to give her the gift of music, so I did.'"

That "gift of music" stuck. Ilsey is now a Grammy-nominated singer/songwriter.

Recording the Album

Ravi's daughter Anoushka Shankar conducted the musicians at the *Chants of India* recording sessions, which took place January and April 1996 in Madras, India (now Chennai), at Sruthilaya Media Artists Studio, and July to August 1996 at George Harrison's home studio at Friar Park: F.P.S.H.O.T.

While in India in April, George and his Hare Krishna cohorts, Mukunda Das and Shyamasundar Das, visited the holy city of Vrindavan, Krishna's birthplace. This pilgrimage demonstrated George's continued devotion to Krishna.[924]

In front of Jiva Goswami memorial in Vrindavan; l. to r.: George, Shyamasundar Das, and Mukunda Goswami.

Anoushka Shankar playing sitar.

Ravi Shankar with his second wife Sukanya, Karnatak vocalist. Trinity Mirror/Mirrorpix/Alamy Stock Photo.

Ronu Majumdar playing bansuri bamboo flute.

Ravi Shankar composed the arrangements, played sitar, and was the director. George Harrison performed on acoustic guitar, bass, autoharp, vibraphone, percussion, and backing vocals. Ravi's second wife Sukanya, a singer trained in the Karnatak tradition, was a vocalist. Ronu Majumdar played bansuri (bamboo flute). Bickram Ghosh was on tabla (drums). Tarun Bhattacharaya played santoor (hammered dulcimer). Sri M. Balachandar ("Bala") played mridangam (double-headed drum).

The following Indian instruments were also played: tambura (drone lute), *morsing* (jaw harp), veena (stringed instrument) and *samvadini* (harmonium: hand-pumped organ). About sixty Indian and British musicians played or sang on the album.

Maestro Bickram Ghosh playing tabla, and Pandit Tarun Bhattacharya playing santoori. Photo courtesy of Bob Haddad. Photo by Greg Plachta.

Legendary tabla player Shankar Ghosh is credited as playing on *Wonderwall Music*. His son, superstar film music director Bickram Ghosh, whom George Harrison nicknamed "The Prince of Tabla," scored dozens of films, pioneered Indo-fusion music, and played on many Grammy-nominated albums. Bickram told me he first met George in 1996 when he stayed for ten days in a hotel just outside Friar Park. One of the castles on the estate was Dark Horse Studios, where Bickram rehearsed and recorded with Ravi, Anoushka, and other musicians every day of his stay. George was very fond of Bickram and his playing. He attended Ravi Shankar's Barbican Centre concert in London every year, where Bickram would perform.

Closing a Chapter with Ravi

Chants of India was the final collaboration between Ravi and George, who was diagnosed with cancer soon after its release. After

George's death, at the "Concert for George" in November 2002, Ravi incorporated selections from *Chants of India*, including "Sarve Shaamm," performed by Ravi's daughter Anoushka Shankar, as a tribute to George.

While promoting the album on May 16, 1997, George said, "It was a great excuse to be able to surround myself with these great musicians, and the great words that have been said in Sanskrit. It is a spiritual experience, but it's all down to the individual what you can manifest within yourself. The whole of life should be a spiritual experience because we're actually spirits in bodies."[925] "I like producing Ravi's music, because for me it's educational as well as a joy to work with. It's actually soothing to your soul, and it helps you to focus or transcend."[926]

J.J. Hurtak, Ph.D., author, composer, and member of the original Critical Studies and Music faculty at Cal Arts with Ravi Shankar, told me: "One time in the early seventies, George Harrison and I were visiting Ravi's home in Los Angeles, where we discussed Vedic wisdom and the importance of musical mantras. We all agreed that meditation must precede any performance to create the proper atmosphere for a higher musical vibration.

"Ravi then described his own powerful paraphysical events that occurred while playing his sitar. Sometimes they were so intense that he could leave his physical body and project his consciousness body into the audience and watch himself perform. His ten fingers became like ten cosmic elephant trunks crocheting the air waves, opening a dimensional door whereby he could leave his body while playing onstage. He rode on his own musical waves to join the audience. Ravi said that meditation, combined with sacred music, was key to activating the power of the seven chakras for this experience of consciousness projection.

"In joy and humble excitement, Ravi, George and I enjoyed discussing the profound Vedic tradition. We agreed it had allowed George to make a shift towards a deeper spirituality that he had found nowhere else."

George once said he felt some outside force guiding down the path of hearing and meeting Ravi Shankar: "I got into India. I think that was the one thing in my life. I could have done without everything else. But that one thing of getting in touch with what's inside through Maharishi and Ravi Shankar and Indian music."[927] Ravi recalled that following a playback of some of the tracks, George was so moved that he "embraced me with tears in his eyes and simply said, 'Thank you, Ravi, for this music.'"[928]

Brainwashed (album)

Written: 1988 to 2002
Released: November 18, 2002

George Harrison's album *Brainwashed* was released one year after his death and fifteen years after his previous album. This unfinished work was completed by George's son Dhani and record producer Jeff Lynne, co-founder of ELO: Electric Light Orchestra and co-founder of the band Traveling Wilburys with George Harrison, Bob Dylan, Roy Orbison, and Tom Petty. Lynne, who also co-produced George's *Cloud Nine* album, was involved with the memorial *Concert for George* and subsequent album that won a Grammy.

"Any Road"

Every solo album that George made was profoundly infuenced by India. *Brainwashed* is no exception. Its first track, "Any Road," which was Harrison's final single, is about the wheel of karma that we all travel on, and the consequences of our actions. No matter which path we take, all roads lead to God-realization. The way out of the karmic wheel is to go within. The song's fourth verse refers to what the Upanishads describe as: "Which is soundless, touchless, formless, undecaying, also tasteless, eternal and scentless, beginningless, endless, beyond the intellect, and constant, knowing that, man escapes from the mouth of Death."[929]

Scan this code to
read the lyrics.

"Brainwashed/Namah Parvati"

Bickram Ghosh, who played tabla on the final track "Brainwashed/
Namah Parvati," told me that in 1999, while staying at a guesthouse
in Kilburn, London, the landlord yelled, "Hey Bickram, there's a
'George' calling." It was George Harrison! "Bickram, I want you to
play the title track on my album. I'm recording after many many
years." A few days later, George sent a limousine, and Bickram was
driven to Friar Park to record with George and his engineer.

Bickram spent the whole day with George. "We talked about
so many things, from Indian classical music to my music, what he
felt about music, The Beatles. He took me around his garden and
showed me his trees; he was heavily into gardening. We had a great
conversation because we had a lot of time. And we had a meal, just
him and me. So that was one of the most special days of my life.
I remember he was such a warm person, so humble, so down to
earth, so spiritual, such a great energy—one of the most beautiful
people I've met, for sure. That is a beautiful memory I still have."

George in his garden. Photo courtesy of Gurudas.

Bickram Ghosh playing tabla. Photo courtesy of Bickram Ghosh by Greg Plachta.

 Scan this code to
read the lyrics.

The Lyrics

The song "Brainwashed/Namah Parvati" is one of George's dia-
tribes against the material world and a plea for God's connection,
salvation, and grace. It speaks of the corrupt nature of institutions
that brainwash us and thereby turn off our spiritual light. A verse
in the song quotes Swami Vivekananda's translation and commentary on Patanjali's *Yoga Aphorisms*, Chapter II: Concentration: Its
Practice, Verse 18, from his book *Raja Yoga*, which Ravi Shankar's
brother Raju had given George in 1966:

"The Purusha [our higher Self] does not love, it is love itself. It does not exist, it is existence itself. The Soul does not know, it is knowledge itself. It is a mistake to say the Soul loves, exists, or knows. Love, existence, and knowledge are not the qualities of the Purusha, but its essence. When they get reflected upon something, you may call them the qualities of that something. They are not the qualities but the essence of the Purusha, the great Atman, the Infinite Being, without birth or death, established in its own glory."[930]

Appropriately, this final song on George's final album ends with a Hindu chant, Namah Parvati, in praise of Lord Shiva, who destroys ignorance and awakens supreme truth. It was double-tracked with the voice of his son Dhani.

This Sanskrit hymn translates as follows (without repetition):

I bow to Parvati's husband, the Great God Shiva, who removes all afflictions.

I bow to Parvati's husband, who removes all afflictions.

Lord Shiva, Lord Shiva, the beneficent Great God Shiva.

The Great Lord Shiva, the destroyer of darkness.

PART VII

AND IN THE END

CHAPTER 14

THE LOVE YOU MAKE

"People Want Peace"

Recorded: January 2016 to February 2018
Released: September 7, 2018: Egypt Station

Several of Paul McCartney's solo songs reflect India's influence. "Maybe I'm Amazed" (April 17, 1970) and "Motor of Love" (June 5, 1989) speak of both worldly and heavenly love. "Junk" and "Teddy Boy" (both April 17, 1970), written in India at Maharishi's ashram, invoke nostalgia, inevitability of death, and remembrance of life's fleeting moments. As per Paul, "Listen to What the Man Said" (May 16, 1975) might be about God. "With a Little Luck" (March 20, 1978) speaks of positive motivation.

Paul's "Coming Up" (April 11, 1980) espouses the universal message of love and peace central to the Beatles. When John Lennon could not get "Coming Up" out of his head, he came out of retirement and made the *Double Fantasy* album. In 1992, Paul sang about "Hope of Deliverance" (December 28, 1992) from the darkness that surrounds us.

Paul continued to chant the Beatles' message of peace in his 2018 album, *Egypt Station*, with his anthem "People Want Peace." He recalled that as a child, he was seeing reports of wars in newspapers and television. So he asked his dad, "What is it? Do people want peace or do they just like to fight?"

Paul's father very quietly answered, "No, no, son, people want peace. It's the politicians and the leaders who get into wars. It's not the people."[931]

 Scan this code to read the lyrics.

In October 2018, *Mojo* magazine reported that "People Want Peace" was inspired by Paul's controversial decision to play a gig in Tel Aviv in 2008, which friends had cautioned him against. When people told Paul "You can't go," it just made him more eager to go there.

When Paul traveled to Israel, he met a group of young adults called OneVoice Movement, which supports activists who seek a just and negotiated resolution to the Israeli-Palestinian conflict. They told Paul, "All we want to do is just live in peace, raise our families, and be able to just get on with our lives in peace." Paul and his band performed his concert in Tel Aviv while endorsing OneVoice and wearing the group's badges.

"Riding into Jaipur"

Written: February 16, 2001
Recorded: February 16 to June 2001
Released: November 12, 2001: Driving Rain

Paul McCartney said he wrote "Riding into Jaipur" while on holiday with his wife Linda: "I had a back-packing guitar, a little Martin travel guitar that is absolutely slimmed down to nothing and weighs sort of zero ounces. Linda had got me [that] as a prezzie; and I took it when she and I went to The Maldives for a holiday.

"My particular back-packer—and I haven't noticed this on other people's—seems to have a bit of a sound on certain frets like a sitar, and because I was in the middle of the Indian Ocean, the two came together in that song. I didn't have a title for the song, but when I went to India [in 2001], I took a train to Jaipur. It was a very exotic overnight train journey and I did some words that were in the same vein as that original melody. So those two things came together."[932]

In this lovely, rare, surprising McCartney raga-rock track, Paul played a Martin "Backpacker" acoustic guitar then overdubbed Hofner bass guitar and sang a melody with an Indian flair. Abe Laboriel, Jr., played a Roland Handsonic with African drum samples, which mimicked an Indian tabla. Rusty Anderson played tambura then overdubbed Gibson electric twelve-string guitar. Gabe Dixon played piano. David Kahne overdubbed a synthesizer.

Scan this code to read the lyrics.

More McCartney Raga Rock

"Taxman"

On April 21, 1966, when George Harrison could not work out a guitar solo on "Taxman" for the album *Revolver*, George Martin grew impatient and asked Paul to have a go. Harrison left the studio for a couple of hours while Paul recorded his amazing solo, described by Geoff Emerick as "stunning in its ferocity—his guitar playing had a fire and energy that his younger band mates rarely matched—and was accomplished in just a take or two."[933]

George later described, "I was pleased to have Paul play that bit on 'Taxman.' If you notice, he did like a little Indian bit on it for me," referring to what author Ian MacDonald described as "a savage seven-bar affair that picks up the octave jump in the riff, adding a scintillating pseudo-Indian descending passage en route."[934]

"Auraveda"

On Paul's "Fireman" album *Rushes* (released September 21, 1998), the instrumental track "Auraveda" features harmonium, sitar, and tabla. Its title is a take-off on Ayurveda—the folk medicine of India. Paul blended the words *aura* (the human energy field) and *Veda* (the ancient wisdom of India) to create the title "Auraveda."

"Tragedy"

Paul played sitar on his cover of the 1959 hit by Gerald H. Nelson and Fred B. Burch, originally performed by Thomas Wayne and the DeLons. Paul and his group Wings recorded the song on March 13, 1972, for the planned *Red Rose Speedway* double album. That LP was released without "Tragedy." This raga-rock track with Paul's amateur-yet-effective sitar accompaniment (similar to George on "Norwegian Wood") was officially released December 7, 2018 in the *Red Rose Speedway Archive Collection*.

Y Not (album)

Written: 2009
Recorded: 2009
Released: January 12, 2010

The breakup of The Beatles hit Ringo harder than the other band members. He drowned his anger in a haze of alcohol and cocaine blackouts, piled atop chain-smoking. He even beat his wife Barbara Bach while in a drunken coma. In 1988, he finally recovered, after the couple entered rehab.

Ringo now lives a healthy lifestyle, exercises with a personal trainer, eats organic vegan food, practices meditation, looks twenty years younger than his age, and has found that God is love. He declares, "God is my life."

Peace and Love

In 2008, a few days before Ringo's birthday, a reporter asked him, "What would you like for your birthday?"

Ringo recalled, "I don't know where it came from, but I said, 'I'd like more peace and love, and I'd love it if at noon on my birthday everyone would say, 'Peace and love.'"[935] This started Ringo's annual "Peace and Love birthday initiative." The tradition began in Chicago in 2008, with sixty to one hundred people attending, but is now a worldwide phenomenon.

Every year on Ringo's birthday, July 7, he asks fans to chant "Peace and love" precisely at noon in every time zone across the globe. Ringo said, "It keeps getting bigger every year. My dream—my fantasy—is that one day in the future everyone on the planet will stop at noon and say, 'Peace and love.' The world has always been violent. All I can do is my part, and part of that is to keep saying 'Peace and love.'"[936] The "Ringo Starr Peace and Love Fund," founded in 2015, supports various charities.

Ringo, wearing a peace symbol on his neck, and making a peace sign with his hand, declares "Peace and Love."

In 2019 Ringo recorded a lovely song to convey his "Peace and Love" message: "Send Love Spread Peace," from his 2019 album *What's My Name*. On the official video, Ringo made the peace sign and also bowed in namaskar (with palms together) in the Indian tradition.

John Lennon said, "If someone thinks that peace and love are just a cliché that must have been left behind in the sixties, that's a problem. Peace and love are eternal."[937] Though Ringo's musical expressions might not be as eloquent as his Beatle-mates, his message is still the same: The Beatles were sent to this earth to bring peace and love. Here are comments about some of Ringo's spiritual songs, most from the album *Y Not*.

"Y Not"

The idea of this song is we ask "Why?" too much and ask "Why not?" too little. Rather than living in a "cannot" world, Ringo suggests we live in a "can do" world. We make excuses that keep us stuck in self-inflicted boundaries rather than stepping out of our comfort zone and experiencing life to the fullest. Nothing lasts, not even sadness. So if we get up off our ass, we can create a better day.

Tina Sugandh (a.k.a. "Tabla Girl"), an Indian musician who lives in New Jersey, chanted and played tabla on this song. The Hindi lyrics she sang, *aajah pyar shanti pyar*, translate as "Come, love, peace, love."[938] Ringo said, "Over the years, I got to love the [Indian] music myself and now I'm a Christian Hindu with Buddhist tendencies. Thanks to George, who opened my eyes as much as anyone else's."[939]

 Scan this code to read the lyrics for "Y Not."

Scan this code for a short
video about the Hindi
lyrics in "Y Not."

"Peace Dream"

This nostalgic walk through memory lane, recalling John and Yoko's bed-in, describes Ringo's dream of world peace and harmony, free from war, without hunger or pain. Ringo is hopeful that we could make that dream a reality.

Scan this code to
read the lyrics.

"Everyone Wins"

This optimistic song is about letting go of the competitive nature of the ego and instead realizing what really makes the world go around—love. When we experience silence in meditation, our light shines to touch everything around us. Then the world can really change. The song promotes the message that whatever happens is meant to be, and all is part of the greater plan. Eventually all doubts will disappear, and we will know life will get better.

Scan this code to
read the lyrics.

"Walk with You"

Ringo said this song was intended as a gospel track. But when he called Van Dyke Parks to collaborate on it, Parks said he would not write about God. However, though the lyrics appear to be about faithful friendship, it seems obvious that the "You" is God. When we walk and talk with God, we know that all is well. Paul McCartney sang harmonies on the track.

 Scan this code to read the lyrics.

"Can't Do It Wrong"

This song conveys a message that, even if we are uncertain about our decisions, all is well and we cannot make a mistake. Once again, no matter what the question, love is always the answer. As long as we keep singing, keep giving, and keep carrying on, we can never go wrong. The spiritual message here is to keep going, no matter what, and not dwell in self-incrimination or regrets.

 Scan this code to read the lyrics.

"Give More Love"

Recorded: 2017
Released: September 15, 2017: Give More Love

"Give More Love" is Ringo's summation of everything The Beatles were about. Though it is hard to know what we can do about those who are in pain, we can give more love. Though many are suffering from broken heartedness, we can reach out and give more love. We can make a change and create a better world, just by giving more love. The simplest message is to give more love.

 Scan this code to read the lyrics.

Passing of John

According to Alan Weiss, an ABC TV Producer who happened to be there, "All My Loving" was playing on the sound system at Roosevelt Hospital Emergency Room when John Lennon was pronounced dead after being shot on December 8, 1980. Coincidentally, "All My Loving" had been The Beatles' opening song on *The Ed Sullivan Show*, February 9, 1964.

After The Beatles' breakup, John and Paul had been at war, insulting each other in song: "Too Many People" by Paul, and "How Do You Sleep?" by John. But eventually, much was forgiven and they renewed their bond, forged in childhood. In a heartfelt performance after John's death, Paul dedicated the song "Here Today" to his boyhood mate: "I still remember how it was before. And I am holding back the tears no more. I love you."

Ringo told Michael Aspel on British TV that he saw John twice after his death. One time in Los Angeles, when Ringo was "down and miserable," John's spirit appeared to him in the corner of a hotel room and asked, "What are you doing?"

Ringo replied, "Being miserable."

John told him, "Come on, get it together."[940]

As for John, his star has not diminished, and his music never fades. With the radiance of his intellect, the brilliance of his wit, the sincerity of his intentions, and the devotion in his heart, it shines on, "like the moon and the stars and the sun... on and on, and on and on."

Passing of George

Ringo described the final time he saw George Harrison: "I went to see him, and he was very ill. He could only lay down."

Ringo told George that he had to go to Boston to see his daughter, Lee Starkey, who had a brain tumor. Ringo recalled, emotionally, "Phew, it's the last words I heard him say, actually, and he said, 'Do you want me to come with you?'"[941]

Ravi Shankar described his final visit to George: "We spent the day before with him, and even then he looked so peaceful, surrounded by love."[942]

George recognized Ravi as "the person who influenced my life the most."[943]

George passed on November 29, 2001. His wife Olivia described, "There was a profound experience that happened when he left his body. It was visible. Let's just say, you wouldn't need to light the room, if you were trying to film it. He just…lit the room."[944]

His family released this statement: "He left this world as he lived in it—conscious of God, fearless of death, and at peace."[945]

Olivia said, "He gave his life to God a long time ago. He wasn't trying to hang on to anything. He was fine with it. George dedicated a lot of his life to obtain a good ending and I don't have any doubt that he was successful."[946]

Hours after his death in Los Angeles, George was cremated at Hollywood Forever Memorial Park. We would assume his ashes were scattered in the River Ganges, but no official ceremony took place, though thousands gathered at the sacred sites of Varanasi and Allahabad in expectation.

When George received his posthumous star on the Hollywood Walk of Fame on April 14, 2009, Olivia described him as "a beautiful mystical man living in a material world."[947]

Tom Hanks declared, "All things must pass, sure. But George is going to live forever."[948]

ADDITIONAL PHOTO CREDITS

ENDNOTES

1   "A day in the life: The Beatles' first appearance on American television," *NBC News*, Nov. 18, 2013, nbcnews.com/nightly-news/day-life-beatles-first-appearance-american-television-flna2D11612597.

2   Beatles, The, and Brian Roylance. *The Beatles Anthology* (San Francisco: Chronicle Books, 2000).

3   Kruth, John. *This Bird Has Flown: The Enduring Beauty of Rubber Soul, Fifty Years On* (Lanham, MD: Backbeat, 2015).

4   Schjeldahl, Peter, "The Outlaw," *The New Yorker*, Jan. 26, 2014, newyorker.com/magazine/2014/02/03/the-outlaw.

5   Ibid.

6   "Jack Kerouac (1922-1969): Poems," *Terebess Asia Online (TAO)*, web.archive.org/web/20090722025344/terebess.hu/english/kerouac.html.

7   "The Beat Papers of Al Aronowitz," *The Blacklisted Journalist*, Jun. 1, 1997, blacklistedjournalist.com/column22.html.

8   Lavezzoli, Peter. *The Dawn of Indian Music in the West* (New York: Continuum, 2006).

9   Wilentz, Sean. *Bob Dylan in America* (New York: Anchor Books, 2011), 50.

10 Harris, Ben and Sebastian Raatz, *George Harrison: Tribute to the Rock & Roll Legend*, Music Spotlight Collector's Edition: Centennial Media, LLC. 2021, 17.

11 Beatles and Roylance, *The Beatles Anthology*, 41.

12 Ganguly, Suranjan, "Allen Ginsberg in India: An Interview," *Ariel*, Oct. 1, 1993, journalhosting.ucalgary.ca/index.php/ariel/article/view/33620.

13 van't Hooftm, Merel, "The Beats and the Beatles: Two Sides of the Same Coin," *Beatdom*, May 26, 2015, beatdom.com/the-beats-and-the-beatles-two-sides-of-the-same-coin.

14 Sheff, David, "John Lennon Interview: Playboy 1980," beatlesinterviews.org/dbjypb.int4.html.

15 Cott, Jonathan and Christine Doudna, eds. *The Ballad of John and Yoko* (Garden City, NY: Doubleday, 1982), 68.

16 "Khandogya-Upanishad: Sixth Prapathaka, Second Khanda," *InfoPlease*, infoplease.com/primary-sources/ philosophy-religion/the-upanishads/second-khavda.

17 Miles, Barry. *Paul McCartney: Many Years From Now* (New York: Henry Holt and Company, 1997, 1998).

18 Gaines, Steven S. and Peter Brown. *The Love You Make: An Insider's Story of the Beatles* (New York: New American Library, 1984), 143.

19 *The Beatles Bible*, beatlesbible.com.

20 Ibid.

21 Miles, *Paul McCartney: Many Years From Now*.

22 Ibid.

23 *The Beatles Bible*, beatlesbible.com.

24 Miles, *Paul McCartney: Many Years From Now*.

25 *The Beatles Bible*, beatlesbible.com.

26 Miles, *Paul McCartney: Many Years From Now*.

27 *The Beatles Bible*, beatlesbible.com.

28 Herbert, Ian, "Revealed: Dentist who introduced Beatles to LSD," *Independent*, Apr. 1, 2009, independent.co.uk/arts-entertainment/music/ news/revealed-dentist-who-introduced-beatles-lsd-6231654.html.

29 Boyd, Pattie, "Patti Boyd: The dentist who spiked my coffee with LSD," DailyMail.com, Aug. 5, 2007, dailymail.co.uk/tvshowbiz/ article-473207/Patti-Boyd-The-dentist-spiked-coffee-LSD.html.

30 Gilmore, Mikal, "Beatles' Acid Test: How LSD Opened the Door to 'Revolver,'" Aug. 25, 2016, rollingstone.com/feature/beatles-acid-test-how-lsd-opened-the-door-to-revolver-251417.

31 Ibid.

32 Love, Robert, Jason Fine, and Jenny Eliscu, eds. *Harrison: By the Editors of Rolling Stone* (New York: Simon & Schuster, 2002), 145.

33 *The Beatles Wiki*, beatles.fandom.com/wiki/The_Beatles_Wiki.

34 Gilmore, Mikal, "Beatles' Acid Test."

35 *The Beatles Bible*, beatlesbible.com.

36 Du Noyer, Paul. *We All Shine On* (New York: HarperCollins, 1997), 75.

37 Beatles and Roylance, *The Beatles Anthology*, 190.

38 *The Beatles Bible*, beatlesbible.com.

39 Beatles and Roylance, *The Beatles Anthology*.

40 Gilmore, Mikal, "Beatles' Acid Test."

41 Beatles and Roylance, *The Beatles Anthology*.

42 *Magic Trip: Ken Kesey's Search for a Kool Place*, directed by Alison Ellwood, Alex Gibney (2011; New York: Magnolia Pictures).

43 McNeil, Legs and Gillian McCain, "The Oral History of the First Two Times the Beatles Took Acid," *Vice*, Dec. 4,

2016, vice.com/en/article/ppawq9/the-oral-history-of-the-beatles-first-two-acids-trips-legs-mcneil-gillian-mccain.

44 Gilmore, Mikal, "Beatles' Acid Test."

45 Beatles and Roylance, *The Beatles Anthology*.

46 Wenner, Jann, "Rolling Stone Interview," *JohnLennon.com*, johnlennon.com/music/interviews/rolling-stone-interview-1970.

47 Fonda, Peter. *Don't Tell Dad: A Memoir* (New York: Hyperion, 1998), 209.

48 Everett, Walter. *The Beatles as Musicians: Revolver Through the Anthology* (New York: Oxford University Press, 1999), 62.

49 Sheff, "John Lennon Interview: Playboy 1980."

50 Gilmore, Mikal, "Beatles' Acid Test."

51 Ibid.

52 "Louise Harrison, Her Kid Brother George, and the 'Harrison Family Curse'—Part Two," *REBEAT*, Aug. 2015, rebeatmag.com/louise-harrison-her-kid-brother-george-and-the-harrison-family-curse-part-two.

53 Havers, Richard, "The Making Of George Harrison's 'Within You Without You,'" *Udiscovermusic*, Mar. 15, 2021, udiscovermusic.com/stories/within-you-without-you.

54 Kumar, Anu, "From Bollywood to Beatles and beyond: The amazing journey of Shiv Dayal Batish," *Scroll.in*, June 24, 2021, scroll.in/global/997581/from-bollywood-to-beatles-and-beyond-the-amazing-journey-of-shiv-dayal-batish.

55 Batish, Pt. Shiv Dayal, "My Episode with the Beatles and George Harrison," *RagaNet*, raganet.com/Issues/3/beatles.html.

56 Ibid.

57 Kumar, "From Bollywood to Beatles and beyond."

58 Batish, S.D. and Ashwin Batish, "Pandit Shiv Dayal Batish—Introduction" *Pandit Shiv Dayal Batish*, batish.com/sd/introduction.html.

59 Love, *Harrison: By the Editors of Rolling Stone*, 174.

60 "Beatles and Ravi Shankar met at Gabor's LSD party," *Zee News*, Apr. 19, 2010, zeenews.india.com/entertainment/celebrity/-beatles-and-ravi-shankar-met-at-gabor-s-lsd-party_59174.html.

61 Nelson, Dean, "Beatles introduced to Ravi Shankar's Music at LSD Party, Byrds singer reveals," *The Telegraph*, Apr. 19, 2010, telegraph.co.uk/culture/music/the-beatles/7603772/Beatles-introduced-to-Ravi-Shankars-music-at-LSD-party-Byrds-singer-reveals.html.

62 Ibid.

63 Lifton, Dave, "How the Beatles Grew Up on 'Rubber Soul.'" *UCR*, Dec. 3, 2015, ultimateclassicrock.com/beatles-rubber-soul.

64 "Phillips, Shawn," *Encyclopedia.com*, encyclopedia.com/education/news-wires-white-papers-and-books/phillips-shawn.

65 Kruth, *This Bird Has Flown*.
66 "Interview: Shawn Phillips," *Hit Channel*, June 4, 2015,
    hit-channel.com/interview-shawn-phillips/83186.
67 Kruth, *This Bird Has Flown*.
68 *SongFacts*, songfacts.com.
69 Badman, Keith. *The Beatles Off the Record: Outrageous Opinions &*
    Unreleased Interviews (London: Omnibus Press, 2000, 2008, 2009), 190.
70 Shankar, Ravi. *Raga Mala: The Autobiography of Ravi Shankar* (New York:
    Welcome Rain, 1999), archive.org/details/ragamalaautobiog00shan.
71 Naqvi, Saeed, "You may say they were dreamers," *Indian Express*, Dec.
    09, 2005, indianexpress.com/full_story.php?content_id=83564.
72 *The Beatles Virtual Museum*, beatlesite.blogspot.com.
73 Ibid.
74 "Ravi Shankar on the *Sitar's* Association With Drugs,"
    The Dick Cavett Show (YouTube channel), Dec. 27,
    2019, youtube.com/watch?v=0HRYbPVOMWY.
75 Beatles and Roylance, *The Beatles Anthology*.
76 Ibid.
77 Ibid.
78 Ibid.
79 Mason, Paul. *The Beatles, Drugs, Mysticism &*
    India (Premanand, 2017), 121.
80 *The Beatles Ultimate Experience*, beatlesinterviews.org.
81 Davies, Hunter. *The Beatles* (New York: W.W. Norton, 1996), 275.
82 Müller, Max and Max Fausböli. *Sacred Books of the East, Vol. 10:*
    The Dhammapada and Sutta Nipata (1881), "Dhammapada,
    Chapter 1," sacred-texts.com/bud/sbe10/sbe1003.htm.
83 *The Beatles Bible*, beatlesbible.com.
84 *The Beatles Wiki*, beatles.fandom.com/wiki/The_Beatles_Wiki.
85 Shotton, Pete and Nicolas Schaffner. *John Lennon: In My*
    Life (Briarcliff Manor, NY: Stein & Day, 1983), 117.
86 Miles, *Paul McCartney: Many Years From Now*.
87 Sheff, "John Lennon Interview: Playboy 1980."
88 "The Varieties of Psychedelic Experience,"
    psychonautdocs.com/docs/thevarieties.pdf.
89 *The Beatles Bible*, beatlesbible.com.
90 *The Beatles Wiki*, beatles.fandom.com/wiki/The_Beatles_Wiki.
91 "John Lennon's last interview, December 8, 1980,"
    Beatles Archive, Dec. 21, 2013, beatlesarchive.net/john-
    lennons-last-interview-december-8-1980.html.

92 Guesdon, Jean-Michel and Philippe Margotin. *All the Songs: The Story Behind Every Beatles Release* (New York: Black Dog & Leventhal, 2013), 311.

93 *In the Life of… The Beatles*, lifeofthebeatles.blogspot.com.

94 Sheff, "John Lennon Interview: Playboy 1980."

95 Miles, *Paul McCartney: Many Years From Now.*

96 Ibid.

97 Ibid.

98 Ibid.

99 Ibid.

100 *The Beatles Ultimate Experience*, beatlesinterviews.org.

101 Miles, *Paul McCartney: Many Years From Now.*

102 Cleave, Maureen, "How a Beatle Lives: from *Evening Standard*, March 25, 1966," *Truth About the Beatles*, truthaboutthebeatlesgirls.tumblr.com/post/64047580055/the-following-is-the-original-article-as-written.

103 Miles, *Paul McCartney: Many Years From Now.*

104 Chan, Dale, "Tomorrow Never Knows," *Dale Chan's Beatles World*, thebeatleshk.com/SongStories/TomorrowNeverKnows.html.

105 Runtagh, Jordan, "When John Lennon's 'More Popular Than Jesus' Controversy Turned Ugly," *Rolling Stone*, July 29, 2016, rollingstone.com/feature/when-john-lennons-more-popular-than-jesus-controversy-turned-ugly-106430.

106 "John Lennon sparks his first major controversy," *History*, Nov. 16, 2009, history.com/this-day-in-history/john-lennon-sparks-his-first-major-controversy.

107 Schaal, Eric, "The Beatles Songs That Got Their Titles From 'Ringo-isms' John Lennon Loved," *Showbiz CheatSheet*, May 15, 2020, cheatsheet.com/entertainment/the-beatles-songs-that-got-their-titles-from-ringo-isms-john-lennon-loved.html.

108 *The Paul McCartney Project*, the-paulmccartney-project.com.

109 Beatles and Roylance, *The Beatles Anthology.*

110 "The Psychedelic Experience," *Psychedelic Frontier*, psychedelicfrontier.com/wp-content/uploads/2014/02/The-Psychedelic-Experience-A-Manual-Based-on-the-Tibetan-Book-of-the-Dead.pdf.

111 *The Paul McCartney Project*, the-paulmccartney-project.com.

112 Mukundananda, Swami, "Chapter 2: Sankhya Yoga," (verses 2:11 and 2:12), *Bhagavad Gita, The Song of God*, holy-bhagavad-gita.org/chapter/2.

113 *The Paul McCartney Project*, the-paulmccartney-project.com.

114 "The Psychedelic Experience," *Psychedelic Frontier.*

115 Ibid.

116 *The Beatles Bible*, beatlesbible.com.

117 "The Psychedelic Experience," *Psychedelic Frontier*.

118 *Beatle Links*, beatlelinks.net.

119 Beatles and Roylance, *The Beatles Anthology*.

120 Ibid.

121 *The Beatles Wiki*, beatles.fandom.com/wiki/The_Beatles_Wiki.

122 Schmidt, Sara, "Paul's LSD interview—when did it happen and why?" *Meet the Beatles for Real*, June 18, 2017, meetthebeatlesforreal.com.

123 *Beatle Links*, beatlelinks.net.

124 Beatles and Roylance, *The Beatles Anthology*.

125 Wenner, Jann, "Rolling Stone Interview," *JohnLennon.com*.

126 *Andrews, Travis M., "He did the impossible and made John Lennon sound like the Dalai Lama," Washington Post*, October 4, 2018. washingtonpost.com /arts-entertainment/2018/10/03/ he-did-impossible-made-john-lennon-sound-like-dalai-lama.

127 *The Beatles Bible*, beatlesbible.com.

128 Emerick, Geoff and Howard Massey. *Here, There and Everywhere: My Life Recording the Music of the Beatles* (New York: Penguin Publishing Group, 2006).

129 Ibid.

130 Ibid.

131 Ibid.

132 Wentzel, Jim. *The Beatles* (New York: Rosen Publishing Group, 2002), 59.

133 Beatles and Roylance, *The Beatles Anthology*, 209.

134 D'Silva, Reynold, *The Beatles and India*, directed by Ajoy Bose and Peter Compton (2021; London: Renoir Pictures/Silva Screen).

135 Beatles and Roylance, *The Beatles Anthology*, 209.

136 "Wouldn't It Be Loverly." Peter Sellers—Topic (YouTube channel). Nov. 21, 2014, youtube.com/watch?v=agDDoOepbaE.

137 Newman, Ray. *Abracadabra! The Complete Story of the Beatles' Revolver* (London: Popkult Books, 2006), 23.

138 Turner, Steve. *Beatles '66: The Revolutionary Year* (New York: HarperLuxe, 2016).

139 Rodriguez, Robert. *Revolver: How the Beatles Reimagined Rock 'n' Roll* (Milwaukee, WI: Backbeat Books, 2012), 114.

140 Womack, Kenneth. *The Beatles Encyclopedia: Everything Fab Four* (Santa Barbara, CA: ABC-CLIO, 2016), 310.

141 Lewisohn, Mark. *The Complete Beatles Chronicle* (Chicago: Chicago Review Press, 1992), 72.

142 Turner, *Beatles '66: The Revolutionary Year*, 231.

143 Shankar, *Raga Mala: The Autobiography of Ravi Shankar*

144 Ibid.

145 "Ravi Shankar teaches George Harrison how to play sitar 1968,"
TheBEATLESMania100n2 (YouTube channel). Sept. 25, 2012,
youtube.com/watch?v=RxI6IkH9Mvo.

146 "Ali Akbar Khan," *National Endowment for the Arts*,
arts.gov/honors/heritage/ali-akbar-khan.

147 Babiuk, Andy. *Beatles Gear: All the Fab Four's Instruments From Stage
to Studio* (Lanham, MD: Backbeat Books, 2001), 202-203.

148 Shankar, *Raga Mala: The Autobiography of Ravi Shankar*.

149 Belmo (Scott Belmer). *George Harrison: His Words, Wit &
Wisdom* (Canada: Belmo Publishing, 2002), 24.

150 Bose, Ajoy, "The 'karmic connection' between The Beatles'
George Harrison and Ravi Shankar," *Quartz India*, Feb.
19, 2018. qz.com/india/1210560/the-karmic-connection-
between-the-beatles-george-harrison-and-ravi-shankar.

151 "Ravi Shankar teaches George Harrison how to play sitar 1968."

152 Beatles and Roylance, *The Beatles Anthology*.

153 *The Beatles Ultimate Experience*, beatlesinterviews.org.

154 Badman, *The Beatles Off the Record*.

155 Norman, Philip. *Shout! The True Story of the
Beatles* (New York: Touchstone, 2005).

156 Frankel, Glenn, "And She Loved Him," *Washington Post*, Oct. 3, 2005,
washingtonpost.com/archive/lifestyle/2005/10/03/and-she-loved-
him/008ecd42-1d14-4a48-a7d5-29ca5c684862.

157 *The Beatles Wiki*, beatles.fandom.com/wiki/The_Beatles_Wiki.

158 Miles, *Paul McCartney: Many Years From Now*.

159 *The Beatles Wiki*, beatles.fandom.com/wiki/The_Beatles_Wiki.

160 Venkatesananda, Swami. *Vasistha's Yoga* (Albany, NY:
State University of New York Press, 1993), 362.

161 Poe, Edgar Allan, "A Dream Within a Dream," *Poetry Foundation*,
poetryfoundation.org/poems/52829/a-dream-within-a-dream.

162 "Life is but a Dream," *All Poetry,* allpoetry.com/Life-is-but-a-Dream

163 "Albert Einstein Quotes," *Brainy Quote*, brainyquote.com/quotes
/albert_einstein_100298.

164 Cott, Jonathan, "John Lennon: The Last Interview," *Rolling Stone*, Dec.
23, 2010-Jan. 6, 2011, rollingstone.com/feature/john-lennon-the-last-
interview-179443.

165 Sheff, "John Lennon Interview: Playboy 1980."

166 *The Beatles Wiki*, beatles.fandom.com/wiki/The_Beatles_Wiki.

167 Beatles and Roylance, *The Beatles Anthology*.

168 Whatley, Jack, "The Beatles song on which John Lennon proved he wasn't a 'lunatic,'" *Far Out*, July 23, 2020, faroutmagazine.co.uk/beatles-song-john-lennon-lunatic-surreal-strawberry-fields-forever.

169 Chadha, Anjani, "Delhi's Lahore Music House embodies remnants of the past," *The New Indian Express*, Oct. 17, 2021. newindianexpress.com/cities/delhi/2021/oct/17/delhis-lahore-music-house-embodies-remnants-of-the-past-2372264.html.

170 Ranjit, S. Sahaya, "Bishan Dass Sharma's perfect note out of musical instruments, manufactured by his establishment," *India Today*, Jan. 14, 2012. indiatoday.in/magazine/offtrack/story/20030519-bishan-dass-sharma-perfect-note-out-of-musical-instruments-by-rikhi-ram-and-sons-759054-2012-01-14.

171 Shankar, Ravi, "On Appreciation of Indian Classical Music," *The Ravi Shankar Foundation*, ravishankar.org/music.html.

172 Austa, Sanjay, "He is instrumental in making music," *The Tribune*, Sept. 14, 2012, tribuneindia.com/2002/20020914/windows/main3.htm.

173 Mallik, Madhusree, "The best Indian musical instrument stores in Delhi," *India Today*, Feb. 14, 2005, indiatoday.in/magazine/supplement/story/20050214-rikhirams-bharat-music-house-marques-and-co-a.godin-and-co-best-indian-musical-instrument-stores-in-delhi-788506-2005-02-14.

174 "Journey of Rikhi Ram," July 17, 2019, *Rikhi Ram*, rikhiram.com/blog/journey-of-rikhi-ram/3.html.

175 Scorsese, Martin, *George Harrison: Living In The Material World*, directed by Martin Scorsese (2011; New York: Sikelia Productions).

176 Runtagh, Jordan, "Beatles' 'Sgt. Pepper' at 50: How George Harrison Found Himself on 'Within You Without You,'" *Rolling Stone.*, May 25, 2017, rollingstone.com/music/music-features/beatles-sgt-pepper-at-50-how-george-harrison-found-himself-on-within-you-without-you-126654.

177 *The Beatles Ultimate Experience*, beatlesinterviews.org.

178 "A Spiritual Tribute to George Harrison ~ Beatle and Devotee of Yogananda," *Yoganandasite*, Nov. 24, 2016, yoganandasite.wordpress.com/2016/11/24/a-spiritual-tribute-to-george-harrison-beatle-and-devotee-of-yogananda.

179 Thomson, Graeme. *George Harrison: Behind the Locked Door* (London: Omnibus Press, 2013).

180 Beatles and Roylance, *The Beatles Anthology*.

181 Cupchik, Jeffrey W, "Polyvocality and Forgotten Proverbs (and Persons): Ravi Shankar, George Harrison and Shambhu Das," *Academia*, 2014, academia.edu/5391509/Polyvocality_and_Forgotten_Proverbs_and_Persons_Ravi_Shankar_George_Harrison_and_Shambhu_Das.

182 Mason, *The Beatles, Drugs, Mysticism & India*, 18.

183 Harrison, George, *Raga*, directed by Howard Worth, (1971; London: Apple Films), Rare Indian Classical Music Programs (YouTube channel), Oct. 30, 2019, youtube.com/watch?v=rCJZ6aDKStQ.

184 Bruns, Prudence Farrow. *Dear Prudence: The Story Behind the Song* (North Charleston, SC: Amazon Digital Services LLC, 2015), 205.

185 Cupchik, "Polyvocality and Forgotten Proverbs."

186 Desborough, Jenny, "The Beatles Ravi Shankar: How George Harrison and Ravi Shankar collaborated," *Express*, Dec. 11, 2020, express.co.uk/entertainment/music/1371540/The-Beatles-Ravi-Shankar-George-Harrison-collaborated-evg.

187 *The Beatles Ultimate Experience*, beatlesinterviews.org.

188 Sheff, "John Lennon Interview: Playboy 1980."

189 "George Harrison in His Own Words," *The Spirit of George Harrison*, beatlesnumber9.com/george.html.

190 Babiuk, Andy. *Beatles Gear: All the Fab Four's Instruments From Stage to Studio*, 202-203.

191 *Self-Realization Magazine*, Spring 1996, Self-Realization Fellowship, Los Angeles, California, yogananda.org.

192 Ibid.

193 Ibid.

194 "George Harrison in His Own Words." *The Spirit*.

195 Jackson, Peter, *Get Back*, directed by Peter Jackson (2021; United States, England, New Zealand: Walt Disney Pictures, Apple Corps, WingNut Films, (Nov. 25, 2021), Disney+ Television. Part 3: 07:06.

196 "Swami VivekanandaQuotesQuotable Quote," *GoodReads*, goodreads.com/quotes/5564260-what-right-has-a-man-to-say-he-has-a.

197 Beatles and Roylance, *The Beatles Anthology*.

198 Thomson, *George Harrison: Behind the Locked Door*.

199 Beatles and Roylance, *The Beatles Anthology*.

200 Ibid.

201 Miles, *Paul McCartney: Many Years From Now*.

202 *The Beatles Ultimate Experience*, beatlesinterviews.org.

203 Greene, Joshua M, "Medley: George Harrison—Beatle, Seeker, Lover of God," *Theosophy Forward*, Dec. 6, 2013, theosophyforward.com/mixed-bag/medley/1059-george-harrison-beatle-seeker-lover-of-god.

204 Runtagh, "Beatles' 'Sgt. Pepper' at 50."

205 *The Beatles Wiki*, beatles.fandom.com/wiki/The_Beatles_Wiki.

206 Boyd, Jenny. *Jennifer Juniper: A journey beyond the muse.* Romsey (United Kingdom: Urbane Publications, 2020).

207 Harris, *George Harrison: Tribute*, 36.

208 "Louise Harrison, Her Kid Brother George.

209 "Swami VivekanandaQuotesQuotable Quote." *Goodreads*. goodreads.com/quotes/68229-each-soul-is-potentially-divine-the-goal-is-to-manifest

210 "George Harrison in His Own Words." *The Spirit*.

211 Lavezzoli, Peter. *The Dawn of Indian Music in the West*, 178.

212 Davies, Hunter. *The Beatles: The Authorised Biography* (London: Heinemann, 1968), 351.

213 Emerick, *Here, There and Everywhere*.

214 Martin, George. *Summer of Love: The Making of Sgt. Pepper* (Basingstoke, UK: Pan Macmillan, 1994).

215 Beatles and Roylance, *The Beatles Anthology*.

216 "University of Sheffield musician helps reveal the last untold Beatles story." *The University of Sheffield News Archive*. June 8, 2017. sheffield.ac.uk/news/nr/beatles-indian-music-concert-george-harrison-sgt-pepper-1.706418.

217 *The Beatles Bible*, beatlesbible.com.

218 Ibid.

219 "Mystery Indian musician on Sgt Pepper album reveals his memories after he's finally identified," *The Herald Scotland*, June 2, 2017, heraldscotland.com/news/15324878.mystery-indian-musician-sgt-pepper-album-reveals-memories-finally-identified.

220 Sheff, "John Lennon Interview: Playboy 1980."

221 DeRiso, Nick, "George Harrison gets deep on 'Within You Without You,'" *UCR*, May 25, 2017, ultimateclassicrock.com/beatles-within-you-without-you.

222 *The Beatles Bible*, beatlesbible.com.

223 "The Beatles in India," *Owl apps*, owlapps.net/owlapps_apps/articles?id=24101956&lang=en.

224 Beatles and Roylance, *The Beatles Anthology*.

225 Thomson, *George Harrison: Behind the Locked Door*.

226 DeRiso, "George Harrison gets deep on 'Within You Without You.'"

227 "John Lennon on 'Lucy In The Sky with Diamonds' and LSD," *The Dick Cavett Show* (YouTube channel), Oct. 5, 2018, youtube.com/watch?v=umF60jXiYBI.

228 "The Beatles' Lucy in the Sky dies, aged 46," *The Guardian*, Sep. 28, 2009, theguardian.com/music/2009/sep/28/beatles-lucy-in-sky-dies.

229 Beatles and Roylance, *The Beatles Anthology*.

230 Ibid.

231 Maeder, Don, "The Incredible Recording Process of Lucy in the Sky with Diamonds and It's Getting Better,"

Beatlemaniac, May 15, 2017, thisbeatlemaniac.blogspot. com/2017/05/the-incredible-recording-process-of.html.

232 Miles, *Paul McCartney: Many Years From Now.*

233 *Beatles Music History*, beatlesebooks.com.

234 Ibid.

235 Sokol, Tony, "The Beatles: Blue Jay Way Is a Hidden Masterpiece," March 13, 2018, denofgeek.com/culture/the-beatles-blue-jay-way-is-a-hidden-masterpiece.

236 *Magic Trip: Ken Kesey's Search for a Kool Place.*

237 *Tripping*, produced and directed by Vikram Jayanti (1999; London: Channel 4 Television), Jeremy Fluff (YouTube channel), Sept. 27, 2016. youtube.com/watch?v=Uh2kK5IfS-8.

238 *Magic Trip: Ken Kesey's Search for a Kool Place.*

239 Kabil, Ahmed, "This magical drug mansion in Upstate New York is where the psychedelic '60s took off," *Timeline*, July 14, 2017, timeline.com/drug-mansion-psychedelic-60s-5116867d5041.

240 St John, Graham, "The Castalians vs the Pranksters," *Reality Sandwich*, Dec. 22, 2015, realitysandwich.com/the-castalians-vs-the-pranksters.

241 *Magic Trip: Ken Kesey's Search for a Kool Place.*

242 Ibid.

243 Ibid.

244 "Ken Kesey Quotes," *Brainy Quote.* brainyquote.com/quotes/ken_kesey_364913.

245 "The Story Behind George Harrison's Psychedelic Mini," *Vintage Everyday*, Dec. 20, 2018, vintag.es/2018/12/george-harrison-psychedelic-mini.html.

246 *The Beatles—Magical Mystery Tour Memories*, directed by David Lambert (2008; Arthouse Pictures), BeforeTheyMakeMeRun 2 (YouTube channel), youtube.com/watch?v=ymmcyH2Zscw.

247 Ibid.

248 *Beatles Music History*, beatlesebooks.com.

249 Miles, *Paul McCartney: Many Years From Now.*

250 *The Beatles Ultimate Experience*, beatlesinterviews.org.

251 *The Beatles Bible*, beatlesbible.com.

252 *The Beatles Ultimate Experience*, beatlesinterviews.org.

253 *The Beatles Bible*, beatlesbible.com.

254 Harrison, George, and Miles, "George Harrison Interview," Fifth Estate, July 1-15, 1967, fifthestate.org/archive/33-july-1-15-1967/george-harrison-interview.

255 *The Beatles Ultimate Experience*, beatlesinterviews.org.

256 Davies, Hunter. *The Beatles: The Authorised Biography* (London: Heinemann, 1968), 351.

257 MacDonald, Ian. *Revolution in the Head: The Beatles' Records and the Sixties* (London: Vintage, 2008).

258 Miles, *Paul McCartney: Many Years From Now.*

259 "Baby You're a Rich Man," *Rolling Stone*, April 10, 2020, rollingstone.com/music/music-lists/100-greatest-beatles-songs-154008/baby-youre-a-rich-man-166209.

260 Emerick, *Here, There and Everywhere.*

261 Beatles and Roylance, *The Beatles Anthology.*

262 "Our World," Programme Index: Radio Times Issue 2276, *BBC One*, Jun 24, 1967, genome.ch.bbc.co.uk/9c4d13f81aaf441aad799a26764f0079.

263 Beatles and Roylance, *The Beatles Anthology.*

264 Schaffner, Nicholas. *The British Invasion: From the First Wave to the New Wave* (New York: McGraw-Hill, 1982), 37.

265 White, Richard. *Come Together: Lennon and McCartney in the Seventies* (London: Omnibus Press, 2016).

266 *Rolling Stones Data*, rollingstonesdata.com.

267 Beatles and Roylance, *The Beatles Anthology.*

268 *The Beatles Ultimate Experience*, beatlesinterviews.org.

269 "Flashback: The Beatles Perform 'All You Need Is Love' Live Via Global Satellite," *Neuhoff Media Lafayette*, June 24, 2020, neuhoffmedialafayette.com/2020/06/24/flashback-the-beatles-perform-all-you-need-is-love-live-via-global-satellite.

270 "Flashback: The Beatles Perform 'All You Need Is Love.'"

271 Smith, Howard, "John Lennon on Love," *Blank on Blank*, blankonblank.org/interviews/john-lennon-love.

272 Miles, Barry. *The Beatles Diary Volume 1: The Beatles Years* (London: Omnibus Press, 2001), 274, 286.

273 Redazione, "George Harrison: the real story behind 'Blue Jay Way,'" *VideoMusik.eu*, July 31, 2018, videomuzic.eu/harrison-th-story-of-blue-jay-way/?lang=en.

274 Davies, Hunter. *The Beatles: The Authorised Biography* (London: Heinemann, 1968), 351.

275 Sokol, "The Beatles: Blue Jay Way Is a Hidden Masterpiece."

276 Boyd, Jenny. *Jennifer Juniper: A journey beyond the muse.*

277 Ibid.

278 Ibid.

279 *The Beatles Ultimate Experience*, beatlesinterviews.org.

280 Clayson, *George Harrison* (London: Sanctuary, 2003), 223.

281 Tillery, Gary. *Working Class Mystic: A Spiritual Biography of George Harrison* (Wheaton, IL: Quest Books, 2011), 54.

282 *The Beatles Ultimate Experience*, beatlesinterviews.org.

283 McCarty, Michael, "Hello Goodbye: Alistair Taylor Reflects on Life with The Beatles," *Monstermikeyaauthor* (blog), Jan. 12, 2017, monstermikeyaauthor.wordpress.com/2017/01/12/hello-goodbye-alistair-taylor-reflects-on-life-with-the-fab-four.

284 Ibid.

285 Miles, *Paul McCartney: Many Years From Now*.

286 Ibid.

287 Blakely, Richard. *The Secret of the Mantras* (Providence, RI: CreateSpace Independent Publishing Platform, 2013).

288 McCartney, Paul and Paul Muldoon, ed. *The Lyrics: 1956 to the Present* (New York: Liveright Publishing Corporation, 2021), 175-176.

289 Miles, *Paul McCartney: Many Years From Now*.

290 Lutes, Charles F. "Memoirs of Charlie Lutes," maharishiphotos.com/memintro.html, chapters 2, 4.

291 Mason, Paul. *The Maharishi: The Biography of the Man Who Gave Transcendental Meditation to the World* (Shaftsbury, Dorset: Element Books Ltd., 1994), 37.

292 Wainwright, Louden, "Invitation to Instant Bliss," *Life*, Nov. 10, 1967, 26.

293 Laughing Crow, "Cosmic Set-Up: How the Beatles First Met Maharishi," *The Beatles In India*, beatlesinindia.blogspot.com/2009/01/cosmic-set-up-how-beatles-first-met.html.

294 Ibid.

295 Mason, *The Beatles, Drugs, Mysticism & India*, 38.

296 Beatles and Roylance, *The Beatles Anthology*.

297 "How The Beatles learned Transcendental Meditation—and what they thought about it." *Transcendental Meditation News & More.* Dec. 10, 2014, tmhome.com/experiences/interview-lennon-and-harrison-on-meditation.

298 Ramanujam, R., "The Guru," *Newsweek*, Dec. 18, 1967, 67.

299 "Maharishi Mahesh Yogi," *The Times*, Feb. 7, 2008, thetimes.co.uk/article/maharishi-mahesh-yogi-xdwdbpbrxcd.

300 Mason, *The Beatles, Drugs, Mysticism & India*, 38.

301 Beatles and Roylance, *The Beatles Anthology*, 260.

302 Gaines and Brown, *The Love You Make*, 231.

303 Badman, *The Beatles Off the Record*.

304 Booth, Robert, "Indian retreat where Beatles learned to meditate opened to public," *The Guardian*, Dec. 9, 2015, theguardian.com/music/2015/dec/09/indian-retreat-where-the-beatles-learned-to-meditate-is-opened-to-the-public.

305 Beatles and Roylance, *The Beatles Anthology*.

306 D'Silva, *The Beatles and India*, directed by Bose and Compton.

307 Ibid.

308 Roberts, Iowerth and Tony Tucker, "The Beatles move in
for a quiet weekend," *Daily Post*, Aug. 26, 1967.

309 "The New Beatles' Mania," *The Prince George Citizen*, Sept. 29, 1967, *The Beatles in the News*, thebeatlesinthenews.blogspot.com/search?q=1967.

310 Mason, *The Beatles, Drugs, Mysticism & India*, 57.

311 *The Beatles Ultimate Experience*, beatlesinterviews.org.

312 Beatles and Roylance, *The Beatles Anthology*.

313 Blakely, *The Secret of the Mantras*.

314 *It Was Fifty Years Ago Today: The Beatles—Sgt. Pepper & Beyond*, directed by Alan G. Parker (2017; London: A Geezer & a Blond Productions).

315 Coleman, Ray. *Lennon* (New York: McGraw Hill, 1984), 339-340.

316 Kennedy, Kostya, ed., *LIFE: The Beatles: Then, Now, Forever*, 57, 67.

317 *The Beatles—Magical Mystery Tour Memories*, directed by David Lambert (2008; Arthouse Pictures)., BeforeTheyMakeMeRun 2 (YouTube channel), youtube.com/watch?v=ymmcyH2Zscw.

318 Wenner, Jann, "Rolling Stone Interview," *JohnLennon.com*.

319 Sheff, "John Lennon Interview: Playboy 1980."

320 Ibid.

321 Lennon, John. *Skywriting by Word of Mouth, and Other Writings, Including The Ballad of John and Yoko* (United Kingdom: Harper & Row, 1986).

322 Kennedy, Kostya, ed., *LIFE: The Beatles: Then, Now, Forever*, 57, 67.

323 "Paul McCartney Carpool Karaoke," Late Late Show with James Corden (YouTube channel), June 22, 2018, youtube.com/watch?v=QjvzCTqkBDQ.

324 *Beatles Music History*, beatlesebooks.com.

325 Harrison, George. *I, Me, Mine* (United States: Chronicle Books, 2002), 142.

326 Ibid.

327 *The Beatles Ultimate Experience*, beatlesinterviews.org.

328 Mason, *The Beatles, Drugs, Mysticism & India*, 79.

329 Shotton and Schaffner, *John Lennon: In My Life*, 139.

330 "On the Newsfronts of the World: The Beatles with their Guru," *Life*, Sept. 8, 1967, 26.

331 Wainwright, "Invitation to Instant Bliss."

332 Howard, Jane, "Year of the Guru," *Life*, Feb. 9, 1968, 52-56.

333 "Mystics: Soothsayer for Everyman," *Time*, Oct. 20, 1967, 86.

334 Lefferts, Barney, "Chief Guru of the Western World," *New York Times Magazine*, Dec. 17, 1967, 44-58.

335 Ramanujam, R., "The Guru," *Newsweek*, Dec. 18, 1967, 67.

336 Hedgepeth, William, "The Non-Drug Turn-On Hits Campus," *Look*, Feb. 6, 1968, 68-78.

337 Horn, Paul, "A Visit with India's High-Powered New Prophet," *Look*, Feb. 6, 1968, 66.

338 Beatles and Roylance, *The Beatles Anthology*.

339 Hurwitz, Matt, "Wonderwall Music," *George Harrison*, Feb. 18, 2020, georgeharrison.com/features/wonderwall-music.

340 Ibid.

341 Ibid.

342 Ibid.

343 Howlett, Kevin. "Wonderwall Music" (liner note essay), *Wonderwall Music* CD booklet (Apple Records, 2014; produced by George Harrison), 8.

344 Wright, Matthew. *Seasick Steve—Ramblin' Man* (United Kingdom: John Blake, 2016).

345 "Beatles: Song featuring George Harrison and Ringo Starr found," *BBC News*, Nov. 10, 2021, bbc.com/news/uk-england-merseyside-59233136.

346 Dasgupta, Priyanka, "Kolkata: 'Lost & found' track with 2 Beatle guest appearances strikes composition row," *The Times of India*, Nov. 15, 2021, timesofindia.indiatimes.com/city/kolkata/lost-found-track-with-2-beatle-guest-appearances-strikes-composition-row/articleshow/87705305.cms.

347 Clayson, *George Harrison*, 206, 235.

348 Howlett, "Wonderwall Music" (liner note essay), 8, 10.

349 Beatles and Roylance, *The Beatles Anthology*.

350 Menon, Bhaskar. Liner notes: *Wonderwall Music* CD (Apple Records, 2014; produced by George Harrison).

351 Ibid.

352 Mason, *The Beatles, Drugs, Mysticism & India*, 127-128.

353 D'Silva, *The Beatles and India*, directed by Bose and Compton.

354 Shukla, Vandana, "Saying bye to Vichitra Veena." *The Tribune*. Apr. 25, 1999, tribuneindia.com/1999/99apr25/sunday/head6.htm.

355 "Ramesh Prem," last.fm/music/Ramesh+Prem/+wiki.

356 Thomson, Graeme, "Macca's banjo, Mellotron and a Monkee: The story of George Harrison's Wonderwall Music," *The Guardian*, Mar. 23, 2017, theguardian.com/music/2017/mar/23/maccas-banjo-mellotron-and-a-monkee-the-story-of-george-harrisons-wonderwall-music?page=with:img-2.

357 Harrison, *I, Me, Mine*, 118-119.

358 Mascaró, Juan. *Lamps of Fire: From the Scriptures and Wisdom of the World* (London: Methuen & Co, Ltd., 1961), 66.

359 Harrison, *I, Me, Mine*, 118.

360 *The Beatles Ultimate Experience*, beatlesinterviews.org.

361 "The Beatles—Arriving in India," *Bienfaits de la méditation*, bienfaits-meditation.com/en/the_beatles_and_tm/the-beatles/the_beatles_anthology/07_arriving_in_india_p281.

362 Walsh, Christopher, "*The Beatles in India* Book review," *Billboard*. Dec. 16, 2000, 28.

363 Hindle, Maurice and Daniel Wiles. "I Say It Just to Reach You." *UNIT*. Interview Dec. 2, 1968, published 1969. keele.ac.uk/media/keeleuniversity/alumni/UNIT%20Lennon%201969%20(1).pdf.

364 "George Harrison in His Own Words." *The Spirit*.

365 Hurwitz, "Wonderwall Music," *George Harrison*.

366 Lewisohn, Mark. *The Complete Beatles Recording Sessions: The Official Story of the Abbey Road Years 1962–1970* (London: Bounty Books, 2005), 72.

367 Emerick, *Here, There and Everywhere*.

368 Nordin, Ingvar Loco, "Maharishi Mahesh Yogi 1967," *Sonoloco*, sonoloco.com/rev/singular/mahesh/mahesh.html.

369 Miles, *Paul McCartney: Many Years From Now*.

370 Ibid.

371 Turner, Steve. *A Hard Day's Write: The Stories Behind Every Beatles Song* (London: Carlton Books Ltd., 1999), 109.

372 Harry, Bill. *The Beatles Encyclopedia: Revised and Updated* (London: Virgin Publishing, 2000).

373 Müller, *Sacred Books of the East*.

374 "Ramakrishna Quotes," *Goodreads*. goodreads.com/author/quotes/1273986.Ramakrishna.

375 Cooke de Herrera, Nancy. *All You Need Is Love: An Eyewitness Account of When Spirituality Spread from East to West* (New York: Open Road, 2005).

376 Cross, Craig. *Beatles-Discography.com: Day-By-Day Song-By-Song Record-By-Record* (Bloomington, Indiana: iUniverse, Inc., 2005), 173.

377 Farrow, Mia. *What Falls Away* (New York: Bantam, 1997), 139.

378 Cooke de Herrera, *All You Need Is Love*.

379 Ibid.

380 Ibid.

381 Ibid.

382 "What a Trip: The Continuing Story of Nancy De Herrera," *WWD*, April 1, 2003, wwd.com/eye/people/what-a-trip-735425.

383 Saltzman, Paul, *Meeting the Beatles in India*, directed by Paul Saltzman (2020; Toronto: Sunrise Films Limited).

384 Farrow, *What Falls Away*, 127.

385 Cooke de Herrera, *All You Need Is Love*.

386 Ibid.

387 Saltzman, *Meeting the Beatles in India*.

388 Ibid.

389 Ibid.

390 *Beatles Music History*, beatlesebooks.com.

391 Cooke de Herrera, *All You Need Is Love*.

392 Mason, *The Beatles, Drugs, Mysticism & India*, 208.

393 Cooke de Herrera, *All You Need Is Love*.

394 Turner, *A Hard Day's Write*, 155.

395 Cooke de Herrera, *All You Need Is Love*.

396 Ibid.

397 Alexander, Phil, ed., "The Beatles White Album Anniversary Edition," *Mojo Magazine*, Sep. 1, 2008.

398 Saltzman, *Meeting the Beatles in India*.

399 Ibid.

400 Sheff, "John Lennon Interview: Playboy 1980."

401 *The Beatles Ultimate Experience*, beatlesinterviews.org.

402 *Beatles Music History*, beatlesebooks.com.

403 Saltzman, *Meeting the Beatles in India*.

404 *SongFacts*, songfacts.com.

405 Saltzman, *Meeting the Beatles in India*.

406 Miles, *Paul McCartney: Many Years From Now*.

407 "Childe of Nature—Hale Village in the footsteps of the McCartneys (and Harrisons)," *There Are Places I Remember* (blog), April 25, 2016, beatlesliverpoollocations.blogspot.com/2016/04/childe-of-nature-hale-village-in.html.

408 Miles, *Paul McCartney: Many Years From Now*.

409 Thomas, Jeff, "Natural Law Party advocates meditation as way to peace," *Colorado Springs Gazette—Telegraph*. Feb. 6, 1996, B.2.

410 "Maharishi on History Channel eng heb," (Stereo: one channel English, the other channel Hebrew) YouTube channel: לאינד רד רקילג. Nov. 5, 2011, youtube.com/watch?v=xcaErBuD9-E.

411 Miles, *Paul McCartney: Many Years From Now*.

412 "Quotes and Transcription of Selected Lectures By His Holiness Maharishi Mahesh Yogi," goldendome.org/Maharishi/quotes/MaharishiQuotes/index.htm.

413 *The Beatles Ultimate Experience*, beatlesinterviews.org.

414 Miles, *Paul McCartney: Many Years From Now*.

415 Ibid.

416 Ibid.

417 Heath, Chris, "The Untold Stories of Paul McCartney," *GQ*, Sept. 11, 2018, gq.com/story/the-untold-stories-of-paul-mccartney.

418 Heath, "The Untold Stories of Paul McCartney."

419 Beatles and Roylance, *The Beatles Anthology*.

420 Harry, *The Beatles Encyclopedia*, 1151.

421 Miles, *Paul McCartney: Many Years From Now*.

422 Mason, *The Beatles, Drugs, Mysticism & India*, 157.

423 Leitch, Donovan. *The Autobiography of Donovan: The Hurdy Gurdy Man* (New York, NY: St. Martin's Press, 2005) 210, 219.

424 Lapham, Lewis H., "There Once Was a Guru from Rishikesh, Part I," *The Saturday Evening Post*, May 4, 1968, 25.

425 "Louise Harrison, Her Kid Brother George." .

426 Norman, *Shout! The True Story of the Beatles*.

427 "Creating World Peace," *Transcendental Meditation at the Maharishi Golden Dome*, goldendome.org.uk/meditate/world-peace.

428 Moore, Toby, "Learn from the Maharishi Effect," *The Oklahoma Herald,* Mar. 7, 2022, oskaloosa.com/opinion/columns/learn-from-the-maharishi-effect/article_246a2fb8-9e61-11ec-923d-033f2bc22f9f.html.

429 Beatles and Roylance, *The Beatles Anthology*.

430 Wenner, Jann, "Rolling Stone Interview," *JohnLennon.com*.

431 Beatles and Roylance, *The Beatles Anthology*,

432 *The Beatles Ultimate Experience*, beatlesinterviews.org.

433 Ibid.

434 Miles, *Paul McCartney: Many Years From Now*.

435 "Toppermost of the Poppermost— UK Number Ones: part 2— The 1960s," *Cooked and Bombd*, June 12, 2019, page 58. cookdandbombd.co.uk/forums/index.php?PHPSESSID=c29odt91a1am5njcf7ger4aos5&topic=73674.1710.

436 *Beatle Links*, beatlelinks.net.

437 Turner, *A Hard Day's Write*, 160.

438 "Transcript of Paul McCartney and Donovan recorded during the sessions for Mary Hopkin's Postcard LP -Jan.'69, as heard on the 'No. 3 Abbey Road N.W. 8' bootleg CD," davidgray101.tripod.com/PaulandDonovan.html.

439 Ibid.

440 Ibid.

441 "Paul McCartney—Blackbird—Little Rock, AR 4/30/16," Chad Jones (YouTube channel), May 1, 2016. youtube.com/watch?v=AIx9NPVDSOI.

442 "Paul McCartney Breaks Down His Most Iconic Songs," *GQ*, Sept. 11, 2018, gq.com/video/watch/paul-mccartney-breaks-down-his-most-iconic-songs.

443 Lifton, Dave, "When the Beatles Refused to Play Before a Segregated Audience," *UCR*, June 8, 2020, ultimateclassicrock.com/beatles-jacksonville-1964.

444 Miles, *Paul McCartney: Many Years From Now.*

445 *The Beatles Ultimate Experience*, beatlesinterviews.org.

446 Ibid.

447 "Al Jardine talks about Transcendental Meditation (July 6, 2013)." *Al Jardine Official* (YouTube channel), Feb. 6, 2014, youtube.com/watch?v=BQK-GCRW4Xk.

448 Mason, *The Beatles, Drugs, Mysticism & India*, 91-92.

449 Love, Mike with James S. Hirsch. *Good Vibrations: My Life as A Beach Boy* (New York: Blue Rider Press, 2016), 179.

450 Taylor, Tom, "When Paul McCartney wrote a Beatles song about a Russian Spy," *Far Out*, Oct. 27, 2021, faroutmagazine.co.uk/when-paul-mccartney-wrote-a-beatles-song-about-a-russian-spy.

451 Love, *Good Vibrations,* 238.

452 Hedegaard, Erik, "The Ballad of Mike Love," *Rolling Stone,* Feb. 17, 2016, rollingstone.com/music/music-news/the-ballad-of-mike-love-170168.

453 Sheff, "John Lennon Interview: Playboy 1980."

454 Mason, *The Beatles, Drugs, Mysticism & India*, 132.

455 Ibid., 132.

456 Ibid., 193.

457 Love, *Good Vibrations,* 189-190.

458 Boyd, Pattie and Penny Junor. *Wonderful Tonight: George Harrison, Eric Clapton, and Me* (New York: Three Rivers Press, 2007), 117.

459 Saxena, Shivani, "A walk down melody lane," *The Times of India*, Oct. 24, 2014, timesofindia.indiatimes.com/city/dehradun/a-walk-down-melody-lane/articleshow/44951760.cms.

460 Bruns, *Dear Prudence: The Story Behind the Song.*

461 Chiu, David, "The Real 'Dear Prudence' on Meeting Beatles in India," *Rolling Stone*, Sept. 4, 2015, rollingstone.com/music/music-news/the-real-dear-prudence-on-meeting-beatles-in-india-74048.

462 Bruns, *Dear Prudence: The Story Behind the Song*, 172.

463 "Prudence Farrow Bruns, on her way to permanent happiness," *Transcendental Meditation News & More*, Nov. 23, 2013, tmhome.com/books-videos/prudence-farrow-bruns-teaches-meditation.

464 Bruns. *Dear Prudence: The Story Behind the Song.*

465 Chiu, "The Real 'Dear Prudence' on Meeting Beatles in India."

466 Bruns, *Dear Prudence: The Story Behind the Song*, 189.

467 Turner, *A Hard Day's Write*, 152.

468 Bruns, *Dear Prudence: The Story Behind the Song*, 205.

469 Chiu, "The Real 'Dear Prudence' on Meeting Beatles in India."

470 Bruns, *Dear Prudence: The Story Behind the Song*, 201-202.

471 Ibid., 203-205.

472 Ibid., 209-210.

473 Turner, *A Hard Day's Write*, 151.

474 Pillai, Ajith, and Pushpinder Singh, "Remains of Yesterday," *Frontline*, Sep. 20, 2013, frontline.thehindu.com/arts-and-culture/remains-of-yesterday/article5085673.ece.

475 Webb, Robert, "Double Take: Dear Prudence—The Beatles/ Souxsie and the Banshees," June 21, 2002, independent.co.uk/ arts-entertainment/music/features/double-take-dear-prudence-the-beatles-souxsie-and-the-the-banshees-180935.html.

476 Miles, *Paul McCartney: Many Years From Now*.

477 Sheff, "John Lennon Interview: Playboy 1980."

478 Kipp, Rachel, "2. Dear Prudence," *The Beatles White Album Project*, thewhitealbumproject.com/songs/side-one.

479 Sheff, "John Lennon Interview: Playboy 1980."

480 Chiu, "The Real 'Dear Prudence' on Meeting Beatles in India."

481 Bruns, *Dear Prudence: The Story Behind the Song*, 212.

482 Blakely, *The Secret of the Mantras*.

483 Ibid.

484 Boyd, *Jennifer Juniper: A journey beyond the muse*.

485 Blakely, *The Secret of the Mantras*.

486 Cooke de Herrera, *All You Need Is Love*.

487 *SongFacts*, songfacts.com.

488 Cooke de Herrera, *All You Need Is Love*.

489 Bruns, *Dear Prudence: The Story Behind the Song*, 214.

490 Dolan, Mike, "Midnight in the Oasis," *Trancenet*, Jul 17, 1997, minet.org/www.trancenet.net/personal/dolan/midnight.shtml.

491 Chiu, "The Real 'Dear Prudence' on Meeting Beatles in India."

492 Ibid.

493 Ibid.

494 Dragemark, Elsa. *The Way to Maharishi's Himalayas* (Forenede Oslo: Trykkerier AS, 1972), 178.

495 Love, *Good Vibrations*, 188.

496 Mason, *The Beatles, Drugs, Mysticism & India*, 222.

497 Beatles and Roylance, *The Beatles Anthology*, 283.

498 Sheff, "John Lennon Interview: Playboy 1980."

499 Badman. *The Beatles Off the Record*, 340.

500 O'Leary, Chris, "Karma Man," *Pushing Ahead of the Dame*, Oct. 19, 2009, bowiesongs.wordpress.com/2009/10/19/karma-man.

501 Badman, *The Beatles Off the Record*, 340.

502 Ibid., 281.

503 Beatles and Roylance, *The Beatles Anthology*.

504 Runtagh, Jordan, "The Beatles' Revelatory White
    Album Demos: A Complete Guide," *Rolling Stone*,
    May 29, 2018, rollingstone.com/music/music-lists/
    the-beatles-revelatory-white-album-demos-a-complete-guide-629178.

505 Coleman, *Lennon*, 339-340.

506 Henke, James. *Lennon Legend: An Illustrated Life of John
    Lennon* (San Francisco: Chronicle Books, 2003), 33.

507 Badman, *The Beatles Off the Record*.

508 Harris, *George Harrison: Tribute,* 97.

509 Greene, "Medley: George Harrison."

510 Runtagh, "Beatles' 'Sgt. Pepper' at 50."

511 *Beatles Music History*, beatlesebooks.com.

512 "RumiQuotesQuotable Quote," *GoodReads*, goodreads.com/
    quotes/109002-love-dogs-one-night-a-man-was-crying-allah-allah.

513 "When You Feel Like Quitting or Giving Up Your Search
    For God, Remember This Advice!" Supreme Yogi (YouTube
    channel), youtube.com/watch?v=azZ8eUpZB9w.

514 Harrison, *I, Me, Mine*, 132.

515 McGuinness, Paul, "'Long, Long, Long': The Story Behind The Song,"
    Udiscovermusic, Oct. 7, 2021, udiscovermusic.com/stories/long-long-long
    -story-behind-song-beatles.

516 Mason, *The Beatles, Drugs, Mysticism & India*, 288.

517 Boyd, *Jennifer Juniper: A journey beyond the muse*.

518 Blakely, *The Secret of the Mantras*.

519 "Meditation Won't Affect Beatles' Career," *Hindustan Times*,
    Feb. 20, 1969.

520 Lennon, Cynthia. *A Twist of Lennon* (New York: Avon Books, 1978),
    169-170.

521 Beatles and Roylance, *The Beatles Anthology*.

522 Ibid., 281.

523 "Will the real Richard Starkey please stand up?" *Melody
    Maker*, Mar. 16, 1968, 12. worldradiohistory.com/UK/
    Melody-Maker/60s/68/Melody-Maker-1968-0316.pdf.

524 Badman, *The Beatles Off the Record*, 340.

525 Coleman, Ray, "Ringo: This is How I Meditate,"
    Disc and Music Echo, Mar. 16, 1968, 1.

526 Boltwood, Derek, "Meditation Is My Cup of Tea." *Record
    Mirror*, Mar. 23, 1968, 7. worldradiohistory.com/UK/
    Record-Mirror/60s/68/Record-Mirror-1968-03-23.pdf

527 Hindle, "I Say It Just to Reach You."

528 Miles, *Paul McCartney: Many Years From Now*.

529 Harnett, Heather, "Paul McCartney Remembers His First Meditation With Maharishi (Part 2)," *TM Blog: Transcendental Meditation*, Apr. 29, 2010, tm.org/blog/maharishi/paul-mccartney-first-meditation-maharishi.

530 Bruns, *Dear Prudence: The Story Behind the Song*, 207.

531 D'Silva, *The Beatles and India*, directed by Bose and Compton.

532 Giuliano, Geoffrey and Avalon Giuliano. *Revolver: The Secret History of the Beatles* (London: John Blake, 2005), 118-119.

533 Beatles and Roylance, *The Beatles Anthology*, 281.

534 Kidd, James, "How The Beatles were affected by their famed trip to India," *The National*, April 25, 2018, thenationalnews.com/arts-culture/how-the-beatles-were-affected-by-their-famed-trip-to-india-1.724805.

535 Beatles and Roylance, *The Beatles Anthology*, 284.

536 Ibid.

537 Boyd, *Wonderful Tonight*, 118.

538 "Will the real Richard Starkey please stand up?" *Melody Maker*.

539 Ibid.

540 "George Harrison & Ringo on Aspel & Co." Steven Rutter (YouTube channel), Oct. 27, 2014, youtube.com/watch?v=JQaqcLPAI_s.

541 Cooke de Herrera, *All You Need Is Love*.

542 "Beatles Journey Off." *The Beatles—The Canberra Times* (newspaper), *The Beatles in the News* (website), April 8th 1968, thebeatlesinthenews.blogspot.com/search?q=1968.

543 Blakely, *The Secret of the Mantras*.

544 Cooke de Herrera, *All You Need Is Love*.

545 Ibid.

546 Ibid.

547 Cooke de Herrera, Nancy. *Beyond Gurus* (Grass Valley, CA: Blue Dolphin Publishing, 1992).

548 Cooke de Herrera, *All You Need Is Love*.

549 Mason, *The Beatles, Drugs, Mysticism & India*, 149.

550 Cooke de Herrera, *All You Need Is Love*.

551 Mason, *The Beatles, Drugs, Mysticism & India*, 181-182.

552 Ibid., 182.

553 Boyd, *Wonderful Tonight*, 119.

554 Farrow, *What Falls Away*, 128-129.

555 Ibid.

556 Wynn, Ned. *We Will Always Live in Beverly Hills: Growing Up Crazy in Hollywood* (New York: William Morrow & Co, 1990), 259.

557 Miles, *Paul McCartney: Many Years From Now*.

558 Gaines and Brown, *The Love You Make*, 188.

559 Chadwick, Jonathan, "Apple Electronics: Inside the Beatles' eccentric 1960s tech subsidiary that spawned color-changing paint, the robotic housewife and the 'memory phone,'" Jan. 13, 2021, dailymail.co.uk/sciencetech/article-9015279/Apple-Electronics-Inside-Beatles-eccentric-technology-subsidiary.html.

560 *The Beatles Bible*, beatlesbible.com.

561 Shotton and Schaffner, *John Lennon: In My Life*, 119.

562 "The Nothing Box," *The Daily Beatle*, May 7, 2021, webgrafikk.com/blog/john-lennon/the-nothing-box.

563 "The Many Faces of 'Magic' Alex Mardas," *Life of the Beatles* (blog), June 2, 2006, lifeofthebeatles.blogspot.com/2006/06/many-faces-of-magic-alex-mardas.html.

564 Shotton and Schaffner, *John Lennon: In My Life*, 159.

565 Beatles and Roylance, *The Beatles Anthology*, 291.

566 Spitz, Bob. *The Beatles: The Biography* (New York: Little, Brown and Company, 2005), 705.

567 "The Many Faces of 'Magic' Alex Mardas," *Life of the Beatles*.

568 Miles, *Paul McCartney: Many Years From Now*.

569 Ibid.

570 "The Many Faces of 'Magic' Alex Mardas," *Life of the Beatles*.

571 Bose, Ajoy. *Across the Universe: The Beatles in India* (New Delhi: Viking Penguin Random House India, 2018).

572 Yogi, Maharishi Mahesh. *Thirty Years Around the World: Volume One, 1957-1964* (Fairfield, IA: MVU Press, 1986), 328.

573 "Maharishi Mahesh Yogi in Athens," Dr. Demetrios Glykas Daily Motion Channel, dailymotion.com/video/x4a06k.

574 Shotton and Schaffner, *John Lennon: In My Life*.

575 Boyd, *Jennifer Juniper: A journey beyond the muse*.

576 "The Many Faces of 'Magic' Alex Mardas," *Life of the Beatles*.

577 Gaines and Brown, *The Love You Make*, 247.

578 Cross, *Beatles-Discography.com*, 176.

579 Klinger, Judd. *It's All Too Much: The Untold Story of a Hollywood Actor's Two Months with the Beatles in India* (Independently published, Dec. 10, 2021).

580 Dolan, "Midnight in the Oasis."

581 Blakely, *The Secret of the Mantras*.

582 Dolan, "Midnight in the Oasis."

583 Mason, *The Beatles, Drugs, Mysticism & India*, 237-238.

584 Klinger, *It's All Too Much*.

585 Ibid.

586 Dolan, "Midnight in the Oasis."

587 Ibid.

588 Mason, *The Beatles, Drugs, Mysticism & India*, 237-238.

589 Klinger, *It's All Too Much.*

590 Boyd, *Wonderful Tonight,* 119.

591 Fitzgerald, Riley, "Jenny Boyd Sheds Light On The Beatles' Relationship With The Maharishi In New Book," *Cosmic*, cosmicmagazine.com.au/news/jenny-boyd-sheds-light-on-the-beatles-relationship-with-the-maharishi-in-new-book.

592 Mardas, Alex, "Statement to *New York Times*," *New York Times* (with editors note appended), March 4, 2010, nytimes.com/2008/02/07/arts/music/07yogi.html. Link to: graphics8.nytimes.com/packages/pdf/arts/Mardas.pdf.

593 Mardas, "Statement to *New York Times*."

594 Wenner, Jann, "Rolling Stone Interview," *JohnLennon.com.*

595 Klinger, *It's All Too Much.*

596 Boyd, *Wonderful Tonight,* 119.

597 Cooke de Herrera, *Beyond Gurus.*

598 Norman, *Shout! The True Story of the Beatles*, 323.

599 Blakely, *The Secret of the Mantras.*

600 Cooke de Herrera, *All You Need Is Love.*

601 Badman, *The Beatles Off the Record,* 345.

602 Cooke de Herrera, *Beyond Gurus.*

603 Cooke de Herrera, *All You Need Is Love.*

604 Cooke de Herrera, *Beyond Gurus.*

605 Massot, Joe, "Identity Crisis," *Meet the Beatles for Real*, May 1, 2013, meetthebeatlesforreal.com/2013/05/identity-crisis.html.

606 Mason, *The Beatles, Drugs, Mysticism & India*, 235.

607 Gaines and Brown, *The Love You Make*, 259.

608 Kane, Larry. *Lennon Revealed* (Philadelphia: Running Press, 2007), 60-61.

609 "The Beatles in India," *Owl apps.*

610 *The Beatles Bible*, beatlesbible.com.

611 Cooke de Herrera, *All You Need Is Love.*

612 Dolan, "Midnight in the Oasis."

613 Giuliano, *Revolver: The Secret History,* 128.

614 Mason, *The Beatles, Drugs, Mysticism & India*, 235-236.

615 Beatles and Roylance, *The Beatles Anthology*, 286.

616 Cross, *Beatles-Discography.com,* 177.

617 Beatles and Roylance, *The Beatles Anthology*, 285.

618 Ibid., 286.

619 Wenner, Jann, "Rolling Stone Interview," *JohnLennon.com.*

620 Ibid.

621 Mardas, "Statement to *New York Times*."

622 Henderson, Stuart, "5. Sexy Sadie." *The Beatles White Album Project*, thewhitealbumproject.com/songs/side-three.

623 Beatles and Roylance, *The Beatles Anthology*, 286.

624 Ibid.

625 Lennon, Cynthia, *A Twist of Lennon,* 176.

626 "Jenny Boyd & The Beatles In India! Author John Gray Was an Assistant to the Maharishi!" *Adika Live!* (YouTube channel), Apr. 20, 2021, youtube.com/watch?v=KSXi23WrbJU.

627 Lennon, Cynthia, *A Twist of Lennon,* 176-177.

628 Klinger, *It's All Too Much.*

629 Cooke de Herrera. *Beyond Gurus.*

630 Cooke de Herrera, Nancy. *All You Need Is Love.*

631 Gaines and Brown, *The Love You Make.* 290.

632 Lennon, Cynthia, *A Twist of Lennon,* 177.

633 Miles, *Paul McCartney: Many Years From Now.*

634 Gaines and Brown, *The Love You Make,* 250.

635 Ibid, 289.

636 Farrow, *What Falls Away*, 128-129.

637 Klinger, *It's All Too Much.*

638 Massot, "Identity Crisis," *Meet the Beatles for Real.*

639 Lennon, Cynthia, *A Twist of Lennon,* 179.

640 Mason, *The Beatles, Drugs, Mysticism, and India,* 241.

641 Fleetwood, Mick. *Fleetwood: My Life and Adventures in Fleetwood Mac* (New York: William Morrow, 1990), 61-63.

642 Miles, *Paul McCartney: Many Years From Now.*

643 Ibid.

644 Ibid.

645 Badman, *The Beatles Off the Record*, 2008.

646 *The Beatles Ultimate Experience*, beatlesinterviews.org.

647 "Lennon & McCartney Interview, *The Tonight Show*," interview with Joe Garagiola, May 14,1968, beatlesinterviews.org/db1968.05ts.beatles.html.

648 Norman. *Shout! The True Story of the Beatles*, 324.

649 Wenner, Jann, "Rolling Stone Interview," *JohnLennon.com.*

650 ITN Factual, Maharishi Mahesh Yogi—Transcendental Meditation Biography, directed by Fiona Procter. (2007; New York: International History Channel), vimeo.com/120745864.

651 Mardas, "Statement to *New York Times*."

652 Miles, *Paul McCartney: Many Years From Now.*

653 Miles, Jeremy, "Hey Bungalow Bill you've not had your fill…" *Dancing Ledge* (blog), Nov. 11, 2014, dancingledge.blog/2014/11/11/hey-bungalow-bill-youve-not-had-your-fill-just-yet/#more-1504.

654 Wenner, Jann, "Rolling Stone Interview," *JohnLennon.com*.

655 Collin-Smith, Joyce. *Call No Man Master: Fifty years of spiritual adventures, in praise of teachers, wary of gurus* (Bath, UK: Gateway Books, 1988), 172.

656 Ibid.

657 Ibid.

658 Faithfull, Marianne. *Faithfull: An Autobiography* (Lanham, MD: Cooper Square Press, 2000), 134-135.

659 Mason, *The Beatles, Drugs, Mysticism & India*, 255.

660 Collin-Smith. *Call No Man Master,* 172.

661 Blakely, *The Secret of the Mantras*.

662 Ibid.

663 Ibid.

664 Ibid.

665 Ibid.

666 Mertens, David, "Sexy romps of the Beatle's giggling guru," *Cult Education Institute*, News of the World, UK, Aug. 23, 1981, culteducation.com/group/1195-transcendental-meditation-movement/20543-sexy-romps-of-the-beatles-giggling-guru.html.

667 Ibid.

668 Ibid.

669 Knapp, John M, "Sex & the Single Guru," *TM-Free Blog*, Jan. 28, 2007, tmfree.blogspot.com/2007_01_28_archive.html.

670 Ibid.

671 Mason, *The Beatles, Drugs, Mysticism & India*, 269.

672 Priddy, Robert, and Reidun Priddy, "Review of Conny Larsson's book: 'The Beatles, Maharishi and I,'" *Conny Larsson on leaving sectarian gurus*, Aug. 21, 2010, maharishisaibaba.wordpress.com.

673 Bennett, Bija, "5 Lessons on Spirituality, Activism, and Humility I Learned from George Harrison," *Rolling Stone*, Dec. 21, 2021, rollingstone.com/culture-council/articles/lessons-spirituality-humility-george-harrison-1274257.

674 "'Beatles are angels on earth,' said Maharishi," *The Times of India*, Feb. 15, 2006, timesofindia.indiatimes.com/india/beatles-are-angels-on-earth-said-maharishi/articleshow/1415351.cms.

675 "When Maharishi threw Beatles Out," *Times of India*, Feb. 15, 2006, timesofindia.indiatimes.com/india/when-maharishi-threw-beatles-out/articleshow/1415230.cms.

676 Dawson, Jeff, "Mia Farrow, A Life Less Ordinary," *Jeff Dawson Blog*, Oct. 4, 2013, jeffdawsonblog.blogspot.com/2013/10/mia-farrow.html.

677 Beatles and Roylance, *The Beatles Anthology*, 285.

678 Ibid., 286.

679 Miles, *Paul McCartney: Many Years From Now*.

680 Beatles and Roylance, *The Beatles Anthology*, 286.

681 Dolan, "Midnight in the Oasis."

682 Beatles and Roylance, *The Beatles Anthology*, 260.

683 Sheff, "John Lennon Interview: Playboy 1980."

684 Mason, *The Beatles, Drugs, Mysticism & India*, 258.

685 De Luca, Jerry, "George Harrison's Letter to His Mother," *Preacher's Illustrative Nuggets*, Nov. 30, 2012, hound-dog-media. com/2012/11/george-harrisons-letter-to-his-mother.html.

686 Lewisohn, *The Complete Beatles Chronicle*, 72, 144, 145, 148, 150.

687 *SongFacts*, songfacts.com.

688 Willman, Chris, "Remembering the one Beatles song about the Maharishi," *Entertainment*, Feb. 6, 2008, ew.com/article/2008/02/06/remembering-the.

689 Sheff, "John Lennon Interview: Playboy 1980."

690 Lennon, Cynthia. *John* (New York: Three Rivers Press, 2005), 226.

691 Ibid.

692 Sheff, "John Lennon Interview: Playboy 1980."

693 Beatles and Roylance, *The Beatles Anthology*.

694 Farrow, *What Falls Away*, 125.

695 "Maharishi on History Channel eng heb."

696 Miles, *Paul McCartney: Many Years From Now*.

697 Farrow, *What Falls Away*, 126.

698 Blakely, *The Secret of the Mantras*.

699 Turner, *A Hard Day's Write*, 149.

700 Beatles and Roylance, *The Beatles Anthology*, 283.

701 Shotton and Schaffner, *John Lennon: In My Life*, 162.

702 Short, Don, *Daily Mirror*, February 19, 1968. britishnewspaperarchive.co.uk.

703 Badman, *The Beatles Off the Record*, 342.

704 Goldman, Albert. *The Lives of John Lennon* (Chicago: A Capella, 2001), 295.

705 Miles, *Paul McCartney: Many Years From Now*.

706 Norman. *Shout! The True Story of the Beatles*, 323.

707 Miles, *Paul McCartney: Many Years From Now*.

708 Lutes, "Memoirs of Charlie Lutes."

709 "Henry Lewy: The Unknown Producer Behind Joni Mitchell, Judee Sill, and Batteaux," *In Sheep's Clothing Hi-Fi.*, March 10, 2021, insheepsclothinghifi.com/henry-lewy.

710 Lennon. *Skywriting by Word of Mouth,* 101.

711 Wenner, Jann, "Rolling Stone Interview," *JohnLennon.com.*

712 Saltzman, Paul. *The Beatles in Rishikesh* (New York: Viking Studio, 2000).

713 Badman, *The Beatles Off the Record,* 340.

714 Green, Jonathon. *Days in the Life: Voices from the English Underground, 1961-1971* (London: William Heinemann Ltd., 1990), 160-161.

715 "Toppermost of the Poppermost— UK Number Ones: part 2.

716 Mason, *The Beatles, Drugs, Mysticism & India,* 198.

717 Miles, *Paul McCartney: Many Years From Now.*

718 Booth, "Indian retreat where Beatles learned to meditate."

719 Boyd, *Wonderful Tonight,* 119.

720 Miles, *Paul McCartney: Many Years From Now.*

721 Wenner, Jann, "Rolling Stone Interview," *JohnLennon.com.*

722 Harry, Bill. *The John Lennon Encyclopedia.* (London: Virgin Publishing, 2000, 683.

723 Rense, Rip, "The Great Lost Lennon Solo Song," *Beatlefan*, Mar. to April. 2018, 29.

724 "Paul McCartney and Ringo Starr Live Webcast Today (April 3)," *Uncut*, Apr. 3, 2009, Uncut.co.uk/news/paul-mccartney-and-ringo-starr-live-webcast-today-april-3-56504.

725 Kaegi, Felix, "Paul McCartney and Ringo Starr Speak Live via Webcast for Meditation Youth Initiative April 3, 12 Noon (EDT)," Apr. 2, 2009, *Good News*, blog.silentadministration.org/2009/04/paul-ringo-at-david-lynch-press.html.

726 *The Paul McCartney Project*, the-paulmccartney-project.com.

727 Kaegi, "Paul McCartney and Ringo Starr Speak Live."

728 "Former Beatles pay tribute to Maharishi," *ABC: Australian Broadcasting Corporation*, Feb. 7, 2008, abc.net.au/news/2008-02-08/former-beatles-pay-tribute-to-maharishi/1036594.

729 D'Silva, *The Beatles and India*, directed by Bose and Compton.

730 Runtagh, "The Beatles' Revelatory White Album Demos."

731 Ibid.

732 Harris, *George Harrison: Tribute,* 37.

733 Morse, Steve, "McCartney Breaks His Silence with a Rock 'n' Roll Album," *Boston Globe*, Oct. 3, 1999, billsartbox.com/id185.html.

734 Miles, *Paul McCartney: Many Years From Now.*

735 Wainwright, "Invitation to Instant Bliss."

736 *The Beatles Ultimate Experience*, beatlesinterviews.org.

737 Miles, *Paul McCartney: Many Years From Now*.

738 Sheff, "John Lennon Interview: Playboy 1980."

739 "George Harrison singing the song Dehradun," CrackBoy (YouTube channel), Oct. 20, 2016, youtube.com/watch?v=D4bAcEIUX0Q.

740 Beatles and Roylance, *The Beatles Anthology*.

741 "While My Guitar Gently Weeps," *Fandom Popular Music Wiki*, popular-music.fandom.com/wiki/While_My_Guitar_ Gently_Weeps. White, Timothy, "A New 'Yellow Submarine Songtrack' Due in September," *Billboard*, June 19, 1999, 77.

742 Beatles and Roylance, *The Beatles Anthology*, 306.

743 Badman, *The Beatles Off the Record*, 2000.

744 "George and Pattie Harrison's home is raided by the Drugs Squad," *Beatles Bible*, beatlesbible.com/1969/03/12.

745 "Happy Birthday George—50 years ago today," *George Harrison*, Feb. 25, 2019, georgeharrison.com/happy-birthday-george-50-years-ago-today.

746 Turner, *A Hard Day's Write*.

747 Spizer, Bruce. *The Beatles on Apple Records* (New Orleans, LA: 498 Productions, LLC, 2003).

748 "Commentary on the Bhagavad Gita by Maharishi Mahesh Yogi." *Transcendental Meditation News & More.* Jan. 20, 2015. tmhome. com/books-videos/commentary-bhagavad-gita-maharishi-yogi.

749 Sikes, James R., "Swami's Flock Chants in Park to Find Ecstasy," *The Prabhupada Connection, The New York Times*, Oct. 10, 1966, 24. nytimes.com/1966/10/10/archives/swamis-flock-chants-in-park-to-find-ecstasy-50-followers-clap-and.html.

750 Goswami, Srila Satsvarupa dasa, "The Mantra-Rock Dance," *Back to Godhead*, August 1981, back2godhead.com/biography-pure-devotee-11.

751 Chryssides, George D. and Margaret Z. Wilkins. *A Reader in New Religious Movements* (London: Continuum International Publishing Group, 2006).

752 "George Harrison Interview: Hare Krishna Mantra–There's Nothing Higher (1982)," *Krishna.org*, April 14, 2021, krishna.org/george-harrison-interview-hare-krishna-mantra-theres-nothing-higher-1982.

753 *The Beatles Ultimate Experience*, beatlesinterviews.org.

754 "George Harrison Interview: Hare Krishna Mantra."

755 Dwyer, Graham and Richard J. Cole, eds. *The Hare Krishna Movement: Forty Years of Chant and Change* (London: I.B. Tauris, 2007), 30-31.

756 Cerrone, Dominick Paul, "The Krishnas: An Unexpected Journey," *IN Wheeling Magazine*, Jan. 7, 2010, 20.

757 Siegel, Roger [a.k.a. Gurudas]. *By His Example: The wit and wisdom of A.C. Bhaktivedanta Swami Prabhupada* (Badger, CA: Torchlight Pub., 2004).

758 Ibid.

759 Das, Anantacharya and Mina Sharma. *A Legacy Begins* (London: Iskcon United Kingdom, no date).

760 Siegel, *By His Example: The wit and wisdom.*

761 Ibid.

762 Cerrone, "The Krishnas: An Unexpected Journey."

763 "George Harrison Interview: Hare Krishna Mantra."

764 Jackson, Peter, *Get Back*, Part 1: 13:20 and 50:58.

765 Giuliano, Geoffrey. *Dark Horse: The Life and Art of George Harrison, rev. ed.* (New York: Da Capo Press, 1997).

766 Das, Shyamasundar. "The Krishna Book Miracle," Sept.-Oct. 2017, *Back to Godhead*, btg.krishna.com/krishna-book-miracle.

767 Harrison, George, "Words From George Harrison," *Krsna, The Supreme Personality of Godhead*, krsnabook.com/george and harekrsna.de/artikel/looking-for-krishna_e.htm.

768 Tillery, *Working Class Mystic: A Spiritual Biography*, 71.

769 Goswami, Satsvarupa dasa. *Prabhupada: He Built a House in Which the Whole World Can Live* (Los Angeles, CA: Bhaktivedanta Book Trust, 1983), 155-156.

770 "George Harrison Interview: Hare Krishna Mantra."

771 "Bhagavad-gita As It Is," *Vaniquotes*, May 16, 2018, vaniquotes.org/wiki/Every_town_and_village.

772 Greene, Joshua M. *Here Comes the Sun,* 143-144.

773 Goswami, *Prabhupada: He Built a House,* 155-156.

774 Taylor, Derek. Liner notes: *The Radha Krsna Temple* CD (Apple/Capitol, 1993; produced by George Harrison).

775 Leng, Simon. *While My Guitar Gently Weeps: The Music of George Harrison* (Milwaukee, WI: Hal Leonard, 2006), 58.

776 Das, *A Legacy Begins.*

777 "George Harrison Interview: Hare Krishna Mantra."

778 Siegel, *By His Example: The wit and wisdom.*

779 O'Dell, Chris with Katherine Ketcham. *Miss O'Dell: My Hard Days and Long Nights with The Beatles, The Stones, Bob Dylan, Eric Clapton, and the Women They Loved* (New York: Touchstone, 2009), 79-81.

780 Allison Jr., Dale C. *The Love There That's Sleeping: The Art and Spirituality of George Harrison* (New York: Continuum, 2006), 153.

781 "George Harrison Interview: Hare Krishna Mantra."

782 Dwyer, *The Hare Krishna Movement*, 31-32.

783 Siegel, *By His Example: The wit and wisdom.*

784 Wenner, Jann, "Rolling Stone Interview," *JohnLennon.com.*

785 Siegel, *By His Example: The wit and wisdom.*

786 Harrison, *I, Me, Mine,* 158.

787 Harry, *The Beatles Encyclopedia*, 233-234.

788 Jackson, Peter, *Get Back*, Part 1: 1:24:40

789 Ibid., Part 2: 2:16:30.

790 Greene, Joshua M. *Here Comes the Sun*, 171, 211.

791 Siegel, *By His Example: The wit and wisdom.*

792 Greene, Joshua M. *Here Comes the Sun*, 170.

793 Castleman, Harry and Walter J. Podrazik, *All Together Now: The First Complete Beatles Discography 1961–1975* (New York: Ballantine Books, 1976), 202.

794 Ibid., 171.

795 Doggett, Peter. *You Never Give Me Your Money: The Beatles After the Breakup* (New York: It Books, 2011), 117.

796 Wenner, Jann, "Rolling Stone Interview," *JohnLennon.com.*

797 Badman, Keith. *The Beatles Off the Record 2: The Dream is Over* (London: Omnibus Press, 2002).

798 "A Spiritual Tribute to George Harrison."

799 *SongFacts*, songfacts.com.

800 *The Beatles Ultimate Experience*, beatlesinterviews.org.

801 Ibid.

802 Badman, Keith. *The Beatles Off the Record 2: The Dream is Over.*

803 "A Spiritual Tribute to George Harrison."

804 *The Beatles Ultimate Experience*, beatlesinterviews.org.

805 "A Spiritual Tribute to George Harrison."

806 "Deepak Chopra on his Friend George Harrison," *Beliefnet*, beliefnet.com/entertainment/music/2001/12/deepak-chopra-on-his-friend-george-harrison.aspx.

807 "George Harrison in His Own Words." *The Spirit.*

808 Hutchinson, Lydia, "George Harrison's 'My Sweet Lord' Copyright Case," *Performing Songwriter: Be Heard*, Feb. 10, 2015, performingsongwriter.com/george-harrison-my-sweet-lord.

809 "George Harrison Interview: Hare Krishna Mantra."

810 Ibid.

811 "A Spiritual Tribute to George Harrison."

812 Ibid.

813 *The Beatles Ultimate Experience*, beatlesinterviews.org.

814 Winn, John C. *That Magic Feeling: The Beatles' Recorded Legacy, Volume Two, 1966–1970* (New York: Three Rivers Press, 2009), 324.

815 Harris, *George Harrison: Tribute*, 54.

816 Harrison, Olivia. *George Harrison: Living in the Material World* (New York: Abrams, 2011), 282.

817 "George Harrison Documentary and Book Announced," *George Harrison*, July 14, 2011, georgeharrison.com/george-harrison-documentary-and-book-announced.

818 Harrison, *I, Me, Mine*, 170.

819 *The Beatles Bible*, beatlesbible.com.

820 "George Harrison Interview: Hare Krishna Mantra."

821 "Ibid.

822 "A Spiritual Tribute to George Harrison."

823 "George Harrison Interview: Hare Krishna Mantra."

824 Greene, "Medley: George Harrison."

825 *Times of India*, "George Left Krishnas Out Of Will," *VNN: Vaishnava News Network*, Feb. 7, 2003, vaishnava-news-network.org/europe/EU0302/EU07-7792.html.

826 Polcaro, Rafael, "What George Harrison thought happened to people after death," *Creem Magazine*, 1987, *Rock and Roll Garage*, Dec. 12, 2020, rockandrollgarage.com/what-george-harrison-thought-happened-to-people-after-death.

827 Short, *Daily Mirror*, February 19, 1968.

828 "George Harrison Interview: Hare Krishna Mantra."

829 Tillery, *Working Class Mystic: A Spiritual Biography*.

830 Love, *Harrison: By the Editors of Rolling Stone*, 40.

831 Greene, Joshua M. *Here Comes the Sun, 184*.

832 Nethercutt, Martin, "Pattie Boyd Admits George Harrison Was The Love Of Her Life – 106.3 The Fox," *McCartney Times: All You Need Is News*, Jan. 22, 2018, mccartney.com/?p=10636.

833 Lewis, Randy, "Olivia Harrison reflects on the music and a book marking what would have been 'quiet Beatles' 74th birthday," *Los Angeles Times*, Feb. 24, 2017, latimes.com/entertainment/music/la-et-ms-george-harrison-autobiography-box-set-20170223-story.html.

834 Harrison, "Words From George Harrison."

835 Castleman, *All Together Now*, 101.

836 Greene, Joshua M. *Here Comes the Sun, ix*.

837 Love, *Harrison: By the Editors of Rolling Stone*, 180.

838 Gambaccini, Paul, "The *Rolling Stone* Interview: Paul McCartney," *Rolling Stone*, Jan. 31, 1974.

839 Harrison, *I, Me, Mine*, 212.

840 "A Short Documentary," *Alla Rakha Foundation*, allarakhafoundation.org/a-short-documentary.

841 "Maestro Ali Akbar Khan," *Ali Akbar College of Music*, aacm.org/ali-akbar-khan.

842 Surti, Aalif, "Annapurna Devi and her music of silence," *Mumbai Mirror,* Oct. 14, 2018, https://mumbaimirror.indiatimes.com/others/sunday-read/the-music-of-silence/articleshow/66199979.cms.

843 Ibid.

844 "The Untold Story of Annapurna Devi (1927-2018)," *Chinar Shade*, March 1, 2020, autarmota.blogspot.com/2020/03/annapurna-devi-with-pandit-ravi-shanker.html.

845 Greene, Joshua M. *Here Comes the Sun,* 85, 149-150.

846 "George Harrison Interview: Hare Krishna Mantra."

847 Razib, Ahmed, "George Harrison—Far East Man." *beatlesnumber9*, beatlesnumber9.com/east.html.

848 Greene, Joshua M. *Here Comes the Sun,* 198-199.

849 Clayson, *George Harrison*, 268.

850 Tillery, *Working Class Mystic: A Spiritual Biography*, 118.

851 O'Dell, Chris with Katherine Ketcham. *Miss O'Dell: My Hard Days and Long Nights with The Beatles, The Stones, Bob Dylan, Eric Clapton, and the Women They Loved* (New York: Touchstone, 2009), 188.

852 "George Harrison—In His Own Words," *Super Seventies Rocksite!* superseventies.com/ssgeorgeharrison.html.

853 *The Beatles Ultimate Experience*, beatlesinterviews.org.

854 "George Harrison in His Own Words." *The Spirit.*

855 "George Harrison Interview: Hare Krishna Mantra."

856 Ibid.

857 Harrison, George, *I, Me, Mine.*

858 "George Harrison Interview: Hare Krishna Mantra."

859 Willman, Chris, *Guitar World 1987, George Harrison Stories*, harrisonstories.tumblr.com/post/69816680964/chris-in-the-70s-i-remember-going-to-airports.

860 Greene, "Medley: George Harrison."

861 "George Harrison Marwa Blues." *Tumbler*, george-harrison-marwa-blues.tumblr.com/post/120569771936/george-with-sri-daya-mata-in-1998-george-was.

862 "Zakir," *Zakir Hussain.* zakirhussain.com/zakir.

863 *The Beatles Bible*, beatlesbible.com.

864 "George HarrisonQuotesQuotable Quote," *Goodreads*, goodreads.com/quotes/23695.

865 Harris, *George Harrison: Tribute,* 89.

866 Harrison, George, "Meeting Srila Prabhupada," *The Prabhupada Connection*, prabhupadaconnect.com/CauselessMercy107.html.

867 "Selections from the *Upanishads*," www2.hawaii.edu/~freeman/courses/phil101/03.%20The%20Upanishads.pdf.

868 Love, *Harrison: By the Editors of Rolling Stone*, 132.

869 "John Lennon's last interview, December 8, 1980," *Beatles Archive*.

870 Tillery, Gary, *The Cynical Idealist: A Spiritual Biography of John Lennon* (Wheaten, IL: Quest Books, 2009), 100.

871 Fawcett, Anthony. *One Day at a Time* (New York: Grove, 1981), 54.

872 Du Noyer, Paul. *John Lennon: The Stories Behind Every Song 1970–1980* (London: Carlton Books Ltd., 2010), 21.

873 Rodriguez, Robert. *Solo in the 70s: John, Paul, George, Ringo: 1970–1980* (Downers Grove, IL: Parading Press, 2013), 8, 21.

874 Blake, John. *All You Needed Was Love: The Beatles After the Beatles* (Middlesex: Hamlyn Paperbacks, 1981), 97.

875 "John Lennon En Mallorca," *Piso Tívoli—Bilbao*, Feb. 9, 2014, pisotivoli.blogspot.com/2014/02/john-lennon-en-mallorca.html.

876 Cullman, Brian, Vic Garbarini, with Barbara Graustark. *Strawberry Fields Forever: John Lennon Remembered* (United Kingdom: Bantam, 1980), 110-111.

877 Norman, Philip. *John Lennon: The Life* (New York: HarperCollins, 2009), 635.

878 Grice, Elizabeth. "John Lennon's Estate | Imagine Disinheritance John Lennon was a hyprocrite, says son." March 7, 2019. *Independent.ie*. May 19, 1998. independent.ie/world-news/ john-lennon-was-a-hypocrite-says-son-26187349.html.

879 Hackard, Mike. *Hackard Law*, hackardlaw.com/ john-lennons-estate-imagine-disinheritance.

880 Giuliano, Geoffrey and Brenda Giuliano. *The Lost Lennon Interviews* (Holbrook, MA: Adams Corporation, 1996), 56.

881 Sheff, "John Lennon Interview: Playboy 1980."

882 Whatley, Jack, "John Lennon becomes the first solo Beatle to appear on Top of the Pops with 'Instant Karma! in 1970," *Far Out*, Feb. 12, 2020, faroutmagazine.co.uk/ john-lennon-instant-karma-top-of-the-pops-1970-video.

883 *The Beatles Bible*, beatlesbible.com.

884 Wenner, Jann, "Rolling Stone Interview," *JohnLennon.com*.

885 Cott, "John Lennon: The Last Interview."

886 Levy, Joe, ed. *Rolling Stone's 500 Greatest Albums of All Time, first paperback ed.* (New York: Wenner Books, 2005), 87.

887 Brackett, Nathan, Ed. *The 500 Greatest Songs of All Time* (New York: Rolling Stone, 2010), 13.

888 Ibid.

889 Blaney, John. *John Lennon: Listen to This Book* (London: Paper Jukebox, 2005), 126.

890 Masters, Robert and Jean Houston. *Mind Games: The Guide to Inner Space, 1st Quest ed.* (Wheaton, Ill.: Theosophical Pub. House, 1998), xii.

891 Sheff, "John Lennon Interview: Playboy 1980."

892 Giuliano, *The Lost Lennon Interviews,* 52.

893 Cott, "John Lennon: The Last Interview."

894 Cullman, *Strawberry Fields Forever*, 176.

895 Ibid., 175.

896 Rodriguez, Robert. *Fab Four FAQ 2.0: The Beatles' Solo Years, 1970–1980* (Milwaukee, WI: Backbeat Books, 2010), 237-238.

897 Harrison, Olivia. *Collaborations*, book accompanying *Collaborations* box set (Dark Horse Records, 2010; produced by Olivia Harrison), 19.

898 Cashmere, Paul, "George Harrison Estate Unveils New Label HariSongs," *Noise 11*, May 3, 2018, noise11.com/news/george-harrison-estate-unveils-new-label-harisongs-20180503.

899 Harrison, Olivia. *Collaborations*, 32.

900 "George Harrison: Transcending The Beatles," University of Liverpool (YouTube channel), youtube.com/watch?v=FTgDD7kPl6Q.

901 "Journey of the Master," *Pandit Hariprasad Chaurasia*, hariprasadchaurasia.com.

902 Varanasi, Anuradha. "George wanted to be reborn in India." *The Week Magazine.* Feb. 25, 2018. theweek.in/theweek/cover/2018/02/17/the-beatles-pandit-hariprasad-chaurasia.html.

903 Pareles, Jon, "Sultan Khan, Indian Classical Musician, Dies at 71," Dec. 5, 2011, *The New York Times*, nytimes.com/2011/12/06/arts/music/sultan-khan-indian-classical-musician-and-sarangi-player-dies-at-71.html.

904 Kalla, Avinash, "Dr. L. Subramaniam—Talking of Now," *the-south-asian.com*, Aug. 2004, the-south-asian.com/aug2004/Subramaniam.htm.

905 "As a guru, he was the king of kindness," *Hindustan Times*, Nov. 22, 2021, hindustantimes.com/india/as-a-guru-he-was-the-king-of-kindness-story-iYt4EDH1S27GqWTO4vkYIP.html.

906 Ghosh, Devarsi. "'All music comes from seven notes': Sitarist Kartick Kumar on his career in film and classical music," *Scroll.in*, Feb. 13, 2022, scroll.in/reel/1017249/all-music-comes-from-seven-notes-sitarist-kartick-kumar-on-his-career-in-film-and-classical-music.

907 Harrison, Olivia, *George Harrison: Living in the Material World,* 302.

908 Harrison, Olivia, *Music Festival from India—Live at the Royal Albert Hall*, directed by Stuart Cooper (2010; London: Dark Horse Records).

909 Harrison, Olivia. *Collaborations*, 25.

910 Harrison, Olivia, *George Harrison: Living in the Material World, 289-299.*

911 Crumlish, Callum, "The Beatles: George 'would NOT' rejoin a band with Paul McCartney," *Express,* Nov. 27, 2020, express.

co.uk/entertainment/music/1365432/the-beatles-george-harrison-death-dead-paul-mccartney-band-reunion-news-interview.

912 Shankar, *Raga Mala: The Autobiography of Ravi Shankar*, 228.

913 Phifer, Evan, "An Ex-Beatle at the White House," *The White House Historical Association*. May 11, 2017. whitehousehistory.org/an-ex-beatle-at-the-white-house.

914 Harrigan, Brian, "Harrison: Eastern Promise," *Melody Maker*, Dec. 21, 1974, 36.

915 Harrison, *I, Me, Mine*, 296-297.

916 Ibid, 297.

917 Ibid., 296.

918 Badman, Keith. *The Beatles Diary Volume 2: After the Break-Up 1970–2001* (London: Omnibus Press, 2001), 144.

919 "Watch George Harrison and Neil Innes perform 'The Pirate Song' on 'Rutland Weekend Television,'" *Far Out*, Dec. 31, 2019, faroutmagazine.co.uk/George-harrison-neil-innes-rutland-weekend-television-pirate-song.

920 Badman, Keith. *The Beatles Diary Volume 2,* 144.

921 Shankar, Ravi. Liner notes: *Chants of India* CD (Angel Records, 1997; produced by George Harrison).

922 "HariSongs—Short Documentary on 'Chants of India.'" George Harrison (YouTube channel), Apr. 27, 2018, youtube.com/watch?v=HR6EKOmXA9M.

923 Shankar, Liner notes: *Chants of India* CD.

924 Greene, Joshua M. *Here Comes the Sun,* 251-253.

925 "USA/ United Kingdom/ India: Ex-Beatle George Harrison and Indian Musician Ravi Shankar Speak About Their New Album," *Reuters*, May 16, 1997. reuters.screenocean.com/record/387035.

926 Huntley, Elliot J. *Mystical One: George Harrison—After the Break-up of the Beatles* (Toronto, ON: Guernica Editions, 2006), 273.

927 D'Silva, *The Beatles and India*, directed by Bose and Compton.

928 Ravi Shankar, *Raga Mala: The Autobiography of Ravi Shankar*, 308.

929 Sitarama Sastri, S. *Katha Upanishad with Shankara's Commentary.* 1928. *Wisdom Library.* wisdomlib.org/hinduism/book/katha-upanishad-shankara-bhashya/d/doc145218.html.

930 Vivekananda, Swami. *The Complete Works of Swami Vivekananda, Volume 1: Raja-Yoga/Patanjali's Yoga Aphorisms—Concentration: Its Practice.* (Wikisource), en.wikisource.org/wiki/The_Complete_Works_of_Swami_Vivekananda/Volume_1/Raja-Yoga/Patanjali%27s_Yoga_Aphorisms_-_Concentration:_Its_Practice.

931 *The Paul McCartney Project*, the-paulmccartney-project.com.

932 Ibid.

933 Emerick, *Here, There and Everywhere.*

934 MacDonald, *Revolution in the Head.*

935 Lewis, Randy, "Ringo Starr celebrates 77th birthday with help from his friends — including Jenny Lewis," *Los Angeles Times,* July 7, 2017, latimes.com/entertainment/music/la-et-ms-ringo-starr-birthday-hollywood-peace-love-20170707-story.html.

936 Ibid.

937 McGrath, Paul, Ed. *Give Peace a Chance: John and Yoko's Bed-in for Peace* (Hoboken, NJ: Wiley, 2009), 4.

938 "Ringo Starr—Y Not (Interview & Performance)," Ringo Starr (YouTube channel). Dec. 7, 2011, youtube.com/watch?v=2A4IAT6eYRg.

939 Mason, *The Beatles, Drugs, Mysticism & India*, 292.

940 "George Harrison & Ringo on Aspel & Co."

941 Hamilton, Giorgina, "Ringo Starr reveals George Harrison's final words to him was a bittersweet joke on his deathbed," *Smooth Radio*, Jan. 18, 2021, smoothradio.com/artists/beatles/ringo-starr-george-harrison-joke-final-words-death-video.

942 "George Harrison 1943-2001," *Surrealist.org*, surrealist.org/prayforpeace/harrison.html.

943 Harrison, Olivia. *Collaborations*, 11.

944 Scorsese, *George Harrison: Living In The Material World.*

945 Boucher, Geoff. "'Quiet Beatle' Sought Spirituality, Privacy," *Los Angeles Times*, Dec. 1, 2001, latimes.com/archives/la-xpm-2001-dec-01-mn-10327-story.html.

946 *Times of India*, "George Left Krishnas Out Of Will."

947 "Paul McCartney Honours George Harrison in Hollywood," *Reuters*, Apr. 14, 2009, reuters.com/article/uk-harrison/paul-mccartney-honours-george-harrison-in-hollywood-idUKTRE53D74J20090414.

948 Ibid.

ACKNOWLEDGMENTS

My greatest gratitude goes to Jeff and Deborah Herman for your constant friendship and loyalty. Thank you to the Permuted Press team, including Jacob Hoye, Clayton Ferrell, Tiffani Rudder, Alana Mills and Heather King for making this book the best it can be. Thank you to Maharishi, to Babaji, and to all my inner teachers who guide me daily. Thank you to Judith Bourque, Conny Larsson, Rob McCutchan, Casey Coleman, Ned Wynn, Billy Clayton, Shannon Dickson, Mike Dolan, Hope and Laurence Juber, Paul Mason, Gurudas a.k.a. Roger Siegel, Richard Blakely, Ted Morano, David Philipson, Bengt Berger, Obadiah McDougall Jones, Mark Lewisohn, Judd Klinger, Pete Compton, Bob Haddad, Carl Roles, J.J. Hurtak, Robert Bartel, Fred Den Ouden, Richard Alexander Cooke III, Ellie Quinn, Mark Ashworth, Chris Turner, and Vitaly Safarov for your valuable contributions.

Thank you to these Indian musicians and their families for permission to print your photos and for sharing your precious memories: Aashish Khan, Hariprasad Chaurasia, Dr. T.V. Gopalakrishnan, Kartick Kumar, Niladri Kumar, Laura Patchen, Mani Biswas, Ashwani Shankar, Akshat Sharma, Pt. Shri Krishan Sharma, Anand Mishra, Bickram Ghosh, Uttank Vora, Ajay Rikhiram, Nitesh Jain, Dr. L. Subramaniam, Ashwin Batish, Lauren Landress of Self-Realization Fellowship, Mary Khan of Ali Akbar Khan Foundation, and Paula Rao of The Music Circle. Thank you to The Beatles for bringing a new sound, a new vibration, and a new spiritual awareness to the planet. This book is my gift to your legacy.

ABOUT THE AUTHOR

Photo by Angela Shin

A pioneer in the human potential field, highly respected spiritual teacher, and tour guide to sacred destinations, Susan Shumsky is an author of twenty spiritual books in English and thirty-six foreign editions. She has won over forty book awards, and her memoir, *Maharishi & Me—Seeking Enlightenment with the Beatles' Guru*, has won thirteen awards. Susan is featured in several documentary films, including *The Beatles and India* and *Here, There and Everywhere*.

In 1970 Susan spent six months in Rishikesh, India studying with Maharishi Mahesh Yogi, guru of The Beatles and founder of Transcendental Meditation. For two decades, she resided in Maharishi's ashrams in the Himalayas, Swiss Alps, and other secluded areas. She served on his personal staff for six of those years in Spain, Mallorca, Austria, Italy, and Switzerland. She then studied New Thought and metaphysics and became a Doctor of Divinity. As a tour guide to sacred destinations, Susan has led many tours to the Kumbh Mela in India, thirty overseas tours, twenty-six holistic retreats, and nineteen conferences at sea. Her websites are drsusan.org and divinetravels.com.